Houghton
Mifflin
Harcourt.

CALIFORNIA

collections

HISTORY.

Houghton
Mifflin
Harcourt

CALIFORNIA
collections

GRADE 7

Program Consultants:

Kylene Beers

Martha Hougen

Carol Jago

William L. McBride

Erik Palmer

Lydia Stack

About Our
Program Consultants

Kylene Beers Nationally known lecturer and author on reading and literacy; 2011 recipient of the Conference on English Leadership Exemplary Leader Award; coauthor of *Notice and Note: Strategies for Close Reading*; former president of the National Council of Teachers of English. Dr. Beers is the nationally known author of *When Kids Can't Read: What Teachers Can Do* and coeditor of *Adolescent Literacy: Turning Promise into Practice*, as well as articles in the *Journal of Adolescent and Adult Literacy*. Former editor of *Voices from the Middle*, she is the 2001 recipient of NCTE's Richard W. Halley Award, given for outstanding contributions to middle school literacy. She recently served as Senior Reading Researcher at the Comer School Development Program at Yale University as well as Senior Reading Advisor to Secondary Schools for the Reading and Writing Project at Teachers College.

Martha Hougen National consultant, presenter, researcher, and author. Areas of expertise include differentiating instruction for students with learning difficulties, including those with learning disabilities and dyslexia; and teacher and leader preparation improvement. Dr. Hougen has taught at the middle school through graduate levels. Recently her focus has been on working with teacher educators to enhance teacher and leader preparation to better meet the needs of all students. Currently she is working with the University of Florida at the Collaboration for Effective Educator Development, Accountability, and Reform Center (CEEDAR Center) to improve the achievement of students with disabilities by reforming teacher and leader licensure, evaluation, and preparation. She has led similar efforts in Texas with the Higher Education Collaborative and the College & Career Readiness Initiative Faculty Collaboratives. In addition to peer-reviewed articles, curricular documents, and presentations, Dr. Hougen has published two college textbooks: *The Fundamentals of Literacy Assessment and Instruction Pre-K–6* (2012) and *The Fundamentals of Literacy Assessment and Instruction 6–12* (2014).

Carol Jago Teacher of English with 32 years of experience at Santa Monica High School in California; author and nationally known lecturer; and former president of the National Council of Teachers of English. Currently serves as Associate Director of the California Reading and Literature Project at UCLA. With expertise in standards assessment and secondary education, Ms. Jago is the author of numerous books on education, including *With Rigor for All* and *Papers, Papers, Papers*, and is active with the California Association of Teachers of English, editing its scholarly journal *California English* since 1996. Ms. Jago also served on the planning committee for the 2009 NAEP Framework and the 2011 NAEP Writing Framework.

William L. McBride Curriculum specialist. Dr. McBride is a nationally known speaker, educator, and author who now trains teachers in instructional methodologies. He is coauthor of *What's Happening?*, an innovative, high-interest text for middle-grade readers, and author of *If They Can Argue Well, They Can Write Well*. A former reading specialist, English teacher, and social studies teacher, he holds a master's degree in reading and a doctorate in curriculum and instruction from the University of North Carolina at Chapel Hill. Dr. McBride has contributed to the development of textbook series in language arts, social studies, science, and vocabulary. He is also known for his novel *Entertaining an Elephant*, which tells the story of a veteran teacher who becomes reinspired with both his profession and his life.

Erik Palmer Veteran teacher and education consultant based in Denver, Colorado. Author of *Well Spoken: Teaching Speaking to All Students* and *Digitally Speaking: How to Improve Student Presentations*. His areas of focus include improving oral communication, promoting technology in classroom presentations, and updating instruction through the use of digital tools. He holds a bachelor's degree from Oberlin College and a master's degree in curriculum and instruction from the University of Colorado.

Lydia Stack Internationally known teacher educator and author. She is involved in a Stanford University project to support English Language Learners, *Understanding Language*. The goal of this project is to enrich academic content and language instruction for English Language Learners (ELLs) in grades K-12 by making explicit the language and literacy skills necessary to meet the Common Core State Standards (CCSS) and Next Generation Science Standards. Her teaching experience includes twenty-five years as an elementary and high school ESL teacher, and she is a past president of Teachers of English to Speakers of Other Languages (TESOL). Her awards include the TESOL James E. Alatis Award and the San Francisco STAR Teacher Award. Her publications include *On Our Way to English*, *Visions: Language, Literature, Content*, and *American Themes*, a literature anthology for high school students in the ACCESS program of the U.S. State Department's Office of English Language Programs.

Additional thanks to the following Program Reviewers

Rosemary Asquino
Sylvia B. Bennett
Yvonne Bradley
Leslie Brown
Haley Carroll
Caitlin Chalmers
Emily Colley-King
Stacy Collins
Denise DeBonis
Courtney Dickerson
Sarah Easley
Phyllis J. Everette
Peter J. Foy Sr.

Carol M. Gibby
Angie Gill
Mary K. Goff
Saira Haas
Lisa M. Janeway
Robert V. Kidd Jr.
Kim Lilley
John C. Lowe
Taryn Curtis MacGee
Meredith S. Maddox
Cynthia Martin
Kelli M. McDonough
Megan Pankiewicz

Linda Beck Pieplow
Molly Pieplow
Mary-Sarah Proctor
Jessica A. Stith
Peter Swartley
Pamela Thomas
Linda A. Tobias
Rachel Ukleja
Lauren Vint
Heather Lynn York
Leigh Ann Zerr

COLLECTION 1
Bold Actions

KEY LEARNING OBJECTIVES

Make inferences.
Determine theme.
Analyze plot, conflict, and setting.
Analyze myths.
Analyze alliteration.

Analyze poetic form.
Cite evidence.
Determine central idea and details.
Analyze and compare news stories.
Determine author's purpose.

Close Reader

eBook *Explore It!*

 ▶ **Video Links**   **Visit hmhfyi.com** for current articles and informational texts.

Perception and Reality

KEY LEARNING OBJECTIVES

Summarize a story.
Identify elements of a folk tale.
Analyze influence of setting on characters.
Analyze use of figurative language.
Analyze use of sound devices.
Analyze poetic form.

Identify and analyze drama elements.
Compare script and performance.
Summarize informational text.
Analyze text features.
Analyze visual media.

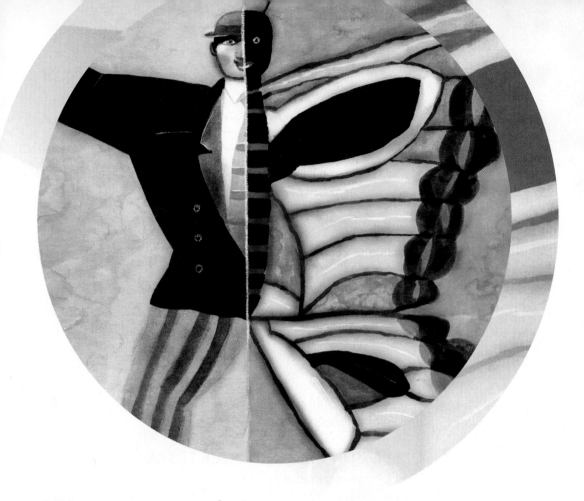

Close Reader

eBook *Explore It!*

 Video Links

 HISTORY

 A&E

 Channel One News®

fyi hmhfyi.com **Visit hmhfyi.com** for current articles and informational texts.

Nature at Work

KEY LEARNING OBJECTIVES

Identify elements of Shakespearean language.
Analyze a soliloquy.
Determine theme.
Analyze figurative language.

Compare and contrast poetic forms.
Identify features of a memoir.
Analyze author's style.
Analyze structure in an expository essay.

Close Reader

eBook *Explore It!*

▶ **Video Links**

Visit hmhfyi.com
for current articles and
informational texts.

COLLECTION **4**

Risk and Exploration

COLLECTION PERFORMANCE TASK

KEY LEARNING OBJECTIVES

Analyze extended metaphor.
Analyze imagery.
Determine central ideas and details.
Analyze sound reasoning.

Analyze tone.
Analyze cause-and-effect relationships.
Trace and evaluate an argument.

Close Reader

Image credits: ©PhotoSpin, Inc/Alamy; (bg) ©Corbis

eBook *Explore It!*

 ▶ **Video Links**   **Visit hmhfyi.com** for current articles and informational texts.

The Stuff of Consumer Culture

KEY LEARNING OBJECTIVES	Determine theme.	Draw conclusions about graphic aids.
	Analyze elements of science fiction.	Analyze author style.
	Compare and contrast poetic forms.	Analyze cause-and-effect organization.
	Make inferences.	

Close Reader

eBook *Explore It!*

▶ **Video Links**

 Visit hmhfyi.com
for current articles and
informational texts.

COLLECTION 6

Guided by a Cause

KEY LEARNING OBJECTIVES

Determine theme.
Analyze characterization.
Analyze flashback.
Analyze author's style.
Analyze multiple points of view.
Compare and contrast genres.

Determine central idea and details.
Analyze elements of a personal essay.
Analyze chronological order.
Determine author's point of view.
Analyze authors' writings on the same topic.
Analyze elements of a documentary.

Close Reader

Image credits: ©Mohd Shahrizan Hussin/Shutterstock

eBook *Explore It!*

 ▶ **Video Links**   **Channel One News®**

fyi
hmhfyi.com

Visit hmhfyi.com
for current articles and
informational texts.

Student Resources

DIGITAL OVERVIEW

Connecting to Your World

Every time you read something, view something, write to someone, or react to what you've read or seen, you're participating in a world of ideas. You do this every day, inside the classroom and out. These skills will serve you not only at home and at school but eventually in your career.

The digital tools in this program will tap into the skills you already use and help you sharpen those skills for the future.

Start your exploration at my.hrw.com

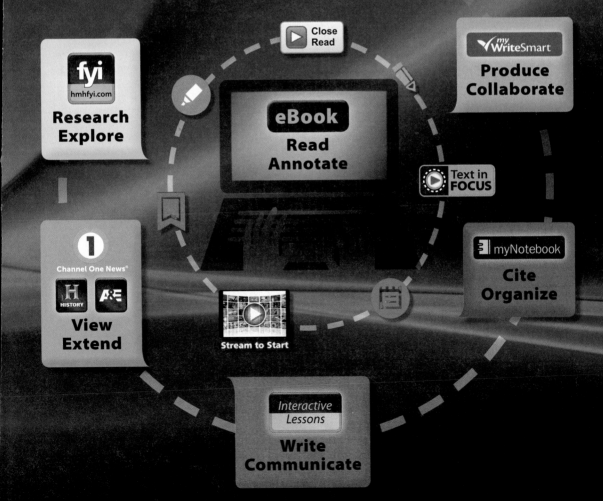

Writing and Speaking & Listening

Communication in today's world requires quite a variety of skills. To express yourself and win people over, you have to be able to write for print, for online media, and for spoken presentations. To collaborate, you have to work with people who might be sitting right next to you or at the other end of an Internet connection.

Available Only in Your eBook

Interactive Lessons

These interactive lessons will help you master the skills needed to become an expert communicator.

Choosing Relevant Evidence

Choose the pieces of evidence that support the reason shown and drag them into the box.

Tip

Reality stars are often placed in situations that cause them to grow or change in a positive way.

One contestant who participated in a fashion reality show remarked, "The show made me a better designer." ✓

The winner of one cooking show won a million dollars.

According to Nielsen ratings for this season, 17 of the top 50 most popular TV shows for viewers between the ages of 18-49 were reality shows.

68% of former contestants on a popular weight-loss show have maintained their goal weight for five years post-show.

You've got it! This quotation shows how one contestant experienced personal growth.

Writing Arguments

Learn how to build a strong argument.

ELA W.7.1, W.7.10
ELD PI.7.4, PI.7.10, PI.7.11, PII.7.1, PII.7.2

Interactive Lessons

Writing Informative Texts

Shed light on complex ideas and topics.

ELA W.7.2, W.7.10
ELD PI.7.4, PI.7.10, PII.7.1

Interactive Lessons

Writing Narratives

A good storyteller can always capture an audience.

ELA W.7.3, W.7.10
ELD PI.7.10, PI.7.12, PII.7.1

Interactive Lessons

Writing as a Process

Get from the first twinkle of an idea to a sparkling final draft.

ELA W.7.4, W.7.5, W.7.10
ELD PI.7.10, PII.7.1

Interactive Lessons

1. Introduction
2. Task, Purpose, and Audience
3. Planning and Drafting
4. Revising and Editing
5. Trying a New Approach

Producing and Publishing with Technology

Learn how to write for an online audience.

ELA W.7.6
ELD PI.7.10

SUBMIT

Interactive Lessons

1. Introduction
2. Writing for the Internet
3. Interacting with Your Online Audience
4. Using Technology to Collaborate

Conducting Research

There's a world of information out there. How do you find it?

ELA W.7.6, W.7.7, W.7.8
ELD PI.7.10

Interactive Lessons

1. Introduction
2. Starting Your Research
3. Types of Sources
4. Using the Library for Research
5. Conducting Field Research
6. Using the Internet for Research
7. Taking Notes
8. Refocusing Your Inquiry

Evaluating Sources

Don't believe everything you read!

ELA W.7.8
ELD PI.7.10

Interactive Lessons	1. Introduction 2. Evaluating Sources for Usefulness	3. Evaluating Sources for Reliability

Using Textual Evidence

Put your research into writing.

ELA W.7.7, W.7.8, W.7.9
ELD PI.7.10

Interactive Lessons	1. Introduction 2. Synthesizing Information 3. Writing an Outline	4. Summarizing, Paraphrasing, and Quoting 5. Attribution

Participating in Collaborative Discussions

There's power in putting your heads together.

ELA SL.7.1
ELD PI.7.1, PI.7.3, PI.7.5

Interactive Lessons	1. Introduction 2. Preparing for Discussion 3. Establishing and Following Procedure	4. Speaking Constructively 5. Listening and Responding 6. Wrapping Up Your Discussion

Analyzing and Evaluating Presentations

Media-makers all want your attention. What are they trying to tell you?

ELA SL.7.2, SL.7.3, SL.7.6
ELD PI.7.5, PI.7.6

Interactive Lessons

1. Introduction
2. Analyzing a Presentation
3. Evaluating a Speaker's Reliability
4. Tracing a Speaker's Argument
5. Rhetoric and Delivery
6. Synthesizing Media Sources

Giving a Presentation

Learn how to talk to a roomful of people.

ELA SL.7.4, SL.7.6
ELD PI.7.4, PI.7.9

Interactive Lessons

1. Introduction
2. Knowing Your Audience
3. The Content of Your Presentation
4. Style in Presentation
5. Delivering Your Presentation

Using Media in a Presentation

If a picture is worth a thousand words, just think what you can do with a video.

ELA SL.7.5
ELD PI.7.9

Interactive Lessons

1. Introduction
2. Types of Media: Audio, Video, and Images
3. Using Presentation Software
4. Practicing Your Presentation

DIGITAL SPOTLIGHT

eBook	▤ myNotebook	**fyi** hmhfyi.com	✓ my WriteSmart

Supporting
21st Century Skills

The amount of information people encounter each day keeps increasing. Whether you're working alone or collaborating with others, it takes effort to analyze the complex texts and competing ideas that bombard us in this fast-paced world. What can allow you to succeed? Staying engaged and organized. The digital tools in this program will help you to think critically and take charge of your learning.

Stream to Start

Ignite your Investigation

You learn best when you're engaged. The **Stream to Start** video at the beginning of each collection is designed to inspire interest in the topics being explored. Watch it and then let your curiosity lead your investigations.

Learn How to Do a Close Read

An effective close read is all about the details; you have to examine the language and ideas a writer includes. See how it's done by accessing the **Close Read Screencasts** in your eBook. Hear modeled conversations about anchor texts.

long after we got here, Papa got a job driving a cab, and Mama worked cleaning people's houses. It was hard for them not to have the respect they were used to from holding government
60 teaching jobs, but they had high regard for the food they could now easily buy at the store.

Six months after we got here, the Boeing Company moved to Chicago and Mr. Bob Campbell got transferred there. When Aunt Madina left with him, it broke Mama's heart. Aunt Madina was the only person we knew from Kazakhstan, and it felt like our family just huddled together on a tiny island in the middle of a great American sea.

I looked at the permission slip, wishing there were some special words I could say to get Mama and Papa to sign it.
70 Around me, everyone in my homeroom was talking excitedly about the Spring Fling. Mama says she thinks the school is

Increase Your Understanding

TEXT IN FOCUS helps you dig deeper into complex texts by offering visual explanations of potential stumbling blocks. Look for **TEXT IN FOCUS** videos in anchor texts.

"sank our roots"

Annotate the Texts

Practice close reading by utilizing the powerful annotation tools in your eBook. Mark up key ideas and observations using highlighters and sticky notes. Tag unfamiliar words to create a personal word list in *my*Notebook.

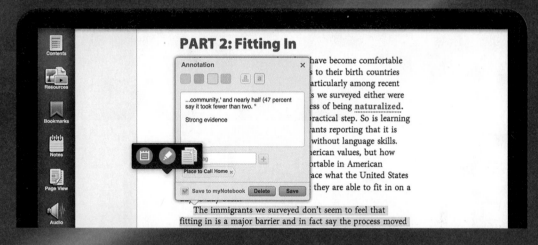

Find More Text Evidence on the Web

Tap into the *fyi* website for links to high-interest informational texts about collection topics. Synthesize information and connect notes and text evidence from any Web source by including it in *my*Notebook

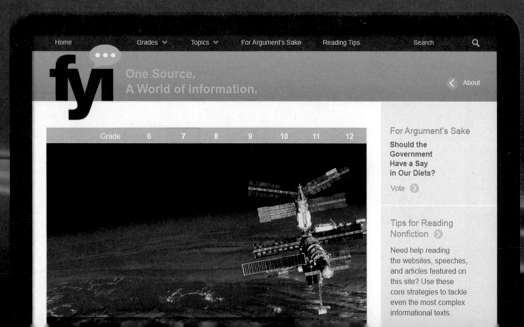

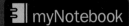 **myNotebook**

Save and Organize Your Notes

Save your annotations to *my*Notebook, where you can organize them to use as text evidence in performance tasks and other writing assignments. You can also organize the unfamiliar words you tagged by creating word lists, which will help you grow your vocabulary.

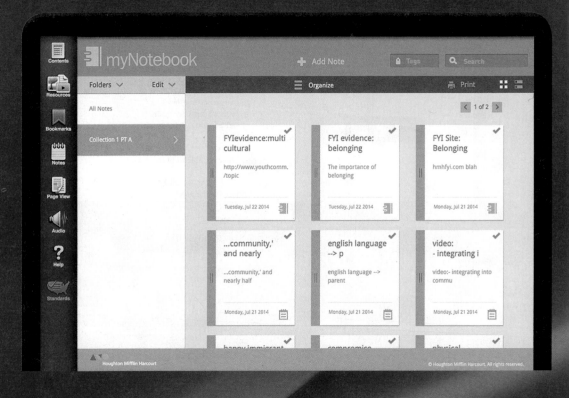

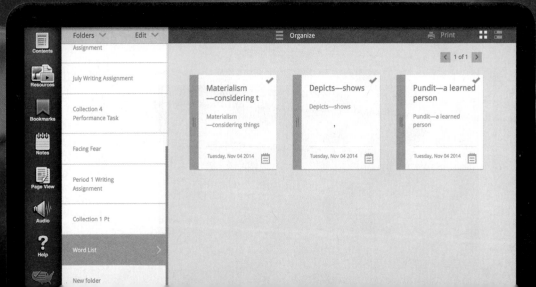

Create, Communicate, and Collaborate

Use the technology provided by the **myWriteSmart** tool to keep track of your writing assignments, create drafts, and collaborate and communicate with peers and your teacher. Use the evidence you've gathered in *my*Notebook to support your ideas.

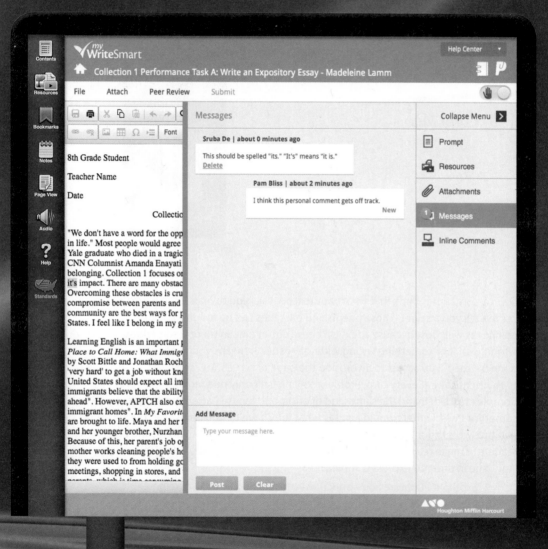

Making Meaning
in the 21st Century ... or Don't Let Complex Texts Get You Down

By Carol Jago

Do you sometimes think that what your teacher asks you to read is too hard? Let me tell you a secret. Those poems and passages can be tough for your teacher as well. Just because a text isn't easy doesn't mean there is something wrong with it or something wrong with the reader. It means you need to do more than skim across the words on the page or screen. You will need to think critically at every turn. Problem solving isn't only needed for math. Complex texts demand the same kind of effort and focused attention. Do you sometimes wish writers would just say what they have to say simply? I assure you that writers don't use long sentences and unfamiliar words to annoy their readers or make readers feel dumb. They employ complex syntax and rich language in order to express complex ideas.

Excellent literature and nonfiction—the kind you will be reading over the course of the year—challenges readers in various ways. Sometimes the background of a story or the content of an essay is so unfamiliar that it is difficult to understand why characters are behaving as they do or to follow the argument a writer is making. By persevering, reading like a detective, and following clues in the text, you will find that your store of background knowledge grows. As a result, the next time you read about global issues, financial matters, political events, environmental news (like the California drought) or health research, the text won't seem nearly as hard. The more you read, the better a reader you will become.

Good readers aren't put off by challenging text. When the going gets rough, they know what to do. Let's take vocabulary, a common measure of text complexity, as an example. Learning new words is the business of a lifetime. Rather than shutting down when you meet a word you don't know, take a moment to think about the word. Is any part of the word familiar to you? Is there something in the context of the sentence or paragraph that can help you figure out its meaning? Is there someone or something that can provide you with a definition? When reading literature or nonfiction from a time period other than our own, the text is often full of words we don't know. Each time you meet those words in succeeding readings you will be adding to your understanding of the word and its use. Your brain is a natural word-learning machine. The more you feed it complex text, the larger a vocabulary you'll have.

Have you ever been reading a long, complicated sentence and discovered that by the time you reached the end you had forgotten the beginning? Unlike the sentences we speak or dash off in a note to a friend, complex text is often full of sentences that are not only lengthy but also constructed in intricate ways. Such sentences require readers to slow down and figure out how phrases relate to one another as well as who is doing what to whom. Remember, rereading isn't cheating. It is exactly what experienced readers know to do when they meet dense text on the page. On the pages that follow you will find stories and articles that challenge you at the sentence level. Don't be intimidated. With careful attention to how those sentences are constructed, their meaning will unfold right before your eyes.

> **"Your brain is a natural word-learning machine. The more you feed it complex text, the larger a vocabulary you'll have."**

That same kind of attention is required for reading the media. Every day you are bombarded with messages— online, offline, everywhere you look. These, too, are complex texts that you want to be able to see through; that is, to be able to recognize the message's source, purpose, context, intended audience, and appeals. This is what it takes to be a 21st century reader.

Another way text can be complex involves the density of the ideas in a passage. Sometimes a writer piles on so much information that you think your head might explode if you read one more detail or one more qualification. At times like this talking with a friend can really help. Sharing questions and ideas, exploring a difficult passage together, can help you tease out the meaning of even the most difficult text. Poetry is often particularly dense and for that reason it poses particular challenges. A seemingly simple poem in terms of vocabulary and length may express extremely complex feelings and insights. Poets also love to use mythological and Biblical allusions which contemporary readers are not always familiar with. The only way to read text this complex is to read it again and again.

You are going to notice a range of complexity within each collection of readings. This spectrum reflects the range of texts that surround us: some easy, some hard, some seemingly easy but in fact hard, some seemingly hard but actually easy. Whatever their complexity, I think you will enjoy these readings tremendously. Remember, read for your life!

Understanding the California Common Core State Standards

What are the California Common Core State Standards for English Language Arts?

The California Common Core State Standards for English Language Arts indicate what you should know and be able to do by the end of your grade level. These understandings and skills will help you be better prepared for future classes, college courses, and a career. For this reason, the standards for each strand in English Language Arts (such as Reading Informational Text or Writing) directly relate to the College and Career Readiness Anchor Standards for each strand. The Anchor Standards broadly outline the understandings and skills you should master by the end of high school so that you are well-prepared for college or for a career.

How do I learn the California Common Core State Standards for English Language Arts?

Your textbook is closely aligned to the California Standards for English Language Arts. Every time you learn a concept or practice a skill, you are working on mastering one of the standards. Each collection, each selection, and each performance task in your textbook connects to one or more of the Standards for English Language Arts listed on the following pages.

The Standards for English Language Arts are divided into five strands: Reading Literature, Reading Informational Text, Writing, Speaking and Listening, and Language.

© Jose Luis Pelaez Inc/Getty Images

Strand	What It Means to You
Reading Literature (RL)	This strand concerns the literary texts you will read at this grade level: stories, drama, and poetry. The Common Core State Standards stress that you should read a range of texts of increasing complexity as you progress through high school.
Reading Informational Text (RI)	Informational text encompasses a broad range of literary nonfiction, including exposition, argument, and functional text, in such genres as personal essays, speeches, opinion pieces, memoirs, and historical and technical accounts. The Common Core State Standards stress that you will read a range of informational texts of increasing complexity as you progress from grade to grade.
Writing (W)	For the Writing strand you will focus on generating three types of texts—arguments, informative or explanatory texts, and narratives—while using the writing process and technology to develop and share your writing. The Common Core State Standards also emphasize research and specify that you should write routinely for both short and extended time frames.
Speaking and Listening (SL)	The Common Core State Standards focus on comprehending information presented in a variety of media and formats, on participating in collaborative discussions, and on presenting knowledge and ideas clearly.
Language (L)	The standards in the Language strand address the conventions of standard English grammar, usage, and mechanics; knowledge of language; and vocabulary acquisition and use.

California Common Core Code Decoder

The codes you find on the pages of your textbook identify the specific knowledge or skill for the standard addressed in the text.

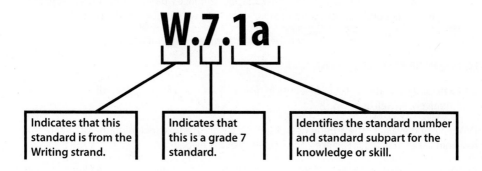

Indicates that this standard is from the Writing strand.	Indicates that this is a grade 7 standard.	Identifies the standard number and standard subpart for the knowledge or skill.

California Common Core State Standards for English Language Arts

Listed below are the standards for English Language Arts that you are required to master by the end of grade 7. We have provided a summary of the concepts you will learn on your way to mastering each standard. The CCR anchor standards and grade-specific standards for each strand work together to define college and career readiness expectations—the former providing broad standards, the latter providing additional specificity.

College and Career Readiness Anchor Standards for Reading

Standards for English Language Arts

KEY IDEAS AND DETAILS

1. Read closely to determine what the text says explicitly and to make logical inferences from it; cite specific textual evidence when writing or speaking to support conclusions drawn from the text.

2. Determine central ideas or themes of a text and analyze their development; summarize the key supporting details and ideas.

3. Analyze how and why individuals, events, and ideas develop and interact over the course of a text.

CRAFT AND STRUCTURE

4. Interpret words and phrases as they are used in a text, including determining technical, connotative, and figurative meanings, and analyze how specific word choices shape meaning or tone.

5. Analyze the structure of texts, including how specific sentences, paragraphs, and larger portions of the text (e.g., a section, chapter, scene, or stanza) relate to each other and the whole.

6. Assess how point of view or purpose shapes the content and style of a text.

INTEGRATION OF KNOWLEDGE AND IDEAS

7. Integrate and evaluate content presented in diverse media and formats, including visually and quantitatively, as well as in words.

8. Delineate and evaluate the argument and specific claims in a text, including the validity of the reasoning as well as the relevance and sufficiency of the evidence.

9. Analyze how two or more texts address similar themes or topics in order to build knowledge or to compare the approaches the authors take.

RANGE OF READING AND LEVEL OF TEXT COMPLEXITY

10. Read and comprehend complex literary and informational texts independently and proficiently.

Reading Standards for Literature, Grade 7 Students

The College and Career Readiness Anchor Standards for Reading apply to both literature and informational text.

Standards for English Language Arts	What It Means to You
KEY IDEAS AND DETAILS	
1. Cite several pieces of textual evidence to support analysis of what the text says explicitly as well as inferences drawn from the text.	You will use information from the text to support its main ideas—both those that are stated directly and those that are suggested.
2. Determine a theme or central idea of a text and analyze its development over the course of the text; provide an objective summary of the text.	You will analyze a text's main ideas and themes by showing how they unfold throughout the text. You will also summarize the main idea of the text as a whole without adding your own ideas or opinions.
3. Analyze how particular elements of a story or drama interact (e.g., how setting shapes the characters or plot).	You will analyze how different parts of a story or drama affect each other.
CRAFT AND STRUCTURE	
4. Determine the meaning of words and phrases as they are used in a text, including figurative and connotative meanings; analyze the impact of rhymes and other repetitions of sounds (e.g., alliteration) on a specific verse or stanza of a poem or section of a story or drama. (See grade 7 Language standards 4–6 for additional expectations.)	You will analyze specific words, phrases, and patterns of sound in the text to determine what they mean and how they contribute to the text's larger meaning.
5. Analyze how a drama's or poem's form or structure (e.g., soliloquy, sonnet) contributes to its meaning.	You will analyze how the form of a drama or poem affects its meaning.
6. Analyze how an author develops and contrasts the points of view of different characters or narrators in a text.	You will analyze how an author contrasts the perspectives of different characters or the points of view of narrators in a text.
INTEGRATION OF KNOWLEDGE AND IDEAS	
7. Compare and contrast a written story, drama, or poem to its audio, filmed, staged, or multimedia version, analyzing the effects of techniques unique to each medium (e.g., lighting, sound, color, or camera focus and angles in a film).	You will compare and contrast how events and information are presented in visual and non-visual texts.

Standards for English Language Arts	What It Means to You
8. (Not applicable to literature)	
9. Compare and contrast a fictional portrayal of a time, place, or character and a historical account of the same period as a means of understanding how authors of fiction use or alter history.	You will recognize and analyze how an author draws from and uses historical source material.

RANGE OF READING AND LEVEL OF TEXT COMPLEXITY

10. By the end of the year, read and comprehend literature, including stories, dramas, and poems, in the grades 6–8 text complexity band proficiently, with scaffolding as needed at the high end of the range.	You will read and understand grade-level appropriate literary texts by the end of grade 7.

Reading Standards for Informational Text, Grade 7 Students

Standards for English Language Arts	What It Means to You
KEY IDEAS AND DETAILS	
1. Cite several pieces of textual evidence to support analysis of what the text says explicitly as well as inferences drawn from the text.	You will cite information from the text to support its main ideas—both those that are stated directly and those that are suggested.
2. Determine two or more central ideas in a text and analyze their development over the course of the text; provide an objective summary of the text.	You will analyze the development of at least two of a text's main ideas by showing how they progress throughout the text. You will also summarize the text as a whole without adding your own ideas or opinions.
3. Analyze the interactions between individuals, events, and ideas in a text (e.g., how ideas influence individuals or events, or how individuals influence ideas or events).	You will analyze the ways in which individuals, events, and ideas in the text interact with one another.

Standards for English Language Arts	What It Means to You

CRAFT AND STRUCTURE

4. Determine the meaning of words and phrases as they are used in a text, including figurative, connotative, and technical meanings; analyze the impact of a specific word choice on meaning and tone. (See grade 7 Language standards 4–6 for additional expectations.)	You will analyze specific words and phrases in the text to determine both what they mean and how they affect the text's tone and meaning as a whole.
5. Analyze the structure an author uses to organize a text, including how the major sections contribute to the whole and to the development of the ideas.	You will examine the major sections of a text and analyze how each one contributes to the whole, including
a. Analyze the use of text features (e.g., graphics, headers, captions) in public documents.	how text features (graphics, headers, and captions) are used in public documents, such as school rules
6. Determine an author's point of view or purpose in a text and analyze how the author distinguishes his or her position from that of others.	You will understand the author's point of view and analyze how the author sets his or her position apart from others.

INTEGRATION OF KNOWLEDGE AND IDEAS

7. Compare and contrast a text to an audio, video, or multimedia version of the text, analyzing each medium's portrayal of the subject (e.g., how the delivery of a speech affects the impact of the words).	You will compare and contrast text to an audio, video, or multimedia version of the text.
8. Trace and evaluate the argument and specific claims in a text, assessing whether the reasoning is sound and the evidence is relevant and sufficient to support the claims.	You will evaluate the strength of the author's claims and reasoning and identify any faults or weaknesses in them.
9. Analyze how two or more authors writing about the same topic shape their presentations of key information by emphasizing different evidence or advancing different interpretations of facts.	You will compare and contrast at least two different authors' treatments of the same subject.

Standards for English Language Arts	What It Means to You
RANGE OF READING AND LEVEL OF TEXT COMPLEXITY	
10. By the end of the year, read and comprehend literary nonfiction in the grades 6–8 text complexity band proficiently, with scaffolding as needed at the high end of the range.	You will demonstrate the ability to read and understand grade-level appropriate literary nonfiction texts by the end of grade 7.

College and Career Readiness Anchor Standards for Writing

Standards for English Language Arts

TEXT TYPES AND PURPOSES

1. Write arguments to support claims in an analysis of substantive topics or texts, using valid reasoning and relevant and sufficient evidence.

2. Write informative/explanatory texts to examine and convey complex ideas and information clearly and accurately through the effective selection, organization, and analysis of content.

3. Write narratives to develop real or imagined experiences or events using effective technique, well-chosen details, and well-structured event sequences.

PRODUCTION AND DISTRIBUTION OF WRITING

4. Produce clear and coherent writing in which the development, organization, and style are appropriate to task, purpose, and audience.

5. Develop and strengthen writing as needed by planning, revising, editing, rewriting, or trying a new approach.

6. Use technology, including the Internet, to produce and publish writing and to interact and collaborate with others.

RESEARCH TO BUILD AND PRESENT KNOWLEDGE

7. Conduct short as well as more sustained research projects based on focused questions, demonstrating understanding of the subject under investigation.

8. Gather relevant information from multiple print and digital sources, assess the credibility and accuracy of each source, and integrate the information while avoiding plagiarism.

9. Draw evidence from literary and/or informational texts to support analysis, reflection, and research.

RANGE OF WRITING

10. Write routinely over extended time frames (time for research, reflection, and revision) and shorter time frames (a single sitting or a day or two) for a range of tasks, purposes, and audiences.

Writing Standards, Grade 7 Students

Standards for English Language Arts	What It Means to You
TEXT TYPES AND PURPOSES	
1. Write arguments to support claims with clear reasons and relevant evidence.	You will write and develop arguments with clear reasons and strong evidence that include
a. Introduce claim(s), acknowledge and address alternate or opposing claims, and organize the reasons and evidence logically.	a clear organization of claims and counterclaims
b. Support claim(s) or counterarguments with logical reasoning and relevant evidence, using accurate, credible sources and demonstrating an understanding of the topic or text.	strong, accurate support for claims
c. Use words, phrases, and clauses to create cohesion and clarify the relationships among claim(s), reasons, and evidence.	use of cohesive words, phrases, and clauses to link information
d. Establish and maintain a formal style.	a formal style
e. Provide a concluding statement or section that follows from and supports the argument presented.	a strong concluding statement that summarizes the argument

Standards for English Language Arts	What It Means to You
2. Write informative/explanatory texts to examine a topic and convey ideas, concepts, and information through the selection, organization, and analysis of relevant content.	You will write clear, well-organized, and thoughtful informative and explanatory texts with
a. Introduce a topic or thesis statement clearly, previewing what is to follow; organize ideas, concepts, and information, using strategies such as definition, classification, comparison/contrast, and cause/effect; include formatting (e.g., headings), graphics (e.g., charts, tables), and multimedia when useful to aiding comprehension.	a clear introduction and organization, including headings and graphic organizers (when appropriate)
b. Develop the topic with relevant facts, definitions, concrete details, quotations, or other information and examples.	sufficient supporting details and background information
c. Use appropriate transitions to create cohesion and clarify the relationships among ideas and concepts.	cohesive transitions to link ideas
d. Use precise language and domain-specific vocabulary to inform about or explain the topic.	precise language and relevant vocabulary
e. Establish and maintain a formal style.	a formal style
f. Provide a concluding statement or section that follows from and supports the information or explanation presented.	a strong conclusion that restates the importance or relevance of the topic
3. Write narratives to develop real or imagined experiences or events using effective technique, relevant descriptive details, and well-structured event sequences.	You will write clear, well-structured, detailed narrative texts that
a. Engage and orient the reader by establishing a context and point of view and introducing a narrator and/or characters; organize an event sequence that unfolds naturally and logically.	draw your readers in with a clear topic that unfolds logically
b. Use narrative techniques, such as dialogue, pacing, and description, to develop experiences, events, and/or characters.	use narrative techniques to develop and expand on events and/or characters
c. Use a variety of transition words, phrases, and clauses to convey sequence and signal shifts from one time frame or setting to another.	use a variety of transition words to clearly signal shifts between time frames or settings

Standards for English Language Arts	What It Means to You
d. Use precise words and phrases, relevant descriptive details, and sensory language to capture the action and convey experiences and events.	use precise words and sensory details that keep readers interested
e. Provide a conclusion that follows from and reflects on the narrated experiences or events.	have a strong conclusion that reflects on the topic

PRODUCTION AND DISTRIBUTION OF WRITING

4. Produce clear and coherent writing in which the development, organization, and style are appropriate to task, purpose, and audience. (Grade-specific expectations for writing types are defined in standards 1–3 above.)	You will produce writing that is appropriate to the task, purpose, and audience for whom you are writing.
5. With some guidance and support from peers and adults, develop and strengthen writing as needed by planning, revising, editing, rewriting, or trying a new approach, focusing on how well purpose and audience have been addressed.	With help from peers and adults, you will revise and refine your writing to address what is most important for your purpose and audience.
6. Use technology, including the Internet, to produce and publish writing and link to and cite sources as well as to interact and collaborate with others, including linking to and citing sources.	You will use technology to share your writing and to provide links to other relevant information.

RESEARCH TO BUILD AND PRESENT KNOWLEDGE

7. Conduct short research projects to answer a question, drawing on several sources and generating additional related, focused questions for further research and investigation.	You will conduct short research projects to answer a question using multiple sources and generating topics for further research.
8. Gather relevant information from multiple print and digital sources, using search terms effectively; assess the credibility and accuracy of each source; and quote or paraphrase the data and conclusions of others while avoiding plagiarism and following a standard format for citation.	You will effectively conduct searches to gather information from different sources and assess the strength of each source, following a standard format for citation.

Writing Standards, Grade 7 Students, continued

Standards for English Language Arts	What It Means to You

9. Draw evidence from literary or informational texts to support analysis, reflection, and research.
 	
   a. Apply *grade 7 Reading standards* to literature (e.g., "Compare and contrast a fictional portrayal of a time, place, or character and a historical account of the same period as a means of understanding how authors of fiction use or alter history").
 	
   b. Apply *grade 7 Reading standards* to literary nonfiction (e.g. "Trace and evaluate the argument and specific claims in a text, assessing whether the reasoning is sound and the evidence is relevant and sufficient to support the claims").
	You will paraphrase, summarize, quote, and cite primary and secondary sources to support your analysis, reflection, and research.

RANGE OF WRITING

10. Write routinely over extended time frames (time for research, reflection, and revision) and shorter time frames (a single sitting or a day or two) for a range of discipline-specific tasks, purposes, and audiences.	You will write for many different purposes and audiences both over short and extended periods of time.

College and Career Readiness Anchor Standards for Speaking and Listening

COMPREHENSION AND COLLABORATION

1. Prepare for and participate effectively in a range of conversations and collaborations with diverse partners, building on others' ideas and expressing their own clearly and persuasively.

2. Integrate and evaluate information presented in diverse media and formats, including visually, quantitatively, and orally.

3. Evaluate a speaker's point of view, reasoning, and use of evidence and rhetoric.

PRESENTATION OF KNOWLEDGE AND IDEAS

4. Present information, findings, and supporting evidence such that listeners can follow the line of reasoning and the organization, development, and style are appropriate to task, purpose, and audience.

5. Make strategic use of digital media and visual displays of data to express information and enhance understanding of presentations.

6. Adapt speech to a variety of contexts and communicative tasks, demonstrating command of formal English when indicated or appropriate.

Speaking and Listening Standards, Grade 7 Students

Standards for English Language Arts	What It Means to You
COMPREHENSION AND COLLABORATION	
1. Engage effectively in a range of collaborative discussions (one-on-one, in groups, and teacher-led) with diverse partners on grade 7 topics, texts, and issues, building on others' ideas and expressing their own clearly.	You will actively participate in a variety of discussions in which you
a. Come to discussions prepared, having read or researched material under study; explicitly draw on that preparation by referring to evidence on the topic, text, or issue to probe and reflect on ideas under discussion.	have read any relevant material beforehand and have come to the discussion prepared
b. Follow rules for collegial discussions, track progress toward specific goals and deadlines, and define individual roles as needed.	work with others to establish goals and processes within the group
c. Pose questions that elicit elaboration and respond to others' questions and comments with relevant observations and ideas that bring the discussion back on topic as needed.	ask and respond to questions and make observations that bring the discussion back to topic as needed
d. Acknowledge new information expressed by others and, when warranted, modify their own views.	respond to different perspectives and adjust your own views if necessary
2. Analyze the main ideas and supporting details presented in diverse media and formats (e.g., visually, quantitatively, orally) and explain how the ideas clarify a topic, text, or issue under study.	You will analyze main ideas and details of various media and relate them to a topic under study.
3. Delineate a speaker's argument and specific claims, and attitude toward the subject, evaluating the soundness of the reasoning and the relevance and sufficiency of the evidence.	You will evaluate a speaker's argument and identify any false reasoning or evidence.

Standards for English Language Arts	What It Means to You
PRESENTATION OF KNOWLEDGE AND IDEAS	
4. Present claims and findings (e.g., argument, narrative, summary presentations), emphasizing salient points in a focused, coherent manner with pertinent descriptions, facts, details, and examples; use appropriate eye contact, adequate volume, and clear pronunciation.	You will organize and present information to your listeners in a logical sequence and engaging style that is appropriate to your task and audience, including
a. Plan and present an argument that: supports a claim, acknowledges counter-arguments, organizes evidence logically, uses words and phrases to create cohesion, and provides a concluding statement that supports the argument presented.	planning and presenting a speech to persuade listeners to support your claim, or position on an issue.
5. Include multimedia components and visual displays in presentations to clarify claims and findings and emphasize salient points.	You will use digital media to enhance and add interest to presentations.
6. Adapt speech to a variety of contexts and tasks, demonstrating command of formal English when indicated or appropriate.	You will adapt the formality of your speech appropriately.

College and Career Readiness Anchor Standards for Language

CONVENTIONS OF STANDARD ENGLISH

1. Demonstrate command of the conventions of standard English grammar and usage when writing or speaking.

2. Demonstrate command of the conventions of standard English capitalization, punctuation, and spelling when writing.

KNOWLEDGE OF LANGUAGE

3. Apply knowledge of language to understand how language functions in different contexts, to make effective choices for meaning or style, and to comprehend more fully when reading or listening.

VOCABULARY ACQUISITION AND USE

4. Determine or clarify the meaning of unknown and multiple-meaning words and phrases by using context clues, analyzing meaningful word parts, and consulting general and specialized reference materials, as appropriate.

5. Demonstrate understanding of figurative language, word relationships, and nuances in word meanings.

6. Acquire and use accurately a range of general academic and domain-specific words and phrases sufficient for reading, writing, speaking, and listening at the college- and career-readiness level; demonstrate independence in gathering vocabulary knowledge when encountering an unknown term important to comprehension or expression.

Language Standards, Grade 7 Students

Standards for English Language Arts	What It Means to You
CONVENTIONS OF STANDARD ENGLISH	
1. Demonstrate command of the conventions of standard English grammar and usage when writing or speaking.	You will correctly understand and use the conventions of English grammar and usage, including
a. Explain the function of phrases and clauses in general and their function in specific sentences.	explaining the function of phrases and clauses
b. Choose among simple, compound, complex, and compound-complex sentences to signal differing relationships among ideas.	using a variety of sentence structures
c. Place phrases and clauses within a sentence, recognizing and correcting misplaced and dangling modifiers.	correctly placing phrases and clauses in sentences
2. Demonstrate command of the conventions of standard English capitalization, punctuation, and spelling when writing.	You will correctly use the conventions of English capitalization, punctuation, and spelling, including
a. Use a comma to separate coordinate adjectives (e.g., *It was a fascinating, enjoyable movie* but not *He wore an old[,] green shirt*).	commas
b. Spell correctly.	spelling

Standards for English Language Arts	What It Means to You
KNOWLEDGE OF LANGUAGE	
3. Use knowledge of language and its conventions when writing, speaking, reading, or listening.	You will apply your knowledge of language in different contexts by
a. Choose language that expresses ideas precisely and concisely, recognizing and eliminating wordiness and redundancy.	choosing precise and concise language to avoid wordiness or stating the same thing more than once
VOCABULARY ACQUISITION AND USE	
4. Determine or clarify the meaning of unknown and multiple-meaning words and phrases based on *grade 7 reading and content,* choosing flexibly from a range of strategies.	You will understand the meaning of grade-level appropriate words and phrases by
a. Use context (e.g., the overall meaning of a sentence or paragraph; a word's position or function in a sentence) as a clue to the meaning of a word or phrase.	using context clues
b. Use common, grade-appropriate Greek or Latin affixes and roots as clues to the meaning of a word (e.g., *belligerent, bellicose, rebel*).	using Greek or Latin roots
c. Consult general and specialized reference materials (e.g., dictionaries, glossaries, thesauruses), both print and digital, to find the pronunciation of a word or determine or clarify its precise meaning or its part of speech or trace the etymology of words.	using reference materials
d. Verify the preliminary determination of the meaning of a word or phrase (e.g., by checking the inferred meaning in context or in a dictionary).	inferring and verifying the meanings of words in context

Standards for English Language Arts	What It Means to You
5. Demonstrate understanding of figurative language, word relationships, and nuances in word meanings.	You will understand figurative language, word relationships, and slight differences in word meanings by
a. Interpret figures of speech (e.g., literary, biblical, and mythological allusions) in context.	interpreting figures of speech in context
b. Use the relationship between particular words (e.g., synonym/antonym, analogy) to better understand each of the words.	analyzing relationships between words
c. Distinguish among the connotations (associations) of words with similar denotations (definitions) (e.g., *refined, respectful, polite, diplomatic, condescending*).	distinguishing among words with similar definitions
6. Acquire and use accurately grade-appropriate general academic and domain-specific words and phrases; gather vocabulary knowledge when considering a word or phrase important to comprehension or expression.	You will learn and use grade-appropriate vocabulary.

California English Language Development Standards

The California English Language Development Standards are designed to be studied and mastered together with the California Common Core State Standards for English Language Arts. *Collections* is closely aligned with the English Language Arts standards. Each selection and each performance task in your textbook also connects to one or more of the English Language Development standards listed on the following pages. Every time you learn a concept or practice a skill, you are working on mastering not only an English Language Arts standard but also an English Language Development standard.

The California English Language Development Standard are divided into three parts.

Development Standards	
I. Interacting In Meaningful Ways	The standards in this part focus on • Using English to participate in conversations, discussions, and writing activities • Understanding and analyzing both written texts and spoken presentations • Producing oral presentations and written texts in English
II. Learning About How English Works	The standards in this part focus on • Understanding how texts are structured • Using language resources • Adding details and improving ideas • Connecting and condensing ideas
III. Using Foundational Literacy Skills	This part focuses on learning foundational concepts such as word recognition and reading fluency.

English Language Development Code Decoder

The codes you find on the pages of your textbook identify the specific skill for the English Language Development standard addressed in the text.

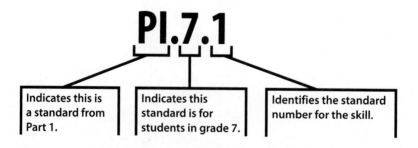

PI.7.1

| Indicates this is a standard from Part 1. | Indicates this standard is for students in grade 7. | Identifies the standard number for the skill. |

Part I: Interacting in Meaningful Ways

English Language Development Standard	Corresponding California Common Core State Standards for English Language Arts
A. COLLABORATIVE	
1. Exchanging information and ideas with others through oral collaborative discussions on a range of social and academic topics	SL.7.1, SL.7.6 L.7.3, L.7.6
2. Interacting with others in written English in various communicative forms (print, communicative technology and multimedia)	W.7.6 SL.7.2 L.7.3, L.7.6
3. Offering and justifying opinions, negotiating with and persuading others in communicative exchanges	W.7.1 SL.7.1, SL.7.4, SL.7.6 L.7.3, L.7.6
4. Adapting language choices to various contexts (based on task, purpose, and audience, and text type)	W.7.4–5 SL.7.6 L.7.1, L.7.3, L.7.6
B. INTERPRETIVE	
5. Listening actively to spoken English in a range of social and academic contexts	SL.7.1, SL.7.3, SL.7.6 L.7.1, L.7.3, L.7.6
6. Reading closely literary and informational texts and viewing multimedia to determine how meaning is conveyed explicitly and implicitly through language	RL.7.1–7, RL.7.9–10 RI.7.1–10 SL.7.2 L.7.1, L.7.3, L.7.6
7. Evaluating how well writers and speakers use language to support ideas and arguments with details or evidence depending on modality, text type, purpose, audience, topic, and content area	RL.7.4–5 RI.7.4, RI.7.6, RI.7.8 SL.7.3 L.7.3, L.7.5–6
8. Analyzing how writers and speakers use vocabulary and other language resources for specific purposes (to explain, persuade, entertain, etc.) depending on modality, text type, purpose, audience, topic, and content area	RL.7.4–5 RI.7.4–5 SL.7.3 L.7.3, L.7.5–6

English Language Development Standard	Corresponding California Common Core State Standards for English Language Arts
C. PRODUCTIVE	
9. Expressing information and ideas in formal oral presentations on academic topics	SL.7.4–6 L.7.1, L.7.3
10. Writing literary and informational texts to present, describe, and explain ideas and information, using appropriate technology	W.7.1–10 L.7.1–6
11. Justifying own arguments and evaluating others' arguments in writing	W.7.1, W.7.8–9 L.7.1–3, L.7.6
12. Selecting and applying varied and precise vocabulary and other language resources to effectively convey ideas	W.7.4–5 SL.7.4, SL.7.6 L.7.1, L.7.3, L.7.5–6

Part II: Learning How English Works

English Language Development Standard	Corresponding California Common Core State Standards for English Language Arts
A. STRUCTURING COHESIVE TEXT	
1. Understanding text structure	RL.7.5 RI.7.5 W.7.1–5, W.7.10 SL.7.4
2. Understanding cohesion	RI.7.5 W.7.1–5, W.7.10 L.7.1, L.7.3–6
B. EXPANDING AND ENRICHING IDEAS	
3. Using verbs and verb phrases	W.7.5 SL.7.6 L.7.1, L.7.3–6
4. Using nouns and noun phrases	W.7.5 SL.7.6 L.7.1, L.7.3–6
5. Modifying to add detail	W.7.4–5 SL.7.6 L.7.1, L.7.3–6

English Language Development Standard	Corresponding California Common Core State Standards for English Language Arts
C. CONNECTING AND CONDENSING IDEAS	
6. Connecting ideas	W.7.1.5 SL.7.4, SL.7.6 L.7.1, L.7.3-6
7. Condensing ideas	W.7.1.5 SL.7.4, SL.7.6 L.7.1, L.7.3-6

Part III: Using Foundational Literacy Skills

Literacy in an Alphabetic Writing System
• Print concepts • Phonological awareness • Phonics and word recognition • Fluency

Bold Actions

"Be bold, take courage . . . and be strong of soul."

—Ovid

Bold Actions

In this collection, you will explore what it means to face challenges fearlessly, even if it means failing in the attempt.

Stream to Start

hmhfyi.com

Channel One News®

COLLECTION

PERFORMANCE TASK Preview

After reading the selections in this collection, you will have the opportunity to complete two performance tasks:

• In one, you will write a fictional narrative with a main character who boldly attempts to overcome a tremendous challenge.

• In the second, you will write and present an argument about the rewards and risks of undertaking bold actions.

ACADEMIC VOCABULARY

Study the words and their definitions in the chart below. You will use these words as you discuss and write about the texts in this collection.

Word	Definition	Related Forms
aspect (ăs´pĕkt) *n.*	a characteristic or feature of something	aspectual
cultural (kul´chər-əl) *adj.*	of or relating to culture or cultivation	agriculture, culture, cultured, multicultural
evaluate (ĭ-văl´yōō-āt´) *v.*	to examine something carefully to judge its value or worth	evaluation, evaluator, evaluative
resource (rē´sôrs´) *n.*	something that can be used for support or help	resources, resourceful, natural resources
text (tĕkst) *n.*	a literary work that is regarded as an object of critical analysis	textbook, textual, texture, textile

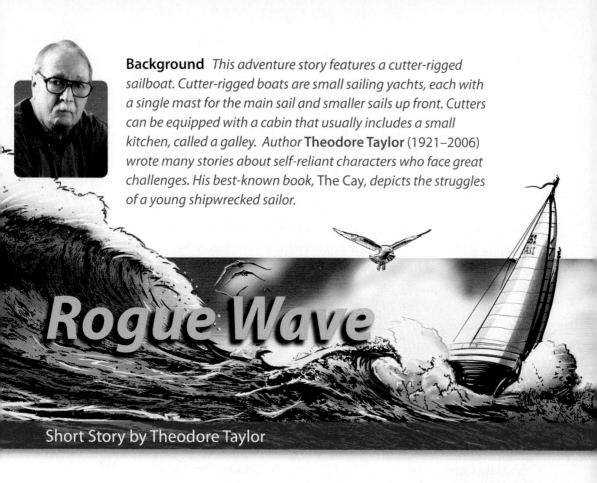

Background *This adventure story features a cutter-rigged sailboat. Cutter-rigged boats are small sailing yachts, each with a single mast for the main sail and smaller sails up front. Cutters can be equipped with a cabin that usually includes a small kitchen, called a galley. Author* **Theodore Taylor** *(1921–2006) wrote many stories about self-reliant characters who face great challenges. His best-known book,* The Cay, *depicts the struggles of a young shipwrecked sailor.*

Rogue Wave

Short Story by Theodore Taylor

SETTING A PURPOSE Pay attention to the details and events that make this story an adventure. As you read, think about how the author builds a sense of excitement and anticipation throughout the short story.

myNotebook

As you read, save new words to *my*WordList.

A killer wave, known to mariners as a "rogue wave," was approaching a desolate area of Baja California below Ensenada. It had been born off the east coast of Australia during a violent storm; it had traveled almost 7,000 miles at a speed of 20.83 miles an hour. Driven by an unusual pattern of easterly winds, it was a little over 800 feet in length and measured about 48 feet from the bottom of its trough to its crest. On its passage across the Pacific, it had already killed thirteen people, mostly fishermen in small boats, but also an
10 entire French family of five aboard a 48-foot schooner . . .

Melissa "Scoot" Atkins went below into the *Old Sea Dog's* tiny galley, moving down the three steps of the companionway, closing the two solid entry doors behind her, always a good idea in offshore sailing. The three horizontal hatch boards that were on top of the doors were also firmly in place, securing the thirty-foot Baba type against sudden invasion of seawater.

Rogues and sneakers have been around since the beginning of the oceans, and the earliest sea literature makes note of "giant" waves. The U.S. Navy manual Practical Methods for Observing and Forecasting Ocean Waves *says, "In any wave system, after a long enough time, an exceptional high one will occur. These monstrous out-sized waves are improbable but still possible and the exact time of occurrence can never be predicted." Naval hydrography[1] studies indicate that waves 15 to 25 feet high qualify for "sneaker" or "sleeper" status; the freak rogue is up to 100 feet or over. As waters slowly warm they seem to be occurring more frequently. In 1995 the* Queen Elizabeth 2 *(the QE2), the great British passenger liner, encountered a 95-foot rogue south of Newfoundland. More than 900 feet long, the QE2 rode over it, but her captain said it looked like they were sailing into the White Cliffs of Dover.*

Sullivan Atkins, Scoot's oldest brother, was steering the cutter-rigged boat on a northerly course about fifteen miles off desolate Cabo Colnett, south of Ensenada. Under a brilliant sun, the glittering blue Pacific rose and fell in long, slick **swells,** a cold light breeze holding steady.

swell
(swĕl) *n.*
A *swell* is a long, unbroken wave.

Below **deck** Scoot was listening to Big Sandy & His Fly-Rite Boys doing "Swingin' West," and singing along with them while slicing leftover steak from last night's meal. They'd grilled it on a small charcoal ring that was mounted outboard on the starboard side[2] at the stern, trailing sparks into the water. The *Sea Dog* had every blessed thing, including a barbecue pit, she marveled.

deck
(dĕk) *n.* The *deck* is the platform on a ship or boat where people stand.

Scoot was learning how to be a deep-water sailor. She was fourteen years old and pretty, with dark hair. Though small in size, not even five feet, she was strong. She'd started off with eight-foot Sabots. On this trip, her first aboard the *Sea Dog,* she'd manned the wheel for most of the three days they'd been under way. She'd stood four-hour watches at night. Sully was a good teacher.

---

[1] **hydrography:** the scientific description and analysis of the earth's surface waters.

[2] **outboard on the starboard side:** positioned outside and on the right side of the boat.

It was one of those perfect days to be out, Sully thought: the three Dacron sails belayed and whispering, white bow waves singing pleasant songs as the fiberglass hull, tilting to starboard, sliced through the ocean. It was a day filled with goodness, peace, and beauty. They'd come south as far as Cabo Colnett, turning back north only an hour ago. They'd sailed from Catalina Island's Avalon Harbor, the *Sea Dog's* home port, out in the channel off Los Angeles. Sully had borrowed the boat from a family friend, Beau Tucker,

60 a stockbroker with enough money to outfit it and maintain it properly. Built by Ta-Shing, of Taiwan, she was heavy and sturdy, with a teakwood deck and handsome teakwood interior, and the latest in **navigation** equipment. Sully had sailed her at least a dozen times. He'd been around boats, motor and sail, for many of his nineteen years. He thought the *Old Sea Dog* was the best, in her category, that he'd ever piloted.

navigation
(năv´ĭ-gā´shən) *n.*
The *navigation* of a ship or boat is the act of guiding it along a planned course.

As he was about to complete a northeast tack, Sully's attention was drawn to a squadron of seagulls diving on

70 small fish about a hundred yards off the port bow, and he did not see the giant wave that had crept up silently behind the *Sea Dog.* But a split second before it lifted the boat like a carpenter's chip, he sensed something behind him and glanced backward, toward the towering wall of shining water.

It was already too late to shout a warning to Scoot so she could escape from the cabin; too late to do anything except hang on to the wheel with both hands; too late even to pray. He did manage a yell as the *Sea Dog* became vertical. She rose up the surface of the wall stern first and then pitch-poled

80 violently, end over end, the bow **submerging** and the boat going upside down, taking Sully and Scoot with it, the forty-foot mast, sails intact, now pointing toward the bottom.

submerge
(səb-mûrg´) *v.*
When something *submerges*, it becomes covered by water.

Scoot was hurled upward, legs and arms flying, her head striking the after galley bulkhead and then the companionway steps and the interior deck, which was now the ceiling. She instantly blacked out.

Everything loose in the cabin was scattered around what had been the overhead. Water was pouring in and was soon lapping at Scoot's chin. It was coming from a four-inch

90 **porthole** that had not been dogged securely and a few other smaller points of entry.

porthole
(pôrt´hōl) *n.* A *porthole* is a circular window on a boat or ship.

Sully's feet were caught under forestay sailcloth, plastered around his face, but then he managed to shove clear and swim upward, breaking water. He looked at the mound of upside-down hull, bottom to the sky, unable to believe that the fine, sturdy *Sea Dog* had been flipped like a cork, perhaps trapping Scoot inside. Treading water, trying to collect his thoughts, he yelled, "Scoot," but there was no answer. Heart pounding, unable to see over the mound of the hull, he circled it, thinking she might have been thrown clear. But there was no sign of her.

> **Maneuvering his body, he pulled on the handles. The doors were jammed.**

He swam back to the point of cabin entry, took several deep breaths, and dove. He felt along the hatch boards and then opened his eyes briefly to see that the doors were still closed. She *was* still inside. Maneuvering his body, he pulled on the handles. The doors were jammed, and he returned to the surface for air.

He knew by the way the boat had already settled that there was water inside her. Under usual circumstances, the hull being upright, there would be four feet, nine inches of hull below the waterline. There would be about the same to the cabin overhead, enabling a six-foot-person to walk about down there.

Panting, blowing, Sully figured there was at least a three-foot air pocket holding the *Sea Dog* on the surface, and if Scoot hadn't been knocked unconscious and drowned, she could live for quite a while in the dark chamber. How long, he didn't know.

In the blackness, water continued to lap at Scoot's chin. She had settled against what had been the deck of the galley alcove, her body in an upright position on debris. Everything not tied down or in a locker was now between the overhead ribs. Wooden hatch covers[3] from the bilges were floating in the water and the naked bilges were exposed. Just aft of her body, and now above it, was the small diesel engine as well as the batteries. Under the water were cans of oil, one of them leaking. Battery acid might leak, too. Few sailors could imagine the nightmare that existed inside the *Sea Dog*. Scoot's pretty face was splashed with engine oil.

130 Over the next five or six minutes, Sully dove repeatedly, using his feet as a fulcrum, and using all the strength that he had in his arms, legs, and back, in an effort to open the doors. The pressure of the water defeated him. Then he thought about trying to pry the doors open with the wooden handle of the scrub brush. Too late for that, he immediately discovered. It had drifted away, along with Scoot's nylon jacket, her canvas boat shoes—anything that could float.

Finally he climbed on top of the keel, catching his breath, resting a moment, trying desperately to think of a way to enter 140 the hull. Boats of the Baba class, built for deep-water sailing, quite capable of reaching Honolulu and beyond, were almost sea-tight unless the sailors made a mistake or unless the sea became angry. The side ports were supposed to be dogged securely in open ocean. Aside from the cabin doors, there was no entry into that cabin without tools. He couldn't very well claw a hole through the inch of tough fiberglass.

He thought about the hatch on the foredeck, but it could only be opened from inside the cabin. Then there was the skylight on the top of the seventeen-foot cabin, used for 150 ventilation as well as a sun source; that butterfly window, hinged in the middle, could be opened only from the inside. Even with scuba gear, he couldn't open that skylight unless he had tools.

He fought back tears of frustration. There was no way to reach Scoot. And he knew what would happen down there. The water would slowly and inevitably rise until the air pocket was only six inches; her head would be trapped between the surface of the water and the dirty bilge. The water would torture her, then it would drown her. Seawater has no heart,

---

[3] **Wooden hatch covers:** door-like coverings made of wood that fit over openings on the deck or hull of a boat.

160　no brain. The *Sea Dog* would then drop to the ocean floor, thousands of feet down, entombing her forever.

Maybe the best hope for poor Scoot was that she was already dead, but he had to determine whether she was still alive. He began pounding on the hull with the bottom of his fist, waiting for a return knock. At the same time, he shouted her name over and over. Nothing but silence from inside there. He wished he'd hung on to the silly scrub brush. The wooden handle would make more noise than the flesh of his fist.

170　Almost half an hour passed, and he finally broke down and sobbed. His right fist was bloody from the constant pounding. Why hadn't *he* gone below to make the stupid sandwiches? Scoot would have been at the wheel when the wave grasped the *Sea Dog*. His young sister, with all her life to live, would be alive now.

They'd had a good brother-sister relationship. He'd teased her a lot about being pint-sized and she'd teased back, holding her nose when he brought one girl or another home for display. She'd always been spunky. He'd taken her sailing locally, in the channel, but she'd wanted an offshore cruise for

180　her fourteenth birthday. Now she'd had one, unfortunately.

Their father had nicknamed her Scoot because, as a baby, she'd crawled so fast. It was still a fitting name for her as a teenager. With a wiry body, she was fast in tennis and swimming and already the school's champion in the hundred-yard dash.

Eyes closed, teeth clenched, he kept pounding away with the bloody fist. Finally he went back into the ocean to try once more to open the doors. He sucked air, taking a half-dozen deep breaths, and then dove again. Bracing his feet against the

190　companionway frames, he felt every muscle straining, but the doors remained jammed. He was also now aware that if they did open, more water would rush in and he might not have time to find Scoot in the blackness and pull her out. But he was willing to take the gamble.

Scoot awakened as water seeped into her mouth and nose. For a moment she could not understand where she was, how she got there, what had happened …Vaguely, she remembered the boat slanting steeply downward, as if it were suddenly diving, and she remembered feeling her body going up.

That's all she remembered, and all she knew at the moment was that she had a fierce headache and was in chill water in total darkness. It took a little longer to realize she was trapped in the *Sea Dog's* cabin, by the galley alcove. She began to feel around herself and to touch floating things. The air was thick with an oil smell. Then she ran her hand over the nearest solid thing—a bulkhead. *That's strange,* she thought—her feet were touching a pot. She lifted her right arm and felt above her—the galley range. The galley range above her? *The boat was upside down.* She felt for the companionway steps and found the entry doors and pushed on them; that was the way she'd come in. The doors didn't move.

Sully crawled up on the wide hull again, clinging to a faint hope that a boat or ship would soon come by; but the sun was already in descent, and with night coming on, chances of rescue lessened with each long minute. It was maddening to have her a few feet away and be helpless to do anything. Meanwhile the hull swayed gently, in eerie silence.

Scoot said tentatively, "Sully?" Maybe he'd been drowned. Maybe she was alone and would die here in the foul water. She repeated his name, but much more loudly. No answer. She was coming out of shock now and fear icier than the water was replacing her confusion. To die completely alone? It went that way for a few desperate moments, and then she said to herself, *Scoot, you've got to get out of here! There has to be some way to get out . . .*

Sully clung to the keel with one hand, his body flat against the smooth surface of the hull. There was ample room on either side of the keel before the dead-rise, the upward slope of the hull. The *Sea Dog* had a beam of ten feet. Unless a wind and waves came up, he was safe enough in his wet perch.

230

Scoot again wondered if her brother had survived and if he was still around the boat or on it. With her right foot she began to probe around the space beneath her. The pot had drifted away, but her toes felt what seemed to be flatware. That made sense. The drawer with the knives and forks and spoons had popped out, spilling its contents. She took a deep breath and ducked under to pick out a knife. Coming up, she held the knife blade, reaching skyward with the handle . . .

Eyes closed, brain mushy, exhausted, Sully heard a faint tapping and raised up on his elbows to make sure he wasn't dreaming. No, there was a tapping from below. He crawled back toward what he thought was the source area, the galley area, and put an ear to the hull. *She was tapping!* He pounded the fiberglass, yelling, "Scoot, Scooot, Scooot . . ."

240

Scoot heard the pounding and called out, "Sully, I'm here, I'm here!" Her voice seemed to thunder in the air pocket.

Sully yelled, "Can you hear me?"

Scoot could only hear the pounding.
"Help me out of here . . ."

Ear still to the hull, Sully shouted again, "Scoot, can you hear me?" No answer. He pounded again and repeated, "Scoot, can you hear me?" No answer. The hull was too thick and the slop of the sea, the moan of the afternoon breeze, didn't help.

250

Though she couldn't hear his voice, the mere fact that he was up there told her she'd escape. Sully had gotten her out of jams before. There was no one on earth that she'd rather have as a rescue man than her oldest brother. She absolutely knew she'd survive.

Though it might be fruitless, Sully yelled down to the galley alcove, "Listen to me, Scoot. You'll have to get out by yourself. I can't help you. I can't break in. Listen to me, I know you're in water, and the best way out is through the skylight. You've got

260

to dive down and open it. You're small enough to go through it . . ." She could go through either section of the butterfly window. "Tap twice if you heard me!"

She did not respond, and he repeated what he'd just said, word for word.

No response. No taps from below.

Scoot couldn't understand why he didn't just swim down and open the doors to the cabin, release her. That's all he needed to do, and she'd be free.

> ## " No response.
> ##   No taps from below. "

Sully looked up at the sky. "Please, God, help me, help us." It was almost unbearable to know she was alive and he was unable to do anything for her. Then he made the decision to keep repeating: "Listen to me, Scoot. You'll have to get out by yourself. I can't break in. Listen to me, the best way out is through the skylight. You've got to dive down and open it. You're small enough to go through it . . ."

He decided to keep saying it the rest of the day and into the night or for as long as it took to penetrate the hull with words. *Skylight! Skylight!* Over and over.

He'd heard of mental telepathy but had not thought much about it before. Now it was the only way to reach her.

Scoot finally thought that maybe Sully was hurt, maybe helpless up on that bottom, so that was why he couldn't open the doors and let her out. That had to be the reason—Sully up there with broken legs. *So I'll have to get out on my own,* she thought.

Over the last two days, when she wasn't on the wheel she had been exploring the *Sea Dog,* and she thought she knew all the exits. Besides the companionway doors, which she knew she couldn't open, there was the hatch on the foredeck for access to the sails; then there was the skylight, almost

270

280

290

in the middle of the long cabin. Sully had opened it, she remembered, to air out the boat before they sailed. As she clung to a light fixture by the alcove, in water up to her shoulders, something kept telling her she should first try the butterfly windows of the skylight. The unheard message was compelling—*Try the skylight.*

300 Sully's voice was almost like a recording, a mantra, saying the same thing again and again, directed down to the position of the galley.

Scoot remembered that an emergency flashlight was bracketed on the bulkhead above the starboard settee, and she assumed it was waterproof. From what Sully had said, Beau Tucker took great care in selecting emergency equipment. It might help to actually see the dogs on the metal skylight frame. She knew she wouldn't have much time to spin them loose. Maybe thirty or forty seconds before she'd have to surface for breath. Trying

310 to think of the exact position of the upside-down flashlight, she again tapped on the hull to let her brother know she was very much alive.

He pounded back.

Sully looked at his watch. Almost four-thirty. About three hours to sundown. Of course, it didn't make much difference to Scoot. She was already in dank night. But it might make a difference if she got out after nightfall. He didn't know what kind of shape she was in. Injured, she might surface and drift away.

320 The mantra kept on.

Scoot dove twice for the boxy flashlight, found it, and turned it on, suddenly splitting the darkness and immediately feeling hopeful. But it was odd to see the *Sea Dog's* unusual overhead, the open hatchways into the bilge and the debris floating on the shining water, all streaked with lubricants; odd to see the toilet upside down. She held the light underwater and it continued to operate.

Every so often, Sully lifted his face to survey the horizon, looking for traffic. He knew they were still within sixteen or

330 seventeen miles of the coast, though the drift was west. There was usually small-boat activity within twenty miles of the shore—fishermen or pleasure boats.

Scoot worked herself forward a few feet, guessing where the skylight might be, and then went down to find the butterfly windows, the flashlight beam cutting through the murk. It took a few seconds to locate them and put a hand on one brass dog. She tried to turn it, but it was too tight for her muscles and she rose up to breathe again.

340 Not knowing what was happening below or whether Scoot was trying to escape, Sully was getting more anxious by the moment. He didn't know whether or not the crazy telepathy was working. He wished she would tap again to let him know she was still alive. It had been more than twenty minutes since she'd last tapped.

Scoot had seen a toolbox under the companionway steps and went back to try to find it. She guessed there'd be wrenches inside it, unless they'd spilled out. Using the flashlight again, she found the metal box and opened it. Back to the surface to breathe again, and then back to the toolbox to extract a wrench.
350 With each move she was becoming more and more confident.

A big sailboat, beating south, came into Sully's view; but it was more than two miles away and the occupants—unless he was very lucky—would not be able to spot the *Sea Dog's* mound and the man standing on it, waving frantically.

Four times Scoot needed to dive, once for each dog; and working underwater was at least five times as difficult as trying to turn them in usual circumstances. She'd aim the light and rest it to illuminate the windows. Finally, all the dogs

were loose and she rose once again. This time, after filling her
360   lungs to bursting, she went down and pushed on the starboard
window. It cracked a little, but the outside sea pressure resisted
and she had to surface again.

Sully sat down, almost giving up hope. How long the air
pocket would hold up was anybody's guess. The boat had
settled at least six inches in the last two hours. It might not last
into the night.

On her sixth dive Scoot found a way to brace her feet against
the ceiling ribs. She pushed with all her strength, and this
time the window opened. Almost out of breath, she quickly
370   pushed her body through and the *Old Sea Dog* released her.
Treading water beside the hull, she sucked in fresh air and
finally called out, "Sully ..."

He looked her way, saw the grin of triumph on the oil-stained
imp face, and dived in to help her aboard the derelict.
        Shivering, holding each other for warmth all night, they
rode and rocked, knowing that the boat was sinking lower
each hour.
        Just after dawn, the *Red Rooster,* a long-range sports
fishing boat out of San Diego bound south to fish for wahoo
380   and tuna off the Revilla Gigedo Islands, came within a
hundred yards of the upside-down sailboat and stopped to
pick up its two chattering survivors.
        The *Red Rooster's* captain, Mark Stevens, asked, "What
happened?"
        "Rogue wave," said Sully. That's what he planned to say to
Beau Tucker as well.
        Stevens winced and nodded that he understood.
        The *Old Sea Dog* stayed on the surface for a little while
longer, having delivered her survivors to safety; then her air
390   pocket breathed its last and she slipped beneath the water,
headed for the bottom.

COLLABORATIVE DISCUSSION How and when did this
adventure tale "hook" you? As it unfolded, what events
helped to keep you anxious about what would happen? With
a partner, review "Rogue Wave" to point out and discuss the
parts that helped to create excitement and anticipation.

Analyze Story Elements: Plot and Setting

ELA RL.7.3
ELD PI.7.6

The power of a story, such as "Rogue Wave," comes from its action and events. Most stories follow a series of events, also known as the **plot.** A story centers around the **conflict,** the struggle between opposing forces. As the characters struggle to resolve a conflict, the plot builds **suspense,** the growing tension and excitement felt by the reader. Most plots have five stages:

- The **exposition** introduces the characters and presents the setting and conflict.
- The **rising action** presents complications that intensify.
- The **climax** is the story's moment of greatest interest—the point where the conflict is resolved.
- In the **falling action,** the story begins to draw to a close.
- The **resolution** reveals the final outcome of the conflict.

Often the plot is influenced by the **setting,** or the time and place of the action. For example, the setting can cause plot complications. In "Rogue Wave," Sully notes that as evening comes, the fading light could hamper his rescue efforts. To understand the influence of setting on the plot in "Rogue Wave," find details that tell where and when the events are happening. Use those details to visualize the setting and follow the action.

Make Inferences

ELA RL.7.1
ELD PI.7.6

Authors do not always fully describe every aspect of a story, setting, or character. They do, however, provide clues that help you to make **inferences,** logical guesses based on facts and one's own knowledge and experience. You make an inference by combining evidence with what you know.

To support your inferences, you may need to **cite textual evidence,** or provide specific information from the text. For example, you can identify story details that indicate a character's feelings, as shown in the chart. Using a chart like this one can help you make inferences throughout a text.

Detail from the Text	My Own Experience	My Inference
In lines 37–39, Scoot is listening to music and singing along.	When I sing along to a song, I usually feel happy.	Scoot feels happy to be sailing with her brother.

Analyzing the Text

ELA RL.7.1, RL.7.3, W.7.3, SL.7.4 ELD PI.7.6, PI.7.9, PI.7.10

Cite Text Evidence Support your responses with evidence from the text.

1. **Infer** Reread lines 218–225. What inference can you make about Scoot's personality, based on these lines?

2. **Connect** How does the information in lines 17–31 help establish the conflict?

3. **Infer** Reread lines 186–194. Describe Sully's emotions at this point.

4. **Infer** Reread lines 328–332. What inference does the author want you to make at this point?

5. **Compare** Fill out a chart like this one to trace the conflicts or complications Scoot and Sully encounter in the story. Review the story events in the text, expanding the chart as necessary to cover the key happenings.

Complication	1	2	3	4	5
Scoot's					
Sully's					

6. **Analyze** Identify the two settings in this story. How does the author's shifting between these settings help build suspense?

7. **Evaluate** Describe the climax of the story. What makes this moment so suspenseful? Explain.

PERFORMANCE TASK

Writing Activity: Movie Outline
Think about how "Rogue Wave" could be adapted as an action movie. Write a four-paragraph movie outline showing how it could be done. Use your completed outline to "pitch"—or present persuasively—your movie idea to a partner or group. In your outline, be sure to include:

- a description of the opening scene that establishes the characters, setting, and conflict.
- a description of each important scene in the plot.
- suggestions for how to shoot each scene to convey the suspense.

Critical Vocabulary

ELA L.7.4a, L.7.4b, L.7.4c
ELD PI.7.6, PI.7.12

swell   deck   navigation   submerge   porthole

Practice and Apply Complete each sentence to show that you understand the meaning of the boldfaced vocabulary word.

1. I can see the water's motion by watching how a **swell** . . .

2. One reason to be on the **deck** of a boat is . . .

3. Sailors need tools for **navigation,** such as . . .

4. When the tide comes in on the beach, it could **submerge** . . .

5. There was a **porthole** in our room on the boat, so we . . .

Vocabulary Strategy: Latin Roots

A **root** is a word part that came into English from an older language. Roots from the ancient language of Latin appear in many English words. Often, by identifying Latin roots, you can figure out the meanings of words that seem unfamiliar. For example, the chart shows two words from "Rogue Wave." Each contains a Latin root having to do with the sea.

Word	Latin Root	Root's Meaning
mariners	*mar*	sea
navigation	*nav*	ship

Mariners, which comes from the Latin root *mar*, are sea sailors. The Latin root *nav*, from which *navigation* comes, appears in words having to do with ships and sailing, such as *navy* (a fleet of ships) and *naval* (having to do with navies). By identifying the roots *mar* and *nav*, you can make a good guess about the meanings of longer words that include them. Relying on a resource such as a print or online dictionary also can help you confirm your ideas.

Practice and Apply Read each sentence. Identify the words with the Latin roots *mar* and *nav*. Tell what each word means. Use a print or online dictionary to check your ideas.

1. Sailors in the navy may spend time in submarines.

2. Mariners long ago navigated using the stars.

3. Using navigation equipment, fishermen found a region of rich marine life.

4. Boats set out from the marina to sail up the river, which is navigable to the waterfalls.

Language Conventions: Sentence Structure

A **clause** is a group of words that has the two main parts of a sentence—a complete subject and a complete predicate. A **complete subject** includes all the words that identify the person, place, thing, or idea that the sentence is about. The **complete predicate** includes all the words that tell or ask something about the subject.

Complete Subject	Complete Predicate
The *Sea Dog*	*had every blessed thing.*
Sully	*was a good teacher.*

A **simple sentence** contains just one main clause.

Sully looked at his watch.

In this sentence, the complete subject is *Sully* and the complete predicate is *looked at his watch*.

A **compound sentence** contains two or more main clauses that are joined either by a comma and coordinating conjunction, such as *and, but, or, for, so, yet,* and *nor,* or are joined by a semicolon.

She pushed with all her strength, and this time the window opened.

In this compound sentence, the simple sentence *She pushed with all her strength* is combined with the sentence *this time the window opened*, using a comma and the coordinating conjunction *and*.

She found the entry doors; they were closed.

In this compound sentence, a semicolon is used to connect two simple sentences.

Practice and Apply Create a compound sentence by joining the two simple sentences with either a comma and a coordinating conjunction or a semicolon.

1. Rogue waves are frightening. They are unpredictable giants.

2. A rogue wave can be very tall. It can travel thousands of miles.

3. Sailors know about the sea's dangers. They follow safety rules.

4. Life at sea has its risks. It also has beauty.

5. Sailors prepare for dangerous weather. They risk dying at sea.

Background *A compelling event in the news can trigger controversy. Through television, the Internet, and print articles, journalists and the general public voice their opinions and ask heated questions that may not have easy answers.*

SETTING A PURPOSE In this lesson, you'll analyze media about a 16-year-old's attempt to become the youngest person to sail solo around the world, an event that sparked worldwide controversy.

MEDIA ANALYSIS

Covering Issues
in the News

Parents of Rescued Teenage Sailor Abby Sunderland Accused of Risking Her Life

Online News Article by Paul Harris

Ship of Fools

Editorial by Joanna Weiss

Was Abby Too Young to Sail?

TV News Interview by CBS News

Parents of Rescued Teenage Sailor Abby Sunderland Accused of Risking Her Life

Sailing experts condemn family for allowing 16-year-old American girl to attempt a solo round-the-world voyage

Paul Harris, New York
The Observer, June 12, 2010

A teenage girl attempting to sail solo around the world was rescued yesterday in a remote spot of the Indian Ocean, bringing to a successful conclusion the dramatic bid to save her life.

Sixteen-year-old American Abby Sunderland was picked up from her stricken vessel by a dinghy[1] launched from the French fishing boat *Ile de la Reunion.*[2]

Her father, Laurence Sunderland, speaking to reporters outside their California home, said his daughter was safe and well: "She got out of her vessel with the clothes on her back, and we are just really excited and ecstatic that Abigail is in safe hands. She was in good spirits . . . she talked to her mother."

However, the same cannot be said of Sunderland's yacht, *Wild Eyes.* The vessel was apparently pounded by gigantic waves that had destroyed its mast,[3] which in turn knocked out her satellite communications equipment. The yacht was then effectively left floundering midway between Africa and Australia. It is likely to be allowed to sink.

Sunderland had activated an emergency beacon[4] which started a huge search and rescue operation involving Australia, America, and France. Numerous ships became involved in the hunt, as well as a chartered jet which spotted the teenager late on Thursday. Sunderland was able to radio the plane and report that she was fit and had food and water supplies.

---

[1] **dinghy:** a small open boat carried as a lifeboat on a larger boat.

[2] *Ile de la Reunion:* the French fishing boat carrying the dinghy that picked up Abby is a large ocean-going ship, 180 feet long, 23 feet wide, and weighing 1295 tons.

[3] **mast:** the tall, vertical pole that supports the sail and rigging of a ship.

[4] **beacon:** a radio or transmitter that emits a guidance signal.

The rescue itself was not without incident as rough seas saw the captain of the French boat fall into the water. "He was fished out in difficult conditions," said a statement from the French territory of Reunion Island.

30   Though the search for Sunderland ended happily, it has caused a debate on the wisdom of such young sailors making dramatic and dangerous journeys. Sunderland was following the achievement of her brother, Zac, who had made the solo journey around the world at the age of 17, becoming the youngest person in the world to do so.

Abby Sunderland on her sailboat *Wild Eyes* in Ensenada, Mexico, during her attempt at a solo round-the-world voyage

Many critics of Sunderland—and her parents—have criticized the decision to let her go on such a journey. "It's not something that a 16-year-old should be able to decide—whether they're capable of doing it. It's potentially
40 irresponsible for the parents," Michael Kalin, junior director of San Francisco's St Francis Yacht Club, told the Associated Press.

Other top figures from the world of sailing joined in the criticism. "In Abby's case she was lucky. It's only a matter of time until we end up with a tragedy on our hands," said Derrick Fries, a world sailing champion and author of *Learn to Sail.*

Such opinions by professionals have been echoed on blogs and comments on news articles as members of the public
50 have called the Sunderlands irresponsible and careless. One commentator on the *Los Angeles Times* website summed up the view of many: "Abby Sunderland was on the wrong type of boat (a racing yacht) in the wrong location (the southern Indian Ocean) at the wrong time of year (winter in the southern hemisphere). Other than those minor details, it was a well-planned voyage."

But the family have robustly defended themselves. They have pointed out that Abby is a highly experienced and highly skilled sailor. They have even used the debate to criticize the
60 too-careful tendency of much modern parenting advice and said that a certain amount of risky challenge was healthy for an adventurous child.

"I never questioned my decision in letting her go. In this day and age we get overprotective with our children," Laurence Sunderland said. "Look at how many teenagers die in cars every year. Should we let teenagers drive cars? I think it'd be silly if we didn't."

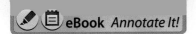

Analyze Structure

ELA RI.7.2, RI.7.5, SL.7.2
ELD PI.7.6, PII.7.1

In a **news report,** whether it's online, in print, or broadcast on television, journalists commonly use the **5 *Ws* and *H* questions**—*who, what, when, where, why,* and *how*—as an outline for writing the news story. Following this structure helps to ensure that writers have covered the necessary details. In turn, readers can use the 5 *Ws* and *H* questions to determine the main idea and supporting details of a news story. The **central idea** is the most important idea about a topic that a writer conveys, and the **supporting details** are the examples, facts, statistics, and anecdotes that provide a basis for the central idea.

Analyzing the Media

ELA RI.7.2, RI.7.5, SL.7.2
ELD PI.7.6, PII.7.1

Cite Text Evidence   Support your responses with evidence from the text.

1. **Summarize** Review the news story and fill out a chart like this one to record the story's 5 *Ws* and *H*.

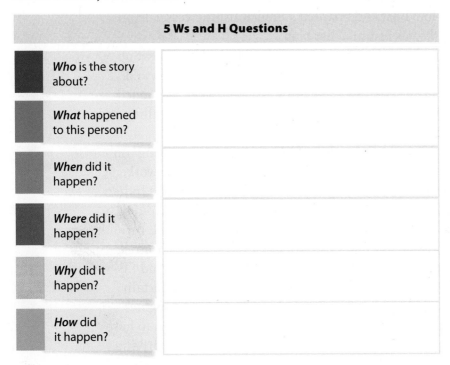

5 Ws and H Questions	
Who is the story about?	
What happened to this person?	
When did it happen?	
Where did it happen?	
Why did it happen?	
How did it happen?	

2. **Infer** What is the central idea of this article? Cite details from the article to support your answer.

Ship of Fools

Protecting a 16-year-old sailor, not enabling
dangerous dreams, is a parent's responsibility

Joanna Weiss, Globe Columnist
The Boston Globe, June 15, 2010

"I THINK it's a parent's job to realize their kids' dreams,"
Abby Sunderland's father told the *Los Angeles Times* last
winter. This was just before he waved his 16-year-old daughter
off on what was to be a six-month voyage alone on a small
boat, her effort to become the youngest person to sail around
the world nonstop and unassisted.

Here's a proposed rule of thumb: any record that requires
more than 10 syllables to explain does not need to be
broken. At any rate, Abby did not succeed. A massive storm
in the Indian Ocean knocked out her mast, launching a
massive international rescue effort. She has since abandoned
her 40-foot boat and boarded a French fishing vessel, from
where she has resumed her blog.

Actually, she has a panoply of interlinked blogs,[1] set up
to track and promote her journey, including one that sold
T-shirts and shoes with an "Abby 16" logo. They're flooded
now with comments offering gratitude and praise, calling her
a role model and an inspiration.

So this is the definition of bravery now? Embarking[2] on
unnecessary risk that jeopardizes the lives of rescue workers?
When I thought of a 16-year-old bobbing alone in the Indian
Ocean, surrounded by 25-foot waves, I didn't feel inspired.
I felt sad. And when I thought about her parents, I felt furious.

Abby's fans would call me a naysayer,[3] I gather from
their posts, and tell me I lack a spirit of adventure. And I'll
admit that parenthood requires one to overcome a certain
intolerance[4] for risk. I can't watch my 5-year-old daughter
climb the monkey bars without feeling like I'm going to have
a coronary. God knows what I'll do when she starts driving.

---

[1] **panoply (păn´ə plē) of interlinked blogs:** an array of blogs that are linked
together.

[2] **Embarking:** setting out.

[3] **naysayer:** one who opposes or takes a negative view.

[4] **intolerance:** condition or quality of not accepting.

30 But parenthood also requires you to invoke[5] maturity where your child lacks it, whether it's telling her that she's too small to slide down the fireman's pole or that her sailing journey will have to wait until she's old enough to come to her senses. It involves helping her figure out the difference between a dream and a fantasy.

Perhaps someone should have stepped in to impose some parenting standards on the Sunderlands; last summer, a court in the Netherlands stopped a 13-year-old girl from making her own unadvised solo sail. Better yet, we could give up a
40 culture that treats accomplishment as a race and turns risk into its own reward. Abby Sunderland couldn't drive without a learner's permit, but her journey on the high seas got her fawning press[6] and endorsement deals. Now, some fans on her site have offered their own money to recover her lost boat. One pledged to play an extra $5 a day in the lottery, just in case.

> " Perhaps someone should have stepped in to impose some parenting standards. "

When will he realize he's simply a pawn in the Sunderlands' audience-building scheme? From onboard the French fishing vessel, Abby has declared, *quelle surprise*,[7] that she's writing a book. Her father also disclosed that he's been
50 shopping a reality show with the working title "Adventures in Sunderland." (What good fortune this family has, to have a name that lends itself to puns.)

parent's resonsibility

---

[5] **invoke:** to call (a higher power) for assistance or support.
[6] **fawning press:** favor-seeking press.
[7] ***quelle surprise*:** What a surprise!

Childhood fame is always some mix of the child's dream and the parents'; so it was with Jessica Dubroff, the 7-year-old who died in 1996, trying to pilot a plane across the country.

With the growing temptations of book deals and TV series, the balance may be shifting even more. We'll surely hear more from Jordan Romero, the 13-year-old who just became the youngest person to climb Mount Everest. We
60 probably haven't heard the last of the Heenes of Colorado,[8] who at least had the sense not to actually put their child inside the Mylar balloon.

But while there's clearly a market for immature stars, we shouldn't confuse "youngest" with significant "first," and we shouldn't call these publicity stunts anything but what they are. Abby Sunderland may find a way to convert her misadventures into lingering fame. But while she seems to be a skilled junior sailor, calm in the face of danger, that doesn't make her a hero. It just makes her very, very lucky.

---

[8] **Heenes of Colorado:** a reference to a widely reported incident in 2009 in which a six-year-old boy was said to have floated away in a helium balloon. The report turned out to be false.

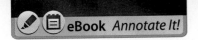

ELA RI.7.2, RI.7.5, RI.7.8
ELD PI.7.6, PI.7.7, PII.7.1

Trace and Evaluate an Argument

An **editorial** is an opinion piece that usually appears in the opinion and commentary section of a newspaper. An editorial is a type of argument in which the writer expresses one or more opinions about an issue and uses facts to support those opinions. A **fact** is a statement that can be proved. An **opinion** is a statement of belief or feeling. Like an argument, an editorial can include a **claim,** which is the writer's position or opinion; **reasons and evidence** that support the claim; and **counterarguments,** or responses to differing opinions.

Analyzing the Media

Cite Text Evidence   Support your responses with evidence from the text.

1. **Cite Evidence** Reread the editorial and fill in a chart like this one to cite the facts and opinions you find.

Type of Evidence	Examples
Facts	
Opinions	

2. **Identify** Which sentence in the editorial represents the writer's claim?

3. **Analyze** In the first quote, Abby's father says, "I think it's a parent's job to realize their kids' dreams." What is the editorial writer's counterargument to this statement?

4. **Summarize** What point does the editorial writer make in lines 41–62?

5. **Evaluate** How effectively does the editorial writer convey her opinion? Evaluate how clearly and convincingly the writer presents her evidence and ideas and concludes the editorial.

Was Abby Too Young to Sail?

TV News Interview by Harry Smith, CBS News

Running Time: 3:40 minutes

AS YOU VIEW The news interview you are about to view was first broadcast June 11, 2010, on the CBS Morning News as news broke that Abby Sunderland had been found in the Indian Ocean and was being rescued. In the segment you are about to view, journalist Harry Smith interviews the Sunderland family. Video clips of Abby and her sailboat before the trip are included.

COLLABORATIVE DISCUSSION Consider the choices the director makes about arranging the split-screen and including media features such as video clips. What is the effectiveness and impact of using video segments while the interviewees are speaking? What new information or insights do you learn from the interview about Abby's voyage and her preparedness? Discuss these choices and questions with your group and cite segments from the newscast to support your ideas.

©BBC Motion Gallery

Analyze Structure

ELA RI.7.2, RI.7.5, SL.7.2
ELD PI.7.6, PII.7.1

In a **TV news interview,** a journalist asks questions of and discusses issues with one or more people who may be experts, eyewitnesses, informed persons, or others close to the subject of the news interview. An interview includes video of the discussion between the interviewer and interviewee and may also include video or visuals of related information that tell the viewer more about the subject. The visual elements usually illustrate or emphasize important information by showing rather than telling what happened. These images can create positive or negative views of the topic or individuals.

When gathering information from a television interview, note the questions and listen carefully to the information provided in each interviewee's response.

Analyzing the Media

ELA RI.7.2, RI.7.5, SL.7.2
ELD PI.7.6, PII.7.1

Cite Text Evidence   Support your responses with evidence from the media.

1. **Identify** As you view the interview, use a chart like the one shown below to record information provided by each interviewee.

2. **Interpret** What overall impression of the Sunderland family does the interview create? Cite specific examples from the interview to support your response.

3. **Analyze** The video segments of Abby that appear at certain points during the interview were recorded before her trip. How do these video segments and the video overall characterize Abby?

Analyze Ideas in Diverse Media

ELA RI.7.2, RI.7.3, RI.7.5, RI.7.6, RI.7.8, RI.7.9, SL.7.2 ELD PI.7.6, PI.7.7, PII.7.1

You've just read coverage of a single topic in three different formats—a news article, an editorial, and a television interview—by different writers who provide their own unique evidence and interpretations of Abby Sunderland's rescue.

To analyze the information from these varied sources, examine the purpose and the ideas presented in each. The writer's purpose is his or her reason for writing the report or story: to inform, to persuade, to entertain, or to express thoughts or feelings. Often there is more than one purpose.

Analyzing the Media

ELA RI.7.2, RI.7.3, RI.7.5, RI.7.6, RI.7.8, RI.7.9, SL.7.2, W.7.6 ELD PI.7.6, PI.7.7, PI.7.8, PI.7.10, PII.7.1

Cite Text Evidence   Support your responses with evidence from the media.

1. **Analyze** Use a chart like this one to analyze the purpose and key information presented in each of the selections.

Type	News Article	Editorial	TV News Interview
Purpose			
Central Idea(s) or Claim(s)			
Support or Evidence			

2. **Synthesize** What idea about Abby's trip is emphasized in the editorial but not in the other two reports? How does this emphasis change your view of Abby's story?

3. **Analyze** What did you learn from the news interview that you did not learn from the articles? Cite specific evidence from each media piece to support your answer.

PERFORMANCE TASK

Media Activity: Blog With your classmates, create a class blog to discuss what you think would be an appropriate age to pursue such an undertaking. To build the blog, map out your home page and plan one or more discussion threads.

Begin the blog by writing your own opinion of Abby's solo adventure. Was it foolish or wise for someone her age to attempt such a trip alone? Refer to any of the three news pieces for evidence. Encourage classmates to post to the blog.

Background *Today we think of myths as stories that have been passed down through countless generations. In the ancient civilization of Greece, myths were the basis of an elaborate system of beliefs. Myths explained their mystifying world and offered wisdom on how to live in it. The myth of Daedalus and his son Icarus is one example.*

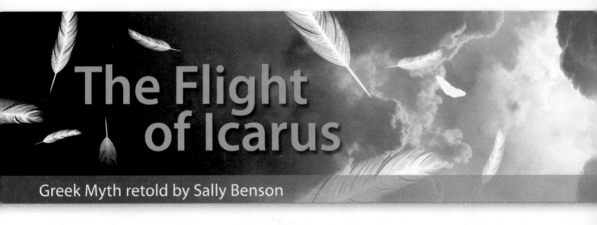

The Flight of Icarus

Greek Myth retold by Sally Benson

SETTING A PURPOSE As you read, pay close attention to the choices Icarus and his father make. What do these choices reveal? Write down any questions you may have while reading.

When Theseus escaped from the labyrinth, King Minos flew into a rage with its builder, Daedalus, and ordered him shut up in a high tower that faced the lonely sea. In time, with the help of his young son, Icarus, Daedalus managed to escape from the tower, only to find himself a prisoner on the island. Several times he tried by bribery to stow away on one of the vessels sailing from Crete, but King Minos kept strict watch over them, and no ships were allowed to sail without being carefully searched.

10   Daedalus was an ingenious artist and was not discouraged by his failures. "Minos may control the land and sea," he said, "but he does not control the air. I will try that way."

He called his son, Icarus, to him and told the boy to gather up all the feathers he could find on the rocky shore.

As thousands of gulls soared over the island, Icarus soon collected a huge pile of feathers. Daedalus then melted some wax and made a skeleton in the shape of a bird's wing. The smallest feathers he pressed into the soft wax and the large ones he tied on with thread. Icarus played about on the beach
20   happily while his father worked, chasing the feathers that blew away in the strong wind that swept the island and sometimes taking bits of the wax and working it into strange shapes with his fingers.

It was fun making the wings. The sun shone on the bright feathers; the breezes ruffled them. When they were finished, Daedalus fastened them to his shoulders and found himself lifted upwards, where he hung poised in the air. Filled with excitement, he made another pair for his son. They were smaller than his own, but strong and beautiful.
30   Finally, one clear, wind-swept morning, the wings were finished, and Daedalus fastened them to Icarus's shoulders and taught him how to fly. He bade him watch the movements of the birds, how they soared and glided overhead. He pointed out the slow, graceful sweep of their wings as they beat the air steadily, without fluttering. Soon Icarus was sure that he, too, could fly and, raising his arms up and down, skirted over the white sand and even out over the waves, letting his feet touch the snowy foam as the water thundered and broke over the sharp rocks. Daedalus watched him proudly but
40   with misgivings. He called Icarus to his side and, putting his arm round the boy's shoulders, said, "Icarus, my son, we are about to make our flight. No human being has ever traveled through the air before, and I want you to listen carefully to my instructions. Keep at a **moderate** height, for if you fly too low, the fog and spray will clog your wings, and if you fly too high, the heat will melt the wax that holds them together. Keep near me and you will be safe."

He kissed Icarus and fastened the wings more securely to his son's shoulders. Icarus, standing in the bright sun, the
50   shining wings dropping gracefully from his shoulders, his golden hair wet with spray, and his eyes bright and dark with excitement, looked like a lovely bird. Daedalus's eyes filled with tears, and turning away, he soared into the sky, calling to Icarus to follow. From time to time, he looked back to see that the boy was safe and to note how he managed his wings in his flight. As they flew across the land to test their **prowess** before

moderate
(mŏd´ər-ĭt) *adj.* When something is kept moderate, it is kept within a certain limit.

prowess
(prou´ĭs) *n.* Prowess is the strength and courage someone has.

setting out across the dark wild sea, plowmen below stopped their work and shepherds gazed in wonder, thinking Daedalus and Icarus were gods.

Father and son flew over Samos and Delos, which lay on their left, and Lebinthus,[1] which lay on their right. Icarus, beating his wings in joy, felt the thrill of the cool wind on his face and the clear air above and below him. He flew higher and higher up into the blue sky until he reached the clouds. His father saw him and called out in alarm. He tried to follow him, but he was heavier and his wings would not carry him. Up and up Icarus soared, through the soft, moist clouds and out again toward the glorious sun. He was bewitched by a sense of freedom and beat his wings **frantically** so that they would carry him higher and higher to heaven itself. The blazing sun beat down on the wings and softened the wax. Small feathers fell from the wings and floated softly down, warning Icarus to stay his flight and glide to earth. But the enchanted boy did not notice them until the sun became so hot that the largest feathers dropped off and he began to sink. Frantically he fluttered his arms, but no feathers remained to hold the air. He cried out to his father, but his voice was submerged in the blue waters of the sea, which has forever after been called by his name.

Daedalus, crazed by **anxiety**, called back to him, "Icarus! Icarus, my son, where are you?" At last he saw the feathers

frantic
(frăn′tĭk) *adj.* If you do something in a frantic way, you do it quickly and nervously.

anxiety
(ăng-zī′ĭ-tē) *n.* Anxiety is an uneasy, worried feeling.

---

[1] **Samos . . . Delos . . . Lebinthus:** (sā′mŏs′. . . dē′lŏs′. . . lŭbĭn′thŭs′): small Greek islands in the eastern Aegean Sea.

floating from the sky, and soon his son plunged through the clouds into the sea. Daedalus hurried to save him, but it was too late. He gathered the boy in his arms and flew to land, the tips of his wings dragging in the water from the double burden they bore. Weeping bitterly, he buried his small son and called the land Icaria in his memory.

Then, with a flutter of wings, he once more took to the air, but the joy of his flight was gone and his victory over the
90 air was bitter to him. He arrived safely in Sicily, where he built a temple to Apollo and hung up his wings as an offering to the god, and in the wings he pressed a few bright feathers he had found floating on the water where Icarus fell. And he mourned for the birdlike son who had thrown caution to the winds in the exaltation of his freedom from the earth.

COLLABORATIVE DISCUSSION In the last sentence, the author says that Icarus "had thrown caution to the winds"—he had made a bold and risky move. How had both Icarus and Daedalus made bold and risky moves? Share your ideas with your group.

Analyze Story Elements: Myth

"The Flight of Icarus" is a **myth,** a traditional story that attempts to answer basic questions about human nature, origins of the world, mysteries of nature, and social customs. A myth is also a form of entertainment that people have enjoyed since ancient times. Most myths share these elements:

- gods and other supernatural beings with special powers
- supernatural events and settings
- a lesson about life or human nature

Myths may also explain the origins of natural phenomena, such as volcanoes or constellations, or warn against the consequences of human error. Often, myths reveal the values that are of greatest cultural importance to a society, such as honesty, cleverness, and moderation, which means acting within reasonable limits. Myths were used to guide ancient people's behavior in a way that reflected these values and beliefs.

Explain how each of these statements is true for "The Flight of Icarus":

- In a myth, events occur that cannot happen in real life.
- A mythical character has unusual abilities.
- A myth shows the values of a culture.

Determine Theme

A **theme** is a message about life or human nature that a writer shares with the reader. An example of a theme might be "beauty fades" or "greed can lead to ruined lives." Authors might state a theme directly. More often, however, a reader must analyze the story events and characters' actions to infer, or make logical guesses about, the theme.

A myth often contains more than one theme, and often the theme reflects the cultural values of the society in which the myth was first told. By analyzing the behavior of mythic characters in unusual situations, we can learn lessons about the traits that mattered to a culture. This chart provides helpful questions for determining a myth's likely themes.

Your answers to the third question can lead you to ideas about life lessons or other big ideas—the themes—in a myth.

Finding the Theme of a Myth	1. What do the characters want?	2. What do the characters do to reach that goal?	3. How well do they succeed, and why?

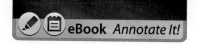
Analyzing the Text

ELA RL.7.1, RL.7.2, RL.7.3, RL.7.4, W.7.3, W.7.7 **ELD** PI.7.6, PI.7.8, PI.7.10

Cite Text Evidence   Support your responses with evidence from the text.

1. **Infer** Reread lines 1–9. How do you think Daedalus is reacting to his situation at this point?

2. **Interpret** Think about Daedalus's advice to Icarus in lines 41–47. What do these lines suggest about the kind of behavior that ancient Greeks valued?

3. **Interpret** Reread lines 56–59. What does the sentence suggest about one of the themes of this myth?

4. **Cite Evidence** What text clues does the author provide to hint at the outcome of Icarus's flight?

5. **Analyze** Reread lines 67–71, and identify descriptive words and phrases. What do these descriptions suggest about Icarus's experience?

6. **Connect** People today may refer to someone "who flew too close to the sun" as a cautionary tale. What does this expression mean and what does it have to do with the myth of Icarus? Explain.

PERFORMANCE TASK

Writing Activity: Graphic Comic
"The Flight of Icarus" begins with references to Theseus and his escape from the labyrinth built by Daedalus. Retell your own version of the myth in the form of a graphic comic. In this kind of text, both verbal and visual elements work together.

- Research retellings of the myth of Theseus and the Minotaur.

- Redo the text of the myth in your own words. Try to keep any character speeches or descriptions as brief as possible.
- Make sure that the words don't crowd the art space.
- Plan how your characters will look. Use any descriptions you find in the text version of the myth to help you.
- Do a rough sketch of your ideas before creating finished pages.

Critical Vocabulary

ELA L.7.4c
ELD PI.7.6, PI.7.12

moderate   **prowess**   **frantic**   **anxiety**

Practice and Apply Answer each question with *yes* or *no*. With your group, use examples and reasons to explain your answers.

1. Are most professional basketball players of **moderate** height?

2. Is **prowess** related to pride?

3. Is it possible to speak in a **frantic** way?

4. Would you look forward to having **anxiety**?

Vocabulary Strategy: Noun Suffixes *-ty* and *-ity*

A **suffix** is a word part that appears at the end of a word or root. Readers can use their knowledge of suffixes to figure out word meanings. Some suffixes signal that a word is a naming word, or **noun**. Notice the word with a noun suffix in this sentence from "The Flight of Icarus."

> **Daedalus, crazed by anxiety, called back to him, "Icarus! Icarus, my son, where are you?"**

The word *anxiety* ends with the suffix *-ty*, which signals that *anxiety* is a noun. Another form of the suffix is *-ity*. These suffixes add the meaning "state or condition of" to a word.

Anxiety means "the state of feeling anxious."

> The word *anxious* is an **adjective,** a word that modifies a noun or a pronoun.

The suffix *-ty* changes the adjective into a noun.

Practice and Apply The bold words in these items are adjectives. Change each adjective into its noun form by using the suffix *-ty* or *-ity*. Consult a resource, such as a print or online dictionary, for words that are unfamiliar.

1. Things that are **similar** are alike. A likeness is a _____.

2. Something that is **frail** may break. It has _____.

3. A **loyal** friend can be trusted. Friends share _____.

4. **Cruel** words hurt. Their speaker shows _____.

5. To be free from danger is to feel **secure.** This freedom is called _____.

Language Conventions: Commas and Coordinate Adjectives

Writers use **adjectives** to modify, or describe, nouns. Often, a writer will use more than one adjective to modify the same noun, such as in this phrase from "The Flight of Icarus": *one clear, wind-swept morning.*

Notice that the adjectives *clear* and *wind-swept* are separated by a comma. These are called **coordinate adjectives,** adjectives of equal effect that modify the same noun. Here is another example from the story: *the slow, graceful sweep of their wings.*

The comma acts like the word *and* between the coordinate adjectives. When you write, you can use a comma to replace *and.* Sometimes, however, two or more adjectives that modify the same noun do not have equal effect. Then no comma is needed.

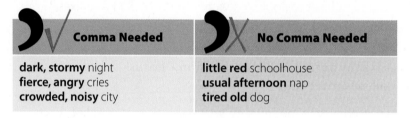

Comma Needed	No Comma Needed
dark, stormy night **fierce, angry** cries **crowded, noisy** city	**little red** schoolhouse **usual afternoon** nap **tired old** dog

You can determine whether adjectives modify equally with these tests:
- Swap the position of the adjectives. If the sentence makes sense, the adjectives modify equally: *the stormy, dark night*
- Insert the word *and* between the adjectives. If the sentence still reads well, the adjectives modify equally: *the dark **and** stormy night*

Practice and Apply   Find the nouns *sun, wings, hair, eyes,* and *bird* in this sentence from "The Flight of Icarus." Write two coordinate adjectives to describe each noun, using commas where needed. Consult resources such as a print or online dictionary for words that are unfamiliar to you.

> Icarus, standing in the bright sun, the shining wings dropping gracefully from his shoulders, his golden hair wet with spray, and his eyes bright and dark with excitement, looked like a lovely bird.

Background *From ancient times to present, writers have been fascinated by the characters of myths. They have featured famous mythic characters in such forms as dramas, stories, and poetry. Whether powerful or weak, noble or flawed, these characters have a hold on writers' imaginations. "Icarus's Flight" is a poem that reflects a poet's fascination with the myth of Icarus, the son of Daedalus who flew too close to the sun.*

Icarus's Flight

Poem by Stephen Dobyns

Stephen Dobyns (b. 1941) *has written numerous, critically acclaimed poetry collections. While he is also the author of other popular works of fiction, including novels and mysteries, he considers himself first and foremost a poet. In fact, he has claimed that he thinks of poetry twenty-four hours a day and that being a successful poet requires constant focus on the craft. Dobyns has also taught writing at a number of colleges throughout the United States.*

SETTING A PURPOSE As you read this poem, think about the way the poet portrays Icarus and his true intention.

Icarus's Flight

What else could the boy have done? Wasn't
flight both an escape and a great uplifting?
And so he flew. But how could he appreciate
his freedom without knowing the exact point

5 where freedom stopped? So he flew upward
and the sun dissolved the wax and he fell.
But at last in his anticipated plummeting
he grasped the confines of what had been

his liberty. You say he flew too far?
10 He flew just far enough. He flew precisely
to the point of wisdom. Would it
have been better to flutter ignorantly

from petal to petal within some garden
forever? As a result, flight for him was not
15 upward escape, but descent, with his wings
disintegrating around him. Should it matter

that neither shepherd nor farmer with his plow
watched him fall? He now had his answer,
laws to uphold him in his downward plunge.
20 Cushion enough for what he wanted.

COLLABORATIVE DISCUSSION According to the poet, what did
Icarus really want? Do you think Icarus achieved it? Discuss your
ideas with a partner.

Analyze Form: Poetry

Poetry is a type of literature in which words are carefully chosen and arranged to create certain effects. **Form** in poetry is the way the words are arranged on the page. Here are two basic elements of form in poetry:

- The **line** is the main unit of all poems. Poets play with line length to emphasize meaning and to create rhythm. **Rhythm** is a pattern of stressed and unstressed syllables in a line of poetry, similar to the rhythmic beats in music.
- Lines are arranged in a group called a **stanza.** A single stanza may express a separate idea or emotion, but each stanza contributes to the overall meaning of a poem.

Crafting a poem's form involves careful choices of words, rhythms, and sounds. To understand how form can help create an effect such as rhythm in a poem, ask yourself these questions.

 How long are the lines?

 Do the lines rhyme?

Do the sentences always end at the end of a line?

How many lines are in each stanza?

Determine Meaning of Words and Phrases: Alliteration

Poetry is often created to be spoken and heard. Reading a poem aloud can give readers a better sense of the feeling and sounds that the poet intended.

Poets often choose different words for their sounds. **Alliteration** is the repetition of consonant sounds at the beginning of words. It can establish rhythms in a poem that create feelings or emphasize ideas and images.

Read aloud these lines from "Icarus's Flight." Listen for the alliterative sounds. What do the repeated sounds suggest to you? How do they create rhythm and add emphasis to ideas or images in text?

> **As a result, flight for him was not**
> **upward escape, but descent, with his wings**
> **disintegrating around him. Should it matter**

Notice how the alliterative words of *descent* and *disintegrating* not only emphasize similar sounds, but they create a sense of falling *downward*—another word that begins with the same sound.

Analyzing the Text

ELA RL.7.2, RL.7.4, RL.7.5, W.7.2, SL.7.4 **ELD** PI.7.6, PI.7.8, PI.7.9, PII.7.1

Cite Text Evidence   Support your responses with evidence from the text.

1. **Identify** Look closely at how certain sentences of the poem extend from one stanza into the next one. What effect is created by extending a sentence into the next line or into the next stanza?

2. **Analyze** Examine the question in lines 3–5. Based on what you know about the Icarus myth, where is the "exact point where freedom stopped"? How would you answer this question?

3. **Analyze** Look at the third stanza and identify the alliterative words. What idea does this alliteration emphasize or draw attention to?

4. **Interpret** What does the poet mean by the two sentences in lines 10 and 11?

5. **Analyze** Find the sentence that begins within line 18 and read it aloud. What examples of alliteration do you see? Why do you think the poet uses alliteration here?

6. **Compare** Consider what you already knew about the mythological character, Icarus, before reading this poem. How does this poem cause your perception of Icarus to change? Explain.

PERFORMANCE TASK

Speaking Activity: Response to Literature The poet asks a number of questions throughout the poem, as if speaking directly to readers. What is the purpose of these questions? Do they cause you to consider Icarus's actions in a new light? Share your views in an oral response.

- Think about the questions and views the poet presents.
- Identify evidence from the poem to support your views.
- Make sure your points are clear and convincing. Use verbal and nonverbal techniques to enhance your points.

Background *In the early 1900s, flying in "aeroplanes"—fixed-winged, self-propelled flying machines—was a bold undertaking. Male pilots were dashing heroes. However, female aviators—especially African American women—had to struggle for acceptance.* **Patricia and Fredrick McKissack** (b. 1944; b. 1939) *have written over 100 biographies and nonfiction books, most focusing on the achievements of African Americans.*

Women in Aviation

Informational Text by Patricia and Fredrick McKissack

SETTING A PURPOSE As you read, pay attention to the details that describe what it was like for a woman to become a pilot during this period. What obstacles did each pilot face? Write down any questions you may have while reading.

American aviation was from its very beginnings marred with sexist and racist assumptions. It was taken for granted that women were generally inferior to men and that white men were superior to all others. Flying, it was said, required a level of skill and courage that women and blacks lacked. Yet despite these prevailing prejudices, the dream and the desire to fly stayed alive among women and African-Americans.

10   The story of women in aviation actually goes back to the time of the hot-air balloons. A number of women in Europe and America gained fame for their skill and daring. Sophie Blanchard made her first solo balloon flight in 1805. She grew in fame and was eventually named official aeronaut of the empire by Napoleon. By 1834, at least twenty women in Europe were piloting their own balloons.

Though she did not fly, Katherine Wright was a major supporter of her brothers' efforts. Orville so appreciated his sister's help that he said, "When the world speaks of the Wrights, it must include my sister. . . . She inspired much of our effort."

Although Raymonde de la Roche of France was the first woman in the world to earn her pilot's license, Harriet Quimby held the distinction of being the first American woman to become a licensed pilot.

On August 1, 1911, Quimby, who was described as a "real beauty" with "haunting blue-green eyes," strolled off the field after passing her pilot's test easily. To the male reporters who **inundated** her with questions, Quimby fired back answers with self-confidence. Walking past a group of women who had come to witness the historic event, Quimby was overheard to quip with a smile and a wink: "Flying is easier than voting." (The Woman's Suffrage Amendment wasn't passed until 1920.)

As difficult as it was for women to become pilots in significant numbers, it was doubly hard for African-Americans, especially black women. That's why Bessie Coleman, the first African-American to earn her pilot's license, is such an exciting and important figure in aviation.

Bessie Coleman was born in 1893 in Atlanta, Texas, the twelfth of thirteen children. Her mother, who had been a slave, valued education and encouraged all of her children to attend school in order to better themselves. The encouragement paid off, because Coleman graduated from high school, a feat not too many black women were able to accomplish in the early 1900s.

Bessie Coleman refused to accept the limitations others tried to place on her. She attended an Oklahoma college for one semester but ran out of money. Accepting the offer of one of her brothers to come live with him and his family in Chicago, Coleman found a job as a manicurist. She fully intended to return to school after saving enough money. But she never did. While in Chicago she learned about flying and made a new set of goals for herself. She wanted to be a pilot.

Coleman learned about flying from reading newspaper accounts of air battles during World War I. She tried to find a school that would accept her as a trainee. But no American instructor or flying school was willing to teach her.

inundate
(ĭn´ŭn-dāt´) v. To *inundate* is to give a huge amount of something.

When the war ended, a friend, Robert S. Abbott, the founder of the *Chicago Defender*, one of the most popular black-owned and -operated newspapers in the country, suggested that Coleman go to France, where racial prejudice was not as **restrictive** as it was in America. Even though the United States was the birthplace of flight, it was slower than other countries to develop an organized aviation program. European leaders immediately saw the commercial and military advantages of a strong national aviation program. Bessie knew from her reading that both French and German aircraft were among the best in the world.

restrictive
(rĭ-strĭk´tĭv) *adj.*
When something is *restrictive*, it is limiting in some way.

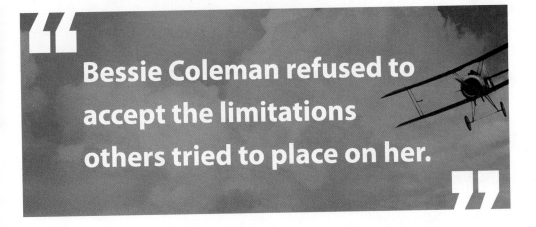

"Bessie Coleman refused to accept the limitations others tried to place on her."

Coleman had also read about Eugene Jacques Bullard, the well-decorated[1] and highly honored native of Georgia who had become the first African-American to fly an airplane in combat as a member of the French Lafayette Flying Corps during World War I. Other blacks had gone to Europe to get their training, too. Coleman realized that if she were ever going to get a chance to fly, she, too, would have to go to France. But she didn't have any money to get there, and besides, she couldn't speak a word of French.

For almost two years, Coleman worked part-time as a manicurist and as a server in a Chicago chili parlor and saved every penny to finance her trip to France. Meanwhile she learned to speak French, so when the time came, she'd be able to understand her instructors.

---

[1] **well-decorated:** term used to describe a person in the military who has received many awards.

Aviator Bessie Coleman posed for this photograph in 1920.

In 1921, Coleman made it to France, where she found an instructor who was one of Tony Fokker's chief pilots. Fokker, the famous aircraft manufacturer, said Coleman was a "natural talent." On June 15, 1921, Coleman made history by becoming the first black woman to earn her wings, thus joining the ranks of the handful of American women fliers.

90   Returning to the United States determined to start a flying school where other African-American pilots could be trained, Coleman looked for ways to finance her dream. There were very few jobs in the aviation industry for women or blacks. She soon learned that there was little or no support for a black woman who wanted to start a flying school. To call attention to aviation and to encourage other women and African-Americans to take part in the new and growing field,

Coleman gave flying **exhibitions** and lectured on aviation. She thrilled audiences with daredevil maneuvers, just as Quimby had done before her.

100   Along with racism, Coleman encountered the burden of sexism, but she made believers out of those who doubted her skill. "The color of my skin," she said, "[was] a drawback at first. . . . I was a curiosity, but soon the public discovered I could really fly. Then they came to see *Brave Bessie*, as they called me."

    The strict rules and regulations that govern aviation today didn't exist during the first three decades of flying. For example, it wasn't uncommon for aviators to ignore safety belts and fly without parachutes. One of these simple
110 safety **precautions** might have saved the lives of both Harriet Quimby and Bessie Coleman.

    On a July morning in 1912, Quimby, and a passenger named William P. Willard, set out to break an over-water speed record. When Quimby climbed to five thousand feet, the French-made Blériot monoplane[2] suddenly nosed down. Both Quimby and Willard were thrown from the plane and plunged to their deaths in the Boston Harbor.

    The *New York Sun* used the opportunity to speak out against women fliers:

120   Miss Quimby is the fifth woman in the world killed while operating an aeroplane (three were students) and their number thus far is five too many. The sport is not one for which women are physically qualified. As a rule they lack strength and presence of mind and the courage to excel as aviators. It is essentially a man's sport and pastime.

    Fourteen years later, Bessie Coleman died in a similar accident. With almost enough savings to start her school, Coleman agreed to do an air show in Florida on May Day
130 for the Negro Welfare League of Jacksonville. At 7:30 P.M. the night before, Coleman, accompanied by her publicity agent, William Wills, took her plane up for a test flight. When she reached an altitude of about five thousand feet, her plane flipped over. Coleman was thrown from the plane and

exhibition
(ĕk´sə-bĭsh´ən) *n.*
An *exhibition* is an organized presentation or show.

precaution
(prĭ-kô´shən) *n.*
A *precaution* is an action taken to avoid possible danger.

---

[2] **monoplane:** an airplane with only one pair of wings.

plunged to her death April 30, 1926. Wills died seconds later when the plane crashed.

Once again critics used the tragedy to assert that neither women nor blacks were mentally or physically able to be good pilots. "Women are often penalized by publicity for their every mishap," said Amelia Earhart, the most famous female pilot in aviation history. "The result is that such emphasis sometimes directly affects [a woman's] chances for a flying job," Earhart continued. "I had one manufacturer tell me that he couldn't risk hiring women pilots because of the way accidents, even minor ones, became headlines in the newspapers."

Although Bessie Coleman died tragically, her plans to open a flight training school for blacks were continued by those she had inspired.

COLLABORATIVE DISCUSSION What obstacles did Quimby, Coleman, and other early female pilots face that their male counterparts did not face? In a group, share ideas about what motivated these women to achieve in spite of difficulties.

Determine Author's Purpose

An **author's purpose** is the reason the author wrote a particular work. Usually an author writes for one or more purposes, as shown in this chart:

Author's Purpose	Examples of Written Works
To inform or explain	encyclopedia entries, informational articles, how-to articles, biographies, and other factual, real-world examples
To persuade	editorials, opinion essays and blogs, advertisements, and other works in which the author shares an opinion and tries to persuade readers to agree
To entertain	stories, novels, plays, essays, and literary works that engage the reader with qualities such as humor, suspense, and intriguing details
To express thoughts or feelings	poems, personal essays, journals and other texts in which the author shares insights, emotions, and descriptions

To determine an author's purpose in informational texts, examine the facts and quotations. An author may have a main purpose for writing, as well as other purposes. For example, "Women in Aviation" provides facts, so it is written mainly to inform. But the authors have other purposes, too, revealed by their word choices and their examples.

Cite Evidence and Draw Conclusions

When you **draw conclusions,** you make judgments or take a position on a topic. To support conclusions, readers cite **textual evidence**—information from the text in the form of facts and details. To draw conclusions in an informational text, follow these steps:

- Look for statements in the text that support your conclusion.
- Consider your own experience and knowledge about the topic.
- Make a judgment based on evidence and your own knowledge.

Informational texts contain details readers can use as textual evidence. For example, here's a quote from "Women in Aviation" that describes Katherine Wright, the sister of famous aviators Orville and Wilbur Wright:

> **"When the world speaks of the Wrights, it must include my sister. . . . She inspired much of our effort."**

Katherine Wright wasn't a pilot. However, based on this text, what conclusion can you draw about her contribution to the Wright brothers' achievements?

Analyzing the Text

ELA RI.7.1, RI.7.3, RI.7.6, W.7.2, W.7.6, W.7.10 **ELD** PI.7.6, PI.7.7, PI.7.10

Cite Text Evidence Support your responses with evidence from the text.

1. **Cite Evidence** Based on the first sentence in "Women in Aviation," what do you think the authors' purpose might be? Which words or phrases indicate this purpose?

2. **Interpret** Reread lines 26–33. What impression do the authors create of Harriet Quimby by using facts and quotations?

3. **Draw Conclusions** Reread lines 69–82. What conclusion can you draw about Bessie Coleman's personality, based on the information in these paragraphs? Fill out a chart to show how you came to your conclusion. Use chart headings like these:

Textual Evidence	My Experience	Conclusion

4. **Compare** In what ways were Harriet Quimby and Bessie Coleman probably most alike? Explain.

5. **Analyze** You've learned that authors may have more than one purpose in mind for a text. For "Woman in Aviation," it's clear that the authors' main purpose is to inform. What secondary purpose do you think is evident in the text?

6. **Evaluate** What do you think is the most important idea the authors want to convey about the efforts of women aviators in the early 20th century? Support your view with evidence from "Women in Aviation."

PERFORMANCE TASK

my **WriteSmart**

Writing Activity: Informative Report Do further research on one of the figures from "Women in Aviation." Then present your research in the form of a report.

- Use text, online, and digital resources such as encyclopedias, web searches, and other texts to find facts and details.

- Include details about the pilot's achievements and their importance.
- Be sure to include additional quotes either directly from or about the aviator you chose.

Critical Vocabulary

inunnate   restrictive   exhibition   precaution

Practice and Apply Which of the two situations best matches the meaning of the vocabulary word? Explain your choice.

1. **inundate**
   a. More than 400 customers call the hot line one morning.
   b. One or two visitors come to a museum.

2. **restrictive**
   a. The gate to the park is locked at six o'clock.
   b. The gate to the park has a rusty lock.

3. **exhibition**
   a. A crowd gathered at a store advertising a one-day sale.
   b. The crowd watched a holiday cooking demonstration.

4. **precaution**
   a. The state lets voters send in their ballots before Election Day.
   b. The state requires motorcyclists to wear safety helmets.

Vocabulary Strategy: Connotations and Denotations

A word's **denotation** is its literal dictionary meaning. A word's **connotation** comes from the ideas and feelings associated with the word. The authors of "Women in Aviation" chose words based on connotation and denotation.

> On August 1, 1911, Quimby, who was described as a "real beauty" with "haunting blue-green eyes," strolled off the field after passing her pilot's test easily.

Notice how the specific word choice of *strolled* suggests an easy, confident way of walking. This paints a picture of an accomplished young pilot. Words can have a positive or a negative connotation. The context of a phrase, sentence, or paragraph can help you determine the connotation of a word.

Practice and Apply For each item that follows, choose the word you think better expresses the meaning of the sentence. Use a print or online dictionary to help you with unfamiliar words. Then write the reason for your choice.

1. Bessie Coleman refused to give up. She was (**stubborn, determined**).

2. Early pilots performed stunts. The pilots were (**daring, reckless**).

3. Women had barriers. Yet female pilots (**followed, pursued**) their dreams.

4. Coleman died as a pioneer. Her efforts (**inspired, helped**) future generations.

Language Conventions: Subordinate Clauses

Think of clauses as building blocks for sentences. A sentence is an **independent clause** because it can stand alone and express a complete thought. A **subordinate clause** cannot stand alone in a sentence because it is subordinate to, or dependent on, a main clause. Subordinate clauses are also called **dependent clauses.**

Subordinate Clause	Independent Clause
Because it's stormy,	the flight is delayed.
When the skies are clear,	we'll take off.

You can recognize a subordinate clause because it begins with a **subordinating conjunction.** Common subordinating conjunctions are *after, although, as, because, before, even though, if, since, so that, though, unless, until, when, where,* and *while.*

The subordinating conjunction *even though* introduces the subordinating clause in this sentence from "Women in Aviation":

> **Even though the United States was the birthplace of flight, it was slower than other countries to develop an organized aviation program.**

When you write, be careful not to confuse a subordinate clause with a complete sentence; a subordinate clause cannot stand alone. A subordinate clause can appear anywhere in a sentence. If you position it before the independent clause, set it off with a comma.

Practice and Apply Write a complete sentence, using each of these subordinate clauses. You can review the text of "Women in Aviation" for details to include.

1. because flying was a new and exciting sport

2. until aviation was regulated

3. when World War I ended

4. although Bessie Coleman died tragically

PERFORMANCE TASK A

Interactive Lessons
To help you complete this task, use *Writing Narratives*.

Write a Fictional Narrative

ELA W.7.3a–e, W.7.4, W.7.5, W.7.10, L.7.3a
ELD PI.7.4, PI.7.10, PI.7.12, PII.7.1, PII.7.3

Use the texts in the collection as models for writing your own story in which the characters take bold actions in the face of a seemingly overwhelming challenge.

A successful fictional narrative

- introduces and develops characters and a setting
- contains a plot with a well-structured and logical sequence
- establishes, develops, and resolves a conflict
- uses dialogue, pacing, and relevant descriptive details
- utilizes transitions to convey sequence
- provides a conclusion that reflects a message about life

Mentor Text See how this example from "Rogue Wave" uses descriptive details to introduce a character and the setting.

> " Sullivan Atkins, Scoot's oldest brother, was steering the cutter-rigged boat on a northerly course about fifteen miles off desolate Cabo Colnett, south of Ensenada. Under a brilliant sun, the glittering blue Pacific rose and fell in long, slick swells. . . . "

myNotebook

Use the annotation tools in your eBook to mark up key details that you might want to include. Save each detail to your notebook.

PLAN

Establish Story Elements A fictional narrative describes experiences and events that you imagine.

- Brainstorm ideas for your characters. How do the characters act, speak, and relate to each other?
- Determine the setting—the time and place the narrative occurs. How will the setting cause your character to confront his or her fear?
- Establish the conflict. How does this challenge give your main character the opportunity to take bold actions?

ACADEMIC VOCABULARY

As you plan, write, and review your draft, try to use the academic vocabulary words.

aspect
cultural
evaluate
resource
text

List Plot Events Fill out a plot diagram to plan your story.

- Use the exposition to introduce the characters, setting, and conflict.
- Introduce obstacles for the characters in the rising action.
- At the climax, tell the most important or exciting event. This is where your character is about to overcome the challenge.
- End with the falling action and resolution to show how the conflict is resolved.
- As you plan, keep pacing in mind. In a well-paced story, the action transitions smoothly from one event to the next.

Interactive Lessons
To help you plot out your narrative, use:
· Writing Narratives: Narrative Structure

Climax

Rising Action   **Falling Action**

Exposition   **Resolution**

Consider Your Purpose and Audience Who will read or listen to your story? What effect do you want the story to have on readers? Do you want simply to entertain them?

> PRODUCE

WriteSmart

Write your rough draft in *my*WriteSmart. Focus on getting your ideas down, rather than perfecting your choice of language.

Write Your Narrative Review your plot diagram as you begin your draft.

- Establish your point of view by introducing a narrator.
- Create the sequence of events, building suspense with transition words and phrases that clearly show the order of events and signal any shifts in setting.
- Leave the audience with a message to reflect on.

Language Conventions: Active and Passive Voice

A verb in the **active voice** describes an action performed by the subject. A verb in the **passive voice** describes an action received by its subject, using a form of the verb *be*.

Passive Voice "Scoot *was hurled* upward, legs and arms flying. . . ."

Active Voice "Scoot *dove* twice for the boxy flashlight. . . ."

Notice how the passive voice verb "was hurled" emphasizes that Scoot was not in control of her body, while the active voice verb "dove" emphasizes that Scoot is working to escape. Consider how you can use verbs to achieve a particular effect.

Have your partner or a group of peers review your draft in *my*WriteSmart. Ask your reviewers to note any scenes that do not help build suspense.

Review Your Draft
Have your partner or group of peers review your draft. Use the following chart to revise your draft.

Questions	Tips	Revision Techniques
Does the narrative have a well-developed plot?	**Underline** each element: conflict, rising action, climax, and resolution.	**Add** or **elaborate** on plot elements. **Delete** events that do not help move the story to its climax.
Are the characters well developed and convincing? Does the story establish a specific setting?	**Underline** the descriptive details and dialogue that reveal character. **Highlight** details that describe the setting.	**Add** descriptive details, dialogue, and actions that develop characters. **Elaborate** on the setting by adding details.
Are events arranged in a logical sequence? Are transitions used to show order?	**Highlight** the main events. **Underline** transitional words and phrases.	**Rearrange** events that are out of order. **Add** a variety of transitions to show the order of events.
Is the point of view established and maintained throughout the narrative?	**Underline** pronouns that show whether the point of view is first or third person.	**Change** pronouns or details that shift point of view.
Does the story reveal a theme or message?	**Underline** clues that suggest an important idea about life or human nature.	**Add** details or sentences that clarify and reflect on the theme.

Interactive Lessons
To help you revise your draft, use:
- Writing Narratives: Narrative Techniques

Create a Finished Copy
Finalize your story and choose a way to share it with your audience. You might submit your story to the school literary magazine or other online or print literary magazines.

PERFORMANCE TASK A RUBRIC
FICTIONAL NARRATIVE

	Ideas and Evidence	Organization	Language
4	• An engaging conflict is clearly established, developed, and resolved. • The setting is skillfully established and developed and helps shape the conflict. • Characters are compelling and believable. • Dialogue and description are used effectively.	• Event sequence is smooth, is well structured, and creates suspense. • The plot builds to a strong, satisfying conclusion. • Pacing is clear and effective. • Transitions convey sequence and indicate shifts in setting. • The conclusion clearly reflects a theme.	• The story has a consistent and effective point of view. • Words, phrases, and verbs are precise and vivid. • Sensory language reveals the setting and characters. • Spelling, capitalization, and punctuation are correct. • Grammar and usage are correct.
3	• A conflict is introduced, developed, and resolved, but it could better engage the readers. • The setting is established but could be more developed to shape the characters and conflict. • Characters have some believable traits but may need development. • Dialogue and description could be more interesting.	• Event sequence is generally well structured but includes some extraneous events. • The plot builds to a conclusion. • Pacing is somewhat uneven and confusing. • Transitions convey sequence but don't indicate shifts in setting. • The conclusion could more clearly reflect a theme.	• The story has a consistent point of view. • Words, phrases, sensory language, and verbs could be more vivid. • Few spelling, capitalization, and punctuation errors occur. • Some grammatical and usage errors are repeated in the story.
2	• A conflict is introduced but not developed or resolved; it does not engage the reader. • The setting is unclear and does not affect the characters or conflict. • Characters are somewhat clear but undeveloped. • Dialogue and description are insufficient or uninteresting.	• Events are not well structured, are too numerous, or distract from the plot. • The conclusion is unsatisfying, with little suspense, and does not follow from the events. • Pacing is distracting or choppy. • Few transitions are used. • The conclusion does not reflect a theme.	• The story's point of view is inconsistent. • Precise words, sensory language, and effective verbs are mostly lacking. • Spelling, capitalization, and punctuation errors make reading the story difficult. • Grammar and usage are incorrect in many places, but the writer's ideas are still clear.
1	• A conflict is not identifiable. • The setting is not described. • Characters are unclear and underdeveloped. • Dialogue and descriptions are not included.	• Event sequence is not evident. • There is no clear conclusion. • There is no evidence of pacing. • No transitions are used.	• The story's point of view is never clearly established. • Precise words, sensory language, and effective verbs are lacking. • Spelling, capitalization, and punctuation are incorrect throughout. • Many grammatical and usage errors change the meaning of the writer's ideas.

Interactive Lessons

To help you complete this task, use:
• *Writing Arguments*
• *Giving a Presentation*
• *Using Media in a Presentation*

COLLECTION 1
PERFORMANCE TASK B

Present an Argument

This collection depicts the bold actions of daring individuals. The myth "The Flight of Icarus" presents a clear message about the risks and rewards of taking those actions. In the following activity, you will draw from "The Flight of Icarus" and other texts in the collection to prepare and present an argument, either for taking bold actions or for avoiding them.

ELA W.7.1a–e, W.7.8, W.7.9, W.7.10, SL.7.4, SL.7.4a, SL.7.5, SL.7.6, L.7.3
ELD PI.7.4, PI.7.9, PI.7.12, PII.7.2, PII.7.4

A successful argument

- provides an introduction that clearly states your **claim**—the point your argument is making
- includes quotations or examples from the texts to support or illustrate central ideas
- uses good eye contact, volume, and pronunciation
- includes visuals to emphasize salient points
- concludes by restating the claim

Visit hmhfyi.com to explore your topic and enhance your research.

PLAN

Clarify Understanding Review the selections in this collection about people and characters that took bold actions.

- Determine the various opinions or messages expressed about the rewards and risks associated with bold actions.
- Identify the reasons and evidence given to support these opinions and messages.

Make Your Claim Decide whether you think the rewards of bold actions are worth the risks. Make a list of the reasons for your opinion. This will help you determine your claim.

Do Research Gain a better understanding of the topic.

- Search for solid, credible evidence for both sides of the argument.
- Find supporting facts, details, and examples.
- Understand the **counterclaim,** or opposing view, that might keep your audience from agreeing with you.
- Identify any visuals that illustrate your ideas.

Use the annotation tools in your eBook to find evidence to support your ideas. Save each piece of evidence to your notebook.

ACADEMIC VOCABULARY

As you plan and present your argument, be sure to use the academic vocabulary words.

aspect
cultural
evaluate
resource
text

Consider Your Purpose and Audience Who will listen to your report? What do you think your audience will think? Think about that audience as you prepare your commentary. Keep your audience in mind as you determine your tone and word choices.

PRODUCE

Draft Your Argument Although you will be presenting your argument orally, you will need to write it out as a full draft.

- Begin by introducing the topic and stating your claim.
- Express your reasons and support them with credible sources.
- Recognize opposing claims, and use a counterargument to show you've anticipated other viewpoints.
- Use words and phrases such as *because*, *therefore*, and *for that reason* to make your argument clearer and more cohesive.
- Conclude by summarizing your argument.

Language Conventions: Noun Phrases

A **noun phrase** consists of a noun and all the words that modify the noun. The modifiers in noun phrases add details. Read the following passage from the editorial "Ship of Fools."

> " A massive storm in the Indian Ocean knocked out her mast, launching a massive international rescue effort. "

Notice how the modifier *massive* adds emphasis in the two noun phrases in the sentence. Look for places in your argument in which you can add details for emphasis or to make a point more vivid.

Prepare Visuals Consider using multimedia and visual displays to emphasize your key points.

- Be sure each visual has a purpose and is interesting.
- Check that all visuals are large and clearly readable.

my WriteSmart

Write your rough draft in *myWriteSmart*. Focus on getting your ideas down, rather than perfecting your choice of language.

Interactive Lessons

For help in writing your draft, use:
· Writing Arguments: Creating a Coherent Argument

Interactive Lessons

For help with visuals, use:
· Using Media in a Presentation

Have your partner or a group of peers review your draft in *my*WriteSmart. Ask your reviewers to note any reasons that do not support your argument or lack sufficient evidence.

Practice Your Argument Use your draft to practice on your own. Then practice with a partner, keeping these suggestions in mind.

- Speak loudly, varying your pitch and tone.
- Look directly at individuals in your audience.
- Use gestures and facial expressions to emphasize ideas.

Evaluate Your Argument Work with your partner to determine whether your presentation is effective. Use this chart to make adjustments to the draft based on your evaluation.

Questions	Tips	Revision Techniques
Does the introduction clearly state my claim?	**Highlight** the claim.	**Revise** the existing claim to make it clear and focused.
Are my reasons supported by effective examples?	**Underline** each reason. **Highlight** your evidence.	**Add** additional quotes or examples to support your reasons.
Have I included noun phrases to enrich sentences?	**Highlight** sensory details.	**Insert** adjectives in order to add details to your ideas.
Did I anticipate a counterargument?	**Underline** opposing claims.	**Add** any opposing claim that may not have been addressed.
Does my conclusion restate my claim and sum up my position?	**Underline** the conclusion.	**Add** a restatement, if needed, to clarify.

Interactive Lessons
For help in practicing your presentation, use:
- Giving a Presentation: Delivering Your Presentation

Deliver Your Argument Finalize your argument and present it to the class. You might also want to use these additional formats to present it:

- Use a computer presentation program to create an interactive version of your argument.
- Make a video recording of yourself presenting your argument, and share it on your class or school website.

PERFORMANCE TASK B RUBRIC
ARGUMENT

	Ideas and Evidence	Organization	Language
4	• The introduction immediately grabs the audience's attention; the speaker clearly states his or her claim. • Logical reasons and relevant evidence from the texts and multiple, credible sources convincingly support the speaker's claim. • The opposing claim is anticipated and effectively addressed. • The conclusion effectively sums up the argument and leaves a lasting impression.	• The reasons and evidence are organized consistently and logically throughout. • Uses words and phrases in a cohesive manner to connect reasons and evidence. • Visuals and graphic aids are visible, well organized, and support key points.	• The argument reflects a formal speaking style. • The speaker uses precise and concise language. • Sentence beginnings, lengths, and structures vary and have a rhythmic flow. • Expands on noun phrases to enrich sentence meanings.
3	• The introduction could do more to grab the reader's attention; the speaker states a claim. • Most reasons support the speaker's claim but could be more convincing; most reasons are supported with evidence from the texts and research sources. • The opposing claim is anticipated but could be better refuted. • The conclusion restates the claim.	• The organization of reasons and evidence is confusing in some places. • A few more words and phrases are needed to connect the ideas cohesively. • Visuals and graphic aids could be clearer and more complete; they don't always support important points.	• The style becomes informal in a few places. • The speaker's use of language could be more precise and concise. • Sentence beginnings, lengths, and structures vary somewhat. • Misses one or two opportunities to expand on noun phrases.
2	• The introduction is ordinary; the speaker's claim is unclearly stated. • The reasons are not always logical or relevant. • The speaker uses poor, unclear evidence from just a few sources. • The opposing claim is anticipated but not logically addressed. • The conclusion provides an incomplete or unclear summary of the argument.	• The organization of reasons and evidence is logical in some places, but it often doesn't follow a pattern. • Many more words and phrases are needed to connect reasons and evidence cohesively. • Few visuals or graphic aids are used; those used are unclear, poorly organized, and don't support important points.	• The style frequently becomes informal. • Language used is vague, unnecessarily wordy, and unclear in many places. • Sentence structures barely vary, and some fragments or run-on sentences are present. • Grammar and usage are incorrect in many places, but the ideas are clear.
1	• The introduction is confusing and contains no claim. • Supporting reasons are missing. • The speech contains no evidence from the texts or research sources. • The opposing claim is neither anticipated nor addressed. • The concluding section is missing.	• There is no logical organization; reasons and evidence are presented randomly. • No cohesive words or phrases are used, making the argument difficult to understand. • No visuals or graphic aids are used.	• The style is inappropriate. • Language used makes the argument confusing. • Repetitive sentence structure, fragments, and run-on sentences make the argument hard to follow. • Many grammatical and usage errors change the meaning of ideas.

Perception and Reality

❝ *Now* I do not know whether it was then
I dreamt I was a butterfly, or whether I am now a butterfly,
dreaming I am a man. **❞**

—Chuang Tzu

Perception and Reality

In this collection, you will explore how things in life are not always how we perceive them to be.

Stream to Start

hmhfyi.com

Channel One News®

COLLECTION

PERFORMANCE TASK Preview

After reading the selections in this collection, you will have the opportunity to complete two performance tasks:

• In one, you will write an argument expressing your opinion of the saying, "Seeing is believing," using evidence from the literature to support your opinion.

• In the second, you will give a summary presentation that shows an understanding of the drama *Sorry, Wrong Number.*

ACADEMIC VOCABULARY

Study the words and their definitions in the chart below. You will use these words as you discuss and write about the texts in this collection.

Word	Definition	Related Forms
abnormal (ăb-nôr´məl) *adj.*	not typical, usual, or regular; not normal	normal, normalcy, normality, normalize, paranormal, subnormal
feature (fē´chər) *n.*	a prominent or distinctive part, quality, or characteristic	feature article, featured, featureless, featuring, text feature
focus (fō´kəs) *v.*	to direct toward a specific point or purpose	autofocus, focused, refocus, unfocused
perceive (pər-sēv´) *v.*	to become aware of something directly through any of the senses	misperceive, misperception, perception, unperceived
task (tăsk) *n.*	an assignment or work done as part of one's duties	multitask, taskmaster

Background *Between the 1600s and 1800s, millions of Africans were taken forcibly to the Americas as enslaved people. Their labor spurred the growth of large-scale farming in the colonies. Despite the hardships of oppression, these people nurtured a strong sense of tradition, passing stories from generation to generation.* **Virginia Hamilton** *(1934–2002) grew up listening to such stories. As an adult, she put many of them into writing and wrote a number of her own books about African American history and culture.*

The People Could Fly

Folk Tale by Virginia Hamilton

SETTING A PURPOSE As you read, think about what this folk tale says about the importance of hope in the lives of oppressed people.

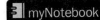 **myNotebook**

As you read, mark up the text. Save your work to **myNotebook**.

- Highlight details
- Add notes and questions
- Add new words to **myWordList**

They say the people could fly. Say that long ago in Africa, some of the people knew magic. And they would walk up on the air like climbin' up on a gate. And they flew like blackbirds over the fields. Black, shiny wings flappin' against the blue up there.

Then, many of the people were captured for Slavery. The ones that could fly shed their wings. They couldn't take their wings across the water on the slave ships. Too crowded, don't you know.

10   The folks were full of misery, then. Got sick with the up and down of the sea. So they forgot about flyin' when they could no longer breathe the sweet scent of Africa.

Say the people who could fly kept their power, although they shed their wings. They kept their secret magic in the land of slavery. They looked the same as the other people from Africa who had been coming over, who had dark skin. Say you couldn't tell anymore one who could fly from one who couldn't.

One such who could was an old man, call him Toby. And standin' tall, yet afraid, was a young woman who once had wings. Call her Sarah. Now Sarah carried a babe tied to her back. She trembled to be so hard worked and scorned.

The slaves labored in the fields from sunup to sundown. The owner of the slaves callin' himself their Master. Say he was a hard lump of clay. A hard, glinty coal. A hard rock pile, wouldn't be moved. His Overseer[1] on horseback pointed out the slaves who were slowin' down. So the one called Driver cracked his whip over the slow ones to make them move faster. That whip was a slice-open cut of pain. So they did move faster. Had to.

Sarah hoed and chopped the row as the babe on her back slept.

Say the child grew hungry. That babe started up bawling too loud. Sarah couldn't stop to feed it. Couldn't stop to soothe and quiet it down. She let it cry. She didn't want to. She had no heart to **croon** to it.

"Keep that thing quiet," called the Overseer. He pointed his finger at the babe. The woman scrunched low. The Driver cracked his whip across the babe anyhow. The babe hollered like any hurt child, and the woman fell to the earth.

The old man that was there, Toby, came and helped her to her feet.

"I must go soon," she told him.

"Soon," he said.

Sarah couldn't stand up straight any longer. She was too weak. The sun burned her face. The babe cried and cried, "Pity me, oh, pity me," say it sounded like. Sarah was so sad and starvin', she sat down in the row.

"Get up, you black cow," called the Overseer. He pointed his hand, and the Driver's whip snarled around Sarah's legs. Her sack dress tore into rags. Her legs bled onto the earth. She couldn't get up.

Toby was there where there was no one to help her and the babe.

croon
(kro͞on) v. When someone *croons*, that person hums or sings softly.

---

[1] **Overseer** (ō´vər-sē´ər): a person who directs the work of others; a supervisor. During the time of slavery, the overseer was usually a white man.

"Now, before it's too late," panted Sarah. "Now, Father!"

"Yes, Daughter, the time is come," Toby answered. "Go, as you know how to go!"

He raised his arms, holding them out to her. *"Kum . . . yali, kum buba tambe,"* and more magic words, said so quickly,
60 they sounded like whispers and sighs.

The young woman lifted one foot on the air. Then the other. She flew clumsily at first, with the child now held tightly in her arms. Then she felt the magic, the African mystery. Say she rose just as free as a bird. As light as a feather.

The Overseer rode after her, hollerin'. Sarah flew over the fences. She flew over the woods. Tall trees could not **snag** her. Nor could the Overseer. She flew like an eagle now, until she was gone from sight. No one dared speak about it. Couldn't believe it. But it was, because they that was there
70 saw that it was.

snag
(snăg) *v.* If you *snag* something, you catch it quickly and unexpectedly.

Say the next day was dead hot in the fields. A young man slave fell from the heat. The Driver come and whipped him. Toby come over and spoke words to the fallen one. The words of ancient Africa once heard are never remembered completely. The young man forgot them as soon as he heard them. They went way inside him. He got up and rolled over on the air. He rode it awhile. And he flew away.

> ## 66 She flew clumsily at first, with the child now held tightly in her arms. 99

Another and another fell from the heat. Toby was there. He cried out to the fallen and reached his arms out to them. *"Kum* 80 *kunka yali, kum . . . tambe!"* Whispers and sighs. And they too rose on the air. They rode the hot breezes. The ones flyin' were black and shinin' sticks, wheelin' above the head of the Overseer. They crossed the rows, the fields, the fences, the streams, and were away.

"Seize the old man!" cried the Overseer.

"I heard him say the magic *words.* Seize him!"

The one callin' himself Master come runnin'. The Driver got his whip ready to curl around old Toby and tie him up. The slave owner took his hip gun from its place. He meant to 90 kill old black Toby.

But Toby just laughed. Say he threw back his head and said, "Hee, hee! Don't you know who I am? Don't you know some of us in this field?" He said it to their faces. "We are ones who fly!"

And he sighed the ancient words that were a dark promise. He said them all around to the others in the field under the whip, ". . . *buba yali . . . buba tambe . . ."*

There was a great outcryin'. The bent backs straightened up. Old and young who were called slaves and could fly joined 100 hands. Say like they would ring-sing. But they didn't **shuffle** in a circle. They didn't sing. They rose on the air. They flew in a flock that was black against the heavenly blue. Black crows or black shadows. It didn't matter, they went so high. Way above the **plantation**, way over the slavery land. Say they flew away to *Free-dom.*

And the old man, old Toby, flew behind them, takin' care of them. He wasn't cryin'. He wasn't laughin'. He was the seer. His gaze fell on the plantation where the slaves who could not fly waited.

shuffle
(shŭf´əl) *v.* When you *shuffle*, you move with short sliding steps.

plantation
(plăn-tā´shən) *n.* A *plantation* is a large farm or estate on which crops are raised.

110   *"Take us with you!"* Their looks spoke it, but they were afraid to shout it. Toby couldn't take them with him. Hadn't the time to teach them to fly. They must wait for a chance to run.

     "Goodie-bye!" the old man called Toby spoke to them, poor souls! And he was flyin' gone.

So they say. The Overseer told it. The one called Master said it was a lie, a trick of the light. The Driver kept his mouth shut.

     The slaves who could not fly told about the people who could fly to their children. When they were free. When they
120 sat close before the fire in the free land, they told it. They did so love firelight and *Free-dom*, and tellin'.

     They say that the children of the ones who could not fly told their children. And now, me, I have told it to you.

COLLABORATIVE DISCUSSION Sarah, Toby, and the others hold onto hope in the most difficult of circumstances. With a partner, discuss what this folk tale says about the nature of hope.

Analyze Story Elements: Folk Tales

ELA RL.7.3
ELD PI.7.6

Folk tales are stories passed down by word of mouth from generation to generation. "The People Could Fly" is a folk tale that would have been around a long time as an oral tradition before it was finally recorded.

Folk tales can vary from culture to culture, but often have these elements:

- supernatural events set in the distant past
- talking animals or other characters with supernatural abilities
- lessons about what is important to the culture of origin

Folk tales are often told using **dialect**—a form of language that is spoken in a particular place or by a particular group of people—to suggest real people talking. In "The People Could Fly," Virginia Hamilton uses dialect to suggest the folksy speech of the African American storyteller. The use of dialect helps to draw the reader or listener more fully into the setting.

Choose one of the listed features of folk tales. Tell how the feature is shown in "The People Could Fly."

Summarize Text

ELA RL.7.2
ELD PI.7.10

A **summary** of a story is a brief retelling that gives only the most important details. When you summarize a story, you use your own words to answer the basic questions *who? when and where?* and *what happens?* A story map like the one shown can help you organize your answers.

Title and Genre (kind of story):	Setting:

Conflict:

Main Events (several events in order):

Outcome/Resolution:

Here is a possible first sentence of a summary of the story you have read:

> "The People Could Fly" is a folk tale that **originated among people held captive as slaves.**

What would you write as the next sentence of the summary?

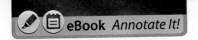
Analyzing the Text

ELA RL.7.2, RL.7.3, RL.7.4, RL.7.10,
SL.7.6 **ELD** PI.7.6, PI.7.8, PI.7.9,
PI.7.10

Cite Text Evidence   Support your responses with evidence from the text.

1. **Interpret** Folk tales often feature lessons that are important to a culture or group of people. What is the lesson of this folk tale? How would enslaved Africans have perceived the lesson as being important?

2. **Summarize** Early in the folk tale, the narrator says, "The folks were full of misery, then." Review the first half of the tale to find details about the conditions under which the slaves lived. Then in your own words, describe these conditions.

3. **Summarize** Fill out a story map for "The People Could Fly." Use your completed map to summarize the plot of the folk tale. Compare your summary with that of a classmate.

4. **Analyze** Reread lines 1–10 to identify examples of dialect. What effect does the use of dialect achieve at the beginning of the story?

5. **Analyze** Reread lines 23–30. What is the Master compared to? What is the whip compared to? Why might the author have included these figurative comparisons?

6. **Analyze Theme** Reread lines 98–105. What theme is expressed in this paragraph?

PERFORMANCE TASK

Speaking Activity: Dramatic Reading With a small group, do a dramatic reading of "The People Could Fly," using the text of the folk tale as a script. Follow these tips for preparing and performing:

- Rehearse the reading several times.
- Make sure your voices fit the personalities of the characters you portray.
- Deliver lines with the appropriate emotion.
- Keep in mind how the tale begins somberly but builds in intensity.

Critical Vocabulary

ELA L.7.4b, L.7.4d
ELD PI.7.6, PI.7.12

croon   snag   shuffle   plantation

Practice and Apply Identify the vocabulary word that is tied in meaning to the italicized word in each question. Provide reasons for your choices.

1. Which word goes with *song*? Why?

2. Which word goes with *farm*? Why?

3. Which word goes with *thorn*? Why?

4. Which word goes with *feet*? Why?

Vocabulary Strategy: Latin Suffixes

A **suffix** is a word part added to the end of a root or base word to form a new word. Readers can use their knowledge of suffixes to analyze words and find familiar parts to determine the meaning of a word. Many suffixes in English words come from Latin. Look at the meanings of the suffixes in the chart.

Suffix	Example Words
-ure	exposure, lecture
-ery/-ary	nursery, military
-ence/-ance	violence, reliance
-ive/-ative	selective, talkative
-ion/-ation	tension, imagination

For example, notice the word with a Latin suffix in this sentence from "The People Could Fly."

> His gaze fell on the plantation where the slaves who could not fly waited.

You can see that *plantation* is made of the base word *plant* and the suffix *-ation*. The meaning of *plantation* is "a farm where crops are planted."

Practice and Apply Choose a suffix from the chart to complete each word. Use a print or online dictionary to find the meanings of unfamiliar words and to confirm your answers.

1. To be enslaved is to live in **mis** _____ .

2. Human flight is an unusual form of **transport** _____ .

3. The people stood up and straightened their **post** _____ .

4. When confronting evil, story characters show **defi** _____ .

5. The solutions in folk tales may be magical and **creat** _____ .

A&E BIO

Background *"The Song of Wandering Aengus" was inspired by Aengus, the Irish god of love and inspiration. In the original myth, Aengus falls in love with a girl he has dreamed about, but when he is unable to find her, he becomes ill. His parents go searching for her, and after three years the couple is finally united.*

The Song of Wandering Aengus

Poem by W. B. Yeats

Sonnet 43

Poem by William Shakespeare

William Butler Yeats (1865–1934) *was an Irish poet and playwright, and one of the most notable literary figures of the 20th century. As a boy, Yeats lived in a rural region in Ireland called Sligo. There he enjoyed local stories about Irish heroes, heroines, and magical creatures. In Yeats's later life as a poet and playwright, the region and its folklore inspired his poetry and drama. "The Song of Wandering Aengus" is an example of this inspiration.*

William Shakespeare (1564–1616) *was an English playwright, poet, and actor. While Shakespeare is widely regarded as the greatest playwright in the English language, he was also just as influential as a poet. He began writing poetry when theaters shut down during an outbreak of the plague in London. Adapting and refining the sonnet form, he produced 154 of his own sonnets. Now the Shakespearean sonnet is itself a unique poetic form.*

SETTING A PURPOSE As you read, think about what each poem has to say about the absence of a loved one. How does each poem convey a sense of loss and longing?

The Song of Wandering Aengus
by W. B. Yeats

I went out to the hazel wood,
Because a fire was in my head,
And cut and peeled a hazel wand,
And hooked a berry to a thread;
5　And when white moths were on the wing,
And moth-like stars were flickering out,
I dropped the berry in a stream
And caught a little silver trout.

When I had laid it on the floor
10　I went to blow the fire aflame,
But something rustled on the floor,
And someone called me by my name:
It had become a glimmering girl
With apple blossom in her hair
15　Who called me by my name and ran
And faded through the brightening air.

Though I am old with wandering
Through hollow lands and hilly lands,
I will find out where she has gone,
20　And kiss her lips and take her hands;
And walk among long dappled¹ grass,
And pluck till time and times are done,
The silver apples of the moon,
The golden apples of the sun.

---

¹ **dappled:** marked with many spotted colors or light.

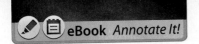

Determine the Impact of Rhyme

ELA RL.7.4, RL.7.5
ELD PI.7.6, PI.7.8, PII.7.1

A poem is a combination of sound and meaning. Poets choose their words carefully, since word choice, or **diction,** affects a poem's meaning and the way it sounds. **Rhyme** is the repetition of sounds at the end of words, as in *more* and *roar*. Words rhyme when their accented vowels and the letters that follow have identical or similar sounds.

Poets use rhyme for a number of purposes:

to make a poem songlike or playful

to emphasize sounds that suggest feelings

to create rhythms that help convey sensory feelings, such as a sense of motion

End rhyme refers to words that rhyme at the ends of lines of poetry. For example, the second and fourth lines from "The Song of Wandering Aengus" contain end rhymes:

> I went out to the hazel wood,
> Because a fire was in my head,
> And cut and peeled a hazel wand,
> And hooked a berry to a thread;

The end rhymes are *head/thread*. Reread the first stanza of the poem to listen for and identify a second pair of end rhymes.

Analyzing the Text

ELA RL.7.1, RL.7.4, RL.7.5
ELD PI.7.6, PI.7.8, PII.7.1

Cite Text Evidence   Support your responses with evidence from the text.

1. **Summarize** What are the primary actions that take place in each of the three stanzas of the poem?

2. **Identify Patterns** Find end rhymes and other examples of repetition in the second stanza. What effects do those forms of repetition have? Do they emphasize a particular meaning?

3. **Interpret** What is the quest of Aengus in this poem?

4. **Analyze** What words suggest that Aengus is chanting a song?

Sonnet 43
by William Shakespeare

When most I wink, then do mine eyes best see,
For all the day they view things unrespected;[1]
But when I sleep, in dreams they look on thee,
And, darkly bright, are bright in dark directed.
5 Then thou, whose shadow shadows doth make bright,
How would thy shadow's form form happy show
To the clear day with thy much clearer light,
When to unseeing eyes thy shade shines so!
How would, I say, mine eyes be blessèd made
10 By looking on thee in the living day,
When in dead night thy fair imperfect shade
Through heavy sleep on sightless eyes doth stay!
　　All days are nights to see till I see thee,
　　And nights bright days when dreams do show thee me.

COLLABORATIVE DISCUSSION Each of these two poems is, in a sense, a love poem. With a partner, discuss how effectively each poet expresses his feelings about love and loss.

---

[1] **they view things unrespected:** during the day the poet's eyes are looking at things that are insignificant or unimportant.

eBook *Annotate It!*

Analyze Form: Sonnet

ELA RL.7.4, RL.7.5
ELD PI.7.6, PII.7.1

The deliberate arrangement of words is the mark of a well-crafted poem. The **form** of a poem is the arrangement of its words and lines on a page. One established form is a 14-line poem called a **sonnet.** The sonnet is a form that originated in Italy but was altered by English poets, especially William Shakespeare. The Shakespearean sonnet is named for the best-known user of the form.

A Shakespearean sonnet has these features:

- The whole poem develops a single idea.
- The idea is developed in three parts, each made of four lines.
- The **rhyme scheme** is the pattern of end rhymes: a-b-a-b, c-d-c-d, e-f-e-f, g-g. The matching letters refer to the pairs of end rhymes.
- The final pair of lines, called a **couplet,** completes the poet's message with a strong impact and helps focus the reader's attention on the theme.

A sonnet may also have a specified **meter,** which is a regular pattern of stressed and unstressed syllables. Notice where the stress falls in this line of the poem.

> **When most I wink, then do mine eyes best see,**

Look again at the sonnet you have just read. How does the punctuation at the end of the lines show how the ideas are organized?

Analyzing the Text

ELA RL.7.2, RL.7.4, RL.7.5, SL.7.1a–e,
SL.7.4, SL.7.6. **ELD** PI.7.6, PI.7.8, PII.7.1

Cite Text Evidence   Support your responses with evidence from the text.

1. **Identify Patterns** Explain what you notice about the rhyme scheme of this poem.

2. **Summarize** A **paradox** is a statement that seems to contradict itself. What paradox presented in the first line is developed throughout the sonnet? (Note that the word *wink* means "to close one's eyes to sleep.")

3. **Interpret** Reread the final couplet. Restate its message in your own words.

4. **Analyze** Reread line 5. How should it be read aloud to express its meaning?

Sonnet 43   **75**

Determine Meanings

ELA RL.7.4, RL.7.5
ELD PI.7.8

Figurative language is the use of words in imaginative ways to express ideas that are not literally true. Poets use figurative language to convey meaning and achieve certain effects. This chart shows three common types of figurative language with examples from "The Song of Wandering Aengus."

Types of Figurative Language	Examples	Effect
Simile is a comparison between two unlike things using the words *like* or *as*.	*moth-like stars*, line 6	The twinkling stars look like moths fluttering.
Metaphor is a comparison of two unlike things without the words *like* or *as*.	*a fire was in my head*, line 2	A feverish, uneasy feeling is likened to a fire in the head.

The figurative language in "Sonnet 43" seems subtler than that in the Yeats poem. In Shakespeare's sonnet, which words help create a metaphor for the absence of the poet's loved one?

Analyzing the Text

ELA RL.7.2, RL.7.4, RL.7.5,
SL.7.1a–d, SL.7.4, SL.7.6
ELD PI.7.1, PI.7.6, PI.7.8

> **Cite Text Evidence** Support your responses with evidence from the texts.

1. **Identify Patterns** What is the rhyme scheme of the Yeats poem and how does it differ from the rhyme scheme of "Sonnet 43"?

2. **Compare** An **extended metaphor** compares two unlike things at length and in a number of ways, sometimes throughout an entire work. In each poem, the poet uses an extended metaphor. What is the metaphor in each poem and what words does the poet use to extend it?

3. **Analyze** Read each poem aloud to hear and feel the unstressed and stressed syllables in each line. What qualities does the meter contribute to each poem? Explain.

PERFORMANCE TASK

Speaking Activity: Discussion With a small group, discuss which speaker of these two poems seems more affected by what he perceives. To prepare for your discussion:

- Consider what each speaker is longing for.
- Think about the words used to express the speaker's longing in each poem.

Background *Brain scientists* **Susana Martinez-Conde** *and* **Stephen L. Macknik** *study how the human visual system responds to and perceives the world around us. They see science at work behind magicians' techniques. A good magician relies on the inner workings of the brain to create all kinds of sensory illusions. By studying how these tricks work, scientists are learning more about the brain. Their work has led them to start a new area of science that they call* neuromagic.

Magic
and the Brain

Magazine Article by Susana Martinez-Conde and Stephen L. Macknik

SETTING A PURPOSE As you read, think about the term *neuromagic* and its usefulness as a new field of scientific study. Write down any questions you may have during reading.

The spotlight shines on the magician's assistant. The woman in the tiny white dress is a luminous beacon of beauty radiating from the stage to the audience. The Great Tomsoni announces he will change her dress from white to red. On the edge of their seats, the spectators strain to focus on the woman, burning her image deep into their retinas. Tomsoni claps his hands, and the spotlight dims ever so briefly before reflaring in a blaze of red. The woman is awash in a flood of redness.

10   Whoa, just a moment there! Switching color with the spotlight is not exactly what the audience had in mind. The magician stands at the side of the stage, looking pleased at his little joke. Yes, he admits, it was a cheap trick; his favorite kind, he explains devilishly. But you have to agree, he did turn her dress red—along with the rest of her. Please, indulge him

and direct your attention once more to his beautiful assistant as he switches the lights back on for the next trick. He claps his hands, and the lights dim again; then the stage explodes in a supernova of whiteness. But wait! Her dress really has turned red. The Great Tomsoni has done it again!

The trick and its explanation by John Thompson (aka the Great Tomsoni) reveal a deep intuitive[1] understanding of the **neural** processes taking place in the spectators' brains—the kind of understanding that we **neuroscientists** can appropriate for our own scientific benefit. Here's how the trick works. As Thompson introduces his assistant, her skintight white dress wordlessly lures the spectators[2] into assuming that nothing— certainly not another dress—could possibly be hiding under the white one. That reasonable assumption, of course, is wrong. The attractive woman in her tight dress also helps to focus people's attention right where Thompson wants it—on the woman's body. The more they stare at her, the less they notice the hidden devices in the floor, and the better adapted their retinal neurons[3] become to the brightness of the light and the color they perceive.

All during Thompson's patter after his little "joke," each spectator's visual system is undergoing a brain process called neural adaptation. The responsiveness of a neural system to a constant stimulus (as measured by the firing rate of the relevant **neurons**) decreases with time. It is as if neurons actively ignore a constant stimulus to save their strength for signaling that a stimulus is changing. When the constant stimulus is turned off, the adapted neurons fire a "rebound" response known as an after discharge.

In this case, the adapting stimulus is the redlit dress, and Thompson knows that the spectators' retinal neurons will rebound for a fraction of a second after the lights are dimmed. The audience will continue to see a red afterimage in the shape of the woman. During that split second, a trap door in the stage opens briefly, and the white dress, held only lightly in place with fastening tape and attached to invisible cables leading under the stage, is ripped from her body. Then the lights come back up.

neural
(nŏŏr´əl) *adj.* Anything that is *neural* is related to the nervous system.

neuroscientist
(nŏŏr´ō-sī´ən-tĭst) *n.* A *neuroscientist* is a person who studies the brain and the nervous system.

neuron
(nŏŏr´ŏn´) *n.* A *neuron* is a nerve cell.

---

[1] **intuitive** (ĭn-tōō´ĭ-tĭv): having the ability to know or understand something without evidence.

[2] **spectators:** the people who are watching the event.

[3] **retinal neurons** (rĕt´n-əl´nŏŏr´ŏnz´): the cells in the retina of the eye that convert light into images.

VISUAL ILLUSIONS
FOOLING MIND OR EYE?

An illusion created by an image like this one often induces a false sense of flowing movement in the concentric rings (start at the center dot in the pictures). But does the illusion originate in the mind or in the eye? The evidence was conflicting until the authors and their colleagues showed in October that the illusory motion is driven by microsaccades—small, involuntary eye movements that occur during visual fixation. Knowing the roles of eye and mind in magic can be used as experimental tools **neuroscience.**

neuroscience
(noŏr´ō-sī´əns) *n.*
Neuroscience is any of the sciences that study the nervous system.

Two other factors help to make the trick work. First, the lighting is so bright just before the dress comes off that when it dims, the spectators cannot see the rapid motions of the cables and the white dress as they disappear underneath the stage. The same temporary blindness can overtake you when you walk from a sunny street into a dimly lit shop. Second, Thompson performs the real trick only after the audience thinks it is already over. That gains him an important cognitive advantage—the spectators are not looking for a trick at the critical moment, and so they slightly relax their scrutiny.

The New Science of Neuromagic

Thompson's trick nicely illustrates the essence of stage magic. Magicians are, first and foremost, artists of attention and awareness. They manipulate the focus and intensity of human attention, controlling, at any given instant, what

60

(Spiral) ©Atypeek Design/Shutterstock; (human eye) © Corbis RF

we are aware of and what we are not. They do so in part by
70   employing bewildering combinations of visual illusions (such
as afterimages), optical illusions (smoke and mirrors), special
effects (explosions, fake gunshots, precisely timed lighting
controls), sleight of hand, secret devices and mechanical
artifacts ("gimmicks").

"Neuroscience is becoming familiar with the methods of magic."

But the most versatile instrument in their bag of tricks
may be the ability to create cognitive illusions. Like visual
illusions, cognitive illusions mask the perception of physical
reality. Yet unlike visual illusions, cognitive illusions are not
sensory in nature. Rather they involve high-level functions
80   such as attention, memory and causal inference. With all
those tools at their disposal, well-practiced magicians make
it virtually impossible to follow the physics of what is actually
happening—leaving the impression that the only explanation
for the events is magic.

Neuroscientists are just beginning to catch up with the
magician's facility in manipulating attention and cognition.
Of course the aims of neuroscience are different from those of
magic, the neuroscientist seeks to understand the brain and
neuron underpinnings of cognitive functions, whereas the
90   magician wants mainly to exploit cognitive weaknesses. Yet
the techniques developed by magicians over centuries of stage
magic could also be subtle and powerful probes in the hands
of neuroscientists, supplementing and perhaps expanding the
instruments already in experimental use.

Neuroscience is becoming familiar with the methods of
magic by subjecting magic itself to scientific study—in some
cases showing for the first time how some of its methods work
in the brain. Many studies of magic conducted so far confirm
what is known about cognition and attention from earlier
100   work in experimental psychology. A **cynic** might dismiss such
efforts: Why do yet another study that simply confirms what is

cynic
(sĭn´ĭk) n. A cynic is
a person who has
negative opinions
about other people
and what they do.

already well known? But such criticism misses the importance and purpose of the studies. By investigating the techniques of magic, neuroscientists can familiarize themselves with methods that they can adapt to their own purposes. Indeed, we believe that cognitive neuroscience could have advanced faster had investigators probed magicians' intuitions earlier. Even today magicians may have a few tricks up their sleeves that neuroscientists have not yet adopted.

By applying the tools of magic, neuroscientists can hope to learn how to design more robust experiments and to create more effective cognitive and visual illusions for exploring the neural bases of attention and awareness. Such techniques could not only make experimental studies of cognition possible with clever and highly attentive subjects; they could also lead to diagnostic and treatment methods for patients suffering from specific cognitive deficits—such as attention deficits resulting from brain trauma, ADHD (attention-deficit hyperactivity disorder), Alzheimer's disease, and the like. The

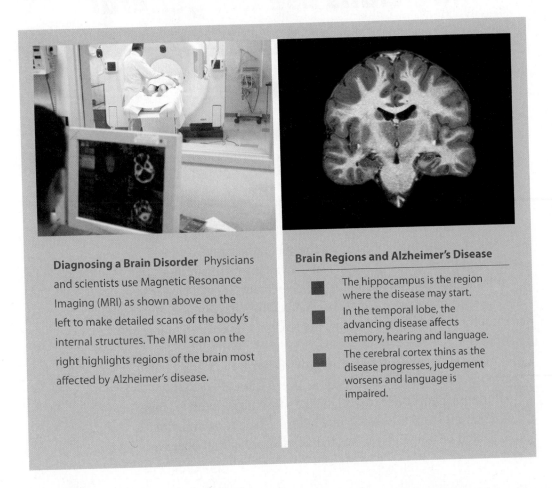

Diagnosing a Brain Disorder Physicians and scientists use Magnetic Resonance Imaging (MRI) as shown above on the left to make detailed scans of the body's internal structures. The MRI scan on the right highlights regions of the brain most affected by Alzheimer's disease.

Brain Regions and Alzheimer's Disease

- The hippocampus is the region where the disease may start.
- In the temporal lobe, the advancing disease affects memory, hearing and language.
- The cerebral cortex thins as the disease progresses, judgement worsens and language is impaired.

¹²⁰ methods of magic might also be put to work in "tricking" patients to focus on the most important parts of their therapy, while suppressing distractions that cause confusion and disorientation.

Magicians use the general term "misdirection" to refer to the practice of diverting the spectator's attention away from a secret action. In the lingo of magic, misdirection draws the audience's attention toward the "effect" and away from the "method," the secret behind the effect. Borrowing some terms from cognitive psychology, we have classified misdirection as

¹³⁰ "overt" and "covert." The misdirection is overt if the magician redirects the spectator's gaze away from the method—perhaps simply by asking the audience to look at a particular object. When the Great Tomsoni introduces his lovely assistant, for instance, he ensures that all eyes are on her.

Magicians use the general term 'misdirection' to refer to the practice of diverting the spectator's attention.

"Covert" misdirection, in contrast, is a subtler technique; there, too, the magician draws the spectator's attentional spotlight—or focus of suspicion—away from the method, but without necessarily redirecting the spectator's gaze. Under the influence of covert misdirection, spectators may be looking

¹⁴⁰ directly at the method behind the trick yet be entirely unaware of it.

Cognitive neuroscience already recognizes at least two kinds of covert misdirection. In what is called change blindness, people fail to notice that something about a scene is different from the way it was before. The change may be expected or unexpected, but the key feature is that observers do not notice it by looking at the scene at any one instant in time. Instead the observer must compare the postchange state with the prechange state.

150   Inattentional blindness differs from change blindness in that there is no need to compare the current scene with a scene from memory. Instead people fail to notice an unexpected object that is fully visible directly in front of them. Psychologist Daniel J. Simons invented a classic example of the genre. Simons and psychologist Christopher F. Chabris, both then at Harvard University, asked observers to count how many times a "team" of three basketball players pass a ball to each other, while ignoring the passes made by three other players. While they concentrated on counting, half of the
160 observers failed to notice that a person in a gorilla suit walks across the scene (the gorilla even stops briefly at the center of the scene and beats its chest!). No abrupt interruption or distraction was necessary to create this effect; the counting task was so absorbing that many observers who were looking directly at the gorilla nonetheless missed it.

Controlling Awareness in the Wired Brain

The possibilities of using magic as a source of cognitive illusion to help isolate the neural circuits responsible for specific cognitive functions seem endless. Neuroscientists recently borrowed a technique from magic that made
170 volunteer subjects incorrectly link two events as cause and effect while images of the subjects' brains were recorded. When event A precedes event B, we often conclude, rightly or wrongly, that A causes B. The skilled magician takes advantage of that predisposition by making sure that event A (say, pouring water on a ball) always precedes event B (the ball disappearing). In fact, A does not cause B, but its prior appearance helps the magician make it seem so. Cognitive psychologists call this kind of effect illusory correlation.

    In an unpublished study in 2006 Kuhn and cognitive
180 neuroscientists Ben A. Parris and Tim L. Hodgson, both then at the University of Exeter in England, showed videos of magic tricks that involved apparent violations of cause and effect to subjects undergoing functional magnetic resonance imaging. The subjects' brain images were compared with those of a control group: people who watched videos showing no

apparent causal violations. The investigators found greater activation in the anterior cingulate cortex among the subjects who were watching magic tricks than among the controls. The finding suggests that this brain area may be important for interpreting causal relationships.

The work of Kuhn and his colleagues only begins to suggest the power of the techniques of magic for manipulating attention and awareness while studying the physiology of the brain. If neuroscientists learn to use the methods of magic with the same skill as professional magicians, they, too, should be able to control awareness precisely and in real time. If they correlate the content of that awareness with the functioning of neurons, they will have the means to explore some of the mysteries of consciousness itself.

COLLABORATIVE DISCUSSION The authors have invented the term *neuromagic*. Why do they think it is a useful term? Talk about your ideas with other group members.

Analyze Structure: Text Features

ELA RI.7.4, RI.7.5
ELD PII.7.1

Text features are elements of a text that help organize and call attention to important information. Informational texts such as "Magic and the Brain" often contain one or more text features, such as those shown in the chart.

Text Features in Informational Texts	
titles, headings, subheadings	The **title** of a piece of writing is the name that is attached to it. It often identifies the topic of the whole text and is sometimes referred to as a **heading. Subheadings** appear at the beginning of sections within the text and indicate the focus of that section.
sidebar	A **sidebar** is a box alongside or within an article that provides additional information that is related to the article's main text.
boldface type	**Boldface type** is dark, heavy print that is used to draw attention to unfamiliar vocabulary.
footnotes	**Footnotes,** which appear at the bottom of the page, provide definitions or additional information about terms in the text.

Graphic aids, such as maps, charts, diagrams, graphs, and pictures are visual text features that can help you understand ideas or processes.

Text features may be used to highlight **technical language**—terms used in a specialized field such as science or technology. If there is no definition for a technical term, use context to determine its meaning. You can confirm the meaning in such resources as print or online dictionaries and encyclopedias.

Look at the top of page 79 of "Magic and the Brain." Identify the text feature that appears there.

ELA RI.7.2
ELD PI.7.10

Summarize Text

When you **summarize** a text, you briefly retell the central ideas in your own words. An **objective summary** reports what the original writer intended, without opinions or unnecessary details. Do not include opinions or commentary. Use headings and subheadings to help you organize ideas.

To summarize a paragraph, find and restate the main idea. To summarize a section, turn the heading into a question. Answer the question using the main idea and important details in the paragraph. To summarize an article, combine your section summaries. Add a sentence to sum up the central idea of the whole article.

Reread lines 1–20 of "Magic and the Brain." How would you complete a summary of that section?

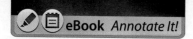

Analyzing the Text

ELA RI.7.2, RI.7.4, RI.7.5, W.7.7, SL.7.4 **ELD** PI.7.6, PI.7.10, PII.7.1

Cite Text Evidence Support your responses with evidence from the text.

1. **Summarize** Reread lines 124–141. Write a summary of these paragraphs to explain how magic tricks work through the techniques of "misdirection."

2. **Draw Conclusions** Reread the sidebar on page 79. What discovery did the authors make about the origin of illusion? Why is it important?

3. **Interpret** Reread the heading on page 83. Use the information in that section to explain what is meant by "the wired brain."

4. **Summarize** Reread lines 85–94. In your own words, describe how the aims of a magician might differ from those of a neuroscientist.

5. **Infer** Reread lines 154–165. What is the most surprising detail about the counting task that is performed by the test subjects?

6. **Compare** Reread lines 65–80. What is the difference between a cognitive illusion and a visual illusion?

7. **Synthesize** Reread lines 110–123. Why do the authors want neuroscientists to use "tools of magic"?

PERFORMANCE TASK

Speaking Activity: Demonstration
Do research to find an easily performed "magic trick" that is based on a science principle. Follow the step-by-step directions for the trick and practice performing it. Determine the principle that makes the trick work. Then demonstrate the trick in a performance for your classmates. Follow these suggestions during the demonstration:

- If necessary, perform the trick a second time, but more slowly, indicating whatever you're doing to distract their attention.
- At the end of the performance, explain the principle at work in the trick and how it relates to the article "Magic and the Brain."
- Invite feedback. Discuss with your classmates whether the demonstration increases their understanding of neuromagic.

Critical Vocabulary

ELA L.7.4a, L.7.4b, L.7.4c
ELD PI.7.6, PI.7.12

neural   neuroscientist   neuron   neuroscience   cynic

Practice and Apply Answer each question.

1. How is a **neural** network like and different from a computer network?

2. How is a **neuroscientist** like and different from a brain surgeon?

3. How is a **neuron** like and different from a blood cell?

4. How is **neuroscience** like and different from medical science?

5. How is a **cynic** like and different from a critic?

Vocabulary Strategy: The Greek Prefix *neuro-*

A **root** is a word part that came into English from an older language, such as ancient Latin or Greek. The Greek word for "cord" or "nerve" was *neuron*. The Greek root *neuro* appears as a prefix at the start of many English words about nerves and the nervous system.

This sentence comes from "Magic and the Brain"; notice the two words with the prefix *neuro-*:

> The responsiveness of a neural system to a constant stimulus (as measured by the firing rate of the relevant neurons) decreases with time.

Restate the sentence, replacing each word with *neuro* with another term that includes *nerve* or *nervous*.

Practice and Apply Use the context and your knowledge of the root *neuro* to write a likely meaning for each bold word. Use a print or online dictionary to look up unfamiliar words or word parts and to confirm word meanings.

1. A patient with an abnormal tingling in one arm may consult a **neurologist.**

2. Some snakes paralyze their prey by injecting a **neurotoxin.**

3. People with a **neuromuscular** disorder may have difficulty with tasks such as unscrewing a jar lid.

4. The **neurosurgeon** removed a tumor from the patient's brain.

Language Conventions: Adverb Clauses

An **adverb** is a part of speech that modifies a verb, an adjective, or another adverb. It answers the question *When? Where? How?* or *To what extent?* A **clause** is a group of words that contains a subject and a predicate—the two main parts of a complete sentence. An **adverb clause** is a subordinate clause that completes the same task as an adverb: it modifies a verb, an adjective, or another adverb.

Adverb clauses start with a connecting word called a **subordinating conjunction,** such as *after, although, as, because, before, even though, if, since, so that, though, unless, until, when, where, while.* Notice the subordinating conjunction and adverb clause in this sentence from "Magic and the Brain."

> **When the constant stimulus is turned off, the adapted neurons fire a "rebound" response known as an afterdischarge.**

The phrase *When the constant stimulus is turned off* modifies the verb *fire* in the rest of the sentence. The clause tells when the "neurons fire." It begins with the subordinating conjunction *when.*

When you write, be careful not to confuse an adverb clause with a complete sentence; an adverb clause cannot stand alone. If you position an adverb clause before the main clause, set it off with a comma.

Sentence Fragment	Complete Sentence
Because not enough research had been done	The science of magic could not be used in medicine because not enough research had been done.
After the lights on stage flashed	After the lights on stage flashed, a set of cables switched the dresses worn by the assistant.

Practice and Apply Identify the adverb clause in each of these sentences and tell whether it modifies a verb, an adjective, or an adverb. Tell which question the adverb clause answers: *When? Where? How?* or *To what extent?*

1. After the magician's "little joke," the real illusion took place.

2. The trick was as complicated as any the magician had ever performed.

3. The magician and his assistant stood here, where they usually performed their act.

4. Before the assistant left the stage, the magician handed her his hat.

Julian Beever (b. 1959) *creates unusual chalk drawings on public sidewalks. Beever started drawing pavement art as a way to make money while traveling. Since then, he has gained international recognition. Beever chooses to draw on sidewalks so that everyone can have access to his art. He says, "My work appeals literally to the man (and woman) in the street and is not confined in galleries or limited by the gallery system."*

MEDIA ANALYSIS

Pavement Chalk Art

Public Art by Julian Beever

SETTING A PURPOSE Beever has developed a special technique of using distortion to unequally magnify images in his work. When seen from one special angle, these images come together to create the illusion that his "anamorphic" drawings are truly three dimensional. Viewed this way, his drawings seem to come to life.

Beever's pavement art gives viewers the impression that they are entering a very real, physical place that exists in the drawings. As you view the two drawings, think about what it would be like to be a passerby who suddenly walks across—or into—one of Beever's works. Write down any questions you have as you view.

A Slight Accident in a Railway Station

AS YOU VIEW Artists make choices about the works they produce and the techniques they use to create those works. **Perspective** is the technique that artists use to give the illusion of three-dimensional space on a two-dimensional surface, which in Beever's case is the sidewalk. One way that Beever creates this illusion is through his use of lines. Beever uses thick and thin as well as long and short lines to frame the stairway in the drawing. Notice how the lines make the stairs look thinner the farther away they seem to get from the viewer.

©Julian Beever

Meeting Mr. Frog

AS YOU VIEW In addition to lines, Beever uses colors and shadows to create the illusion that we are seeing something real. Artists can use color to create mood and to create images that imitate life. Notice how the colors Beever uses at the top of the frog seem brighter or lighter. He uses shadows, or shading, at the bottom of the drawing where the frog sits on the lily pad. Color and shadow work together to give the whole image a sense of shape and depth.

COLLABORATIVE DISCUSSION Beever's drawings focus on the sudden collision of perception and reality. With a partner, discuss your reactions to one of Beever's drawings.

Analyze Diverse Media

ELA SL.7.2
ELD PI.7.6

Art is created with an audience in mind. The **audience** is the group of people who view an exhibit or performance. Because Beever produces art that is viewed in public outdoor spaces, his audience is everyday passersby.

Artists also have a **message,** an idea or point, that they want to convey through their art. Beever uses various artistic elements and techniques, such as lines, perspective, and distortion, to convey his message and to make his illusions come to life.

Analyzing the Media

ELA SL.7.2, SL.7.5, W.7.6
ELD PI.7.2, PI.7.6

Cite Text Evidence   Support your responses with evidence from the media.

1. **Analyze** How do the colors and lines in "A Slight Accident in a Railway Station" create a feeling of movement and make the image seem real?

2. **Analyze** Choose one of Beever's drawings. Tell how Beever uses the elements of line, color, perspective, shadow, and distortion to create effects. As shown in the graphic below, explain what effect each element creates.

Element **Effect**

3. **Compare** Both drawings create the illusion of depth. What are some ways the two drawings are different?

4. **Synthesize** Why do you think Beever chooses to create this style of art to put in public spaces? What message or messages does Beever convey through his art?

PERFORMANCE TASK

Media Activity: Poster Working in small groups, create a poster or a flyer that announces an exhibit of Beever's art in a city. Use your favorite design software program to lay out your work, including images and text.

- Highlight the effectiveness of Beever's drawings as public art.

- Promote the advantages of having sidewalk art in a city.
- Present your completed flyer or poster to the other groups, explaining what you intend to communicate with it and how you accomplished that goal.

Background *When **Cory Doctorow** (b. 1971) first saw the movie* Star Wars *at the age of six, he was inspired to rewrite the entire story as a self-made book. The movie sparked his desire to be a science fiction writer. Publishing his first story at 17, Doctorow has since produced many science fiction novels, short stories, and magazine articles. The author has an online presence as a blogger and makes most of his books available online for free.*

Another Place, Another Time

Short Story by Cory Doctorow

SETTING A PURPOSE Science-based ideas are important in this story. As you read, think of the significance of these ideas to the characters—especially to Gilbert.

Gilbert hated time. What a tyrant it was! The hours that crawled by when his father was at sea, the seconds that whipped past when he was playing a brilliant game in the garden with the Limburgher children. The eternity it took for summer to arrive at the beach at the bottom of the cliffs, the flashing instant before the winter stole over them again and Father took to the sea once more.

"You can't hate *time*," Emmy said. The oldest of the three Limburghers and the only girl, she was used to talking

10   younger boys out of their foolishness. "It's just *time*."

Gilbert stopped pacing the tree house floor and pointed a finger at her. "That's where you're wrong!" He thumped the book he'd taken out of his father's bookcase, a book fetched

home from London, heavy and well made and swollen with the damp air of the sea-crossing home to America. He hadn't read the book, but his tutor, sour Señor Uriarte, had explained it to him the day before while he was penned up inside, watching summer whiz past the study's windows. "Time isn't just time! Time is also space! It's also a dimension." Gilbert
20 thumped the book again for emphasis, then opened it to the page he'd marked with a wide blade of sawgrass.

"See this? This is a point. That's one dimension. It doesn't have length or depth. It's just a dot. When you add another dimension, you get *lines*." He pointed at the next diagram with a chewed and dirty fingernail. "You can go back and you can go forward, you can move around on the surface, as though the world were a page. But you can't go up and down, not until you add another dimension." He pointed to the diagram of the cube, stabbing at it so hard, his finger dented the page. "That's
30 three dimensions, up and down, side to side, and in and out."

Emmy rolled her eyes with the **eloquence** of a thirteen-year-old girl whose tutor had already explained all this to her. Gilbert smiled. Em would always be a year older than he was, but that didn't mean he would always be dumber than she was.

"And Mr. Einstein, who is the smartest man in the whole history of the world, he has proved—absolutely *proved*—that time is just *another dimension*, just like space. Time is what happens when you can go up and down, side to side, in and
40 out, and *before and after*."

Em opened her mouth and closed it. Her twin brothers, Erwin and Neils, snickered at the sight of their sister struck dumb. She glared at them, then at Gilbert. "That's stupid," she said.

"You're calling *Einstein* stupid?"

"Of course not. But you must not understand him properly. Space is space. Time is time. Everyone knows that."

Gilbert pretended he hadn't heard her. "But here's the part no one knows: why can we move through space in any
50 direction—"

"You can't go up!" Em said, quickly.

"You got up into my tree house," he said, putting a small emphasis on *my*. "And you could go back *down*, too."

eloquence
(ĕl′ə-kwəns) *n.* If someone behaves or speaks with *eloquence*, he or she uses persuasive, powerful expression.

Emmy, who was a better fighter than any of them, put her fists on her hips and mimed *Make me*. He pretended he didn't see it.

"Why can we move through space in *almost* any direction, but time only goes in one direction, at one speed? Why can't we go faster? Slower? Backwards?"

60   "Sideways?" Neils said. He didn't speak often, but when he did, what he said was usually surprising.

"What's sideways in time?" his twin asked.

Neils shrugged. "Sideways is sideways."

"This is dumb," Emmy declared, but Gilbert could see that she was getting into the spirit of the thing—starting to understand how it had made him all so angry.

Outside Gilbert's house the summer roared past like a three-masted schooner before a gale,[1] with all sails bellied out. Inside the study, the hours crawled by. And then, in between, there

70 were the breakfasts and dinners with Gilbert's father, who was home for the summer, whose kind eyes were set into an ever-growing net of wrinkles and bags, who returned from his winter voyages each year a little thinner, a little more frail.

"And what did you learn today, my boy?" he said, as he tucked in to the mountain of lentils and beans made by the housekeeper, Mrs. Curie (who was so old that she had actually once served as Father's nanny and changed his diapers, which always made Gilbert giggle when he thought of it). Father was a strict vegetarian and swore by his diet's life-enhancing

80 properties, though that didn't seem to stop him from growing older and older and older.

Gilbert stopped fussing with his lentils, which he didn't like very much. "Geography," he said, looking at his plate. "We're doing the lowlands." He looked out at the sunset, the sun racing for the other side of the planet, dragging them all back toward the winter. "Belgium. Belgium, Belgium, Belgium."

His father laughed and smacked his hands on his thighs. "Belgium! Poor lad. I've been **marooned** there once or twice.

90 Land of bankers and cheese-makers. Like hitting your head, Belgium, because it feels so good when you stop. What else?"

---

[1] **three-masted schooner before a gale:** a vessel with three sails, moving fast because of a forceful wind.

maroon
(mə-rōōn´) *v.* To *maroon* is to abandon or leave someone in a place that is hard to get away from.

"I *want* to do more physics, but Señor says I don't have the math for it."

His father nodded **judiciously**. "He would know. Why physics?"

judicious
(jōō-dĭsh´əs) *adv.* If you are *judicious*, you have good judgment.

"Time," he said, simply. They'd talked of time all summer, in those few hours when Gilbert wasn't with his tutor and when Father wasn't sitting at his desk working at his accounts, or riding into town to huddle over the telephone, casting his
100 will over place and time, trying to keep his ships and their cargos in proper and correct motion.

"Why time, Gil? You're eleven, son! You've got lots of time! You can worry about time when you're an old man."

Gilbert pretended he hadn't heard. "I was thinking of more ways that time is like space. If I was at sea, standing on the deck of a ship, I could see a certain ways before me, and if I turned around, I could see a small ways behind me. But the horizon cuts off the view in both directions. Time is like that. I can think back a certain ways, and the further back I
110 try to remember, the fuzzier it gets, until I can't see at all. And I can see forward—we'll have cobbler soon, go to bed, wake tomorrow. But no further."

His father raised his furry eyebrows and smiled a genuine and delighted smile. "Ah, but things separated by time affect each other the way that events separated by space can't. A star dying on the other side of the universe, so far away that its light hasn't yet had time enough to crawl all the way to us, can't have any effect on us. But things that happened hundreds of years ago, like the planting of the seed that grew the oak
120 that made this table . . ." He rattled his saucer on it, making his coffee sway like a rough chop. He waggled his eyebrows again.

"Yikes," Gilbert said. That hadn't occurred to him. "What if time moved in every direction and at every speed—could you have a space where events at the far end of the galaxy affected us?" He answered his own question. "Of course. Because the events could travel backwards in time—or, uh . . ." He fumbled, remembered Neils. "Sideways." He swallowed.

"What's sideways in time?"

130 He shrugged. "Sideways is sideways," he said.

"WHAT IF TIME MOVED IN EVERY DIRECTION AND AT EVERY SPEED?"

His father laughed until tears rolled down his cheeks, and Gilbert didn't have the heart to tell him that the phrase had been Neils's, because making his father laugh like that was like Christmas and his birthday and a day at the beach all rolled into one.

And then his father took him down to the ocean, down the rough goat trail cut into the cliff, as surefooted as a goat himself. They watched the sun disappear behind the waves, and then they moved among the tidepools, swirling their
140   hands in the warm, salty water to make the bioluminescent² speck-size organisms light up like fireworks. They sat out and watched the moon and the stars, lying on their backs in the sand, Gilbert's head in the crook of his father's arm, and he closed his eyes and let his father tell him stories about the sea and the places he went in the long, lonely winters, while the waves went *shhh, shhh,* like the whisper of the mother who'd died giving birth to him.

Then they picked their way back up the cliff by moonlight that was so bright, it might have been day, a blue-white noon
150   in shades of gray, and his father tucked him up into bed as if he were three years old, smoothing the covers and kissing him on the forehead with a whiskery kiss.

As he lay along a moment that stretched sleepily out like warm taffy, suspended on the edge of sleep, the thought occurred to him: *What if space moved in only one direction, in two dimensions, like time?*

---

² **bioluminescent** (bī´ō-loo´mə-něs´ənt): visible light, caused by chemical reactions, that emits from a living organism.

The year passed. For so long as Gilbert could remember, summer's first messenger had been the postmaster, Mr. Ossinger, who rode his bicycle along the sea road to the house
160   to deliver his father's telegram advising of his expected arrival in port and the preparations to be made for him. Mrs. Curie usually signed for the letter, then knocked on the study door to deliver it into Gilbert's eager hands.

But this year, while the wind and rain howled outside the window, and Señor Uriarte plodded through the formation of igneous rock,[3] Mrs. Curie did not come and deliver the letter, rescuing him from geography. She didn't come to the door, though Señor had finished rocks and moved on to algebra and then to Shakespeare. Finally, the school day ended. Gilbert left
170   Señor stirring through the coals of the study fire, adding logs against the unseasonal winds outside.

Gilbert floated downstairs to the kitchen as though trapped in a dream that compelled him to seek out the housekeeper, even though some premonition told him to hide away in his room for as long as possible.

From behind, she seemed normal, her thin shoulders working as she beat at the batter for the night's cake, cranking the mixer's handle with slow, practiced turns. But when the door clicked shut behind him, she stopped working the
180   beater, though her shoulders kept working, shuddering, rising, falling. She turned her face to him and he let out a cry and took a step back toward the door. It was as though she had been caught by an onrush of time, one that had aged her, turning her from an old woman to an animated corpse. Every wrinkle seemed to have sunk deeper, her fine floss hair hung limp across her forehead, her eyes were red and leaked steady rills of tears.

She took a step toward him, and he wanted to turn and run, but now he was frozen. So he stood, rooted to the
190   spot, while she came and took him up in her frail arms and clutched at him, sobbing dry, raspy sobs. "He's not coming home," she whispered into his ear, the whiskers on her chin tickling at him. "He's not coming home, Gilbert. Oh, oh, oh." He held her and patted her and the time around him seemed to crawl by, slow enough that he could visualize every sweet moment he'd had with his father, time enough to visualize

---

[3] **igneous rock** (ĭg′nē-əs rŏk): rock formed when melted rock, called magma, cools and solidifies above or below the earth.

every storm his father had ever narrated to him. Had all that
time and more before Señor Uriarte came downstairs for his
tea and found them in the kitchen. He gathered up frozen
Gilbert and carried him to his bedroom, removed his shoes,
and sat with him for hours until he finally slept.

When morning dawned, the storm had lifted. Gilbert went
to his window to see the stupid blue sky with its awful yellow
sun and realized that his father was now gone forever and
ever, to the end of time.

Emmy and her brothers were queasy of him for the first week
of summer, playing with him as though he were made of china
or tainted with plague. But by the second week, they were back
to something like normal, scampering up the trees and down
the cliffs, ranging farther and farther afield on their bicycles.

Most of all, they were playing down at the switchyards,
the old rail line that ran out from the disused freight docks a
few miles down the beach from their houses. Señor and Mrs.
Curie didn't know what to do with him that summer, lacking
any direction from Father, and so Gilbert made the most of
it, taking the Limburghers out on longer and longer trips,
their packs bursting with food and water and useful tools:
screwdrivers, crowbars, cans of oil.

Someone probably owned the switchyard, but whoever
that was, he was far away and had shown no interest in it in
Gilbert's lifetime. It had been decades since the freighters
came into this harbor and freight trains had taken their cargos
off into the land on the rusted rails. The rusted padlocks on
the utility sheds crumbled and fell to bits at the lightest touch
from the crowbars; the doors squealed open on their ancient
hinges.

Inside, the cobwebby, musty gloom yielded a million
treasures: old time-tables, a telegraph rig, stiff denim coveralls
with material as thick as the hall carpet at home, ancient
whiskey bottles, a leather-bound journal that went to powder
when they touched it, and . . .

A handcar.[4]

"It'll never work," said Emmy. "That thing's older than the
dinosaurs. It's practically rusted through!"

---

[4] **handcar:** a small, open railroad car that is propelled by a hand pump.

Gilbert pretended he hadn't heard her. He wished he could move the car a little closer to the grimy windows. It was almost impossible to make sense of in the deep shadows of the shed. He pushed hard on the handle, putting his weight into it. It gave a groan, a squeal, and another groan. Then it moved an inch. That was a magic inch! He got his oilcan and lavishly applied the forty-weight oil to every bearing he could find. Neils and Erwin held the lamp. Emmy leaned in closer. He pushed the handle again. Another groan, and a much higher squeal, and the handle sank under his weight. The handcar rumbled forward, almost crushing Emmy's foot—if she hadn't been so quick to leap back, she'd have been crippled. She didn't seem to mind. She, her brothers, and Gilbert were all staring at the handcar as if to say, "Where have you been all my life?"

> ## "THE HANDCAR RUMBLED FORWARD, ALMOST CRUSHING EMMY'S FOOT."

They christened it *Kalamazoo* and they worked with oil and muscle until they had moved it right up to the doorway. It cut their fingers to ribbons and turned their shins into fields of bruises, but it was all worth it because of what it promised: motion without end.

The track in the switchyard went in two directions. Inland, toward the nation and its hurrying progress and its infinite hunger for materials and blood and work. And out to sea, stretching out on a rockbed across the harbor, to the breakers where the great boats that were too large for the shallow harbor used to tie up to offload. Once they had bullied *Kalamazoo* onto the tracks—using blocks, winches, levers, and a total disregard for their own safety—they stood to either side of its bogey handle and stared from side to side. Each knew what the others were thinking: Do we pump for the land, or pump for the sea?

"Tomorrow," Gilbert said. It was the end of August now, and lessons would soon begin again, and each day felt like something was drawing to a close. "Tomorrow," Gilbert said. "We'll decide tomorrow. Bring supplies."

270   That night, by unspoken agreement, they all packed their treasures. Gilbert laid out his sailor suit—his father bought him a new one every year—and his book about time and space and stuffed a picnic blanket with Mrs. Curie's preserves, hardtack bread, jars of lemonade, and apples from the cellar. Mrs. Curie—three quarters deaf—slept through his raid. Gilbert then went to his father's study and took the **spyglass** that had belonged to his grandfather, who had also been lost at sea. He opened the small oak box holding Grandad's **sextant**, but as he'd never mastered it, he set it down. He took

280   his father's enormous silver-chased[5] turnip watch, and tried on his rain boots and discovered that they fit. The last time he'd tried them on, he could have gotten both feet into one of them. Time had passed without his noticing, but his feet had noticed.

He hauled the bundles out to the hedgerow at the bottom of the driveway, and then he put himself to bed and in an instant he was asleep. An instant later, the sun was shining on his face. He woke, put on his sailor suit, went downstairs, and shouted hello to Mrs. Curie, who smiled a misty smile to

290   see him in his sailor suit. She gave him hotcakes with butter and cherries from the tree behind Señor's shed, a glass of milk and a mountain of fried potatoes. He ate until his stomach wouldn't hold any more, said goodbye to her, and walked to the bottom of the hedgerow to retrieve his secret bundle. He wrestled it into his bike's basket and wobbled down to the Limburghers' gate to meet his friends, each with a bundle and a bike.

The half-hour ride to the switchyard took so little time that it was over even before Gilbert had a chance to think

300   about what he was doing. Time was going by too fast for thoughts now, like a train that had hit its speed and could now only be perceived as a blur of passing cars and a racket of wheels and steam.

spyglass
(spī´glăs´) *n.* A *spyglass* is a small telescope.

sextant
(sĕk´stənt) *n.* A *sextant* is an instrument used to determine location by measuring the position of the stars and sun.

---

[5] **silver-chased:** Silver-chasing is a technique used in engraving silver. The silver is moved, rather than removed, with a small pointed tool and mallet to create a design or texture.

Kalamazoo was still beaded with dew as they began to unload their bundles onto its platform. Gilbert set his down at the end farthest from the sea, and Emmy set hers down at the end farthest from the land, and when they stood to either side of the pump handle, it was clear that Emmy wanted to push for the land while Gilbert wanted to push them out to sea.

Naturally.

Emmy looked at Gilbert and Gilbert looked at Emmy. Gilbert took out his grandfather's spyglass, lifted off the leather cap from the business end, extended it, and pointed it out to sea, sweeping from side to side, looking farther than he'd ever seen. Wordlessly, he held it out to Emmy, who turned around to face the bay and swept it with the telescope. Then she handed it off to Neils and Erwin, who took their turns.

Nothing more had to be said. They leaned together into the stiff lever that controlled *Kalamazoo's* direction of travel, threw it into position, and set to pumping out to sea.

What the spyglass showed: waves and waves, and waves and waves, and, farther along, the curvature of the planet itself as it warped toward Europe and Africa and the rest of the world. It showed a spit of land, graced with an ancient and crumbling sea fort, shrouded in mist and overgrown with the weeds and trees of long disuse. And beyond it, waves and more waves.

The gentle sea breeze turned into a stiff wind once they'd pumped for an hour, the handcart at first rolling slowly on the complaining wheels. Then, as the rust flaked off the axles and the bearings found their old accommodations, they spun against one another easily. The pumping was still hard work, and even though they traded off, the children soon grew tired and sore and Emmy called for a rest stop and a snack.

As they munched their sandwiches, Gilbert had a flash. "We could use this for a sail," he said, nudging his picnic blanket with one toe. Neils and Erwin—whose shorter arms suffered more from the pumping labor—loved the idea, and set to rigging a mast from their fishing poles and the long crowbar they'd lashed to *Kalamazoo's* side. Emmy and Gilbert let them do the work, watching with the wisdom of age, eating sandwiches and enjoying the breeze that dried their sweat.

As they started up again, *Kalamazoo* seemed as refreshed from the rest as they were, and it rolled more easily than ever, the sail bellied out before the mast. When Gilbert and Emmy stopped to trade pumping duties back to the twins, Kalamazoo continued to roll, propelled by the stiff wind alone. All four children made themselves comfortable at the back of the pump car and allowed the time and the space to whip past them as they would.

350 "We're moving through space like time," Gilbert said.

Emmy quirked her mouth at him, a familiar no-nonsense look that he ignored.

"We are," he said. "We are moving in a straight line, from behind to in front, at a rate we can't control. Off to the sides are spaces we could move through, but we're not. We're on these rails, and we can't go sideways, can't go back, can't go up or down. We can't control our speed. We are space's slaves. This is just how we move through time."

Emmy shook her head. Neils seemed excited by the idea,
360 though, and he nudged his twin and they muttered in their curious twinnish dialect to one another.

The sea fort was visible with the naked eye now, and with the spyglass, Gilbert could make out its brickwork and the streaks of guano that ran down its cracked walls. The rails ran right up to the fort—last used as a customs inspection point— and past it to the hidden docks on the other side of the spit.

"Better hope that the wind shifts," Emmy said, holding a wetted finger up to check the breeze.

"Otherwise we're going to have a devil of a time pumping
370 ourselves home in time for supper."

Gilbert drew out the turnip watch, which he'd set this morning by the big grandfather clock in the front hall, carefully winding its spring. He opened its face and checked the second hand. It seemed to be spinning a little more slowly, but that could have been his imagination. According to the watch, it was nearly eleven, and they'd been on the rails for three hours.

"I think we'll make the fort in time for lunch," he said.

At the mention of food, Neils and Erwin clamored for
380 snacks, and Emmy found them cookies she'd snitched from the big jar in the Limburgher kitchen.

Gilbert looked at the watch for a moment. The second hand had stopped moving. He held it up to his ear, and it wasn't precisely ticking any longer, but rather making a sound like a truck-wheel spinning in spring mud. He closed the lid again, and held it so tight that the intricate scrolling on the case dug into his palm.

Time passed.

And then it didn't.

390 And then it did again.

"Oh!" said Neils and Erwin together.

> **"GILBERT LOOKED AT THE WATCH FOR A MOMENT. THE SECOND HAND HAD STOPPED MOVING."**

To either side of the car, stretching into infinity, were more tracks, running across the endless harbor, each with its own car, its own sail, its own children. Some were edging ahead of them. Some were going backwards. A racket overhead had them all look up at once, at the tracks there, too, the rails and the cars and the Limburghers and the Gilberts in them. Some children were older. Some were younger. One Gilbert was weeping. One was a girl.

400 Gilbert waved his hand, and a hundred Gilberts waved back. One made a rude gesture.

"Oh!" said Emmy. To her right, another Emmy was offering her a sandwich. She took it and handed over the last of her cookies and Emmy smiled at herself and said thank you as politely as you could wonder.

"Sideways is sideways," Neils and Erwin said together.

Emmy and Gilbert nodded.

Gilbert pulled out his spyglass and looked ahead at the fort. All the rails converged on it, but without ever meeting.

410 And some stretched beyond. And out there, somewhere, there was time like space and space like time. And somewhere there was a father on a ship that weathered a storm rather than succumbed to it.

Gilbert turned to his friends and shook each of their hands in turn. Neils was crying a little. Emmy gave Gilbert a friendly punch in the shoulder and then a hug.

There was another *Kalamazoo* to the right, and Gilbert was pretty sure he could easily make the leap from his car to it. And then to the next car, and the next. And beyond, into

420 the infinite sideways.

If there was an answer, he'd find it there.

COLLABORATIVE DISCUSSION Why is Gilbert so interested in the dimension of time? Talk about your ideas with other group members. Discuss how time interacts with and changes Gilbert.

Analyze Story Elements: Character

The characters of "Another Place, Another Time" bring amazingly complex happenings down to a human level. **Characters** are the people, animals, or other creatures who take part in a story. A short story often has a **main character,** whose problem or goal drives the plot. The behavior and action of all the characters affects what happens. In addition, the **setting** of the story, or the time and place of the action, can affect the characters' traits, motivations, and actions.

When you analyze how characters act and change throughout a story, consider the chart below.

Character traits are the qualities shown by a character. Traits may be physical (blond hair) or expressions of personality (fearlessness).	The writer may directly state the character's traits, or you may have to infer traits based on the character's words, thoughts, actions, appearance, or relationships.
Character motivations are the reasons for a character's behavior.	To understand a character's obvious or hidden desires and goals, notice what makes the character take or avoid action.

Think about the main character, Gilbert, in "Another Place, Another Time." Use one or two words to describe his traits. How do the setting and events change him as the story unfolds?

Determine Meaning of Words and Phrases

A **symbol** is a person, a place, an object, or an activity that stands for something beyond itself. Often, a symbol represents an important idea or concept, such as freedom, love, or loneliness. For example, a dove is often a symbol of peace. Characters, objects, conflicts, and settings can serve as symbols for important ideas in a story.

You can identify symbols and determine their meanings by analyzing details in the text.

- Look for people, places, things, or actions that the writer emphasizes or mentions frequently.
- Think about the importance of these details to the characters.

The sea setting is a major feature in "Another Place, Another Time." The sea stands for at least one idea or feeling that is important to Gilbert. Reread lines 138–147 of the story. What might the sea represent for Gilbert here?

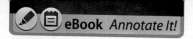
Analyzing the Text

ELA RL.7.1, RL.7.3, RL.7.4, RL.7.5, W.7.9a **ELD** PI.7.6, PI.7.8, PI.7.10

Cite Text Evidence   Support your responses with evidence from the text.

1. **Infer** What does the story title have to do with the setting and the main character's motivations?

2. **Interpret** Reread lines 1–7. What words or phrases describe time? What do these descriptions suggest about the story's **theme,** the message about life or human nature?

3. **Cite Evidence** How might Albert Einstein be a motivating factor in Gilbert's quest?

4. **Infer** Reread lines 353–358. What does this speech reveal about Gilbert and how he perceives reality?

5. **Interpret** Examine lines 408–413. What do these lines suggest about Gilbert's emotional state at this point of the story?

6. **Synthesize** Use a web like the one shown to explore symbolism in the story. In the central circle, write *handcar, father's watch,* or the name of something else from the story that works as a symbol. Fill out the web by recording your ideas about what the symbol represents.

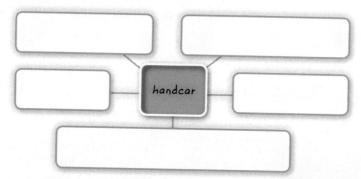

PERFORMANCE TASK

Writing Activity: Character Analysis With a partner, find and record references to the passage of time that connect to key experiences for Gilbert. For each important reference, also note what is happening to Gilbert. Together, write a one-page character profile of Gilbert, including details that answer these questions:

- What are Gilbert's personal traits?
- What motivates Gilbert's actions?
- What life-changing events occur in his life?
- When and where is he at the start of the story? At the end?
- How has he changed by the end of the story?

Critical Vocabulary

eloquence   maroon   judicious   spyglass   sextant

Practice and Apply Complete each sentence to show that you understand the meaning of the vocabulary word.

1. Everyone was impressed by the **eloquence** of . . .

2. The sailors were **marooned** on . . .

3. Before the travelers set out, they were **judicious** about . . .

4. The way to use a **spyglass** is to . . .

5. Sailors long ago needed a **sextant** to . . .

Vocabulary Strategy: Reference Aids

A **dictionary** is a valuable resource for anyone who is checking and expanding their vocabulary. The searching and browsing methods differ for print and digital dictionaries, but users can find the same basic information about each entry word.

- pronunciation
- part of speech label
- one or more definitions
- related forms

> **in•tri•cate** (ĭn´trĭ-kĭt) *adj.* **1.** Having many complexly arranged elements; elaborate. **2.** Difficult to understand, analyze, or solve for having many interconnected elements. —**in´tri•cate•ly** *adv.* —**in´tri•cate•ness** *n.*

Synonyms are words with similar meanings. The dictionary entry shown for *intricate* includes a synonym within the definition: *elaborate*. Some dictionaries provide a list of synonyms after an entry. A **thesaurus** is a reference aid that lists synonyms. Writers can use a print or digital thesaurus to help find the exact word they need.

> **intricate** *adj.* complicated, complex, elaborate, involved, convoluted

Practice and Apply Find the sentence with *judiciously* in line 94 of "Another Place, Another Time." Look up the word *judicious* and find the related form in an available dictionary and thesaurus. Use your own words to tell what the sentence means. Then rewrite the sentence using an appropriate synonym.

Language Conventions: Spell Correctly

ELA L.7.2b
ELD PI.7.10

When you proofread your writing for accuracy, you should check the spelling of every word. If you are using computer software to write, you will find that the spellchecker catches most misspellings—but not all. So, you still need to check the spelling in your work. In particular, be attentive to the spelling of proper nouns, proper adjectives, personal titles, and abbreviations, which are less likely to be corrected by a spellchecker.

Read these sentences from "Another Place, Another Time."

He thumped the book he'd taken out of his father's bookcase, a book fetched home from London, heavy and well made and swollen with the damp air of the sea-crossing home to America. He hadn't read the book, but his tutor, sour Señor Uriarte, had explained it to him the day before . . .

Note the capitalization and spelling of the geographical names *London* and *America*; a personal title, *Señor*; and a proper name, *Uriarte*.

The chart shows categories of words to check for correct spelling and capitalization.

Category	Examples
geographical names	Madagascar, Kaskaskia River, Cincinnati, Sagamore Boulevard
personal titles and names	Madame Thibeau, Professor Moriarty, Señorita Madariaga
proper adjectives	Parisian, Colombian, Shakespearean, Einsteinian
abbreviations	Mme., Mr., Dr., Ave., Sq., Blvd.

Practice and Apply These sentences include errors in spelling and capitalization. In each sentence, identify the misspellings and write the words correctly. Refer to "Another Place, Another Time" and to other reference resources to check spellings.

1. Cory Docorow, the author of "Another Place, Another Time," tells how the children named the handcar *Kamalazoo*.

2. In this story, Gilbert is friends with Emmy Limberger and her twin brothers, Neils and Irwin.

3. Gilbert's tutor, Señor Uriate, and his housekeeper, Mme. Curie, care for him when his father is crossing the Altantic ocean.

4. Profesor Einstein's book leaves a deep impression on Gilbert, who wants to understand how the newtonion view of the universe has changed.

Background *Long before cell phones, telephone service went over wires. People called the operator, who connected them to a number. Occasionally, malfunctions resulted in "crossed" wires, allowing a caller to hear other people's phone conversations.* **Lucille Fletcher** *(1912–2000) wrote novels, radio plays, stage plays, and screenplays. She is best remembered for her radio play* Sorry, Wrong Number, *which was first broadcast in 1943. The play became a sensation, capturing the imaginations of mystery fans around the world.*

Sorry, Wrong Number

Drama by Lucille Fletcher

SETTING A PURPOSE A drama is mainly intended to be performed for an audience. As you read, pay attention to the stage directions to help you imagine the plot events as if they were being performed by live actors. Write down any questions you have while reading.

Cast of Characters

Mrs. Stevenson	4th Operator
1st Operator	5th Operator
1st Man	Information
2nd Man	Hospital Receptionist
Chief Operator	Western Union
2nd Operator	Sergeant Duffy
3rd Operator	A Lunchroom-Counter Attendant

Scene: *As the curtain rises, we see a divided stage, only the center part of which is lighted and furnished as* Mrs. Stevenson's *bedroom. Expensive, rather fussy furnishings. A large bed, on which* Mrs. Stevenson, *clad in a bedjacket, is lying. A nighttable close by, with phone, lighted lamp, and pill bottles.*
10 *A mantel, with clock, R. A closed door, R. A window, with curtains closed, rear. The set is lit by one lamp on nighttable. Beyond this central set, the stage on either side is in darkness.*

Mrs. Stevenson *is dialing a number on the phone as the curtain rises. She listens to the phone, slams down the receiver in irritation. As*
20 *she does so, we hear the sound of a train roaring by in the distance. She reaches for her pill bottle, pours herself a glass of water, shakes out a pill, swallows it, then reaches for the phone again, dials the number nervously.* Sound: *Number being dialed on the phone. Busy signal.*

Mrs. Stevenson (*a querulous, self-centered neurotic*). Oh, *dear!*
30 (*Slams down receiver. Dials* Operator. *A spotlight, L. of side flat, picks up out of peripheral darkness the figure of* 1st Operator *sitting with headphones at small table.*)

Operator. Your call, please?

Mrs. Stevenson. Operator? I've been dialing Murray Hill 4-0098 for the last three quarters of an hour and the line is always busy.
40 But I don't see how it *could* be busy that long. Will you try it for me, please?

Operator. Murray Hill 4-0098? One moment, please. (*She makes gesture of plugging in call through a switchboard.*)

Mrs. Stevenson. I don't see how it could be busy all this time. It's my husband's office. He's working late
50 tonight and I'm all alone here in the house. My health is very poor and I've been feeling so nervous all day.

Operator. Ringing Murray Hill 4-0098. (Sound: *Phone buzz. It rings three times. Receiver is picked up at the other end. Spotlight picks up a figure of a heavy-set man seated at a desk with a phone on R. side of dark periphery of stage. He is*
60 *wearing a hat. Picks up phone.*)

Man. Hello.

Mrs. Stevenson. Hello? (*a little puzzled*) Hello. Is Mr. Stevenson there?

Man (*into phone, as though he has not heard*). *Hello.* (louder) Hello. (*Spotlight on L. now moves from* Operator *to another man,* George—*a killer type, also wearing*
70 *a hat, but standing as in a phone booth.*)

2nd Man (*slow heavy quality, faintly foreign accent*). Hello.

1st Man. Hello? George?

George. Yes, sir.

Mrs. Stevenson (*louder and more imperious, to phone*). Hello. Who's this? What number am I calling, please?

1st Man. We have heard from our client. He says the coast is clear for tonight.

George. Yes, sir.

1st Man. Where are you now?

George. In a phone booth.

1st Man. Okay. You know the address. At eleven o'clock, the private patrolman goes around to the bar on Second Avenue for a beer. Be sure that all the lights downstairs are out. There should be only one light visible from the street. At eleven-fifteen, a subway train crosses the bridge. It makes a noise in case her window is open and she should scream.

Mrs. Stevenson (*shocked*). Oh— hello! What number is this, please?

George. Okay. I understand.

1st Man. Make it quick. As little blood as possible. Our client does not wish to make her suffer long.

George. A knife okay?

1st Man. Yes. A knife will be okay. And remember—remove the rings and bracelets, and the jewelry in the bureau drawer. Our client wishes it to look like simple robbery.

George. Okay—I get—(*Spotlight suddenly goes out on* George. *Sound: A bland buzzing signal. Spotlight goes off on* 1st Man.)

Mrs. Stevenson (*clicking phone*). Oh! (*Bland buzzing signal continues. She hangs up.*) How awful! How unspeakably—(*She lies back on her pillows, overcome for a few seconds, then suddenly pulls herself together, reaches for phone.* Sound: *Dialing. Phone buzz. Spotlight goes on at* 1st Operator's *switchboard.* 1st *and* 2nd Man *exit as unobtrusively as possible, in darkness.*)

Operator. Your call, please?

Mrs. Stevenson (*unnerved and breathless, into phone*). Operator, I—I've just been cut off.

Operator. I'm sorry, madam. What number were you calling?

Mrs. Stevenson. It was supposed to be Murray Hill 4-0098, but it wasn't. Some wires must have crossed—I was cut into a wrong number. And I've just heard the most dreadful thing—a—a murder—and (*imperiously*) you'll simply have to retrace that call at once, Operator.

Operator. I beg your pardon, madam, I don't quite—

Mrs. Stevenson. Oh, I know it was a wrong number and I had no business listening, but these two men—they were cold-blooded fiends and they were going to murder somebody—some poor innocent woman who was all alone—in a house near a bridge. And we've got to stop them—

Operator (*patiently*). What number were you calling, madam?

Mrs. Stevenson. That doesn't matter. This was a *wrong* number.

And *you* dialed it. And we've got to find out what it was—immediately!

Operator. But, madam—

Mrs. Stevenson. Oh, why are you so stupid? Look—it was obviously a case of some little slip of the finger. I told you to try Murray Hill 4-0098 for me—you dialed it but your finger must have slipped and I was connected with some other number. I could hear them, but they couldn't hear me. I simply fail to see why you couldn't make that same mistake again—on purpose. Why you couldn't *try* to dial Murray Hill 4-0098 in the same careless sort of way—

Operator (*quickly*). Murray Hill 4-0098? I will try to get it for you, madam.

Mrs. Stevenson (*sarcastically*). Thank you. (*She bridles, adjusts herself on her pillows, reaches for a handkerchief and wipes her forehead, glancing uneasily for a moment toward the window. Sound of ringing and busy signal.*)

Operator. I'm sorry. Murray Hill 4-0098 is busy.

Mrs. Stevenson (*frantically clicking receiver*). Operator—Operator!

Operator. Yes, madam?

Mrs. Stevenson (*angrily*). You *didn't* try to get that wrong number at all. I asked explicitly and all you did was dial correctly.

Operator. I'm sorry. What number were you calling?

Mrs. Stevenson. Can't you forget what number I was calling and do something specific? I want to trace that call. It's my civic duty—it's *your* civic duty—to trace that call and to apprehend those dangerous killers. And if *you* won't—

Operator (*glancing around wearily*). I will connect you with the Chief Operator.

Mrs. Stevenson. *Please!* (*Sound of ringing. Operator puts hand over mouthpiece of phone, gestures into darkness.*)

Operator (*a half whisper*). Miss Curtis, will you pick up on seventeen, please? (*Miss Curtis, Chief Operator, enters. Middle-aged, efficient, pleasant. Wearing headphone.*)

Miss Curtis. Yes, dear. What's the trouble?

Operator. Somebody wanting a call traced. I can't make head nor tail of it.

Miss Curtis (*sitting down at desk as* Operator *gets up*). Sure, dear. (*She makes gesture of plugging in her headphone, coolly and professionally.*) This is the Chief Operator.

Mrs. Stevenson. Chief Operator? I want you to trace a call. Immediately. I don't know where it came from, or who was making it, but it's absolutely necessary that it be tracked down. It was about a murder, a terrible, cold-blooded murder of a poor innocent woman—tonight, at eleven-fifteen.

Chief Operator. I see.

Mrs. Stevenson (*high-strung, demanding*). Can you trace it for me? Can you track down those men?

Chief Operator. It depends, madam.

Mrs. Stevenson. Depends on what?

Chief Operator. It depends on whether the call is still going on. If it's a live call, we can trace it on the equipment. If it's been disconnected, we can't.

Mrs. Stevenson. Disconnected?

Chief Operator. If the parties have stopped talking to each other.

Mrs. Stevenson. Oh, but of course they must have stopped talking to each other by *now*. That was at least five minutes ago.

Chief Operator. Well, I can try tracing it. (*She takes a pencil out of her hair.*) What is your name, madam?

Mrs. Stevenson. Mrs. Elbert Stevenson. But listen—

Chief Operator (*writing*). And your telephone number?

Mrs. Stevenson (*more irritated*). Plaza 4-2295. But if you go on wasting all this time—(*She glances at clock on the mantel.*)

Chief Operator. And what is your reason for wanting this call traced?

Mrs. Stevenson. My reason? Well, for heaven's sake, isn't it obvious? I overhear two men planning to murder this woman—it's a matter for the police!

Chief Operator. Have you told the police?

Mrs. Stevenson. No. How could I?

Chief Operator. You're making this check into a private call purely as a private individual?

Mrs. Stevenson. Yes. But meanwhile—

Chief Operator. Well, Mrs. Stevenson, I seriously doubt whether we could make this check for you at this time just on your say-so as a private individual. We'd have to have something more official.

Mrs. Stevenson. Oh, for heaven's sake! You mean to tell me I can't report a murder without getting tied up in all this red tape? It's perfectly idiotic. All right, then I *will* call the police. (*She slams down the receiver. Spotlight goes off two* Operators.) Ridiculous! (*Sound of dialing as* Mrs. Stevenson *dials phone and two* Operators *exit unobtrusively in darkness. On R. of stage, spotlight picks up a* 2nd Operator, *seated like first, with headphone at table—same one vacated by* 1st Man.)

2nd Operator. Your call, please?

Mrs. Stevenson (*very annoyed*). The Police Department—please.

2nd Operator. Ringing the Police Department. (*Ring twice. At table L. spotlight now picks up* Sergeant Duffy, *seated in a relaxed position. Just entering beside him is a young man in a cap and apron, carrying a large brown-paper parcel, delivery boy for a local lunch counter. Phone is ringing.*)

Lunchroom Attendant. Here's your lunch, Sarge. They didn't have no jelly doughnuts, so I got French crullers, okay?

Duffy. French crullers. I got ulcers. Whyn't you make it apple pie? (*picks up phone*) Police Department, Precinct 43, Duffy speaking.

Lunchroom Attendant (*anxiously*). We don't have no apple pie, either, Sarge.

Mrs. Stevenson. Police Department? Oh. This is Mrs. Stevenson—Mrs. Elbert Smythe Stevenson of 53 North Sutton Place. I'm calling to report a murder. (Duffy *has been examining lunch, but double-takes suddenly on above.*)

Duffy. Eh?

Mrs. Stevenson. I mean, the murder hasn't been committed yet, I just overheard plans for it over the telephone—over a wrong number the operator gave me. (Duffy *relaxes, sighs, starts taking lunch from bag.*) I've been trying to trace the call myself, but everybody is so stupid—and I guess in the end you're the only people who could *do* anything.

Duffy (*not too impressed*). Yes, ma'am. (Attendant *exits.*)

Mrs. Stevenson (*trying to impress him*). It was perfectly *definite* murder. I heard their plans distinctly. (Duffy *begins to eat sandwich, phone at his ear.*) Two men were talking, and they were going to murder some woman at eleven-fifteen tonight—she lived in a house near a bridge.

Duffy. Yes, ma'am.

Mrs. Stevenson. There was a private patrolman on the street who was going to go around for a beer on Second Avenue. And there was some third man, a client, who was paying to have this poor woman murdered. They were going to take her rings and bracelets—and use a knife. Well, it's unnerved me dreadfully—and I'm not well.

Duffy. I see. (*He wipes his mouth with a paper napkin.*) When was all this, ma'am?

Mrs. Stevenson. About eight minutes ago. Oh—(*relieved*)—then you *can* do something? You *do* understand.

Duffy. And what is your name, ma'am? (*He reaches for a pad of paper.*)

Mrs. Stevenson (*impatiently*). Mrs. Stevenson. Mrs. Elbert Stevenson.

Duffy. And your address?

Mrs. Stevenson. 53 North Sutton Place. *That's* near a bridge. The Queensboro Bridge, you know—and *we* have a private patrol-man on *our* street. And Second Avenue—

390 **Duffy.** And what was that number you were calling?

Mrs. Stevenson. Murray Hill 4-0098. (Duffy *writes it down.*) But that wasn't the number I overheard. I mean Murray Hill 4-0098 is my husband's office. (Duffy, *in exasperation, holds his pencil poised.*) He's working late tonight and I was trying to reach 400 him to ask him to come home. I'm an invalid, and it's the maid's night off, and I *hate* to be alone even though he says I'm perfectly safe as long as I have the telephone right beside my bed.

Duffy (*stolidly*). Well, we'll look into it, Mrs. Stevenson, and see if we can check it with the telephone company.

410 **Mrs. Stevenson** (*getting impatient*). But the telephone company said they couldn't check the call if the parties had stopped talking. I've already taken care of that.

Duffy. Oh—yes? (*He yawns slightly.*)

Mrs. Stevenson. Personally, I feel you ought to do something far more immediate and drastic than

420 just check the call. What good does checking the call do if they've stopped talking? By the time you track it down, they'll already have committed the murder.

Duffy (*he reaches for a paper cup of coffee*). Well, we'll take care of it, lady. Don't worry. (*He begins to remove the top of the coffee container.*)

430 **Mrs. Stevenson.** I'd say the whole thing calls for a complete and thorough search of the whole city. (Duffy *puts down the phone to work on the cup as her voice continues.*) I'm very near a bridge, and I'm not far from Second Avenue. And I know I'd feel a whole lot better if you sent around a radio car to *this* neighborhood at once.

440 **Duffy** (*picks up phone again, drinks coffee*). And what makes you think the murder's going to be committed in your neighborhood, ma'am?

Mrs. Stevenson. Oh, I don't know—the coincidence is so

horrible. Second Avenue—the bridge—

Duffy. Second Avenue is a very long street, ma'am. And do you

450 happen to know how many bridges there are in the city of New York? How do you know there isn't some little house out on Staten Island— on some little Second Avenue you never heard about? (*He takes a long gulp of coffee.*) How do you know they were even talking about New York at all?

Mrs. Stevenson. But I heard

460 the call on the New York dialing system.

Duffy. How do you know it wasn't a long-distance call you overheard? Telephones are funny things. (*He sets down coffee.*) Look, lady, why don't you look at it this way? Supposing you hadn't broken in on that telephone call? Supposing you'd got your husband the way

470 you always do? Would this murder have made any difference to you then?

Mrs. Stevenson. I suppose not. But it's so inhuman—so cold-blooded—

Duffy. A lot of murders are committed in this city every day, ma'am. If we could do something to stop 'em, we would. But a clue of

480 this kind that's so vague isn't much more use to us than no clue at all.

Mrs. Stevenson. But surely—

Duffy. Unless, of course, you have some reason for thinking this call is phony, and that someone may be planning to murder *you?*

Mrs. Stevenson. *Me?* Oh, no—I hardly think so. I mean—why should anybody? I'm alone all day and night. I see nobody except my maid Eloise—she's a big two-hundred-pound woman too lazy to bring up my breakfast tray—and the only other person is my husband Elbert. He's crazy about me—adores me—waits on me hand and foot. He's scarcely left my side since I took sick twelve years ago—

Duffy. Well, then, there's nothing for you to worry about, is there? (*The* Lunchroom-Counter Attendant *has entered. He is carrying a piece of apple pie on a plate and points it out to* Duffy *triumphantly.*) And now, if you'll just leave the rest of this to us—

Mrs. Stevenson. But what will you *do?* It's so late—it's nearly eleven o'clock.

Duffy (*firmly*). We'll take care of it, lady.

Mrs. Stevenson. Will you broadcast it all over the city? And send out squads? And warn your radio cars to watch out—especially in suspicious neighborhoods like mine. (*The* Attendant, *in triumph, has put the pie down in front of* Duffy.)

Duffy (*more firmly*). Lady, I *said* we'd take care of it. Just now I've got a couple of other matters here on my desk that require my immediate—

Mrs. Stevenson. Oh! (*She slams down the receiver hard.*) Idiot! (Duffy *listening at the phone, hangs up and shrugs, then attacks his pie as spotlight fades out.* Mrs. Stevenson, *in bed, looks at the phone nervously.*) Why did I do that? Now he'll think I *am* a fool. (*She sits tensely, then throws herself back against the pillows, lying there a moment, whimpering with self-pity.*) Oh, why doesn't Elbert come home? *Why* doesn't he? (*We hear sound of train roaring by in the distance. She sits up, reaching for phone. Sound of dialing operator. Spotlight picks up* 2nd Operator, *seated R.*)

Operator. Your call, please?

Mrs. Stevenson. Operator—for heaven's sake—will you ring that Murray Hill 4-0098 number again? I can't think what's keeping him so long.

Operator. Ringing Murray Hill 4-0098. (*rings—busy signal*) The line is busy. Shall I—

Mrs. Stevenson (*nastily*). I can hear it, you don't have to tell me it's busy! (*Slams down receiver. Spotlight fades off on* 2nd Operator. Mrs. Stevenson *sinks back against the pillows again, whimpering to herself fretfully. She glances at the clock, then, turning, punches her pillows up, trying to make herself comfortable. But she isn't and she whimpers to herself as she squirms restlessly in bed.*) If I could get out of this bed for a little while. If I could get a breath of fresh air—or just lean out the window—and see the street. (*She sighs, reaches for pill bottle, and shakes out a pill. As she does, the phone rings and she darts for it instantly.*) Hello, Elbert? Hello. Hello. Hello. Oh—what's the *matter* with this phone? *Hello? Hello?* (*Slams down the receiver and stares at it tensely. The phone rings again. Once. She picks it up.*) Hello? Hello! Oh, for heaven's sake, who *is* this? Hello. Hello. *Hello.* (*Slamming down the receiver, she dials the operator. Spotlight comes on* L. *showing* 3rd Operator, *at spot vacated by* Duffy.)

3rd Operator. Your call, please?

Mrs. Stevenson (*very annoyed and imperious*). Hello, Operator, I don't know what's the matter with this telephone tonight, but it's positively driving me crazy. I've never seen such inefficient, miserable service. Now, look. I'm an invalid, and I'm very nervous, and I'm *not* supposed to be annoyed. But if this keeps on much longer—

3rd Operator (*a young, sweet type*). What seems to be the trouble, madam?

Mrs. Stevenson. *Everything's* wrong. The whole world could be murdered for all you people care! And now my phone keeps ringing!

Operator. Yes, madam?

Mrs. Stevenson. Ringing and ringing and ringing every five seconds or so, and when I pick it up there's no one there!

Operator. I'm sorry, madam. If you'll hang up, I'll test it for you.

Mrs. Stevenson. I don't want you to test it for me, I want you to put through that call—whatever it is—at once.

Operator (*gently*). I'm afraid that's not possible, madam.

Mrs. Stevenson (*storming*). Not possible? And why, may I ask?

Operator. The system is automatic, madam. If someone is trying to dial your number, there's no way to check whether the call is coming through the system or not—unless the person who is trying to reach you complains to his particular operator.

Mrs. Stevenson. Well, of all the stupid, complicated—And meanwhile *I've* got to sit here in my bed, *suffering* every time that phone rings, imagining everything!

Operator. I'll try to check it for you, madam.

Mrs. Stevenson. Check it! Check it! That's all anybody can do. Of all the stupid, idiotic—(*She hangs up.*) Oh, what's the use! (3rd Operator *fades out of spotlight as* Mrs. Stevenson's *phone rings again. She picks up the receiver.*) Hello! *Hello!* Stop ringing, do you hear me? Answer me? What do you want? Do you realize you're driving me crazy? (*Spotlight goes on* R. *We see a* Man *in eyeshade and shirtsleeves at a desk with a phone and telegrams.*) Stark, staring—

Western Union (*dull, flat voice*). Hello. Is this Plaza 4-2295?

Mrs. Stevenson (*catching her breath*). Yes. Yes. This is Plaza 4-2295.

650 **Western Union.** This is Western Union. I have a telegram here for Mrs. Elbert Stevenson. Is there anyone there to receive the message?

Mrs. Stevenson (*trying to calm herself*). I am Mrs. Stevenson.

Western Union (*reading flatly*). The telegram is as follows: "Mrs. Elbert Stevenson, 53 North Sutton Place, New York, New York.
660 Darling. Terribly sorry. Tried to get you for last hour, but line busy. Leaving for Boston eleven P.M. tonight on urgent business. Back tomorrow afternoon. Keep happy. Love. Signed, Elbert."

Mrs. Stevenson (*breathlessly, aghast, to herself.*) Oh, no—

Western Union. That's all, madam. Do you wish us to deliver a copy of
670 the message?

Mrs. Stevenson. No—no, thank you.

Western Union. Thank you, madam. Goodnight. (*He hangs up the phone. Spotlight on* Western Union *immediately out.*)

Mrs. Stevenson (*mechanically, to phone*). Goodnight. (*She hangs up slowly, suddenly bursting into*)
680 No—no—it isn't true! He couldn't do it! Not when he knows I'll be all alone! It's some trick—some

fiendish—(*We hear the sound of a train roaring by outside. She half rises in bed, in panic, glaring toward the curtains. Her movements are frenzied. She beats with her knuckles on the bed, then suddenly stops and reaches for the phone.*
690 *Spotlight picks up* 4th Operator, *seated L.*)

Operator (*coolly*). Your call, please?

Mrs. Stevenson. Operator—try that Murray Hill 4-0098 number for me just once more, please.

Operator. Ringing Murray Hill 4-0098. (*Call goes through. We hear ringing at the other end, ring
700 after ring.*)

Mrs. Stevenson. He's gone. Oh, Elbert, how could you? How could you? (*She hangs up, sobbing pityingly to herself, turning restlessly. Spotlight goes out on* 4th Operator.) But I can't be alone tonight, I can't! If I'm alone one more second— (*She runs her hands wildly through her hair.*) I don't care what he
710 says, or what the expense is, I'm a sick woman—I'm entitled! (*With trembling fingers she picks up the receiver again and dials* Information. *The spotlight picks up* Information Operator, *seated R.*)

Information. This is Information.

Mrs. Stevenson. I want the telephone number of Henchley Hospital.

720 **Information.** Henchley Hospital? Do you have the address, madam?

Mrs. Stevenson. No. It's somewhere in the Seventies. It's a small, private, and exclusive hospital where I had my appendix out two years ago. Henchley. H-E-N-C—

Information. One moment, please.

Mrs. Stevenson. Please—hurry. And please—what's the time?

Information. I don't know, madam. You may find out the time by dialing Meridan 7-1212.

Mrs. Stevenson (*irritated*). Oh, for heaven's sake, couldn't you—?

Information. The number of Henchley Hospital is Butterfield 7-0105, madam.

Mrs. Stevenson. Butterfield 7-0105. (*She hangs up before she finishes speaking and immediately dials the number as she repeats it. Spotlight goes out on* Information. *Phone rings. Spotlight picks up* Woman *in nurse's uniform, seated at desk L.*)

Woman (*middle-aged, solid, firm, practical*). Henchley Hospital, good evening.

Mrs. Stevenson. Nurses' Registry.

Woman. Who was it you wished to speak to, please?

Mrs. Stevenson (*high-handed*). I want the Nurses' Registry at once. I want a trained nurse. I want to hire her immediately. For the night.

Woman. I see. And what is the nature of the case, madam?

Mrs. Stevenson. Nerves. I'm very nervous. I need soothing—and companionship. My husband is away and I'm—

Woman. Have you been recommended to us by any doctor in particular, madam?

Mrs. Stevenson. No. But I really don't see why all this catechizing is necessary. I want a trained nurse. I was a patient in your hospital two years ago. And, after all, I *do* expect to pay this person—

Woman. We quite understand that, madam. But registered nurses are very scarce just now and our superintendent has asked us to send people out only on cases where the physician in charge feels it is absolutely necessary.

Mrs. Stevenson (*growing hysterical*). Well, it is absolutely necessary! I'm a sick woman. I'm very upset! Very! I'm alone in this house—and I'm an invalid—and tonight I overheard a telephone conversation that upset me dreadfully. About a murder—a poor woman who was going to be murdered at eleven-fifteen tonight. In fact, if someone doesn't come at once, I'm afraid I'll go out of my mind!

Woman (*calmly*). I see. Well, I'll speak to Miss Phillips as soon as she comes in. And what is your name, madam?

Mrs. Stevenson. When do you expect Miss Phillips in?

Woman. I really don't know, madam. She went out to supper at eleven o'clock.

Mrs. Stevenson. Eleven o'clock. But it's not eleven yet. (*She cries out.*) Oh, my clock *has* stopped. I *thought* it was running down. What time is it? (Woman *glances at wristwatch.*)

Woman. Just fourteen minutes past eleven. (*Sound of phone receiver being lifted on same line as* Mrs. Stevenson's. *A click.*)

Mrs. Stevenson (*crying out*). What's *that*?

Woman. What was what, madam?

Mrs. Stevenson. That—that click just now—in my own telephone? As though someone had lifted the receiver off the hook of the extension phone downstairs.

Woman. I didn't hear it, madam. Now, about this—

Mrs. Stevenson (*scared*). But I *did*. There's someone in this house! Someone downstairs in the kitchen! And they're listening to me now—they're (*She puts hand over her mouth, hangs up the phone, and sits in terror, frozen, listening.*) I won't pick it up, I won't let them hear me. I'll be quiet—and they'll think—(*with growing terror*) But if I don't call someone now while they're still down there, there'll be no time! (*She picks up the receiver. There is a bland, buzzing signal. She dials the operator. On the second ring, spotlight goes on* R. *We see* 5th Operator.)

Operator (*fat and lethargic*). Your call, please?

840 **Mrs. Stevenson** (*a desperate whisper*). Operator—I—I'm in desperate trouble—

Woman. I cannot hear you, madam. Please speak louder.

Mrs. Stevenson (*still whispering*). I don't dare. I—there's someone listening. Can you hear me now?

Operator. Your call, please? What number are you calling, madam?

850 **Mrs. Stevenson** (*desperately*). You've got to hear me! Oh, please! You've got to help me! There's someone in this house—someone who's going to murder me! And you've got to get in touch with the—(*Click of receiver being put down on* Mrs. Stevenson's *line. She bursts out wildly.*) Oh—there it is—he's put it down! He's coming! **860** (*She screams.*) He's coming up the stairs! (*She thrashes in the bed. The phone cord catching in the lamp wire, the lamp topples, goes out. Darkness. Hoarsely.*) Give me the Police Department (*We see on the dark C. stage the shadow of the door opening.* Mrs. Stevenson *screams.*) The police! (*On stage, there is the swift rush of a shadow advancing to* **870** *the bed—the sound of her voice is choked out as*)

Operator. Ringing the Police Department. (*Phone is rung. We hear the sound of a train beginning to fade in. On the second ring,* Mrs. Stevenson *screams again, but the roaring of the train drowns out her voice. For a few seconds we hear nothing but the roaring of the* **880** *train, then, dying away, the phone at Police Headquarters ringing. Spotlight goes on* Duffy, *L. stage.*)

Duffy. Police Department. Precinct 43. Duffy speaking. (*Pause. Nothing visible but darkness on C. stage*) Police Department. Duffy speaking. (*Now a flashlight goes on, illuminating the open phone to one side of* Mrs. Stevenson's **890** *bed. Nearby hanging down, is her lifeless hand. We see the second man,* George *in black gloves, reach down and pick up the phone. He is breathing hard.*)

George. Sorry, wrong number. (*He replaces the receiver on the hook quietly and exits as* Duffy *hangs up with a shrug and the curtain falls.*)

COLLABORATIVE DISCUSSION *Sorry, Wrong Number* was originally performed as a radio play. With a partner, discuss how you would translate this drama into a radio or stage production. How would you direct the actors to bring the mystery story to life in performance?

Analyze Form: Drama

The play you have just read is a **drama,** a form of literature meant to be performed by actors in front of an audience. Like other forms of literature, a drama presents a series of events, called the **plot,** and establishes the time and place of those events, called the **setting.** The plot centers on a **conflict,** a struggle between opposing forces, and unfolds through the characters' words and actions.

Unlike other forms of literature, a drama usually includes the following elements:

- **cast of characters**—a list of all the characters in the drama; the cast appears at the beginning of the drama.
- **dialogue**—the words that the characters say; the character's name precedes his or her lines of dialogue.
- **stage directions**—instructions for how the drama is to be performed in front of an audience; the instructions are often set in parentheses.

Because dramas are primarily meant to be performed, reading the script requires you to focus on the dialogue and stage directions to picture the action and understand the drama's meaning. Use a graphic organizer to keep track of the plot as you read and to help you analyze how the elements of the drama interact.

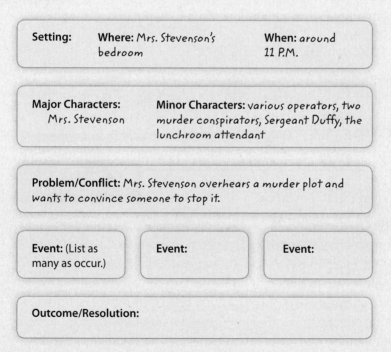

Setting: **Where:** Mrs. Stevenson's bedroom   **When:** around 11 P.M.

Major Characters: Mrs. Stevenson   **Minor Characters:** various operators, two murder conspirators, Sergeant Duffy, the lunchroom attendant

Problem/Conflict: Mrs. Stevenson overhears a murder plot and wants to convince someone to stop it.

Event: (List as many as occur.)   **Event:**   **Event:**

Outcome/Resolution:

Return to *Sorry, Wrong Number* and complete the graphic organizer to show the Plot Events and Outcome/Resolution.

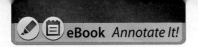
ELA RL.7.1, RL.7.2, RL.7.3, RL.7.5,
RL.7.7, RL.7.10, W.7.2, W.7.4,
W.7.9a, W.7.10, SL.7.2 ELD PI.7.1,
PI.7.6, PI.7.10, PII.7.1

Analyzing the Text

Cite Text Evidence Support your responses with evidence from the text.

1. **Infer** Reread the stage directions in lines 16–27. What do Mrs. Stevenson's actions reveal about her physical condition?

2. **Cause/Effect** Reread lines 328–531. How does Sergeant Duffy react to Mrs. Stevenson's call and how does his reaction affect Mrs. Stevenson?

3. **Summarize** Create a plot diagram like the one shown. Then place the events of *Sorry, Wrong Number* in their correct position on the diagram.

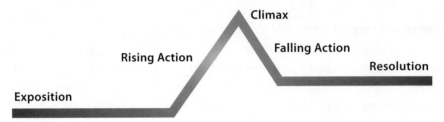

Climax

Falling Action

Rising Action

Resolution

Exposition

4. **Analyze** When a writer provides hints that suggest future events in a story, it's called **foreshadowing.** Go back through the drama and find examples of foreshadowing. For each example, provide a description of what eventually happens.

5. **Analyze and Evaluate** How do the setting and other details from the drama show that perception and reality do not always match up?

Speaking and Listening

Watch the clip from the film version of *Sorry, Wrong Number*. How is seeing the drama as a film different from reading it? With a partner, discuss the differences between the use of stage directions in the drama and the filmmakers' use of film techniques to create suspense and a feeling of terror.

PERFORMANCE TASK

Writing Activity: Character Analysis Write a three-paragraph character analysis of Mrs. Stevenson. Support your analysis with examples of her actions, as expressed in the dialogue and stage directions. Try to answer these questions.

- How does she perceive herself?

- How does she perceive other people such as the operators, police sergeant, and hospital workers?

- What parts of her personality might have been misunderstood or allow her to be misunderstood by others?

- How do her actions affect the drama's plot?

Interactive Lessons

To help you complete this task, use *Writing Arguments*.

Write an Argument

ELA W.7.1a–e,W.7.4, W.7.5, W.7.9, W.7.10
ELD PI.7.4, PI.7.10, PI.7.11, PI.7.12, PII.7.1, PII.7.2

Folk tales like "The People Could Fly" often make readers reflect on the ways we perceive our world. Consider the common saying "seeing is believing" and its meaning. After reading the texts in this collection, do you believe this saying is true? You will draw from "The People Could Fly" and other texts in the collection to write an argument that states and supports your position.

A successful argument

- contains an engaging introduction that clearly states the claim, or opinion
- supports the opinion with logical reasoning and relevant evidence
- presents and refutes opposing claims, or viewpoints
- uses language that effectively conveys ideas and adds interest
- concludes with a restatement of the claim

PLAN

myNotebook

Use the annotation tools in your eBook to find evidence to support your claim. Save each piece of evidence to your notebook.

Form a Claim Revisit the texts in the collection. Consider your answers to the following questions as you form your claim:

- How and why do the characters or people perceive the things that happen?
- How does this information relate to the meaning of the saying "seeing is believing"?

Gather Information Focus on the selection(s) that have information you can cite to support your claim.

- Consider the points of view or opinions that are expressed.
- Make a list of the reasons you have for your claim.
- Identify evidence in the texts that supports your reasons.

ACADEMIC VOCABULARY

As you plan, write, and review your draft, be sure to use the academic vocabulary words.

abnormal

feature

focus

perceive

task

Organize Your Ideas Think about organizing your argument. A graphic organizer like this one can help present ideas logically.

Interactive Lessons
For help in organizing your ideas, use:
• Writing Arguments: Building Effective Support

Consider Your Purpose and Audience Think about who will read or listen to your argument. What do you want them to understand? What will be most convincing to them? Keep these questions and your answers in mind as you prepare to write.

PRODUCE

Write Your Argument Review the information in your notes as you begin your draft.

- Begin by introducing the topic and stating your claim. Include an attention-grabbing lead.

- Write your reasons and support them with evidence, such as facts and examples. Organize your argument logically.

- Be aware of any **counterclaims,** or opinions that oppose your position.

- Include words and phrases such as *because, therefore*, and *for that reason* that will link your opinion, reasons, and evidence and make your argument clearer and more coherent.

- Establish and maintain a formal style and tone.

- Summarize your argument, repeating the most important reasons and evidence, and leave a lasting impression.

Write your rough draft in *my*WriteSmart. Focus on getting your ideas down, rather than perfecting your choice of language.

Interactive Lessons
For help in developing your argument, use:
• Writing Arguments: Creating a Coherent Argument

Language Conventions: Connect Ideas

Words like *and, but,* and *or* can help to combine ideas in a sentence. Read the following example from "Magic and the Brain."

> " Tomsoni claps his hands, and the spotlight dims ever so briefly before reflaring in a blaze of red. "

Notice how the word *and* connects two clauses to form a compound sentence. Look for places in your argument where you can add words to make connections between ideas.

REVISE

Evaluate Your Draft
Work with your partner to determine whether your argument is effective. Use this chart to help you.

Have your partner or a group of peers review your draft in *my*WriteSmart. Ask your reviewers to note any reasons or evidence that does not support your claim.

Questions	Tips	Revision Techniques
Does my introduction clearly state the claim?	**Underline** the claim.	**Clarify** the claim to make it hard to miss.
Is my claim supported by reasons and evidence?	**Highlight** each reason, and **underline** your evidence.	**Add** facts, statistics, and examples to strengthen your claim.
What words or phrases are helping to make my argument clear?	**Highlight** words that help to connect your reasons and evidence.	**Use** words like *and, but, so,* and *because* to connect ideas and to create cohesion.
Have I addressed counterclaims?	**Underline** your claim. **Consider** what an opposing claim might be and how to address it.	**Include** a visible counterargument to show you understand and can address an opposing view.
Is the tone of my argument formal?	**Highlight** any contractions and use of casual wording.	**Change** the contractions. **Revise** so the tone sounds objective.
Does the conclusion restate my claim and end convincingly?	**Underline** the restatement.	**Summarize** your main points in a restatement that tells the audience what you want it to believe or understand.

Interactive Lessons
For help in refining your argument, use:
• Writing Arguments: Concluding Your Argument

PRESENT

Create a Finished Copy
Finalize your argument and choose a way to share it with your audience. Consider these options:

• Post it as a blog on a personal or school website.
• Present your ideas in a debate with someone who has an opposing claim.

PERFORMANCE TASK A RUBRIC
ARGUMENT

	Ideas and Evidence	Organization	Language
4	• The introduction is engaging; it clearly states the writer's claim about the statement. • Logical reasons and relevant evidence from the texts convincingly support the writer's claim. • Opposing claims are anticipated and effectively refuted. • The concluding section effectively summarizes the claim and leaves a lasting impression.	• The reasons and evidence are organized logically and consistently throughout the argument. • Words and phrases logically connect reasons and evidence to the writer's claim.	• The writing reflects a formal style and tone. • The use of clear, succinct language effectively conveys the writer's ideas. • Sentence beginnings, lengths, and structures vary and have a rhythmic flow. • Spelling, capitalization, and punctuation are correct. • Grammar and usage are correct.
3	• The introduction could do more to grab the reader's attention; the introduction states the writer's claim. • Most reasons and relevant evidence from the texts support the writer's claim, but they could be more convincing. • Opposing claims are anticipated, but they could be more effectively refuted. • The concluding section restates the claim, but it is not very memorable.	• The organization of reasons and evidence is confusing in a few places. • A few more words and phrases are needed to connect reasons and evidence to the writer's claim.	• The style and tone become informal in a few places. • Sentence beginnings, lengths, and structures vary somewhat. • Few spelling, capitalization, and punctuation mistakes occur. • Some grammatical and usage errors are repeated in the argument.
2	• The introduction is ordinary; the writer's claim is not clearly stated. • The reasons and evidence are not always relevant or logical. • Opposing claims are anticipated but not addressed logically. • The concluding section includes an incomplete summary of the claim.	• The organization of reasons and evidence is generally logical, but it frequently doesn't follow a pattern. • Many more words and phrases are needed to connect reasons and evidence to the writer's claim.	• The style and tone become informal in many places. • Sentence structures barely vary, and some fragments or run-on sentences are present. • Several spelling and capitalization mistakes occur, and punctuation is inconsistent. • Grammar and usage are incorrect in many places.
1	• The introduction is missing. • Supporting reasons and evidence are missing. • Opposing claims are neither anticipated nor addressed. • The concluding section is missing.	• A logical organization is not used; reasons and evidence are presented randomly. • Connecting words and phrases are not used.	• The style and tone are inappropriate for an argument. • Repetitive sentence structure, fragments, and run-on sentences make the writing hard to follow. • Spelling and capitalization are often incorrect, and punctuation is missing. • Many grammatical and usage errors occur.

Give a Summary Presentation

ELA W.7.2a–f, W.7.4,
W.7.5, W.7.6, W.7.10,
SL.7.4
ELD PI.7.4, PI.7.9, PI.7.10,
PI.7.12, PII.7.5

Sorry, Wrong Number is a drama chockful of actions and shifting perceptions. In the following activity, you will draw from *Sorry, Wrong Number* to deliver a summary presentation.

A successful summary presentation

- includes the title and author of the work being summarized
- restates in your own words the **theme,** or main idea, and its supporting details
- shows a comprehensive understanding of the source
- interests listeners through the use of effective verbal and nonverbal techniques

PLAN

myNotebook

Use the annotation tools in your eBook to mark up key details that you might want to include. Save each detail to your notebook.

Review and Take Notes The first step in presenting a summary is making sure you fully understand the work that you are summarizing. Review *Sorry, Wrong Number* closely to identify key details.

- Jot down notes about the setting, the characters' personalities, and the major plot events.
- Look for details that help you decide what point the writer is making. Reread for details that support this point.
- Consider that not every detail will be important enough to include.
- Sum up the details in your own words in a statement about the **theme,** or main idea, the writer has expressed.

Consider Your Purpose and Audience Think about who will see your presentation and what you want them to understand. Keep in mind the essential information you want to share and how to capture your audience's attention.

ACADEMIC VOCABULARY

As you plan your summary, try to use the academic vocabulary words.

abnormal
feature
focus
perceive
task

Write your rough draft in myWriteSmart. Focus on getting your ideas down before condensing your summary.

Draft Your Summary Review your notes as you begin a draft of your summary. Your draft should

- cite the drama's title and author
- clearly identify the theme by stating it in your own words
- include the most important details that support the theme
- present this information in a condensed, short passage
- show that you fully understand the source

Language Conventions: Modifying to Add Details

An **adverbial phrase** is a group of words that modifies much like a simple adverb. There are different categories of adverbial phrases. Adverbial phrases of time describe when an action occurs, how often, or to what extent. Read the following speech from *Sorry, Wrong Number*.

> **Mrs. Stevenson.** Operator? I've been dialing Murray Hill 4-0098 for the last three quarters of an hour and the line is always busy.

The phrase *for the last three quarters of an hour* modifies the verb *dialing,* telling how long Mrs. Stevenson has waited and revealing her impatience.

Have your partner or a group of peers review your draft in *my*WriteSmart. Ask your reviewers to suggest possible cuts.

Practice Your Delivery Once you have a firm grasp of your summary, you are ready to practice how you'll present it. Practice until you know your summary well. The tips below will help you make your summary presentation more engaging.

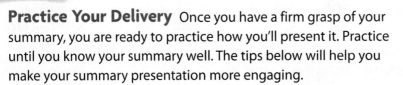

Verbal Elements	Nonverbal Signals
Enunciation: Pronounce your words clearly.	**Eye contact:** Look into the eyes of your audience members.
Inflection: Let your voice rise and fall naturally as you speak.	**Facial expressions:** Look serious, look intense, or raise an eyebrow.
Pace: Match the speed of your delivery to the mood of what you are describing.	**Gestures:** Use your hands, shrug, nod, or shake your head.

Interactive Lessons
For help in practicing your presentation, use:
- Giving a Presentation: Delivering Your Presentation

Evaluate Your Summary To help you smooth out any rough spots, have a partner view a practice run of your presentation. Use the following chart to help you.

Interactive Lessons

For help in refining your presentation, use:
• Giving a Presentation: Style in Presentation

Questions	Tips	Revision Techniques
Are the author and title included in your summary?	**Highlight** the author and title.	**Mention** the author and title at or near the beginning of the summary.
Does your summary state the theme of the drama in your own words?	**Underline** the theme.	**Check** to be sure you have used your own words.
How well do the details in the summary support the theme?	**Highlight** supporting details.	**Revise** the details so that the connections to the theme are clear.
How effective are your nonverbal and verbal techniques?	**Pair** with a partner to find out how you are using your body language and voice.	**Improve** your delivery by trying out any suggestions.

PRESENT

Create a Finished Copy Finalize your summary presentation for a wider audience. You might present it to the class or record it as a video to post on an approved website.

PERFORMANCE TASK B RUBRIC
SUMMARY PRESENTATION

	Ideas and Evidence	Organization	Language
4	• The summary cites the work's title and author. • The summary states the work's theme in the presenter's own words. • The summary reflects the presenter's full understanding of the work.	• The theme is supported strongly by relevant details. • The summary consists of a condensed, short passage.	• The presentation quite effectively conveys the work's theme and supporting ideas. • The presenter's verbal and nonverbal techniques engage the audience. • The summary features rich details through use of strong modifiers.
3	• The summary doesn't include both the title and author. • The summary states the theme of the work but it could be less wordy. • The summary shows a sufficient understanding of the work.	• There is sufficient support for the theme. • The summary passage, though short, could use some tightening.	• The presentation needs more work to convey the theme and supporting ideas well. • The presenter shows a decent grasp of verbal and nonverbal techniques. • Improved use of modifiers would add more detail to the summary.
2	• The title is mentioned in the summary but not the author. • The theme that is stated seems relatively minor. • The summary could do more to show a better understanding of the work.	• One or two supporting details seem randomly chosen. • The summary includes too many repeated words and phrases.	• The work's theme and supporting ideas are not evident. • The verbal and nonverbal techniques are minimal. • The summary needs modifiers in more places.
1	• Neither the title nor the author is included. • The theme is missing. • The details show no understanding of the work.	• The supporting details for the theme are missing. • Due to lack of detail, the summary shows no understanding of the work.	• There is no communication of the work's theme and supporting ideas. • The presenter uses no verbal or nonverbal techniques to engage the audience. • There is little or no use of modifiers.

COLLECTION **3**

©Franz Pritz/Picture Press/Getty Images

Nature at Work

" Those who dwell . . . among the beauties and mysteries of the earth are never alone or weary of life. **"**

—Rachel Carson

Nature at Work

In this collection, you will explore the beauty, power, and mystery of nature.

Stream to Start

fyi
hmhfyi.com

Channel One News®

COLLECTION

PERFORMANCE TASK Preview

After reading the selections in this collection, you will have the opportunity to complete two performance tasks:

• In one, you will write a personal narrative about an experience in a natural setting that is meaningful to you.

• In the second, you will write a poetry analysis of poems about nature.

ACADEMIC VOCABULARY

Study the words and their definitions in the chart below. You will use these words as you discuss and write about the texts in this collection.

Word	Definition	Related Forms
affect (ə-fĕkt´) v.	to have an influence on or effect a change in something	affectation, affection, affective, affects, disaffected, unaffected
element (ĕl´ə-mənt) n.	a part or aspect of something	elemental, elementally, elementary, elements
ensure (ĕn-shŏŏr´) v.	to make sure or certain	ensured, ensuring
participate (pär-tĭs´ə-pāt´) v.	to be active and involved in something or to share in something	participant, participation, participator
specify (spĕs´ə-fī´) v.	to state exactly or in detail what you want or need	nonspecific, specific, specific gravity, specific heat

Eddy Harris (b. 1956) *is a writer, adventurer, and seeker who spent his early years in New York City before moving to St. Louis. His first book,* Mississippi Solo, *chronicles the canoe trip he took down the entire length of the Mississippi River in the 1980s—a risky trip that this city dweller was unprepared for. He has also written about adventurous journeys in other southern regions and in Africa.*

from Mississippi Solo

Memoir by Eddy Harris

SETTING A PURPOSE Pay attention as you read to how the author recounts a special moment from his life while he canoed by himself down the Mississippi River. What makes his experience so meaningful for him?

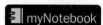

As you read, mark up the text. Save your work to **myNotebook**.

- Highlight details
- Add notes and questions
- Add new words to **myWordList**

Too many marvelous days in a row and you begin to get used to it, to think that's the way it's supposed to be. Too many good days, too many bad days—you need some break in the monotony of one to appreciate the other. If you only get sunshine, someone said, you end up in a desert.

I guess I'd had enough hard days to last me for a while, enough scary times to be able to appreciate the peaceful, easy, glorious days. On the way to Natchez,[1] I had another one, and I took full advantage of it to do absolutely nothing. 10 No singing, no thinking, no talking to myself. Just feeling. Watching the river, noticing the changes in color, seeing the way it rises and falls depending on the wind and on what lies

---

[1] **Natchez** (năch´ĭz): a city in southwest Mississippi on the Mississippi River.

on the river bed. Each change had something to say, and I
listened to the river. The river was talking to me, changing
colors from puce[2] to brown to thick, murky green. Saying
nothing. The idle chatter you get when you walk with your
favorite niece or nephew going no place in particular with
nothing special on your minds and the little kid just jabbers
away because it's comfortable and he feels like it. The river was
20   like that to me. A comfortable buddy sharing a lazy day.

Nothing else mattered then. Going someplace or not.
Arriving in New Orleans or shooting past and landing
in Brazil. I didn't care about anything. The river kept me
company and kept me satisfied. Nothing else mattered.

Then the river whispered, "Get ready. Get ready."

The day turned gray and strange. Clouds rolled overhead
in wild swirls like batter in a bowl. I could see the rainstorm
forming off in the distance but swirling rapidly toward me
like a dark gray **avalanche**. I felt the river dip down and up—a
30   shallow dale[3] in the water. I passed from the cool moisture
surrounding me and into a pocket of thin air hot and dry. It
was as though a gap had opened in the clouds and the sun
streamed through to boil the water and heat up this isolated
patch of river a scant[4] thirty yards long. My first thought was
to shed a shirt and stay cool, but when I passed through the
far curtain of the **insulated** air, I knew I had better do just the
opposite. I drifted and donned my yellow rain suit and hood.
The sky above grew serious and advanced in my direction
with the speed of a hurricane. Looking for a place to land, I
40   scanned the shore. There was no shore. Only trees. Because
of the heavy rains and high water, the shore had disappeared,
and the new shoreline of solid earth had been pushed back
through the trees and beyond the woods. How far beyond, I
couldn't tell. I looked across to the other side of the river half
a mile away. No way could I have made it over there. Halfway
across and the wind would have kicked up and trapped me in
the middle.

The leading edge of the storm came, and the first sprinkles
passed over like army scouts. The wooded area lasted only
50   another hundred yards or so, and I thought I could easily get
there before the rains arrived. I could then turn left and find

avalanche
(ăv´ə-lănch´) *n.* An
avalanche is a large
mass of snow, ice,
dirt, or rocks falling
quickly down the side
of a mountain.

insulate
(ĭn´sə-lāt´) *v.*
When you *insulate*
something, you
prevent the passage
of heat through it.

---

[2] **puce** (pyoos): purplish brown.
[3] **dale:** valley.
[4] **scant:** just short of.

ground to pull out and wait out the storm. But the voice of the river came out and spoke to me teasingly but with a chill of seriousness down my spine. I could have ignored it, but as if reading my thoughts and not wanting me to fight it, the river grabbed the end of the canoe and turned me toward the trees. I thought I was looking for land. I wasn't. I was looking for shelter.

"The day turned gray and strange."

The urge to get into the trees came on me quite suddenly
60 and really without thought or effort on my part. Almost an instinct.

No sooner had I ducked into the trees than the sky split open with a loud crash and a **splintery** crackle of lightning. I was not going to make it through the trees. The wind came in at hurricane strength. The tips of the trees bent way over and aimed toward the ground, like fishing rods hooked on a big one. Water flooded like the tide rushing upstream. The trees swooshed loudly as the leaves and branches brushed hard together. Branches fell. Rains came and poured down
70 bucketfuls.

The trees were tall and no more than three feet around. I maneuvered the canoe as best I could in the wind and rushing water, turned it to face upstream, and kept my back to the rain, which slanted in at a sharp angle. I reached out for the sturdiest tree I could get my arms around and I held on.

Water everywhere.[5] The river sloshed over the side and into the canoe. I tried to keep the stern pointed right into the flow so the canoe could ride the waves, but it didn't work. The canoe was twisted about, and water poured over the side. The

splinter
(splĭn´tər) v. To *splinter* means to break up into sharp, thin pieces.

---

[5] **Water everywhere:** The author is referring to the line "water, water, everywhere" from *The Rime of the Ancient Mariner*, a widely known poem about a sailor recounting supernatural events at sea.

80   rain was heavier than any I had ever been in or seen before.
It really was more like a tropical storm. The heavy winds, the
amount of water, the warmth of the air, and the cold rain.
Only my neck was exposed to the rain. When the rain hit my
neck, it ran under the rain suit and very cold down my back.

    The wind shifted as the storm came directly overhead.
Water streamed straight down. I was drenched, and the canoe
was filling up quickly. Anything in the canoe that could float
was floating. If the rain continued for long or if the wind kept
up strong and the rain kept spilling into the canoe, I would
90   sink. But I was not worried, hardly more than concerned. In
fact I enjoyed the feeling of the water all around me and on
me, enveloping me like a cocoon, and despite the drama I
felt no real threat. I was more amazed than anything, trying
to analyze the voice I had heard or whatever instinct or
intuition it was that urged me to park in these trees. It had
been something so very definite that I could feel it and yet
so **ethereal** that I could not put my finger on it. So I stopped
trying and just sat there patiently waiting and hugging my
tree. I was one with this river, and nothing could happen to
100   me.

    The storm slid forward, and the rain slanted in on my face.
Then it moved on farther up the river to drench someone else.
It was gone as suddenly as it had arisen. Only the trailing edge
was left, a light rain that lasted almost until I reached Natchez.

ethereal
(ĭ-thîr′ē-əl) *adj.* If
something is *ethereal,*
it is light and airy.

COLLABORATIVE DISCUSSION What do you think made this
experience on the river affect the author so strongly? Talk about
your ideas with other group members.

Analyze Text: Memoir

ELA RI.7.3
ELD PI.7.6

A **memoir** is a form of autobiographical writing in which a writer shares his or her personal experiences and observations of significant events or people. Memoirs are often written in the first person. Authors of memoirs often

- "talk" to readers, using informal language and sharing personal feelings
- recall actual events and emphasize their reactions to them
- show how their experiences changed their attitudes and lives

What feature of a memoir appears in the first sentence of the excerpt from *Mississippi Solo*?

Analyze the Meanings of Words and Phrases

ELA RI.7.4
ELD PI.7.8

The author's **style** is the manner of writing—*how* something is said rather than what is said. Readers can analyze an author's style by making observations about these elements:

- word choice
- sentence types
- sentence length
- sentence fragments
- repetition of one or more words
- descriptive details

An author's style can be **formal,** using complex language and sentence structures, or **informal,** using simpler language, sentences, and fragments.

Figurative language is an imaginative use of words to express ideas that are not literally true but that are meaningful and can have an emotional impact. This chart shows three common kinds of figurative comparisons.

Comparison	Example	Effect
simile: a comparison of two unlike things using the word *like* or *as*	Clouds rolled overhead in wild swirls like batter in a bowl. (lines 26–27)	vivid image of changing sky
metaphor: a comparison of two unlike things that have qualities in common, without using *like* or *as*	. . . the far curtain of the insulated air . . . (lines 35–36)	warmth that is trapped inside a barrier
personification: the giving of human qualities to an animal, object, or idea	The river was talking to me . . . (line 14)	a feeling of connectedness

Find another example of a simile in this memoir. What does it help you understand?

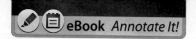
Analyzing the Text

ELA RI.7.1, RI.7.2, RI.7.3, RI.7.4, W.7.2b,
W.7.9 **ELD** PI.7.6, PI.7.8, PI.7.10

Cite Text Evidence   Support your responses with evidence from the text.

1. **Interpret** Reread lines 85–100. What seems unexpected about the author's reactions during this experience?

2. **Compare** Reread lines 13–20 to find what the author compares to walking with a favorite niece or nephew. What does that comparison suggest?

3. **Cite Evidence** Reread lines 1–10. What does the author reveal about himself?

4. **Analyze** Reread line 25. What kind of figurative language is the author using, and what does it suggest about his connection to his environment?

5. **Analyze** Find an example of one or more sentence fragments. Why might the author have chosen to use fragments instead of complete sentences, and what does it suggest about the style of his writing?

6. **Analyze** Reread lines 62–70. What word choices and figurative language help you picture the scene?

PERFORMANCE TASK

Writing Activity: Literary Analysis
Look back through the memoir to list examples of how the author uses similes and personifies the river. Focusing on examples from your list, write a two-to four-paragraph literary analysis that explains how the author uses figurative language in this memoir.

- Support your main points by using quotes from the text as examples.
- Explain the meanings of the examples and how they contribute to important ideas of the memoir.
- Discuss what impressions you have about the author's writing style, based on his use of figurative language.

Critical Vocabulary

ELA L.7.5a
ELD PI.7.6, PI.7.8

avalanche   insulate   splinter   ethereal

Practice and Apply Choose the situation that is the better match with the meaning of the vocabulary word. Give your reasons.

1. **avalanche**
   a. Snow fell for two days, covering the rooftops and streets.
   b. Snow on a mountainside suddenly loosened and slid.

2. **insulate**
   a. On a hot day, a car with closed windows heats up quickly.
   b. An old, drafty house is expensive to heat in winter.

3. **splinter**
   a. People stroll on the boardwalk that crosses the wetland.
   b. River water breaks up into many streams and smaller creeks.

4. **ethereal**
   a. The desert travelers came to an area with palm trees and shade.
   b. The desert travelers mistakenly thought they saw a lake ahead.

Vocabulary Strategy: Figures of Speech

An author may make an **allusion,** a reference to a famous person, place, event, or work of literature. Although an allusion is not explained, the reader may recognize its source and meaning, or may do research to learn about it. Look for the allusions in these examples:

> Poppa's shoe store closed after only a year, and he lost money. Poppa worked hard, but he just didn't have the Midas touch.

> All of my cousins were strong and good-looking; I was unhappily aware of my ugly duckling status from an early age.

In the first example, the phrase *the Midas touch* is an allusion to the Greek myth about King Midas, who was briefly able to turn everything he touched into gold. The second example includes an allusion to the fairy tale "The Ugly Duckling," by Hans Christian Andersen. In that tale, an odd-looking duckling endures abuse until it grows up to find its true family of beautiful swans.

Practice and Apply Reread the paragraph that begins on line 76 of the memoir. The first sentence of that paragraph is an allusion to a well-known quotation from the long poem *The Rime of the Ancient Mariner*, by Samuel Taylor Coleridge. Find the poem and identify the famous lines in Part II. What meaning from the poem might Harris have tried to connect to his own experience?

Language Conventions: Precise Language

ELA L.7.3a
ELD PI.7.12

When you write, choose words carefully to ensure that readers picture what you see and understand what you mean. Use precise words to express exact meanings and to be concise, using only necessary words. Compare these two sentences:

> I moved the canoe in the water, which was rushing very fast.

> I maneuvered the canoe in the rushing water.

You can tell that the second sentence is the stronger one. The word *maneuvered* is more precise than *moved*. In the clause *which was rushing very fast*, the words *very fast* are unnecessary because they repeat the meaning of *rushing*. The single word *rushing* conveys the same meaning.

This sentence appears in the excerpt from *Mississippi Solo*. Note how the author has used vivid language and precise words—*gap, streamed, boil, isolated patch, a scant thirty yards long*—to help the reader participate in the scene.

> It was as though a gap had opened in the clouds and the sun streamed through to boil the water and heat up this isolated patch of river a scant thirty yards long.

Practice and Apply Each of these sentences is not as strong as it could be. Rewrite the sentence to make it more precise and concise.

1. The clouds in the sky overhead moved very slowly and looked interesting.

2. All at once, a streak of lightning suddenly traveled down from a big cloud.

3. I heard the thunder, which was loud and shook the ground under my feet a lot.

4. I looked around for a place that would be safe and went into a building that was nearby.

Background The Tempest, *from which this excerpt is taken, is believed to be the last play Shakespeare wrote alone. In* The Tempest, *Prospero, the duke of Milan and a powerful magician, was exiled from Italy and left to die at sea by his brother, Antonio, and Alonso, the king of Naples. After twelve years, Fortune finally sends Antonio and Alonso within Prospero's reach. He conjures a powerful storm, the tempest, causing his enemies to shipwreck on his island. Prospero then seeks to use his magic to make these lords restore him to his rightful position.*

from
The Tempest

Soliloquy by William Shakespeare

William Shakespeare (1564–1616) *is generally considered the greatest playwright in the English language. From about 1592 on, he performed in and wrote plays in London. The location most closely associated with him is the Globe Theatre, shown here. Most of Shakespeare's early plays are about historical figures, although he also wrote more light-hearted comedies. Later, Shakespeare penned his famous tragedies, including* Hamlet *and* Macbeth.

SETTING A PURPOSE In *The Tempest*, Prospero, who has learned to cast spells from a book of magic, rules over a mystical island. As you read, think about what Prospero plans to do with his power and what that means for his character.

from **The Tempest**

ACT 5, Scene 1

Prospero. Ye elves of hills, brooks, standing lakes and groves,
And ye that on the sands with printless foot
Do chase the ebbing Neptune,[1] and do fly him
When he comes back; you demi-puppets that
5   By moonshine do the green sour ringlets make
Whereof the ewe not bites; and you whose pastime
Is to make midnight mushrooms, that rejoice
To hear the solemn curfew; by whose aid,
Weak masters[2] though ye be, I have bedimmed
10   The noontide sun, called forth the mutinous winds,
And 'twixt the green sea and the azured vault
Set roaring war—to the dread rattling thunder
Have I given fire, and rifted Jove's stout oak[3]
With his own bolt; the strong-based promontory
15   Have I made shake, and by the spurs plucked up
The pine and cedar; graves at my command
Have waked their sleepers, oped, and let 'em forth
By my so potent art. But this rough magic
I here abjure. And when I have required
20   Some heavenly music—which even now I do—
To work mine end upon their senses that
This airy charm[4] is for, I'll break my staff,
Bury it certain fathoms in the earth,
And deeper than did ever plummet sound
25   I'll drown my book.

COLLABORATIVE DISCUSSION What does Prospero plan to do
with his source of power? What does that tell you about Prospero's
character? Share your ideas with other group members.

---

[1] **ebbing Neptune:** Neptune was the mythical Roman god of water and the sea; "ebbing Neptune" suggests waves flowing away from shore. Like tiny seabirds on a beach, the elves chase the ocean waves as they flow away from the shore, and "fly" or run from them as they flow back to shore.

[2] **Weak masters:** supernatural spirits that do not work powerful evil.

[3] **rifted Jove's stout oak:** Jove was the mythical Roman king of the gods for whom the oak tree was sacred. Jove was identified with thunderbolts, too. Here the image is of lightning splitting the oak.

[4] **airy charm:** magical music.

Determine Meanings

ELA RL.7.4
ELD PI.7.8

The English language we use today is different from the language used by writers in the 1600s. To understand a Shakespearean play, you need to analyze how Shakespeare uses the language of his time to create rhythm and meaning. These elements all appear in the excerpt from *The Tempest*.

Grammar Shakespeare used familiar pronouns such as *you, yourself, your,* and *yours,* but he also used other forms of *you: thou, thee, thy, thine,* and *ye.* Shakespeare used *my* or *mine* before a noun, but we no longer say phrases such as *mine eyes.*

Word Order The positions of words and phrases in Shakespearean language can sound strange to modern ears. Prospero says:

> the strong-based promontory
> Have I made shake, and by the spurs plucked up
> The pine and cedar;

A modern English speaker might use this sentence structure: "I have made the strong-based promontory shake, and plucked up the pine and cedar by the spurs."

Vocabulary Shakespeare's vocabulary included words that modern English speakers either no longer use or use differently. What is a "strong-based promontory"? It's the strong rocky base that holds the "spurs," or roots, of pine and cedar trees.

Blank Verse Shakespeare wrote many of his plays, including *The Tempest,* in **blank verse,** or unrhymed iambic pentameter. In blank verse, the final words of the lines do not rhyme, and each line consists of ten syllables alternating unstressed and stressed.

Analyze Form

ELA RL.7.5
ELD PI.7.6, PII.7.1

In a drama, a **soliloquy** is a speech given by a character alone on a stage. It is different from a **monologue,** which is a speech that is often directed to another character.

In soliloquies, characters seem to be thinking aloud, revealing thoughts, feelings, and plans. It is almost as if the characters are talking to themselves. In lines 18–19 of his soliloquy, Prospero announces his plan with the words, "But this rough magic / I here abjure." He is saying that he will no longer work his magic.

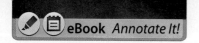
Analyzing the Text

ELA RL.7.2, RL.7.4, RL.7.5, SL.7.1, SL.7.6
ELD PI.7.1, PI.7.6, PI.7.8, PII.7.1

Cite Text Evidence   Support your responses with evidence from the text.

1. **Interpret** In lines 4–6, Prospero refers to "green sour ringlets." These rings were said to be a poisonous trail made by fairies dancing in the night. (Today, a circle of mushrooms that sprouts overnight is still called a fairy ring.) How would you restate Prospero's words in modern English?

2. **Interpret** What words in lines 5–8 help you understand when fairies and other magical creatures were free to come out?

3. **Cause/Effect** In lines 9–18, Prospero vividly describes the powerful things he has accomplished with magic. What are some of the effects of his spells?

4. **Interpret** What does Prospero mean in line 18, when he says, "By my so potent art"?

5. **Analyze** Shakespeare wrote Prospero's soliloquy in blank verse. How does this form contribute to the meaning of the text?

6. **Draw Conclusions** How might an actor playing Prospero use his voice and gestures to convey the meanings of the text in these three main sections: lines 1–8, lines 9–18, lines 19–25?

7. **Evaluate** This excerpt from *The Tempest* includes many examples of imagery—the words and phrases that appeal to the five senses. Evaluate the impact the imagery has on your understanding of the text.

PERFORMANCE TASK

Speaking Activity: Dramatic Reading
Divide the lines of this soliloquy among the members of a small group so that each participant has several lines that express one idea or related ideas.

- Together, discuss and analyze the Shakespearean vocabulary and sentence structure.
- Use your analysis to rewrite Prospero's soliloquy in your own words.
- Then, as a group, deliver your version of the soliloquy to the class.

Naomi Shihab Nye (b. 1952) *was born to a Palestinian father and an American mother. During her adolescence, she lived in St. Louis, Missouri; Jerusalem; and San Antonio, Texas; and she has traveled extensively as an adult. Influenced by her heritage and the cultural diversity of the places she has known, Nye has written books of poetry as well as fiction for younger audiences.*

Allied with Green

Short Story by Naomi Shihab Nye

SETTING A PURPOSE As you read, consider the author's use of the word *green*. How is she using the term to describe something that Lucy, the story's main character, feels very strongly about?

For her paper on "What I Believe In," Lucy writes first "the color green."

That's how everything starts. A tiny shoot of phrase prickling the mind . . .

Then she runs around for a few days doing other things but noticing the green poking up between buildings, on sides of roads, in front of even the poorest homes, how pots of green lined on rickety front porches, hanging baskets of green on light posts downtown, the new meticulous xeriscape[1] beds of
10 puffy green grasses and plants alongside the river, are what seem to keep everything else going. If people could not see

---

[1] **xeriscape** (zĭr´ ĭ-skāp´): landscaping that saves water and protects the environment.

green from the windows of the hospital, the hospital might fall down. She believes this.

Once she starts making a list, it will not stop.

Green has had a terrible summer. Threatened by the longest drought and highest heat in recorded history, green has had many second thoughts.

Lucy's family could only water with a sprinkler on Wednesday evenings between eight and ten. When she and her mom wash lettuce, blueberries, peaches, they carry the plastic tubs of fruit water outside to pour onto a plant. It's ritual now. It's holy water. The city had a water waster hotline. It made the national news. You could turn people in for excessive watering.

Last semester, when asked to write a paper on **addictions**, Lucy wrote about trimming and got a C. Her teacher scrawled across the top of the paper, "What is this?" But Lucy often feels happiest with pruning shears in her hand, heading toward an overgrown jasmine vine.

It's a clear task, trimming. The longer you've done it, the more you know how it encourages green, in the long run. Also, you can have fine ideas while trimming. Queen's crown, germander, plumbago. *Snip, snip, snip.*

She knew it had been mentioned before, but thought she ought to include how cities assault their green for two reasons: money and greed. Later, feeling remorseful, or sickened by the new view, they name everything for green—Oak Meadows, Lone Pine. You could find it almost anywhere now.

Lucy's father demonstrated against developments when he was in college. She had a faded black and white picture of him holding a NO! sign, his hair bushy and wild. Highways slashing through green space—he now drives one of those highways almost every day, feeling guilty. He plants free trees in scrappy **medians**, as an apology. Sometimes people steal them. When he planted four little palms in pots as a gift to Freddy's Mexican Restaurant, they got plucked from the soil overnight. Obviously some people were desperate for green. And surely, with all the population issues now, some developments were necessary, but look at what happened before you knew it—hills sheared, meadows plucked, fields erased, the world turns into an endless series of strip centers— yo, Joni Mitchell! Joni sang about parking lots when the world

addiction
(ə-dĭk´shən) *n.* An *addiction* is a habit one is dependent on.

median
(mē´dē-ən) *n.* A *median* is a dividing area between opposing lanes of traffic on a highway or road.

had probably half the number it has now. Her dad told her that. She likes Joni Mitchell.

The boulevard wakes up when a strip of green is planted down its center.

The sad room smiles again when a pot of green is placed on a white tablecloth.

No one goes to Seattle to see the concrete.

60   An exhausted kid says, I'm going outside—sick of her mother's voice, she knows she will feel better with bamboo.

In Dallas people run around the lake or refresh themselves at the **arboretum**.

San Antonians send their kids to summer digging classes at the botanical gardens. The kids come home with broccoli. After a while.

Patience is deeply involved with green.

It's required.

So, why don't people respect green as much as they should?

70   This was the serious question growing small fronds and tendrils at the heart of Lucy's paper. She knew her teacher might turn a snide nose up at it. Oh, blah blah, isn't this rather a repeat of what you wrote last semester?

People took green for granted. They assumed it would always be skirting their ugly office buildings and residences

arboretum
(är´bə-rē´təm) *n.*
An *arboretum* is a
place where many
trees are grown
for educational or
viewing purposes.

and so they didn't give it the attention it deserved. Somewhat like air. Air and green, close cousins.

Lucy truly loved the words *pocket park*.[2]

She loved community gardeners with purple bandannas
80 tied around their heads. She loved their wild projects—rosemary grown so big you could hide in it.

She loved roofs paved with grass.

She loved the man in New York City—Robert Isabell—who planted pink impatiens on the metal overhang of his building. He had started out as a florist, at seventeen, in Minnesota—green state in the summer, not so green in December. Then he moved to New York City and became a major party planner, incorporating flowers, lighting, tents, fabrics, to create magical worlds of festivity. He didn't attend
90 his own parties. He disappeared once he got everything set up. Sometimes he hid behind a giant potted plant to see what people liked. Lucy found his **obituary** in the newspaper, clipped it out, and placed it on her desk. She wished she could have worked for him just to learn how he put flowers together on tables, how he clipped giant green stalks and placed them effectively around a tent to make Morocco, Italy, the French Riviera. Transporting. Green could take you away.

Save you. But you had to care for it, stroke it, devote yourself to it, pray to it, organize crews for it, bow down to it.
100 You had to say the simple holy prayer, rearranging the words any way you liked best—"Dig, Grow, Deep, Roots, Light, Air, Water, Tend."

Tend was a more important verb than most people realized.

You had to carry a bucket.

obituary
(ō-bĭch´oo-ĕr´ē) *n*. An *obituary* is a public notice of a death.

COLLABORATIVE DISCUSSION What is unusual about the author's use of the word *green*, and why does she use it that way? Talk about your ideas with other group members.

---

[2] **pocket park:** a small park accessible to the general public.

Determine Theme

In short stories like "Allied with Green," authors often use the characters to share a theme with the reader. A **theme** is a message about life or human nature. In works of fiction, themes are the "big ideas" that readers infer based on evidence from the text. The following statements are examples of themes that might be found in short stories:

- A person can gain more by giving than by taking.
- We may not appreciate what we have until it is gone.

Often the theme of a story is not stated directly. It's usually implied. You have to analyze the text to see what it reveals about the theme. To determine the theme, it is helpful to

- look at the title to see if it contains a significant idea
- analyze the characters' words and actions, especially how characters change
- evaluate whether the setting has special meaning to a character
- look for important statements by the narrator or a character

Determine the Meanings of Words and Phrases

An author's **style** is his or her manner of writing—*how* something is said rather than *what* is said—and it often corresponds to the genre of the writing. Style can be described with words such as *formal, journalistic, literary, flowery,* and *plain.*

Readers can analyze an author's style by making observations about the author's word choice and descriptive details, among other elements. An author may use **imagery**—words and phrases that appeal to the senses—to help readers imagine how things look, feel, smell, sound, and taste.

An author's style may also include **figurative language,** comparisons and expressions that are not literally true but give meaning in imaginative ways. One form of figurative language is **personification,** the giving of human qualities to animals, objects, or ideas. The author of "Allied with Green" uses personification to give human qualities to the color green and other objects.

Review "Allied with Green." How would you describe the style in which it's written?

 eBook *Annotate It!*

Analyzing the Text

ELA RL.7.1, RL.7.2, RL.7.3, RL.7.4,
RL.7.6, W.7.1, W.7.4, W.7.10
ELD PI.7.6, PI.7.8, PI.7.10, PI.7.11

Cite Text Evidence   Support your responses with evidence from the text.

1. **Interpret** In lines 3–4, the author uses the phrase "a tiny shoot of phrase prickling the mind" to describe how everything starts. What does the phrase mean?

2. **Infer** Once Lucy decides on the topic for her school assignment, she can't help but notice the green around her. What does this tell you about her character and how she feels about her topic?

3. **Interpret** Reread lines 18–22 to find what the narrator compares to holy water. What does that comparison suggest?

4. **Predict** Lucy chooses to write about the color green for her school assignment. Based on her teacher's reaction to her paper from last semester, what will her teacher's reaction to this topic probably be?

5. **Draw Conclusions** Reread lines 34–51. What point is the narrator making about developments?

6. **Analyze** What does the personification in lines 55–58 help the reader understand?

7. **Analyze** Use a chart like this one to list examples of imagery, figurative language, and personification that contribute to Naomi Shihab Nye's style.

Elements	Examples
Imagery	
Figurative Language	
Personification	

8. **Draw Conclusions** What is the theme of this story?

PERFORMANCE TASK

✔ *my* WriteSmart

Writing Activity: Argument Look back through "Allied with Green" to take notes on the points Lucy makes in favor of green. Adapt those ideas to develop a three- to four-paragraph argument in support of or against her position.

- Introduce your opinion.
- Specify support for your opinion with reasons and examples.
- Acknowledge a possible argument from an opponent and refute it.
- Conclude with a statement that summarizes your opinion and ties your ideas together.

Critical Vocabulary

addiction   median   arboretum   obituary

Practice and Apply Answer each question with *yes* or *no*. With your group, use examples and reasons to explain your answer.

1. Could someone have an **addiction** to chocolate? Why or why not?

2. Could a single-lane road have a **median?** Why or why not?

3. Is an **arboretum** like a garden? Why or why not?

4. Is an **obituary** like a biography? Why or why not?

Vocabulary Strategy: Using a Glossary

A **glossary** is a list of specialized terms and their definitions. A glossary can exist on its own, or it can be part of a larger text. A text may have more than one glossary if it refers to multiple types of specialized terms that a reader is not assumed to know. Here are more useful details about glossaries.

- When a printed book contains a glossary, words are listed in the back of the book in alphabetical order.
- A digital, or electronic, glossary allows readers to click on a word in the text to see its definition and hear its pronunciation.
- A glossary may contain information about a word's pronunciation and part of speech.

Notice the parts of this glossary entry for the word *median*.

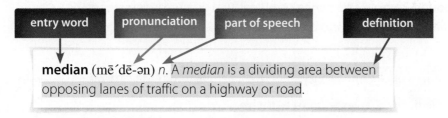

Practice and Apply This literature program contains multiple glossaries. Use the table of contents and the glossaries to answer the following questions.

1. In which glossary would you expect to find a listing for the Critical Vocabulary words that are highlighted in each selection?

2. Which glossary would you use to learn definitions for the literary terms that are used in the instruction?

3. According to the glossary, what is the part of speech for the word *obituary*?

Language Conventions: Sentence Structure

ELA L.7.1b
ELD PII.7.6

When you combine two independent clauses, you make a **compound sentence.** There are two basic ways to combine clauses to make a compound sentence: (1) with a **coordinating conjunction,** such as *and, but,* and *or;* (2) with a semicolon.

Independent Clauses	Urban parks are calm places. City dwellers need them.
Compound Sentence	Urban parks are calm places, and city dwellers need them.
Independent Clauses	The color green suggests life. People are drawn to green.
Compound Sentence	The color green suggests life; people are drawn to green.

When you combine a subordinate clause with an independent clause, you make a **complex sentence.** A subordinate clause begins with a **subordinating conjunction,** such as *after, although, as, because, before, even though, if, since, so that, though, unless, until, when, where,* and *while.*

Independent Clause	Gardens give many rewards.
Subordinate Clause	although gardening requires patience
Complex Sentence	Although gardening requires patience, gardens give many rewards.

A **compound-complex sentence** combines two or more independent clauses and one or more subordinate clauses. Note the three clauses in each example:

> **When trees grow on city sidewalks, people must take care of them, or the trees will fail to thrive.**

> **People love the pocket park because it was green and quiet; they found peace there.**

Practice and Apply The following independent clauses are taken from "Allied with Green." For each independent clause, add more clauses to make a compound sentence and a compound-complex sentence. Then explain how each sentence type signals a different relationship between ideas.

1. He planted four little palms in pots.

2. A pot of green is placed on a white tablecloth.

Douglas Fox *is a science, environmental, and technology writer who lives in northern California. His pursuit of science stories has led him to many exotic places, including Australia, Mauritius, Papua New Guinea, and Antarctica. In addition to writing, Fox sometimes takes photos for his stories, which have appeared in many scientific journals, magazines, and books.*

Big Rocks' Balancing Acts

Expository Essay by Douglas Fox

SETTING A PURPOSE In this article, you'll get familiar with a curiosity in nature. As you read, think about what makes these rock formations so unique and what people can learn from them. Write down any questions you have while reading.

Richard Brune was pretty dizzy the first time he shot photos while leaning out of a flying airplane.

The plane's door had been removed so Brune could ride with one leg outside. As the tiny propeller plane zigzagged over the desert, Brune leaned out over empty air. The 80 mile-per-hour headwind pummeled his face. He looked through his camera and snapped pictures of the rocky desert hundreds of feet below.

10 He got woozy after a few seconds, unsure which way was up. He learned to avoid that feeling by keeping his eyes on the shifting, slanting horizon whenever he could. And just in case he tumbled out of the plane, he wore a parachute. "It's not that bad," says Brune, who has done plenty of skydiving. "From 1,000 feet you've probably got at least nine or 10 seconds [of falling] before you really have to pull the rip cord."

It is estimated this balanced rock has occupied this spot in the Mojave Desert for 15,000 to 20,000 years.

Brune wasn't flying over the desert in southern California to be a daredevil. He was taking pictures of balanced rocks. Big, balanced rocks. Really awkward ones. The kind of rock that looks like it would tip over, roll down a hill and flatten a

20 car if someone were silly enough to lean against it.

ODD HOBBY

Richard and his dad, James Brune, have a passion for balanced rocks. James is a geologist, someone who studies the history and movement of the Earth as recorded in rocks, at the University of Nevada in Reno. He has spent 20 years looking for balanced rocks across the deserts of Nevada and California.

Richard, his son, isn't officially a scientist, but he is good with airplanes, parachutes, cameras, computers—all kinds of gadgets. When he was younger, he would camp in the

30 desert while his dad did scientific work there. Richard, now 46, has helped his dad study balanced rocks for 15 years, photographing them from the air and then hiking into the desert with his dad to find them.

"We've found literally thousands of these rocks," says James. Some of them stand up to 5 meters tall and weigh 15,000 kilograms—real car crushers!

It sounds like an odd hobby, but James, the geologist, is serious about these rocks. He has also studied earthquakes for many years, and he believes that balanced rocks can tell us something important about earthquakes.

STANDING STRONG

An earthquake's tremors can topple balanced rocks. So if you look at these rocks across California, you should find clues about where sizable earthquakes have happened.

In places that haven't experienced large earthquakes, you should find really delicate rocks—ones you could tip over with a finger. But in places that have seen more serious quakes, the only rocks left standing in the balance should be those that are far harder to tip over.

Geologists find these rocks so interesting because they could give clues about the severity of earthquakes over thousands of years. In parts of California, records collected by scientists go back only about 150 years. Historical data on tremor intensities are important when determining how strong a bridge or dam needs to be to survive earthquakes.

HOW OLD IS OLD?

All of this depends, of course, on finding out how long the balanced rocks have been standing.

It's a basic question, really: How quickly does the land change? Maybe you've wondered it yourself. Have you ever walked down a path, kicked a rock and wondered how long that rock had stood there before you knocked it down the hill? Maybe it was there for one year. Maybe 100 years. Perhaps even 10,000 years.

Or maybe you sat on a boulder and wondered who else had sat there. Was the boulder there when the first pioneers rolled their wagons by 200 years ago? Or maybe even when the very first humans arrived in North America 15,000 years ago?

Believe it or not, scientists have clever ways to figure this stuff out.

Earlier this year, Richard Brune went to the Mojave Desert in southern California to find out how long some balanced rocks have been standing.

The desert slopes gently away from a mountain of globby shaped granite rocks. Gravel and lots of prickly plants cover the ground. Richard has parked his Jeep at the end of a bumpy dirt road. He now walks on the sandy bottom of a winding **gully** with Dylan Rood, a geologist from Lawrence Livermore National Laboratory in California.

Speckled granite rocks stacked like giant brown marshmallows tower above the gully on both sides. Now and
80 then, Richard and Rood spot a rock balanced on top of the stack, like a milk jug standing upside down.

> ## "Speckled granite rocks stacked like giant brown marshmallows tower above the gully."

"Be careful," says Richard, as Rood approaches one rock. "That one could go off easily. It wouldn't take much."

Several minutes later, Rood climbs to another rock, this one the size of a TV, sitting on top of the marshmallows. "Woohoo!" he hollers to Richard. "Just with a thumb I can move it."

CARVED BY WATER

People often assume that rocks become balanced after falling on top of each other. But that wasn't the case for these marshmallow stacks—there's nowhere the balanced rocks
90 could have rolled from above.

Instead, scientists think these balanced rocks were probably carved by water. As rivers cut gullies into the granite **bedrock** beneath the desert floor, water chews away the weaker types of rock, leaving only the stronger behind.

Imagine a house built of strong bricks and held together by weak cement—bedrock often has these strong and weak parts, although they aren't always visible. If the house is continuously exposed to running water, the cement will
100 **gradually** wear away. But the bricks will remain. And some of the bricks will be left stacked or balanced on top of each other—like the granite marshmallows in the gully.

bedrock
(bĕd´rŏk´) n. Bedrock is the solid rock that lies under sand, soil, clay, and gravel.

gradual
(grăj´ōō-əl) adj. If something is gradual, it advances little by little.

Rood thinks that most of these rocks were carved out during the last Ice Age.[1] "There was a lot more water," he says. "There were big lakes all over the Mojave Desert." If that's true, it would mean these rocks have been standing like bowling pins in the desert for 15,000 to 20,000 years—four or five times longer than the pyramids of Egypt!

SUNBURNED ROCK

Rood and Richard plan to test this age estimate. Late one afternoon, a couple of days after their walk through the marshmallow gully, they find a refrigerator-sized boulder that looks ready to roll downhill.

Unlike a lot of the other balanced rocks they've seen, this one is on the side of a small mountain, in a place where it *could* have landed after rolling from somewhere higher up. But Richard and Rood have a way of knowing that it didn't. They can tell, in fact, that it's sitting within a few centimeters of where it was eroded out of the surrounding bedrock.

Rood points out a vein of brownish quartz crystals, several fingers thick, that runs through the bedrock a few meters behind the rock. That layer runs for 30 meters before disappearing. It is tilted, like the hour hand of a wall clock at 8 o'clock—but otherwise straight as an arrow. That same layer of quartz runs through the boulder. It is perfectly lined up with the layer in the bedrock. It would be a pretty unlikely **coincidence** if the boulder just rolled down the mountain and landed that way. This rock has to be sitting in its original birthplace.

Rood hangs a tape measure down the boulder, which is 6 feet tall.

He hammers a small piece off of the boulder every few inches from top to bottom. Back at the lab, he'll test these bits of rock to see how long each part of the boulder has been exposed to sunlight.

Rood measures this by using an accelerator-mass spectrometer, a monster machine the size of an 18-wheeler. He'll use this machine to measure tiny amounts—a few quadrillionths of a gram—of a rare radioactive form of the element beryllium.

coincidence
(kō-ĭn´sĭ-dəns) *n.*
A *coincidence* is a sequence of events that although accidental seems to have been planned.

----
[1] **Ice Age:** a time in history when thick sheets of ice covered large areas of land.

This is one section of an accelerator-mass spectrometer, an enormous instrument scientists can use to analyze and collect data about rock samples.

140   This rare form, called beryllium-10, is created when cosmic rays from space hit the rock and split apart larger atoms of oxygen and nitrogen. You might say that when this happens, the rock is getting sunburned. As long as the rock is sitting out in the open, the cosmic rays are hitting it and beryllium-10 is forming in the outer 2 or so centimeters of the rock. But while the rock is buried underground—before running water chews it out of the desert floor—it's shaded from cosmic rays, so no beryllium-10 develops.

OLDEST PLACES

By measuring the sunburn—that is, the amount of
150   beryllium-10 in the rock fragments—scientists can tell how long ago the rock emerged from the surrounding bedrock.

Rood has already used this method, called exposure dating, on one balanced rock in the Mojave Desert. He found that it had been freestanding for 18,000 years—about what he expected if the rock was carved out during the last Ice Age.

Scientists have used exposure dating all over the world. Deserts, usually the oldest places, change the slowest because there is little water to alter the landscape. Once a rock is standing, it can stay still for a long time because there is
160 hardly any water to erode it or wash it away. And during the winter, ice doesn't form inside cracks in the rock and slowly pry it apart.

In places with lots of water, things change quickly. Over the past 150 years, the Missouri River has shifted its winding path by three kilometers in some places, leaving its mark in the landscape.

Antarctica probably has the oldest, most unchanging landscapes on Earth. Ice covers most of the continent, but a few small areas remain ice-free. In one such place, called the
170 Olympus Range, you can sit on boulders that haven't moved in five or six million years! The rocks survived because Antarctica is a desert: It is so cold that it receives hardly any rain or snow. The continent was once warmer and wetter, but when it became cold and dry, it stayed that way.

ROCK TIPPING

Here in California, Rood and Richard need to know not only how long their **precariously** balanced rocks have been standing but also how hard they are to knock over.

These are tough questions. The best way to find out how firmly in place a rock is—simply push it over. But toppling
180 a rock that's been balanced for 18,000 years is sort of like chopping down one of the oldest redwood trees. No one wants to do it.

Once, though, Richard and James Brune had a chance to topple some rocks. They heard about a businessman who was building some houses in the desert and planned to knock over some balanced rocks that were in the way.

The Brunes convinced the developer to let them do it for him. They fastened a steel cable to each rock and used a gadget to measure exactly how much pulling was needed to bring
190 down the boulder. "It was kind of fun," admits James. "They

precarious
(prĭ-kâr´ē-əs) *adj.*
If something is *precarious*, it is dangerous and unstable.

were 7 or 8 feet high and weighed many tons." And each landed with a satisfying thud.

Richard has also found less destructive ways to pull on rocks. Out in the Mojave Desert with Rood, he takes out a camera and begins photographing from all sides the refrigerator-sized boulder they're studying.

Back at home, he'll load the photos into a computer that will stitch the pictures into a three-dimensional model of the rock—a virtual rock.

200   Richard can then run that virtual rock through a computer program that shakes and knocks the rock down many times. By tipping that virtual rock they can ensure that the other one—the real rock—has a fighting chance to stay standing for another 18,000 years.

COLLABORATIVE DISCUSSION What surprising details does the author reveal about how geologists conduct their research? Discuss your ideas with a small group of classmates.

Analyze Structure: Essay

ELA RI.7.2, RI.7.3, RI.7.5
ELD PI.7.6, PII.7.1

"Big Rocks' Balancing Acts" is an **expository essay,** which presents or explains information or ideas. To ensure that informational texts are clear to readers, writers choose a **pattern of organization,** a particular arrangement of ideas and information. Facts and details can be organized in a variety of ways. This chart shows a few common patterns of organization:

Pattern	What It Shows or Highlights	Signal Words or Phrases
chronological order	the order in which actions or events occur	*first, second, then, at the same time*
cause-and-effect order	the relationship between events and their causes	*because, and so, as a result, therefore*
compare-and-contrast order	the similarities and differences of two or more subjects	*like, by contrast, similarly, as opposed to, however*
spatial order	the arrangement of details according to their physical position or relationship	*top, bottom, above, in front of*

A pattern of organization may be used to organize an entire piece of writing or single paragraphs within a longer work. Reread lines 113–118. Identify the pattern of organization within that paragraph and the words or phrases that signal the organization.

Being able to identify patterns of organization can help readers find a writer's main, or central, idea, which is the most important idea in an essay. Often, the **central idea** is not directly stated but is implied by supporting details. As you read, use these strategies to identify and understand central ideas in an expository essay:

- Identify the specific topic of each paragraph or section.
- Examine the details the author includes in that section.
- Look for words that signal an organization.
- Ask what idea or message the details convey about the topic.

Where in "Big Rocks' Balancing Acts" does the author introduce the topic and central idea of the essay?

ELA RI.7.1, RI.7.2, RI.7.3, RI.7.4, RI.7.5, W.7.7, SL.7.4
ELD PI.7.6, PI.7.7, PI.7.9, PI.7.10, PII.7.1

Analyzing the Text

Cite Text Evidence Support your responses with evidence from the text.

1. **Recognize and Analyze** Under the heading "Sunburned Rock," examine lines 119–130. What pattern of organization is evident in these paragraphs? What details help you to recognize it?

2. **Summarize** Reread from the beginning of the essay to the end of the section "Odd Hobby." In your own words, describe the most important idea the author of this expository essay wants readers to understand.

3. **Cite Evidence** Reread the section "Standing Strong." Why is it worthwhile to study balanced rocks?

4. **Analyze** Reread lines 96–102. What comparisons does the author make, and how are they helpful for readers?

5. **Draw Conclusions** Reread lines 57–68. What might be the author's reason in using the pronoun *you* and presenting information in this way?

6. **Analyze** What important idea from the essay is in the concluding sentence?

PERFORMANCE TASK

Speaking Activity: Summary Presentation Choose a concept or term about geology from "Big Rocks' Balancing Acts" (for example: *earthquake tremors, granite, bedrock, accelerator-mass spectrometer, erosion, Ice Age,* or *geology* itself). Think of a question related to that term to explore, such as *"How many ice ages have taken place on Earth?"* Research your topic and present a brief summary of the information you find.

- Find at least two informational print or online articles on the topic. Make sure these sources are credible.
- List the most important ideas you want to present.
- Begin your summary with an introduction that specifies your topic clearly, establishes your central idea, and hooks listeners into listening further.
- Explain the central idea or ideas from your research.

Critical Vocabulary

ELA L.7.4b, L.7.6
ELD PI.7.6, PI.7.12

gully   **bedrock**   **gradual**   **coincidence**   **precarious**

Practice and Apply   Identify the vocabulary word that is tied in meaning to the italicized word in each question. Give your reasons.

1. Which word goes with *patience*? Why?

2. Which word goes with *drill*? Why?

3. Which word goes with *cliff*? Why?

4. Which word goes with *rainstorm*? Why?

5. Which word goes with *chance*? Why?

Vocabulary Strategy: Latin Roots

A **root** is a word part that came into English from an older language. You can check a print or digital dictionary to learn about roots; the entry for a word often gives details about the word's origin. Roots from Latin appear in many English words. This sentence comes from "Big Rocks' Balancing Acts":

> **If the house is continuously exposed to running water, the cement will gradually wear away.**

The word *gradually* contains a root, *grad*, from the Latin word *gradus*, which means "step" or "stage." You can see the root meaning in the different meanings of the word *grade*, which have to do with steps, stages, or levels. The root meaning also appears in the word *gradually*, which describes actions taken step by step. In the example sentence, the cement doesn't disappear all at once, but wears away in stages. By recognizing the root *grad*, you can make a good guess about the meanings of longer words that include it.

Practice and Apply   Read each sentence. Identify the word with the Latin root *grad*. Tell what each word means. Use a print or digital dictionary to check your ideas.

1. After learning camera settings, we graduated to taking nature photos.

2. The hill has a gradient that is perfect for sledding.

3. Until astronomers understood that planets orbit the Sun, they had trouble explaining the retrograde motion of planets during part of the year.

4. The art appears to be red, but a closer look shows gradations of color.

5. Weathering and erosion slowly cause the degradation of mountains.

6. Some products last forever in landfills, while others are biodegradable.

Language Conventions: Prepositional Phrases

A **preposition** is a part of speech that relates one word to another. These are just a few common prepositions: *about, across, against, at, before, beside, between, by, for, from, in, like, next to, of, on, on top of, over, through, to,* and *with.*

A **phrase** is a group of related words that acts like a single word in a sentence. A **prepositional phrase** acts like a **modifier,** a word that changes the sense of another word in a sentence. A prepositional phrase includes a preposition, its object (the noun or pronoun that follows the preposition), and any modifiers. These examples show how the prepositional phrase always modifies or relates to another word in a sentence, telling which one, where, when, how, why, or to what extent.

The scientists fly over the southern California desert.

(The prepositional phrase *over the southern California desert* modifies *fly* and tells *where.*)

modifies

The scientists have a passion for balanced rocks.

(The prepositional phrase *for balanced rocks* modifies *passion* and tells *what kind.*)

One of them shoots photos from the plane.

(The prepositional phrase *of them* modifies *One* and tells *which.* The prepositional phrase *from the plane* modifies *shoots* and tells *where.*)

Writers use prepositional phrases to add information to their sentences. This sentence from "Big Rocks' Balancing Acts" has five prepositional phrases:

And some of the bricks will be left stacked or balanced on top of each other—like the granite marshmallows in the gully.

Practice and Apply Use these prepositional phrases to build sentences that tell about information in "Big Rocks' Balancing Acts." Try to use more than one phrase in a sentence.

- in the desert
- with little water
- on ancient boulders
- by water
- like bowling pins
- for a long time

Background *The topic of nature is popular with poets around the world and throughout history. Two of the most important poets of the 20th century, Pablo Neruda and Mary Oliver, continue this tradition with their poems in this lesson. Neruda's poem "Ode to enchanted light" was written originally in Spanish. Its Spanish title is "Oda a la luz encantada."*

Ode to enchanted light

Poem by Pablo Neruda

Sleeping in the Forest

Poem by Mary Oliver

Pablo Neruda (1904–1973) *was the pen name of Ricardo Eliecer Neftalí Reyes Basoalto. Born in a small town in Chile, Neruda began writing poetry as a child. While a student, he met Gabriela Mistral, a famous poet. She encouraged Neruda to continue writing. Neruda went on to write hundreds of poems and gain a worldwide reputation. He was awarded the Nobel Prize for Literature in 1971 for his lifetime of work.*

Mary Oliver (b. 1935) *was born in Maple Heights, Ohio. She spent a great deal of time in her younger years writing, reading, and walking through the woods where she grew up. Today, Oliver always walks with a notepad so she can write down her thoughts immediately. Oliver's first book of poems was published in 1962. Since then she has written many books and won many awards for her poetry.*

SETTING A PURPOSE As you read, think about how each poet portrays a meaningful experience in nature. Beyond the subject matter, how are the poems similar? How are they different? Write down any questions you have while reading.

Ode to enchanted light

by Pablo Neruda
translated by Ken Krabbenhoft

Under the trees light
has dropped from the top of the sky,
light
like a green
5 latticework of branches,
shining
on every leaf,
drifting down like clean
white sand.

10 A cicada sends
its sawing song
high into the empty air.

The world is
a glass overflowing
15 with water.

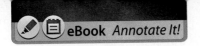

Analyze Form: Ode

Pablo Neruda's poem is an **ode,** a poem that deals with serious themes, such as justice, truth, or beauty. An ode praises or celebrates its subject, which is usually a person, event, thing, or element in nature.

The word *ode* comes from the Greek word *aeidein*, which means to sing or chant. Originally, the ode was written to be accompanied by music and dance. A traditional ode is a long poem with a formal structure, and due to its dignified nature, its language is often formal as well. Many modern poets experiment with the form to make it fresh and interesting for modern readers. What do you notice about the length and arrangement of lines in Neruda's poem?

Analyzing the Text

Cite Text Evidence   Support your responses with evidence from the text.

1. **Infer** What feelings are suggested in lines 1–9 of this poem? How does the poet suggest those feelings?

2. **Analyze** A cicada is an insect that makes a high-pitched, continual sound, usually in summer. Reread lines 10–12. What repeated first sounds, or **alliteration,** do you hear, and how are the sounds connected to the poem's meaning?

3. **Analyze and Evaluate** Does this poem meet the requirements of an ode? Why or why not?

Sleeping in the Forest
by Mary Oliver

I thought the earth
remembered me, she
took me back so tenderly, arranging
her dark skirts, her pockets
5   full of lichens[1] and seeds. I slept
as never before, a stone
on the riverbed, nothing
between me and the white fire of the stars
but my thoughts, and they floated
10   light as moths among the branches
of the perfect trees. All night
I heard the small kingdoms breathing
around me, the insects, and the birds
who do their work in the darkness. All night
15   I rose and fell, as if in water, grappling[2]
with a luminous doom. By morning
I had vanished at least a dozen times
into something better.

COLLABORATIVE DISCUSSION Read the first two lines of each
poem and compare the images they present. What do these lines
say about the speaker's relationship to nature? Share your ideas
with the students in your class.

---

[1] **lichens** (lī´kənz): fungi that grow together with algae and form a crust-like growth on rocks or tree trunks.

[2] **grappling:** struggling.

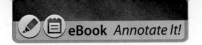

Analyze Form: Lyric Poem

ELA RL.7.4, RL.7.5
ELD PI.7.8, PII.7.1

"Sleeping in the Forest" is a **lyric poem,** a short poem in which a single speaker expresses personal thoughts and feelings. Lyric poetry is a broad category that includes traditional forms such as odes and sonnets, as well as **free verse,** a form that does not use formal structure or rhyme schemes. In fact, in ancient times, lyric poems were created to be sung. Although they aren't sung today, lyric poems do have some elements in common with songs, including

- a sense of rhythm and melody
- imaginative word choice, or **diction**
- the creation of a single, unified impression

What is the single, unified impression conveyed in this poem?

Analyzing the Text

ELA RL.7.1, RL.7.4, RL.7.5
ELD PI.7.6, PI.7.8, PII.7.1

Cite Text Evidence   Support your responses with evidence from the text.

1. **Interpret** Reread the last sentence in the poem. What might the speaker mean by "something better"?

2. **Analyze** Reread lines 5–7. What is compared to "a stone / on the riverbed"? Where else does that image appear in the poem?

3. **Analyze and Evaluate** Identify examples of each of the elements of a lyric poem that appear in "Sleeping in the Forest." Do you think Oliver's poem is a good example of a lyric poem? Why or why not?

ANCHOR TEXT: COMPARE POEMS

Determine Meaning

ELA RL.7.1, RL.7.4
ELD PI.7.8

Through **figurative language,** words are used in an imaginative way to express ideas that are not literally true. The most common types are

simile
a comparison between two unlike things using the word *like* or *as* (*friendship as sturdy as a tree*)

metaphor
a comparison of two things that are basically unlike but have some qualities in common; a metaphor does not contain the word *like* or *as* (*a forest of confused thoughts*)

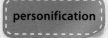
personification
the giving of human qualities to an animal, object, or idea (*the trees stood guard*)

In the poem "Ode to enchanted light," the poet Pablo Neruda states that light is "drifting down like clean / white sand." What type of figurative language does this phrase represent?

Analyzing the Text

ELA RL.7.1, RL.7.4, RL.7.5, W.7.2, W.7.3, W.7.10
ELD PI.7.6, PI.7.8, PI.7.10

Cite Text Evidence   Support your responses with evidence from the texts.

1. **Interpret** Reread lines 13–15 of "Ode to enchanted light." What type of figurative language is represented here, and what is the comparison being made? What feelings does this evoke in the reader?

2. **Analyze** What is personified in lines 1–5 of "Sleeping in the Forest"? Why might the poet have chosen to use this personification?

3. **Compare** Reread lines 8–9 of "Ode" and lines 9–11 of "Sleeping in the Forest." What similarities do you observe in the poets' use of language?

4. **Analyze** How do the images of light differ in these two poems?

PERFORMANCE TASK

Writing Activity: Poem Write a four-stanza poem to describe an experience with nature.

- Base the poem on your own experiences or on an imagined one.
- Experiment with figurative language.

- Consider expressing a theme or message about nature.
- As you create your poem, try reading it aloud to help you refine your choices of words or effects.

Write a Personal Narrative

ELA W.7.3a–e, W.7.4,
W.7.5, W.7.10, SL.7.4
ELD PI.7.4, PI.7.10,
PI.7.12, PII.7.1, PII.7.6

In this collection, you read about the strong and emotional connections that people have with different elements of nature. In particular, consider the experience that Eddy Harris recounts in the excerpt from his memoir, *Mississippi Solo*. Then think about your own interactions with nature. Write a personal narrative about a natural setting that is meaningful to you.

A successful personal narrative

- begins with a captivating lead that clearly establishes the situation
- contains a well-structured event sequence that unfolds naturally and logically
- uses descriptive details that offer insight on significant events and feelings
- creates vivid images in the reader's mind through the use of sensory language
- provides a conclusion that follows from and reflects on the narrated experiences and events

PLAN myNotebook

Use the annotation tools in your eBook to mark up sensory language that you can use as inspiration later. Save each example to your notebook.

Establish the Situation A personal narrative describes a true story from a person's life. Consider what made the sudden rainstorm on the Mississippi River memorable to Eddy Harris. Then think about memorable experiences you have had in a natural setting.

- Consider how the natural setting is important to you. Is it important now, or was it important in the past?
- Determine whether you have a story to tell about yourself and the setting.
- Identify the feelings you have about the setting.
- Think about how the experience with the natural setting changed your feelings or ideas.
- Specify the most important idea you want the reader to know.

ACADEMIC VOCABULARY

As you share your experience, be sure to use the academic vocabulary words.

affect
element
ensure
participate
specify

Organize Your Ideas In a personal narrative, you are the narrator, or the person telling the story. Organize your ideas about the personal narrative under the following categories.

- Setting
- Events
- Sensory Details
- Most Memorable Images
- Emotions and Reactions
- Conclusion

Interactive Lessons
For help in organizing your narrative, use the following lesson:
· Writing Narratives: Narrative Structure

Mentor Text Notice how in this example from *Mississippi Solo*, Eddy Harris uses descriptive words to appeal to the senses.

> " The trees swooshed loudly as the leaves and branches brushed hard together. Branches fell. Rains came and poured down bucketfuls. "

Consider Your Purpose and Audience Think about what you want your audience to understand as you prepare to write.

PRODUCE

✔ myWriteSmart

Write your rough draft in *my*WriteSmart. Focus on getting your ideas down, rather than perfecting your choice of language.

Write Your Personal Narrative Review the information in your notes as you begin your draft.

- Begin by clearly establishing the situation.
- Use first-person point of view to present the events in a clear and logical sequence.
- Write what you see, hear, smell, taste, and feel.
- Elaborate on your ideas, including descriptive details.
- Conclude by reflecting on what the experience meant to you.

Interactive Lessons
For help in drafting your narrative, use the following lesson:
· Writing Narratives: The Language of Narrative

Language Conventions: Connecting Ideas

A compound-complex sentence contains two or more main clauses and one or more subordinate clauses. Sentences like these can connect ideas and enhance descriptive detail. For example, read this description from *Mississippi Solo*.

> " I tried to keep the stern pointed right into the flow *so* the canoe could ride the waves, *but* it didn't work. "

By using the words *so* and *but*, the writer has formed a compound-complex sentence to describe what could happen in attempting to move his canoe. Look for places in your narrative where you can add compound-complex sentences.

Review Your Draft

Review Your Draft Work with a partner to determine if you have described your experience clearly and have used vivid details. Be sure to consider the following points.

Questions	Tips	Revision Techniques
Does my introduction clearly establish the situation and the setting?	**Underline** the opener.	**Add** an attention-grabbing statement. **Add** specific details to the setting to make it more precise.
Have I used the first-person point of view consistently?	**Check** that you have related events from your point of view.	**Change** any third-person pronouns to first-person pronouns.
Have I developed a plot line to make the personal narrative easy to follow?	**Note** whether the events are ordered in a logical sequence.	**Make** the order of events clear by adding such transition words as *next, finally, afterwards.*
Have I included effective descriptive details?	**Highlight** sensory details. **Note** which senses the details appeal to.	**Add** more and various sensory details that appeal to the senses.
Does my personal narrative reveal what an experience means to me?	**Underline** details that show why the experience is meaningful.	**Add** a clearly worded statement that reflects on what the experience means.

Have your partner or a group of peers review your draft in *myWriteSmart*. Ask your reviewers to note any words or phrases that could be replaced with more descriptive language.

Interactive Lessons

For help in revising your narrative, use the following lesson:
• Writing Narratives: Narrative Context

Create a Finished Copy

Create a Finished Copy Finalize your personal narrative and choose a way to share it with your audience. Consider these options:

- Present your personal narrative aloud to your class.
- Post your personal narrative as a blog entry on a personal or school website.
- Dramatize your personal narrative in a one-person performance.

PERFORMANCE TASK A RUBRIC
PERSONAL NARRATIVE

	Ideas and Evidence	Organization	Language
4	• The introduction engagingly and clearly establishes the natural setting and identifies the writer's experience in nature. • Descriptive details, realistic dialogue, and reflection strongly re-create the experience. • The conclusion summarizes the significance of the experience and leaves readers with an interesting thought.	• The organization is effective; ideas are arranged logically, and events are organized chronologically. • Transitions successfully connect ideas and show a naturally flowing sequence of events.	• The first-person point of view is used creatively and consistently. • Sensory language vividly describes people, places, and events. • Sentence beginnings, lengths, and structures vary and have a rhythmic flow. • Spelling, capitalization, and punctuation are correct. • Grammar and usage are correct.
3	• The introduction identifies the experience but could do more to present the natural setting and engage the reader. • Descriptive details and dialogue generally re-create the experience. • The conclusion summarizes most of the writer's ideas and feelings about the experience.	• The organization of ideas is generally logical; the sequence of events is occasionally confusing. • A few more transitions are needed to clarify the sequence of events and give it a more natural flow.	• The narrative occasionally shifts from the first-person point of view. • Sensory language describes people, places, and events but could be used more effectively. • Sentence beginnings, lengths, and structures vary somewhat. • Few spelling, capitalization, and punctuation errors occur. • Some grammatical and usage errors are repeated in the narrative.
2	• The introduction is ordinary; it mentions an experience in nature and hints at the setting. • A few descriptive details create lively scenes, but most details are ordinary; dialogue is lacking. • The conclusion only hints at the significance of the experience.	• The organization of ideas often doesn't follow a pattern, and the sequence of events is confusing in several places. • More transitions are needed throughout to clarify the sequence of events.	• The narrative frequently shifts from the first-person point of view. • The narrative lacks sensory language in several key parts. • Sentence structures barely vary, with some fragments or run-on sentences. • Spelling, capitalization, and punctuation are often incorrect. • Grammar and usage are incorrect in several places.
1	• The introduction does not focus on an experience or establish a setting. • Descriptive details and dialogue are unrelated or missing. • The narrative lacks a conclusion.	• The narrative is not organized; information and details are presented randomly. • Transitions are not used, making the narrative difficult to understand.	• The narrative lacks a consistent point of view. • Sensory language is not used. • Repetitive sentence structure, fragments, and run-on sentences make the writing confusing. • Spelling, capitalization, and punctuation are incorrect throughout. • Several grammatical and usage errors change the meaning of the writer's ideas.

COLLECTION 3
PERFORMANCE TASK B

Interactive Lessons

To help you complete this task, use *Writing Informative Texts*.

Write a Poetry Analysis

ELA W.7.2a–f, W.7.4, W.7.5, W.7.6, W.7.10, SL.7.4
ELD PI.7.4, PI.7.10, PI.7.12, PII.7.1, PII.7.7

"Ode to enchanted light" and "Sleeping in the Forest" are lyric poems that convey an appreciation of nature. In this activity, you will analyze each poet's style by comparing and contrasting elements such as form, structure, and use of figurative language.

A successful poetry analysis

- begins with clear thesis statement
- uses an effective organizational structure and transitions
- analyzes ideas and elements of the text and provides supporting textual evidence
- clearly explains how the poets use figurative language
- provides a conclusion that summarizes main points

PLAN

Identify Stylistic Elements Every poet has his or her own style. Reread each poem. Jot down stylistic elements of each poem as you read.

- Consider each poem's subject. What does the title reveal? What is the poet's attitude toward the subject?
- Study the form and structure of each poem. Note how the lines are organized and grouped. Think about the sound and rhythm. What effects do they create in the poem?
- Examine word choice. Are the words concrete or abstract? Do the word choices make the poem seem happy? sad? funny?
- Identify figurative language, and explain what it means.

Organize Your Ideas To organize and compare your ideas, use a Venn diagram to compare and contrast elements of each poet's style.

ACADEMIC VOCABULARY

As you share your ideas, be sure to use the academic vocabulary words.

affect
element
ensure
participate
specify

Ode to enchanted light   Both   Sleeping in the Forest

Gather Evidence Use the annotation tools in your eBook to find supporting evidence from the poems. Save your evidence to *my*Notebook, in a folder titled *Collection 3 Performance Task*. Try to gather varied stylistic elements, such as figurative language.

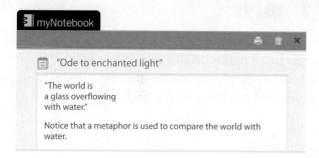

Develop Your Thesis Statement A thesis statement identifies the main points of your analysis. It states what you want to say about the topic. A good thesis statement engages the reader's curiosity or gets the reader to ask questions.

PRODUCE

Write Your Analysis Review the information in your Venn diagram as you begin your draft.

- Start with an engaging introduction that clearly identifies your topic and thesis statement.
- Arrange your information clearly and logically.
- Organize your main points in order of importance.
- Include supporting evidence from the poems.
- Maintain a formal style and use transitions to connect ideas.
- Conclude by summarizing your main points and offering an overall insight about each poet's style and its effects.

Write your rough draft in *my*WriteSmart. Focus on getting your ideas down, rather than perfecting your choice of language.

Interactive Lessons
For help in writing your draft, use:
• Developing a Topic
• Organizing Ideas

Language Conventions: Condensing Ideas

Sometimes a single word can connect one detail to another. Read this passage from the essay, "Big Rocks' Balancing Acts."

> " Geologists find these rocks so interesting because they could give clues about the severity of earthquakes over thousands of years. "

This passage could have been written as two sentences. Using *because* conveys the details more precisely.

Review Your Draft

Review Your Draft Work with a partner or a group of peers to determine whether your analysis is effective. Be sure to consider the following points in each other's drafts.

Questions	Tips	Revision Techniques
Does my introduction have a thesis statement that explains the analysis?	**Underline** the thesis statement.	**Add** a sentence that clearly states the main point and sets up your analysis.
Do the key points presented in the analysis support the thesis statement?	**Highlight** key points throughout the analysis.	**Review** the poems' stylistic elements. **Add** evidence, such as quotations and concrete details.
Is the organization of my analysis easy to follow?	**Note** how the key points are organized.	**Revise** your points to show a comparison and contrast. **Relate** ideas with transitions.
Am I maintaining a formal style?	**Underline** any contractions in the analysis.	**Replace** contractions or other informal language with precise, formal vocabulary.
Does my conclusion summarize the thesis statement and offer an insight into the poems?	**Highlight** the sentence that restates the thesis.	**Reword** the conclusion to include the thesis statement. **Provide** an insight about the effects of each poet's style.

Have your partner or a group of peers review your draft in *my*WriteSmart. Ask your reviewers to note whether the evidence you provide supports your main points.

Interactive Lessons

For help in revising your draft, use:
· Formal Style
· Introductions and Conclusions

Create a Finished Copy

Create a Finished Copy Finalize your analysis and choose a way to share it with your audience. Consider these options:

- In a small group, take turns reading your analyses aloud.
- Post your analysis as a blog on a personal or school website.
- Send your analysis to a source that publishes literary reviews.

PERFORMANCE TASK B RUBRIC
POETRY ANALYSIS

	Ideas and Evidence	Organization	Language
4	• The introduction is interesting; the thesis statement identifies the two poems and sets up a number of literary elements for comparison and contrast. • Specific, well-chosen quotations from the poems support the key points. • A satisfying concluding section summarizes the analysis and offers an original thought about the two poems.	• Key points and supporting text evidence are organized effectively and logically throughout the literary analysis. • The compare/contrast structure is clearly followed. • Transitions successfully show the relationships between ideas.	• The analysis has an appropriately formal style with precise language. • Sentence beginnings, lengths, and structures vary and flow well. Sentences show condensed ideas. • Spelling, capitalization, and punctuation are correct. • Grammar and usage are correct.
3	• The introduction could be more engaging; the thesis statement sets up a few elements for analysis. • A few more relevant quotations from the poems are needed to support key points. • The concluding section summarizes most of the analysis but doesn't leave the reader with a new idea to think about.	• The organization of key points and supporting text evidence is confusing in a few places. • The compare/contrast structure is not followed in some places. • A few more transitions could clarify the relationships between ideas.	• The style becomes informal. There is some imprecise language. • Sentence beginnings, lengths, and structures vary somewhat. Ideas could be condensed more. • Few spelling, capitalization, and punctuation mistakes occur. • Some grammatical and usage errors are repeated.
2	• The introduction is ordinary; the thesis statement only hints at the main comparisons and contrasting points of the analysis. • Quotations from the poems support some key points but are unclear or poorly chosen. • The concluding section restates the thesis statement but gives an incomplete summary of the analysis.	• Most key points are organized logically, but much of the supporting text evidence is out of place or used in a confusing manner. • There are many places where the compare/contrast structure is absent. • More transitions are needed throughout the literary analysis to connect ideas.	• The style is informal in many places, with too much vague and repetitive language. • Sentence structures barely vary, with some fragments or run-on sentences. • Spelling, capitalization, and punctuation are often incorrect. • Grammar and usage are incorrect in several places.
1	• The introduction is missing. • Examples and quotations from the poems are either irrelevant or missing. • The poetry analysis lacks a concluding section.	• A logical organization is not apparent; ideas are presented randomly. • There is no sense of comparing and contrasting ideas. • Transitions are not used, making the literary analysis difficult to understand.	• The style is inappropriate, and the language is inaccurate, repetitive, and too general. • Repetitive sentence structures, fragments, and run-on sentences make the writing confusing. • Spelling, capitalization, and punctuation are incorrect throughout. • Several grammatical and usage errors change the meaning of the writer's ideas.

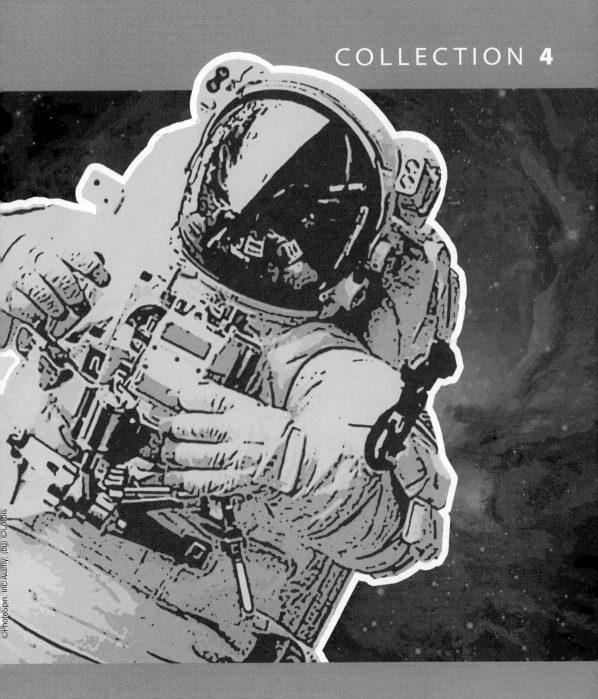

Risk and Exploration

" All adventures, especially into new territory, are scary. "

—Sally Ride

Risk and Exploration

In this collection, you will encounter individuals who must confront a compelling question: How far is too far?

Stream to Start

hmhfyi.com

Channel One News®

COLLECTION
PERFORMANCE TASK Preview

After reading the selections in this collection, you will consider the risks of exploration in extreme conditions and present an argument on whether it is worth the costs.

ACADEMIC VOCABULARY

Study the words and their definitions in the chart below. You will use these words as you discuss and write about the texts in this collection.

Word	Definition	Related Forms
complex (kŏm´plĕks´) *adj.*	consisting of many interwoven parts that make something difficult to understand	complex number, complexity, complicate, complicated
potential (pə-tĕn´shəl) *adj.*	capable of doing or being something; having possibility	potent, potentiality, potential energy
rely (rĭ-lī´) *v.*	to depend on something or someone for support, help, or supply	reliable, reliability, reliance, reliant
stress (strĕs) *v.*	to put emphasis on something	stress fracture, stressed, stressed-out, unstressed, stressful
valid (văl´ĭd) *adj.*	convincing or having a sound reason for something	invalid, invalidation, validate, validation

Background *In 1957, the country then known as the Soviet Union launched the first satellite to orbit Earth. The Soviet Union and the United States were bitter enemies at the time. After becoming the 35th president of the United States in 1961,* **John F. Kennedy** *was determined to equal the Soviet's knowledge of space. Well known for many accomplishments as president, Kennedy is also remembered as an inspirational speaker. He gave this speech the day before his assassination in November 1963.*

Remarks at the
Dedication of the Aerospace
Medical Health Center

Speech by John F. Kennedy

SETTING A PURPOSE As you read, pay attention to the points President Kennedy is making. Why does he think the United States should be involved with space research?

myNotebook

As you read, save new words to *myWordList*.

Mr. Secretary, Governor, Mr. Vice President, Senator, Members of the Congress, members of the military, ladies and gentlemen:

For more than 3 years I have spoken about the New Frontier.[1] This is not a partisan term, and it is not the exclusive property of Republicans or Democrats. It refers, instead, to this Nation's place in history, to the fact that we do stand on the edge of a great new era, filled with both crisis and opportunity, an era to be characterized by achievement and by challenge. It is an era which calls for action and for the best efforts of all those who would test the unknown and the

10

---

[1] **New Frontier:** term Kennedy used in his presidential campaign.

uncertain in every phase of human endeavor. It is a time for pathfinders and pioneers.

I have come to Texas today to salute an outstanding group of pioneers, the men who man the Brooks Air Force Base School of Aerospace Medicine and the Aerospace Medical Center. It is fitting that San Antonio should be the site of this center and this school as we gather to dedicate this complex of buildings. For this city has long been the home of the pioneers

20   in the air. It was here that Sidney Brooks, whose memory we honor today, was born and raised. It was here that Charles Lindbergh and Claire Chennault,[2] and a host of others, who, in World War I and World War II and Korea, and even today have helped demonstrate American mastery of the skies, trained at Kelly Field and Randolph Field,[3] which form a major part of aviation history. And in the new frontier of outer space, while headlines may be made by others in other places, history is being made every day by the men and women of the Aerospace Medical Center, without whom there

30   could be no history.

Many Americans make the mistake of assuming that space research has no values here on earth. Nothing could be further from the truth. Just as the wartime development of radar gave us the transistor, and all that it made possible, so research in space medicine holds the promise of substantial benefit for those of us who are earthbound. For our effort in space is not, as some have suggested, a competitor for the natural resources that we need to develop the earth. It is a working partner and a coproducer of these resources. And

40   nothing makes this clearer than the fact that medicine in space is going to make our lives healthier and happier here on earth.

I give you three examples: first, medical space research may open up new understanding of man's relation to his environment. Examinations of the astronaut's physical, and mental, and emotional reactions can teach us more about the differences between normal and abnormal, about the causes and effects of disorientation, about changes in **metabolism**

metabolism
(mĭ-tăb′ə-lĭz′əm) *n.*
The *metabolism* of a living thing is all the processes that allow for growth and life.

---

[2] **Sidney Brooks . . . Charles Lindbergh . . . Claire Chennault** (shən′ôlt): Sidney Brooks was a young flyer killed in a training accident. Charles Lindbergh was the first transatlantic solo pilot, and Claire Chennault was an important figure in the development of air-war theories.

[3] **Kelly Field and Randolph Field:** airfields in the San Antonio area where many military pilots were trained.

which could result in extending the life span. When you
study the effects on our astronauts of exhaust gases which can
contaminate their environment, and you seek ways to alter
these gases so as to reduce their toxicity, you are working on
problems similar to those we face in our great urban centers
which themselves are being corrupted by gases and which
must be clear.

And second, medical space research may revolutionize
the technology and the techniques of modern medicine.
Whatever new devices are created, for example, to monitor
our astronauts, to measure their heart activity, their breathing,
their brain waves, their eye motion, at great distances and
under difficult conditions, will also represent a major advance
in general medical instrumentation. Heart patients may even
be able to wear a light monitor which will sound a warning if
their activity exceeds certain limits. An instrument recently
developed to record automatically the impact of acceleration
upon an astronaut's eyes will also be of help to small children
who are suffering miserably from eye defects, but are unable to
describe their **impairment**. And also by the use of instruments
similar to those used in Project Mercury, this Nation's private
as well as public nursing services are being improved, enabling
one nurse now to give more critically ill patients greater
attention than they ever could in the past.

And third, medical space research may lead to new
safeguards against hazards common to many environments.
Specifically, our astronauts will need fundamentally new
devices to protect them from the ill effects of radiation which
can have a profound influence upon medicine and man's
relations to our present environment.

Here at this center we have the laboratories, the talent,
the resources to give new **impetus** to vital research in the life
centers. I am not suggesting that the entire space program
is justified alone by what is done in medicine. The space
program stands on its own as a contribution to national
strength. And last Saturday at Cape Canaveral I saw our new
Saturn C-1 rocket booster,[4] which, with its payload,[5] when it
rises in December of this year, will be, for the first time, the
largest booster in the world, carrying into space the largest
payload that any country in the world has ever sent into space.

impairment
(ĭm-pâr´mənt) *n.*
An *impairment* is an
injury or weakness.

impetus
(ĭm´pĭ-təs) *n.* The
impetus is the driving
force or motivation
behind an action.

---

[4] **booster:** a rocket used to launch a spacecraft.
[5] **payload:** the load carried by a rocket or other vehicle.

I think the United States should be a leader. A country as rich and powerful as this which bears so many burdens and responsibilities, which has so many opportunities, should be second to none. And in December, while I do not regard our mastery of space as anywhere near complete, while I recognize that there are still areas where we are behind—at least in one area, the size of the booster—this year I hope the United States will be ahead. And I am for it. We have a long way to go. Many weeks and months and years of long, **tedious** work lie ahead. There will be setbacks and frustrations and disappointments. There will be, as there always are, pressures in this country to do less in this area as in so many others, and temptations to do something else that is perhaps easier. But this research here must go on. This space effort must go on. The conquest of space must and will go ahead. That much we know. That much we can say with confidence and conviction.

Frank O'Connor, the Irish writer, tells in one of his books how, as a boy, he and his friends would make their way across the countryside, and when they came to an orchard wall that seemed too high and too doubtful to try and too difficult to permit their voyage to continue, they took off their hats and tossed them over the wall—and then they had no choice but to follow them.

This Nation has tossed its cap over the wall of space, and we have no choice but to follow it. Whatever the difficulties, they will be overcome. Whatever the hazards, they must be guarded against. With the vital help of this Aerospace Medical Center, with the help of all those who labor in the space endeavor, with the help and support of all Americans, we will climb this wall with safety and with speed—and we shall then explore the wonders on the other side.

Thank you.

tedious
(tē′dē-əs) *adj.*
Something that is *tedious* is boring.

COLLABORATIVE DISCUSSION Kennedy makes several points about why he thinks the United States should be involved with space research. Do you think the points he makes are valid? Does his speech inspire you to support space research? Discuss your ideas with a partner.

Trace and Evaluate an Argument

The speech you've just read is an **argument,** in which the speaker states a claim supported by reasons and evidence. A **claim** is the speaker's position on a problem or an issue. The strength of an argument relies not on the claim but on the support. **Support** consists of reasons and evidence used to prove the claim. **Reasons** are declarations made to explain an action or belief. **Evidence** includes specific facts, statistics, or examples.

To **trace,** or follow the reasoning of, an argument:

- Identify the claim, which may be stated directly or implied.
- Look for reasons and evidence that support the claim.
- Pay attention to the way the author connects the claim, reasons, and evidence.
- Identify **counterarguments,** which are statements that address opposing viewpoints. A good argument anticipates opposing viewpoints and provides counterarguments to disprove the opposing views.

Some arguments have more than one claim, which might only be determined after careful examination of the text. To trace the argument in Kennedy's speech:

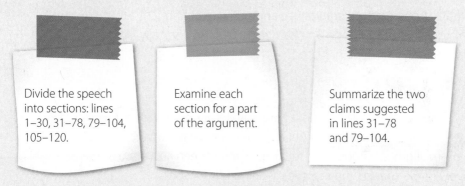

Divide the speech into sections: lines 1–30, 31–78, 79–104, 105–120.

Examine each section for a part of the argument.

Summarize the two claims suggested in lines 31–78 and 79–104.

To **evaluate** an argument, or decide whether it makes sense and is convincing:

- Consider whether the evidence logically supports the claim.
- Examine the logic to ensure the ideas make sense and are in a proper order.
- Consider whether the opposing view has been adequately addressed.
- Identify persuasive techniques such as appeals to emotion.

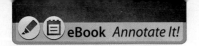
Analyzing the Text

ELA RI.7.1, RI.7.4, RI.7.5, RI.7.7, RI.7.8,
W.7.2, W.7.7, W.7.8, SL.7.3 **ELD** PI.7.1,
PI.7.6, PI.7.7, PI.7.10, PII.7.1

Cite Text Evidence   Support your responses with evidence from the text.

1. **Interpret** Kennedy refers to his audience as *pathfinders* and *pioneers* and mentions the *New Frontier*. Why might Kennedy use these words?

2. **Cite Evidence** Using a chart like the one shown, identify two opposing viewpoints that Kennedy anticipates in lines 31–42 and cite Kennedy's counterarguments to those viewpoints.

Opposing Viewpoints	Kennedy's Counterarguments

3. **Draw Conclusions** Reread lines 64–68. How does Kennedy describe the children who might benefit from medical space technology? What might Kennedy be trying to accomplish through his choice of language?

4. **Draw Conclusions** Examine lines 79–88. Describe Kennedy's shift in focus. Why might Kennedy make this shift in his argument?

5. **Cite Evidence**   Examine lines 112–119. Identify phrases that Kennedy repeats. What ideas is he emphasizing with this repetition?

6. **Evaluate** Considering the audience and purpose of Kennedy's speech, is his argument convincing? Do his conclusions arise logically from the reasons and evidence he has cited?

Speaking and Listening

Listen to an audio version of President Kennedy delivering the speech you have just read. How is hearing the speech different from reading it? With a partner or small group, choose two sections of the speech and discuss how the delivery of the speech conveys the meaning of the words.

PERFORMANCE TASK

my WriteSmart

Writing Activity: Research Report
Research a recent or planned space mission for medical research by NASA (National Aeronautics and Space Administration).

- Identify one mission and write a brief description of its purpose and outcome.
- Explain whether or not it is in keeping with Kennedy's views about space research.
- Share your findings with the class.

Critical Vocabulary

metabolism   impairment   impetus   tedious

Practice and Apply   Choose the response that best answers each question. Then discuss with a partner why the other choices are incorrect.

1. If a person's **metabolism** were not functioning properly, what symptom might be present?
   a. toned muscles
   b. labored breathing
   c. tanned skin
   d. shiny hair

2. Which condition would be considered an **impairment**?
   a. sensitive taste buds
   b. a slight limp
   c. 20/20 vision
   d. a photographic memory

3. Which would NOT serve as an **impetus** to study harder?
   a. a chance to play on a team
   b. a mention on the honor roll
   c. a reward from a parent
   d. a speech on physical fitness

4. Which task might be the most **tedious**?
   a. walking your dog
   b. redecorating your room
   c. shopping for groceries
   d. planning a party

Vocabulary Strategy: Using Context Clues

When you encounter an unfamiliar word, look at its **context**—or the surrounding words, phrases, or sentences—to try to understand its meaning. Look at the following example:

> We have a long way to go. Many weeks and months and years of long, *tedious* work lie ahead.

The work described as "tedious" is also described as "long" and lasting for "many weeks and months and years." Work that lasts a very long time has the potential to be difficult, boring, or tiring. Checking the word's meaning in the dictionary confirms that *tedious* means "tiresome" or "boring."

Practice and Apply   Reread Kennedy's speech and find the following words: *host, substantial, impairment, profound*. Look at the surrounding sentences for clues to each word's meaning. Then fill out a chart like the one shown.

Word	Context Clues	Guessed Definitions	Dictionary Definition
host (lines 21–24)			
substantial (lines 31–36)			
impairment (lines 64–68)			
profound (lines 73–78)			

Language Conventions: Capitalization

ELA L.7.2
ELD PI.7.10

In your writing, you will need to apply the rules of capitalization to **proper nouns**—the names of specific people, places, and things—including organizations, historical documents, and events. In the following example, note which proper nouns are capitalized.

> In "Remarks at the Dedication of the Aerospace Medical Health Center," President Kennedy honored the Brooks Air Force Base School of Aerospace Medicine. He also mentioned that Americans demonstrated "mastery of the skies" in World War I, World War II, and the Korean War.

Note that when writing a title, the articles *and* and *the* remain lowercase, as do the prepositions *at* and *of*. The chart below shows three types of proper nouns that require capitalization. When events or organizations are abbreviated, their abbreviations are also capitalized.

Capitalization of Proper Nouns		Abbreviations
Organizations	American Library Association	ALA
	World Health Organization	WHO
Events	World War II	WW II
	Presidents' Day	
Documents	Bill of Rights	
	Declaration of Independence	

Practice and Apply These sentences include proper nouns that lack correct capitalization. In each sentence, indicate which proper nouns should be capitalized. Consult reference materials for terms or titles that are unfamiliar to you.

1. Each January, the President of the United States delivers a speech called the state of the union.

2. Once a year, we observe Martin Luther King Jr. day to celebrate the great civil rights leader.

3. In 1969, Apollo 11 was the first manned space mission to land on the Moon. The details of the mission are preserved in a document called the Apollo 11 flight plan.

4. In 2011, five top scientists were selected by nasa, the national aeronautics and space administration, to investigate discoveries on the planet Mars.

Background *Today, concerns over the ocean environment and potential economic and technological benefits are spurring greater interest in deep-sea exploration.* **Philippe Cousteau** *(b. 1980) is the grandson of Jacques Cousteau, the explorer whose 1960s television show revealed undersea wonders. Philippe Cousteau shares his grandfather's passion for ocean conservation, and he reports regularly on environmental and humanitarian stories from around the world.*

Why Exploring the Ocean Is Mankind's Next Giant Leap

Commentary by Philippe Cousteau

SETTING A PURPOSE As you read, consider whether Philippe Cousteau's reasons for further ocean exploration are valid. Write down any questions you may have while reading.

"Space . . . the final frontier." Not only has this classic phrase dazzled the many millions of fans of the Star Trek franchise, some could argue it has defined a big part of the American ideal for the last 50 years. The 1960s were dominated by the race to the moon and Americans were rightfully proud to be the first nation to make it there.

However, another incredible feat happened in 1960 that is largely forgotten today. For the first time in history, on January 23, 1960, two men, Lt. Don Walsh and Jacques Piccard,
10 descended to the deepest part of the ocean, the bottom of the Challenger Deep in the Mariana Trench located in the western Pacific Ocean. While this feat made international news, the race to the depths of this planet was quickly overshadowed by the race to the moon—and no one has ever gone that deep since.

And for the last 50 years, we have largely continued to look up. But that trend may be changing.

In July 2011, the space shuttle program that had promised to revolutionize space travel by making it (relatively) affordable and accessible came to an end after 30 years. Those three decades provided numerous technological, scientific and **diplomatic** firsts. With an estimated price tag of nearly $200 billion, the program had its champions and its detractors. It was, however, a source of pride for the United States, capturing the American spirit of innovation and leadership.

With the iconic space program ending, many people have asked, "What's next? What is the next giant leap in scientific and technological innovation?"

Today a possible answer to that question has been announced. And it does not entail straining our necks to look skyward. Finally, there is a growing recognition that some of the most important discoveries and opportunities for innovation may lie beneath what covers more than 70 percent of our planet—the ocean.

You may think I'm doing my grandfather Jacques Yves-Cousteau and my father Philippe a disservice when I say we've only dipped our toes in the water when it comes to ocean exploration. After all, my grandfather co-invented the modern SCUBA system and "The Undersea World of Jacques Cousteau" introduced generations to the wonders of the ocean. In the decades since, we've only explored about 10 percent of the ocean—an essential resource and complex environment that literally supports life as we know it, life on earth.

We now have a golden opportunity and a pressing need to recapture that pioneering spirit. A new era of ocean exploration can yield discoveries that will help inform everything from critical medical advances to **sustainable** forms of energy. Consider that AZT, an early treatment for HIV, is derived from a Caribbean reef sponge, or that a great deal of energy—from offshore wind, to OTEC (ocean thermal energy conservation), to wind and wave energy—is yet untapped in our oceans. Like unopened presents under the tree, the ocean is a treasure trove of knowledge. In addition, such discoveries will have a tremendous impact on economic growth by creating jobs as well as technologies and goods.

diplomat
(dĭp´lə-măt´) *n.*
A *diplomat* is a person appointed by a government to interact with other governments.

sustain
(sə-stān´) *v.* If things *sustain*, they remain in existence.

A submersible, a craft designed for deep-sea research, glides just above the ocean floor.

In addition to new discoveries, we also have the opportunity to course correct when it comes to **stewardship** of our oceans. Research and exploration can go hand in glove[1] with resource management and conservation.

Over the last several decades, as the United States has been exploring space, we've **exploited** and polluted our oceans at an alarming rate without dedicating the needed time or resources to truly understand the critical role they play in the future of the planet. It is not trite to say that the oceans are the life support system of this planet, providing us with up to 70 percent of our oxygen, as well as a primary source of protein for billions of people, not to mention the regulation of our climate.

Despite this life-giving role, the world has fished, mined and trafficked the ocean's resources to a point where we are actually seeing dramatic changes that are seriously impacting today's generations. And that impact will continue as the world's population approaches 7 billion people, adding strain to the world's resources unlike any humanity has ever had to face before.

In the long term, destroying our ocean resources is bad business with devastating consequences for the global economy, and the health and sustainability of all

steward
(stoō′ərd) *n.* A *steward* is a person who supervises and manages something.

exploit
(ĕk′sploit′) *v.* If you *exploit* something, you use it selfishly.

60

70

___
[1] **hand in glove:** in close combination with something else.

80 creatures—including humans. Marine spatial planning, marine sanctuaries, species conservation, sustainable fishing strategies, and more must be a part of any ocean exploration and conservation program to provide hope of restoring health to our oceans.

While there is still much to learn and discover through space exploration, we also need to pay attention to our unexplored world here on earth. Our next big leap into the unknown can be every bit as exciting and bold as our pioneering work in space. It possesses the same "wow" factor:
90 alien worlds, dazzling technological feats and the mystery of the unknown. The United States has the scientific muscle, the diplomatic know-how and the entrepreneurial[2] spirit to lead the world in exploring and protecting our ocean frontier.

Now we need the public demand and political will and bravery to take the plunge in order to ensure that the oceans can continue to provide life to future generations.

Today is a big step in that direction and hopefully it is just the beginning.

COLLABORATIVE DISCUSSION What does Philippe Cousteau want you to realize after reading this commentary? What does he want you to do? Is his evidence convincing? Talk about your ideas with other group members.

---

[2] **entrepreneurial** (ŏn´trə-prə-nŏŏr´ē əl): business-starting.

Analyze Structure: Sound Reasoning

Strong arguments use sound reasoning and evidence to support any claims. A carefully constructed written argument includes the following elements:

- **claim:** the writer's position on an issue or problem
- **reasons:** logical statements that explain an action or belief
- **evidence:** facts, examples, quotations, experiences, and other pieces of information that support the claim
- **counterargument:** reasons and evidence given to disprove an opposing viewpoint

An argument may appear to be persuasive, but it may be based on faulty reasoning. A **logical fallacy** is an error in reasoning that often starts with a false assumption or mistaken beliefs. Here are a few logical fallacies:

Logical fallacy	Definition	Example
Circular reasoning	Repeating an idea rather than providing evidence.	I am too tied to my cell phone because I can't put it down.
Either/or fallacy	A statement that suggests there are only two choices available in a situation that really offers more than two options.	Either the city should provide recycling bins or throw out the Recycling Act.
Overgeneralization	A generalization that is too broad.	A ballet dancer would be a natural at gymnastics.

Assess the reasoning in an argument by determining whether

- the argument presents a clear claim
- the reasons make sense and are presented in a logical order
- the evidence is valid and adequately supports the claim
- there are no instances of logical fallacies or faulty reasoning

Determine Meanings

The **tone** of a written work expresses the author's attitude toward his or her subject. For example, the tone can be described as angry, sad, or humorous. An author's choice of words, phrases, and details signal the tone of the work.

This sentence from Philippe Cousteau's commentary includes words that reveal his attitude about ocean exploration:

> **We now have a golden opportunity and a pressing need to recapture that pioneering spirit.**

What words in this sentence show an enthusiastic tone?

Analyzing the Text

ELA RI.7.1, RI.7.2, RI.7.4, RI.7.5, RI.7.8, W.7.7, W.7.8, SL.7.1, SL.7.4
ELD PI.7.3, PI.7.6, PI.7.7, PI.7.8, PI.7.9

Cite Text Evidence   Support your responses with evidence from the text.

1. **Compare** What comparison does the author develop in the first five paragraphs, and what is his purpose?

2. **Interpret** Reread lines 26–34. Which sentence presents the author's claim? Assess the clearness of the claim by restating it in your own words.

3. **Assess Reasoning** Reread lines 45–56. Do the examples of support seem valid? Explain.

4. **Infer** Reread lines 61–84. What is the author's tone? Which words and phrases in the paragraphs reveal that tone?

5. **Analyze** How does the author describe both past events and future events to persuade readers to agree with him?

6. **Evaluate** Examine lines 85–93. How sound is the author's reasoning here? Explain your assessment.

PERFORMANCE TASK

Speaking Activity: Informal Debate
Philippe Cousteau begins by mentioning the 1960 exploration of the Mariana Trench. Would further exploration of this deep-sea region be worthwhile? Divide your group into two teams to informally debate that question.

In an informal debate, speakers from each side take turns presenting and supporting valid claims and countering opposing claims. The whole group can decide on the rules to follow. You may want to use a moderator, for example, and have a time limit for each speaker.

- First, research the Mariana Trench and any attempts to explore it in recent years.
- Investigate the potential for benefits in exploring the region.
- Identify the potential risks involved. Find out if any issues or problems have been reported.
- Listen well to any opponent's points to help you prepare your responses.

Critical Vocabulary

diplomat	sustain	steward	exploit

Practice and Apply Choose the situation that is the better match with the meaning of the vocabulary word. Give your reasons.

1. **diplomat** **a.** Leaders discuss policy with leaders of other countries.
    b. Political leaders are chosen on Election Day.

2. **sustain** **a.** Laws limit the kinds of fish that can be caught.
    b. Fishing boats overfish local fishing stocks.

3. **steward** **a.** The city ignores its local fishing industry.
    b. Citizens rely on their city to clean up polluted areas.

4. **exploit** **a.** Young children attend school for six hours a day.
    b. Young children work long hours in factories.

Vocabulary Strategy: Prefixes

A **prefix** is a word part added before a word or a root. Readers can use their knowledge of prefixes to analyze words and find familiar parts and relationships. This chart shows two common prefixes.

Prefix	Meaning	Example Words
dis-	not, lack of, opposite of	dishonest, disgrace, disinfect, discourage, dispute, distract
ex-	not, out, away from	exchange, exhale, exclude, expose, extract, external

Notice the words with prefixes in this sentence from Cousteau's commentary:

> You may think I'm doing my grandfather Jacques Yves-Cousteau and my father Philippe a disservice when I say we've only dipped our toes in the water when it comes to ocean exploration.

You can see that *disservice* has the prefix *dis-*. A disservice is the opposite of a helpful service. The word *exploration* has the prefix *ex-* before a Latin root; the original meaning of the Latin word is "to search out."

Practice and Apply Complete each word with the prefix *dis-* or *ex-*. Check a print or digital dictionary to make sure the word makes sense.

1. People have always ___**ploited** natural resources.

2. Marine animals that are ___**posed** to pollutants may become ill.

3. Overfishing may cause some fish to become ___**tinct**.

4. There are ___**tinct** actions to take to protect oceans.

Language Conventions: Adjective Clauses

An **adjective** is a part of speech that modifies a noun or a pronoun. It answers the question *What kind? Which?* or *How many?* A **clause** is a group of words that has a subject and a predicate—the two main parts of a complete sentence. An **adjective clause** acts like an adjective to modify a noun or pronoun in the rest of the sentence.

In an adjective clause, the subject is often a **relative pronoun**—a pronoun that relates, or connects, adjective clauses to the words they modify in a sentence. Relative pronouns include *who, whom, whose, which,* and *that.* Notice the relative pronoun in this sentence from "Why Exploring the Ocean Is Mankind's Next Giant Leap":

> However, another incredible feat happened in 1960 that is largely forgotten today.

The relative pronoun *that* introduces the adjective clause *that is largely forgotten today.* The clause modifies the noun *feat,* answering the question *What kind of feat?*

When you write, you can use adjective clauses to tell more about a noun or a pronoun in a sentence. The adjective clause is underlined in each of these sentences.

> Lt. Don Walsh and Jacques Piccard descended to Challenger Deep, <u>which is the deepest part of the ocean</u>. (The adjective clause tells more about *Challenger Deep.*)

> Jacques Piccard, <u>who was a Swiss engineer</u>, developed underwater vehicles. (The adjective clause tells more about *Jacques Piccard.*)

> More people know about the astronauts <u>who traveled to the moon</u> than about these two explorers. (The adjective clause tells more about *astronauts.*)

Practice and Apply Use the relative pronoun in parentheses to introduce an adjective clause that tells about the underlined noun or pronoun. Write the new sentence.

1. <u>Scientists</u> study the ocean. (who)

2. Ocean exploration will be the next giant <u>leap</u>. (that)

3. Discoveries about ocean life will affect <u>everyone</u>. (who)

4. Our pioneering <u>spirit</u> is still strong. (which)

Background *For many years, it was nearly impossible to study life at the bottom of our oceans. Therefore, very little was known about deep-sea habitats. But recent 20th-century technological advances have allowed scientists to begin to discover surprising forms of life in the ocean depths. In her writing,* **Cheryl Bardoe** *likes to draw back the curtain to reveal how scientists explore the unknown. She presently lives in Chicago, Illinois, where she once worked at the city's famous Field Museum of Natural History.*

from
Living in
the Dark

Science Article by Cheryl Bardoe

SETTING A PURPOSE As you read, notice how scientific study has altered past beliefs about Earth's oceans. Write down any questions you have while reading.

When a Whale Falls

Imagine the moment when a great blue whale, undernourished and exhausted from migrating, grunts out its last breath somewhere in the Pacific Ocean.

Then, as the pressure of the surrounding water squeezes the last air reserves from the whale's lungs, this massive creature begins to sink.

It plunges 700 feet (200 meters) through the ocean's top layer, the warm "sunlight zone" where algae kick-start life's food chain with photosynthesis. It drops another 2,600 feet (800 meters) through the cold twilight zone, where no plants live and fish have extra-large eyes to catch the faintest glimmers of sun. It descends down, down, down through 3,300 feet (1 kilometer) or more of the midnight zone. Here, temperatures hover close to freezing; deep-sea creatures must flash their own lights to break the darkness; and the weight of the water feels like about 500 bowling balls pressing in on every square inch of the whale's carcass.

The tiny flecks of dead plankton that are called marine snow may drift for months before reaching the ocean floor. But this great blue whale plummets so quickly that scavengers barely get a nibble. Its 160-ton carcass thumps down nearly intact, depositing as many nutrients as several thousand years' worth of marine snow—all in one fell swoop.

This **cache** of resources, called a whale fall, will become the center of a unique habitat. First, it attracts deep-sea scavengers. Hagfish—unsightly creatures also called slime eels—wriggle inside the carcass and begin to eat it from the inside out. Squat lobsters, sleeper sharks, and crabs tear at the whale's flesh and scatter crumbs into nearby sediments. Then mollusks colonize those sediments. Meanwhile, fantastical worms, slugs, and bacteria bore into the whale's bones to feast on fatty marrow.

Finally come bacteria that transform the chemicals leaking out of the decaying bones into food for themselves and others. Much as plants use energy from the sun to make their own nourishment, these "chemosynthetic" bacteria use energy from chemical reactions to create the basic building blocks of life. Within months this whale carcass may support more than 40,000 creatures; it might keep this chemosynthetic ecosystem going for up to a century.

The living things that take up residence on this whale fall are similar to those that live near undersea **geysers** (called hydrothermal vents) or cracks that leak natural gas into the ocean (called cold seeps). Together, these three habitats have completely changed how scientists think about the basic rules for life.

cache
(kăsh) *n*. A *cache* is an amount of something that has been hidden away.

geyser
(gī´zər) *n*. A *geyser* is a natural hot spring that shoots hot water and steam into the air.

Life Where Life Isn't Possible

For most of human history, the ocean's secrets have been beyond reach. Gazing across the water's rippling surface, who could have guessed what truly lay beneath? In the 1840s, British naturalist Edward Forbes dredged the Aegean Sea[1] 100 times to find out. The deeper his device went, the less it

---

[1] **Aegean Sea** (ĭ-jē´ən sē): an arm of the Mediterranean Sea between Greece and Turkey.

dragged up, and Forbes concluded that nothing at all lived below 1,600 feet (500 meters) deep. This theory fit perfectly with what others had observed on land. If the extreme climates of the Arctic and high mountain peaks snuffed out life, then the cold, dark, deep sea must be empty too.

> 66 **Within months this whale carcass may support more than 40,000 creatures.** 99

Over the next century, people challenged this theory. Corals were hauled up from 2,500 feet (750 meters) deep; starfish and oysters were gathered from 7,500 feet
60 (2,300 meters). One expedition collected 4,700 new species from as deep as 16,000 feet (5,000 meters)—that's more than three miles underwater! Because photosynthesis isn't possible at such depths, scientists decided that marine snow provided the base of the food chain for these animals. Sure, they acknowledged, life was possible in the deep sea. But scientists assumed that life forms living off such scraps would be **meager**. And so they continued to believe that life couldn't survive in the most extreme ocean-floor conditions.
Then everything changed.
70 In 1977, a team of geologists squeezed into the research mini-sub called *Alvin,* hoping to confirm whether geysers (like Old Faithful in Yellowstone National Park) existed on the ocean floor. The hydrothermal vents were there, all right. So was a "Garden of Eden,"[2] as the scientists called it, of mussels, anemones, and 7-foot (2-meter) worms with crimson, feather-like plumes. The stunned researchers gathered samples and called biologists at the Woods Hole Oceanographic Institute (WHOI) in Massachusetts.

meager
(mē´gər) *adj.* If something is *meager,* it is small or deficient in quantity.

---

[2] **Garden of Eden:** the garden that was the first home of Adam and Eve according to the Bible.

On the sea floor, a spider crab, mussels, and worms are revealed by the light of a submersible vehicle.

"It was predicted that vents would exist," explains Santiago
80   Herrera, a biologist currently working at WHOI. "What wasn't predicted was that there would be anything living there." Scientists had found an ecosystem that didn't rely on the sun for energy. Not only that, but its inhabitants were thriving in a place that would be toxic for any other known organism. Ideas about the origins and requirements for life on Earth were suddenly turned upside down.

Hydrothermal Vents

You can often find undersea volcanic activity where Earth's **tectonic** plates are pulling apart. As the planet's crust stretches thin, molten rock breaks through to create new
90   crust. Meanwhile, water soaks into the crust through nearby cracks, dissolving rocks and heating up to temperatures of 660 degrees Fahrenheit (350 degrees Celsius) before rising again through a "chimney" on the ocean floor. When the mineral-rich, super-hot water from the geyser meets the oxygen-rich, frigid water of the deep sea, a chemical reaction is triggered that forms hydrogen sulfide. This smells like rotten eggs and looks like black smoke spewing into the ocean.

tectonic
(tĕk-tŏn´ĭk) *adj.*
If something is *tectonic*, it relates to the deformation of Earth's rocky crust.

©I. MacDonald/National Oceanic And Atmospheric Administration (NOAA)

Scientists now know that some bacteria release energy by breaking down these sulfides spewing from the geysers. These same bacteria then harness that energy to turn carbon dioxide and oxygen from the ocean water into sugars—that is, food energy. Ta-da! Here's the foundation for an entire deep-sea food chain.

These chemosynthetic bacteria may be food for other creatures themselves, or may live in symbiosis[3] with other deep-sea dwellers. The giant tube worms, for example, have no mouths or stomachs, but get their food by hosting billions of bacteria within their bodies. Many clams and mussels living near these vents get their food the same way.

Hydrothermal vents have been a constant source of surprises, ranging from the single-celled microbe that actually lives *inside* a vent (and tolerates temperatures of 250 degrees Fahrenheit, or 120 degrees Celsius) to the white crab with such furry arms that it was dubbed the "yeti crab."

Cold Seeps

Scientists discovered a second type of deep-sea chemosynthetic habitat in 1984. This time, bacteria were breaking down the hydrogen sulfide and methane that oozed from cracks in the ocean floor near Monterey Bay, California. Scientists have since identified three sources for these "cold seep" communities: large deposits of oil or natural gas beneath the seabed; deep trenches created by one tectonic plate sinking below another; and undersea landslides or erosion that expose chemical deposits in the seabed.

Cold seep communities play a major role in shaping Earth's climate, Herrera says. "If they did not exist, a lot of methane would end up in the atmosphere." Without bacteria breaking down methane from the ocean floor, this greenhouse gas[4] would escape from the ocean and make Earth warmer.

Cold seep habitats develop like those at hydrothermal vents do, but with different species. Chemosynthetic bacteria arrive first, forming large white mats on the sea floor. Crabs and shrimp come to scavenge dead bacteria, and mussels arrive that live with symbiotic bacteria. Over time, the

---

[3] **symbiosis** (sĭm´bē-ō´sĭs): a relationship between two living things that benefits both of them.

[4] **greenhouse gas:** a gas in the atmosphere that traps heat.

chemosynthetic bacteria produce a hard material called carbonate, which offers tube worms a firmer ground to grip than the muddy sea floor. Then tube worms build up their hard, protective branches, providing living space for even more organisms.

Whale Bones, Stepping Stones

So far, whales are the only animals we know of that can affect life on the ocean floor the same way shifting tectonic plates do. Besides their hefty size, whales are unique in that fats make up 60 percent of their bone weight. (For comparison, humans are born with almost no fat in their bones.) In life, this bone fat helps whales float and store energy. In death, these fats are **decomposed** by bacteria that give off hydrogen sulfide—sound familiar? Once the chemosynthetic community that lives off these sulfides is in full swing, whale falls host an average of 185 different species—the highest number yet observed in such deep-sea communities.

decompose (dē´kəm-pōz´) *v.* When things *decompose*, they decay and break down into their basic parts.

Whale falls might explain how species travel across vast ocean spaces from one hydrothermal vent or cold seep to the next. "There are specialists in each habitat, but there is also overlap," says Craig Smith, a professor at the University of Hawaii, who discovered the first whale fall in 1987. "Some species may use whale falls as stepping stones."

Smith says that seeing the same kinds of communities at hydrothermal vents, cold seeps, and whale falls shows us how connected the oceans really are. "The connectivity is across widespread spaces from seemingly isolated habitats."

At the Whims of the Waves

Thirty-five years have passed since the discovery of the first hydrothermal vent—but study of the deep sea has really just begun. The main obstacle is getting there.

Fieldwork in the ocean requires tremendous resources. For starters, scientists need a ship and a crew. Reaching a field site may take weeks at sea. Then scientists need high-tech equipment to open a window onto the watery world. Even if everything comes together, success is at the whims of weather and waves. Herrera remembers one expedition where an unmanned, remotely operated vehicle (called an ROV) drifted into the wrong place at the wrong time and was destroyed

The *Alvin* submersible begins its descent under water.

by the ship's propellers. "Every time you put something overboard on a ship," he says, "it's basically a miracle that you get it back."

Under such conditions, scientists must balance the thrill of discovery with persistence and patience. Smith knows what that's like. His team discovered the first whale fall at the tail end of the last *Alvin* dive on a research trip. "Within ten minutes of *Alvin's* return, we knew what we had," he says, "but we had to wait a year to get back and investigate it."

180   Fortunately, improvements in technology are giving scientists more ocean access than ever. In 2010, Herrera sailed to the Coral Triangle, near Indonesia. This is the most diverse marine ecosystem on the planet, and scientists wonder if the deep-sea communities underlying the coral reefs there might be the reason. Herrera was one of only a few scientists on the ship, but video footage of his ROV dives was transmitted to Massachusetts, Maryland, and Washington, plus Canada

and Indonesia. Dozens of scientists worldwide witnessed and discussed the dives as if they were all present on the ship.

190   The goal of this expedition was to explore unseen waters and identify places worth returning to for in-depth research. Scientists saw far more than they expected. Monitoring video from most exploratory dives means watching hours of flat and empty (which is to say, boring) seabed scroll by, hoping to spot something exciting. But on this expedition, Herrera says, "we were never bored because we were constantly seeing amazing species. We suspect this is one of the areas of highest biodiversity[5] on Earth." Scientists will definitely be going back—just as soon as they can find the money to fund

200   another expedition.

To date, scientists have identified more than 1,300 species in deep-sea chemosynthetic habitats. These organisms have introduced us to completely new ways of life and expanded our view of how adaptable life can be. Yet they raise as many questions as they answer. Smith predicts that scientists will find life popping up in even more surprising locations: "We haven't exhausted the list of processes that create these kinds of ecosystems."

The oceans cover 70 percent of Earth's surface, yet less

210   than 5 percent of this resource has been explored. "This is definitely worth investing your whole life to study," Herrera says.

COLLABORATIVE DISCUSSION The author tells how scientists react to evidence that challenges ideas they had long accepted as possibilities. How have scientists reacted to the discoveries of deep-sea habitats? Talk about your ideas with other group members.

---

[5] **biodiversity:** the range of living things within an environment.

Analyze Structure

ELA RI.7.3, RI.7.5
ELD PI.7.6, PII.7.1

Science writing usually presents relationships between events or ideas. Events can show **cause-and-effect relationships,** in which one event brings about, or causes, the other. The event that happens first is the **cause;** the one that follows is the **effect.**

Readers of science writing can grasp cause-and-effect relationships by thinking about what happens and why. One of the main clues readers can look for are **signal words.** Words or phrases that signal causes are *due to, because of,* or *since.* Words or phrases that signal effects are *as a result, therefore,* and *led to.* Sometimes the cause-and-effect relationship is not obvious, and readers must look deeper for **implied** causes and effects. This involves making inferences based on clues in the text.

Organizing information into a chart can help you to connect causes and effects. This chart shows a cause-and-effect chain based on ideas in the section "Cold Seeps" of the excerpt from "Living in the Dark."

Cause	Effect	Effect	Effect
cold seep communities form	bacteria break down hydrogen sulfide and methane	methane can't escape from ocean floor	potential global warming is reduced

Reread lines 1–13 from the section "When a Whale Falls." Organize the information into a chart that shows a cause-and-effect chain.

Determine Central Ideas and Details

ELA RI.7.2, RI.7.3
ELD PI.7.6

Paraphrasing is the restating of information in your own words. When you read science texts, you may encounter complex ideas and new vocabulary. To check your understanding, use paraphrasing to restate the language in the text. For example, reread lines 33–40 of the excerpt from "Living in the Dark." Then read this paraphrase of the sentence comparing green plants and deep-sea bacteria:

> **Plants make their own food using the sun's energy, but these "chemosynthetic" bacteria use chemical energy to make food.**

Look back at lines 33–40 again. Tell what a "chemosynthetic ecosystem" is in your own words.

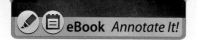
Analyzing the Text

ELA RI.7.1, RI.7.2, RI.7.3, RI.7.5, RI.7.6, W.7.1, W.7.4, W.7.8, W.7.10
ELD PI.7.6, PI.7.10, PI.7.11, PII.7.1

Cite Text Evidence   Support your responses with evidence from the text.

1. **Cause-Effect** What are the major effects of a giant whale's death on ocean life?

2. **Cause-Effect** Reread lines 87–97. Note the cause-and-effect connections in that paragraph. Paraphrase the information in the form of a chart that shows the cause-and-effect chain. Label the first box as "Cause" and complete it with this entry:
   Water soaks into cracks in Earth's stretched crust.

3. **Compare** What are the three types of habitats described in this article, and how are they alike?

4. **Interpret** Reread lines 104–109. How would you paraphrase the information in the first sentence of this paragraph?

5. **Cite Evidence** Reread lines 79–86 from the section "Life Where Life Isn't Possible." What ideas were "suddenly turned upside down," and why?

6. **Evaluate** Why might the author have decided to end the article using the scientist's quotation?

PERFORMANCE TASK

Writing Activity: Argument
Think about Santiago Herrera's statement at the end of the excerpt from "Living in the Dark." Why does he have that opinion? Why might someone else have a different opinion? Do you agree with Herrera's statement? Use your answers to those questions to write a one- to three-paragraph argument.

- In your introduction, state your opinion, or claim, clearly.
- In the rest of the essay, present valid reasons for your opinion and support them with evidence from the text and other sources that you can rely on.
- Try to present and refute one counterargument to your claim.

Critical Vocabulary

cache   geyser   meager   tectonic   decompose

Practice and Apply Complete each sentence to show that you understand the meaning of the vocabulary word.

1. It's wise to keep a **cache** of . . .

2. Scientists study **geysers** to learn . . .

3. If you ate a **meager** meal, you . . .

4. Everywhere on Earth, **tectonic** . . .

5. Bacteria will **decompose** . . .

Vocabulary Strategy: Greek Roots

A **root** is a word part that came into English from an older language. You can check a print or digital dictionary to learn about roots; the entry for a word often gives details about the word's origin. Roots from ancient Greek are often called **combining forms** because they are combined to form words, especially terms in science and technology.

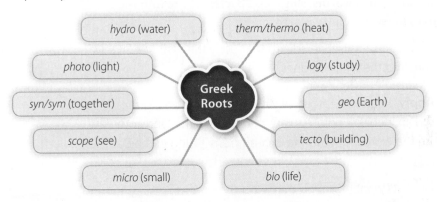

In the excerpt from "Living in the Dark," you read about Earth's tectonic plates. What do tectonic plates have to do with the meaning of the Greek root *tecto*, "building"? The movements of the plates are responsible for building continents, mountains, and oceans.

Practice and Apply Read each phrase and identify the word made from Greek combining forms. Refer to the chart for the root's meaning. Then define the phrase. Use a print or digital dictionary to check your ideas.

1. hydrothermal vents

2. photosynthesis in green plants

3. microscopic organisms

4. symbiotic bacteria

5. hydrogeological events

Language Conventions: Verbal Phrases

A **verbal** is a verb form that is used as a noun, an adjective, or an adverb. An **infinitive** is a verbal that begins with *to* and has the base form of a verb. The infinitive is underlined in each of these sentences.

- Our plan is <u>to sail</u>. (The infinitive acts like a noun and tells what *our plan* is.)
- There may be whales <u>to photograph</u>. (The infinitive acts like an adjective to modify *whales* and tell *what kind*.)
- <u>To breathe</u>, whales come to the surface. (The infinitive acts like an adverb to modify *come* and tell *why*.)

A **verbal phrase** is made of a verbal and any other words that complete its meaning. The **infinitive phrase** is underlined in each of these sentences. The whole phrase in each sentence acts the same way as the infinitive alone.

- Our plan is <u>to sail tomorrow</u>.
- There may be whales <u>to photograph from the boat</u>.
- <u>To breathe the air they need</u>, whales come to the surface.

Note the infinitive phrase in this sentence from "Living in the Dark":

Meanwhile, fantastical worms, slugs, and bacteria bore into the whale's bones <u>to feast on fatty marrow</u>.

The infinitive phrase acts like an adverb to modify the verb *bore*. It tells why bacteria bore into the whale's bones.

Practice and Apply Read each group of words and the question in parentheses. Add an infinitive phrase to answer the question and complete a sentence using the words. Refer to the excerpt from "Living in the Dark" for ideas to include.

1. deep-sea scientists want (What do they want?)

2. fish of the deep sea have extra-large eyes (Why do they have such eyes?)

3. crabs and shrimp come to the ocean floor (Why do they come?)

4. scientists need equipment (What kind of equipment?)

5. the goal of a deep-sea expedition (What is the goal?)

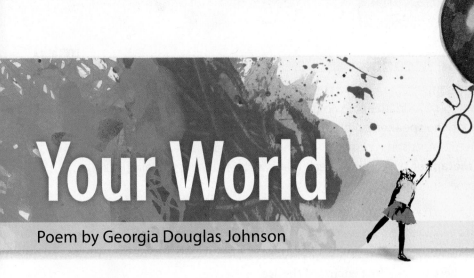

Your World

Poem by Georgia Douglas Johnson

Georgia Douglas Johnson (1880–1966) *was one of the most famous African American women writers of the early 1900s. She is associated with the Harlem Renaissance—an African American literary and cultural movement of the 1920s and 1930s. Johnson wrote four volumes of poetry as well as plays and fiction.*

SETTING A PURPOSE Sometimes a poem contains a message designed to inspire. As you read, consider the poet's message and how it may inspire others to take risks.

Your world is as big as you make it
I know, for I used to abide
In the narrowest nest in a corner
My wings pressing close to my side.

5 But I sighted the distant horizon
Where the sky-line encircled the sea
And I throbbed with a burning desire
To travel this immensity.

I battered the cordons¹ around me
10 And cradled my wings on the breeze
Then soared to the uttermost reaches
With rapture, with power, with ease!

COLLABORATIVE DISCUSSION In what ways does this poem teach a lesson about risk-taking? Share your ideas with other group members.

---

¹ **cordons** (kôr´dnz): lines or borders stretched around an area, indicating that access is restricted.

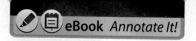

Determine Meanings

ELA RL.7.4
ELD PI.7.8

In the poem "Your World," the poet conveys a comparison of two unlike things through the **speaker,** or the voice that "talks" to the reader. Because this figurative comparison is carried through the entire poem, it is called an **extended metaphor,** a figure of speech that compares two essentially unlike things at some length and in several ways.

The poet also uses **imagery,** words and phrases that appeal to the senses, to engage the reader and develop the extended metaphor. In these two lines, the descriptions encourage readers to use their senses:

line 6: **Where the sky-line encircled the sea**
line 10: **And cradled my wings on the breeze**

Look back at the poem. Find additional examples of imagery and lines that give clues about the extended metaphor.

Analyzing the Text

ELA RL.7.1, RL.7.2, RL.7.4, W.7.2, W.7.9a
ELD PI.7.6, PI.7.8, PI.7.10

Cite Text Evidence   Support your responses with evidence from the text.

1. **Interpret** What words in the second stanza appeal to the senses?

2. **Interpret** What does the speaker mean when she says, "I battered the cordons around me"?

3. **Compare** Through the extended metaphor, what comparison does the poet make?

4. **Draw Conclusions** A poem's **theme** is a message about life or human nature that the poet shares with the reader. What is the theme of "Your World"?

PERFORMANCE TASK

Writing Activity: Analysis Think about the extended metaphor in this poem. Write at least one paragraph analyzing the extended metaphor. These questions may help you organize your thoughts and writing:

- What words and phrases show the comparison throughout the poem?
- Why might the poet have chosen this comparison?
- What feelings are suggested by the comparison?

COLLECTION **4**
PERFORMANCE TASK

Present an Argument

Persuasive speeches such as John F. Kennedy's "Remarks at the Dedication of the Aerospace Medical Health Center" can have powerful effects. In the following activity, you will draw from Kennedy's speech and other texts to prepare and present an argument. You will try to persuade others whether major exploration is worth the risk.

ELA W.7.1a–e, W.7.7, W.7.8, W.7.10, SL.7.4, SL.7.4a, SL.7.5, SL.7.6
ELD PI.7.4, PI.7.9, PI.7.11, PI.7.12, PII.7.1, PII.7.2

A successful argument

- contains an engaging introduction that establishes the claim
- supports key points with reasoning and relevant evidence pulled from a variety of solid, credible sources
- uses language that effectively conveys ideas and adds interest
- concludes by forcefully summing up the claim

Visit hmhfyi.com to explore your topic and enhance your research.

PLAN

myNotebook

Use the annotation tools in your eBook to find evidence that supports your claim. Save each piece of evidence to your notebook.

Choose Your Position Think about the texts you read in this collection and the various points made by the writers concerning risk and exploration. Then choose a position either for or against major exploration based on the risks involved, and write out your claim in a statement.

Gather Information Focus on the selection(s) that have information you can cite to support your position. Jot down important details that support your claim. Consider the following:

- What are your reasons for taking the position you took?
- What evidence can you use as quotes to support your claim?
- What might others say to oppose your claim? How would you try to convince them to agree with you?
- What do you want your audience to understand?

ACADEMIC VOCABULARY

As you plan and present your speech, be sure to use the academic vocabulary words.

complex
potential
rely
stress
valid

Do Further Research Research additional print and digital sources to find solid, credible evidence for your argument.

- Search for facts, quotes, and statistics that support your claim.
- Try to find sources that don't agree with you. Develop a counterargument to address an opposing view.

Organize Your Ideas Think about how you will organize your speech. This can help you to present your ideas coherently.

Mentor Text Read this passage from President Kennedy's speech, which shows how word choices can engage the audience.

Interactive Lessons
For help in incorporating evidence, use:
- Writing Arguments: Creating a Coherent Argument
- Writing Arguments: Persuasive Techniques

> " It is an era which calls for action and for the best efforts of all those who would test the unknown and the uncertain in every phase of human endeavor. It is a time for pathfinders and pioneers. "

PRODUCE

Draft Your Argument Use the information you have gathered to help you write your argument.

- Introduce your claim. Begin with an attention-grabbing comment or an unusual or funny quote, statistic, or story.
- Organize your reasons and evidence logically. For example, will it work better to start with your weakest or strongest argument?
- Be sure to include quotes and other data from your sources.
- Use words and phrases such as *because, therefore,* and *for that reason* to make your argument clearer and more cohesive.
- Conclude your argument. Summarize your main points in a restatement, and connect them to your introduction.

✓ myWriteSmart

Write your rough draft in *my*WriteSmart. Focus on getting your ideas down, rather than perfecting your choice of language.

Language Conventions: Using Pronouns for Cohesion

Cohesive writing flows smoothly from one sentence to another. Using pronouns is a cohesive way to avoid unnecessary repetition. Read the following quotation from the speech "Remarks at the Dedication of the Aerospace Medical Health Center."

> " For this city has long been the home of the pioneers in the air. It was here that Sidney Brooks, whose memory we honor today, was born and raised. "

Notice how the pronoun *It* refers to the noun *city*, in the first sentence. This helps to connect an idea in one sentence to an idea in another.

Prepare Visuals Select multimedia resources to create charts, graphs, or pictures that clarify and strengthen your claim. Make sure that all visuals are large enough to be read easily.

REVISE

Practice Your Argument Present your argument aloud. Try speaking in front of a mirror, or make a recording of your presentation and listen to it. Then practice with a partner.

Evaluate Your Argument Work with your partner to determine whether your argument is effective.

Have your partner or a group of peers review your draft in *my*WriteSmart. Ask your reviewers to note any reasons that do not support the claim or lack sufficient evidence.

Interactive Lessons

For help in practicing your delivery, use:
• Giving a Presentation: Delivering a Presentation

Questions	Tips	Revision Techniques
Did I clearly state my claim?	**Highlight** the claim.	**Revise** the existing claim to make your position more clear.
Is my claim supported logically?	**Underline** the reasons. **Highlight** your evidence.	**Add** more reasons, if your argument lacks support. **Replace** weak evidence with stronger examples, facts, or quotes.
Is the style of my argument formal enough?	**Underline** any use of informal language, such as contractions.	**Focus** on specific words to improve. **Write** out any contractions to sound more precise.
Is my response to an opposing claim understandable?	**Highlight** any counterarguments. **Note** the wording of your response.	**Use** transitions to set off your counterargument from an opposing claim.
Does the conclusion have a strong restatement?	**Underline** the conclusion.	**Add** a restatement of the claim, if needed, to clarify. **Make** your point forcefully.

PRESENT

Deliver Your Speech Finalize your argument and present it to the class.

PERFORMANCE TASK RUBRIC
ARGUMENT

	Ideas and Evidence	Organization	Language
4	• The introduction grabs the audience's attention; the claim clearly states the speaker's position on an issue. • Logical reasons and relevant evidence support the claim. • Opposing claims are anticipated and effectively addressed with counterarguments. • The concluding section effectively summarizes the claim.	• The reasons and evidence are organized logically and consistently throughout the speech. • Transitions logically connect reasons and evidence to the presenter's claim.	• The speech reflects a formal style. • Sentence beginnings, lengths, and structures vary and have a rhythmic flow. • Sentences show cohesion through the use of pronouns to avoid repetition of nouns. • Grammar, usage, and mechanics are correct.
3	• The introduction could do more to grab the audience's attention; the speaker's claim states a position on an issue. • Most reasons and evidence support the speaker's claim, but they could be more convincing. • Opposing claims are anticipated, but counterarguments need to be developed more. • The concluding section restates the claim.	• The organization of key reasons and supporting evidence is logical in some places. • A few more transitions are needed to clarify the relationships between ideas.	• The style becomes informal in a few places. • Sentence beginnings, lengths, and structures vary somewhat. • Could use more pronouns to avoid wordiness in sentences and improve cohesion. • Some grammatical and usage errors are present.
2	• The introduction does not grab the audience's attention; the speaker's claim identifies an issue, but the position is not clearly stated. • The reasons and evidence are not always logical or relevant. • Opposing claims are anticipated but not addressed logically. • The concluding section includes an incomplete summary of the claim.	• The organization of reasons and evidence is confusing in some places, and it often doesn't follow a pattern. • Several more transitions are needed to connect reasons and evidence to the presenter's claim.	• The style becomes informal in several places. • Sentence structures rarely vary, and some fragments or run-on sentences are present. • Sentences lack cohesion. • Grammar and usage are incorrect in several places, but the speaker's ideas are still clear.
1	• The introduction is confusing. • Supporting reasons and evidence are missing. • Opposing claims are neither anticipated nor addressed. • The concluding section is missing.	• A logical organization is not used; reasons and evidence are presented randomly. • Transitions are not used, making the speech difficult to understand.	• The style is inappropriate for the speech. • Repetitive sentence structure, fragments, and run-on sentences make the speech hard to follow. • Several grammatical and usage errors change the meaning of ideas.

The Stuff of Consumer Culture

"We live much of our lives in a realm I call the *buyosphere.*"

—Thomas Hine

The Stuff of Consumer Culture

In this collection, you will take a look at our consumer culture and consider the question: How much is enough?

Stream to Start

hmhfyi.com

Channel One News®

COLLECTION

PERFORMANCE TASK Preview

At the end of this collection, you will research and write an informative essay about consumerism, using information from the selections in the collection as your starting point. Then you will create a multimedia presentation of your essay to share with others.

ACADEMIC VOCABULARY

Study the words and their definitions in the chart below. You will use these words as you discuss and write about the texts in this collection.

Word	Definition	Related Forms
attitude (ăt´ĭ-tōōd´) *n.*	a way of thinking or feeling about something or someone	attitudes, attitudinal, attitudinize
consume (kən-sōōm´) *v.*	to buy things for your own use or ownership	consumed, consumer, consumer good, consuming, consumption
goal (gōl) *n.*	the object toward which your work and planning is directed; a purpose	goals
purchase (pûr´chĭs) *v.*	to buy	purchasable, purchaser, purchasing, purchasing power
technology (tĕk-nŏl´ə-jē) *n.*	the application of science and engineering as part of a commercial or industrial undertaking	technologic, technological, technologist

Background *It's hard to imagine, but less than 100 years ago, television as we know it didn't exist. Then in 1927, Philo T. Farnsworth successfully transmitted an image onto a remote screen. By the early 1950s, TV purchases skyrocketed. Today almost every home in the United States has at least one. This excerpt from* Life at Home in the Twenty-First Century *describes what a team of archaeologists uncovered about TVs when they examined the daily lives of 32 California families.*

from

LIFE at HOME in the TWENTY-FIRST CENTURY

Informational Text by Jeanne E. Arnold

SETTING A PURPOSE Perhaps no other technology is more widely shared as the television. As you read, keep track of how the popularity of this consumer good has changed over time. How will archaeologists of the future track its significance? Write down any questions you have while reading.

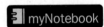
myNotebook

As you read, mark up the text. Save your work to *my*Notebook.

- Highlight details
- Add notes and questions
- Add new words to *my*WordList

Television and Daily Life

In North America, and in as few as three generations, mass media broadcast by analog and digital signal has all but replaced oral history and become the primary conveyor of culturally shared ideas. Broadcast communication, particularly television-streamed content, figures so prominently in economic decisions, political outcomes, and moral reasoning that even at the height of the last U.S. recession, TV advertising expenditures exceeded $50 billion.

10   Television is now so intricately woven into the fabric of the American family experience that few children born during the last two decades will be able to imagine a social world that

has not been partly shaped by the imagery, discourse, and ideas originating from television programming. In fact, many twenty-first century children are born in the physical presence of a TV: most labor, delivery, and recovery rooms in the U.S. now feature large, wall-mounted flat-panel sets. That TVs are witness to such intimate and emotionally bonding experiences speaks volumes about televisions and the American way of being.

20   Currently, 99 percent of U.S. households own a TV, and more than 50 percent own three or more. All of the families in our study have at least one TV, and most have two or more. One set is typically located in a large space used by all family members, such as the living room, family room, or den. The set used by the collective is a compelling example of an object that is not merely a tangible product of otherwise invisible cultural forces but rather an agentive[1] participant in the daily production of social lives. The introduction of a new TV to a living room, for example, shapes the decisions underlying
30   where we locate our furniture, where we direct our gaze, and how we orient our bodies.

At some deeper cognitive level, our relationship to the TV—which includes a relationship to the object itself but also our personal experiences centering on TV media— even shapes the ways that we relate to our built spaces. Our photographs of living room assemblages[2] repeatedly reveal spaces organized around televisions rather than spaces with other primary affordances, such as face-to-face conversation. For all of its influence on the design and organization of
40   space, the TV may as well be a hearth,[3] which until quite recently in human history exerted the most influence on the spatial distribution of social interactions and activities inside homes. Indeed, families often locate the TV immediately adjacent to a wood-burning stove or fireplace, and new homes feature recessed fireplace-like nooks designed for television sets. The TV has ascended to the rank of essential major appliance (alongside the refrigerator, clothes washer, and dryer) around which builders and architects imagine the designs of residential spaces.

---

[1] **agentive:** having the power to cause an effect.
[2] **assemblages:** collections of people or things.
[3] **hearth:** the brick or cement floor of a fireplace that extends into a room.

LOS ANGELES HOUSEHOLDS AND TV OWNERSHIP

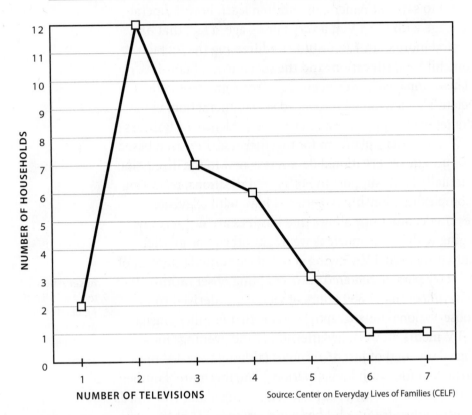

NUMBER OF HOUSEHOLDS

NUMBER OF TELEVISIONS

Source: Center on Everyday Lives of Families (CELF)

This graph is based on data about TV ownership among 32 California families. The data was gathered by researchers from the University of California, Los Angeles (UCLA), and Connecticut College.

50   Families now also routinely equip various bedrooms with televisions. Fully 25 of the 32 CELF[4] families (78 percent) have a TV in the parents' bedroom, and 14 families (47 percent) place a TV in one or more of the bedrooms used by children. Researchers at the Kaiser Family Foundation surveyed 1,051 U.S. households with young children and found that 43 percent place a TV in at least one child's bedroom.

The same Kaiser-funded project reveals that 87 percent of children age four to six years are able to turn on the TV without assistance. Most two- and three-year-olds can do the

---

[4] **CELF:** the Center on the Everyday Lives of Families at the University of California at Los Angeles, which studies how families approach the challenges of everyday life.

60 same (82 percent), and the majority of children belonging
to both age groups are capable of changing the channel.
Suffice it to say that American children learn how to operate
and engage with the TV at a very young age, a fact that has
motivated more than 4,000 studies addressing the impacts of
TV on children, education, and the social lives of families.

These impacts, however, are debated. Some researchers
associate TV viewing with reduced social interaction, while
others report the opposite and even see evidence for families'
use of TV time as a platform for togetherness. Research based
70 on our unique observational data sets is new to the discussion
and actually lends support to both generalizations, reflecting
the complex relationship Americans have with television.
For example, our study shows that families are not actively
engaging with TV as much as we might otherwise predict.
Attentive, focused TV viewing accounts for only 11 percent of
all primary person-centered scan sampling **observations**, and
the careful coding of 380 hours of videotape (derived from
our observational videography) reveals that families engage
with TV media on weekday afternoons and evenings for an
80 average daily total of just 46 minutes (although the TV may
be turned on for much longer periods). Furthermore, families'
viewing is usually a social experience: during about two-thirds
of observations where a child or adult watches TV, at least one
other family member is present.

However, children are slightly more likely than their
parents to watch TV alone. Kids view solo in about 17 percent
of the cases where we record TV viewing as the primary
activity, mothers and fathers watch alone in only 6 percent
and 13 percent of the cases, respectively. We also found that
90 children much more frequently watch TV in a bedroom
(34 percent of primary TV observations, alone or with
others) than either of their parents (9 percent for mothers and
10 percent for fathers). Indeed, the socially isolating potential
of TV appears higher among families that have more than one
TV set in the home. Children in families that have TVs in one
or more bedroom spaces are more likely to watch TV alone
than children in families that do not have a TV in a child's or
parents' bedroom.

observation
(ŏb´zər-vā´shən) *n.*
An *observation* is
the act of watching
something.

> ## *Some researchers associate TV viewing with reduced social interaction.*

The Material Legacy of TV

The **proliferation** of video media technology since the debut of network television in 1946 has had a profound influence on American lifestyles. Indeed, few Americans can imagine everyday life without access to TV. Television is so entrenched in popular culture that we are surprised when we meet people who do not have at least one set. In 1947, U.S. households owned 44,000 TVs, just one set per 3,275 people. During the early 2000s, people purchased about 31 million TVs annually in the U.S., or one new TV for every nine Americans each year.

Of course, sales figures do not reflect the number of sets already found in what archaeologists regard as systemic context (here, the home): the behavioral system in which artifacts[5] participate in everyday life. The full inventory of TVs emerges only when the count includes the sets purchased in years past and still in the house. Only some older TVs are replaced. As is true for most artifacts, the life history of each individual television is entangled in the changing ways that families use them, the availability of similar artifacts in the home, and the desire for newer forms of visual media technologies.

Eventually the life history of a TV, or at least the portion of the life history that overlaps with family use, comes to an end. At that point, the artifact exits the systemic context and enters an archaeological context, a state in which interaction is primarily with the natural environment, such as the city dump. The Environmental Protection Agency estimates that

proliferation
(prə-lǐf´ər-rā´shən) *n.*
A *proliferation* is the fast growth of something.

---

[5] **artifacts:** objects made by humans.

during the mid-2000s, Americans discarded an average of 1.5 billion pounds of TVs each year, in the range of 25 to 27 million sets annually, of which only 4 to 4.5 million were collected for domestic recycling.

An Archaeology of TVs

130 The rate at which TV technology evolves and the sheer volume of television sets people discard both suggest that this artifact will be particularly useful for teasing out discrete generations of household refuse from the materially complex and jumbled strata[6] that constitute our **municipal** landfills. Archaeologists rely on seriation—the sequencing of functionally similar artifacts based on stylistic differences—as a method for ascertaining relative chronology[7] at archaeological sites. Although seriation cannot be used to pinpoint a specific date, it places older and younger materials in order based

140 on the simple assumption that object styles change over time. Frequency seriation thus determines the relative age of each layer.

We expect 1980s-era landfill strata to contain high proportions of black-and-white TVs and color CRT TV sets, but very low proportions of rear-projection TVs and no flat panels. Garbage layers forming today will contain few black-and-white sets, numerous color CRT sets, and (assuming a continued low rate of recycling) an increasing number of flat panels, assuming that household disposal of any particular

150 TV may postdate its purchase by a decade or more.

Archaeologists often use battleship curves to depict frequency seriation patterns. These graphs are particularly useful for showing changes in the proportion of different technological styles of artifacts over time. Interpretation of the curves is straightforward: the width of a horizontal bar for each year represents a percentage of a total count (see right axis opposite). In 1990, for example, 22.6 million TVs were purchased in the U.S. Only 6 percent were black-and-white sets, whereas 46 percent were color CRT models

160 less than 19 inches in size and another 46 percent were large color CRT models. Just 2 percent were the new rear-projection models, and flat panels had not yet debuted.

municipal
(myōō-nĭs´ə-pəl) *adj.*
If something is *municipal*, it relates to a city or town.

---

[6] **strata:** layers.
[7] **chronology** (krə-nŏl´ə-jē): the order of events in time.

DISPOSAL RATE OF TELEVISIONS

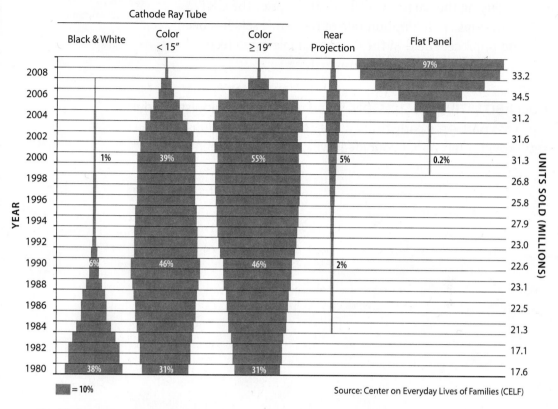

= 10%

Source: Center on Everyday Lives of Families (CELF)

This battleship curve is a graphic aid used by archaeologists to record an artifact's patterns of use across a period of time. Here, the battleship curve indicates periods of popularity and fading use of different styles of TVs.

The shape of each battleship curve is particularly telling, providing an at-a-glance account of changes in the popularity of an artifact style or type over the course of its history. After the artifact's introduction, curves typically become gradually wider as the artifact style becomes more popular. As newer styles enter the material system, the first curve **tapers** and eventually terminates altogether. The maximum widths and rates of tapering (in both directions) summarize the popularity, rapidity of change in preference or supply, and persistence through time.

In the complex story of U.S. television consumption, several well-defined patterns emerge. Black-and-white TV sets persisted until the early 2000s, long after color CRT sets began dominating household assemblages, and rear-projection units enjoyed a long lifespan but never gained popularity. When

taper
(tā´pər) *v.* When things *taper*, they gradually get thinner.

170

significantly better TV technology emerged in the form of flat-panel models, color CRT models declined **precipitously**, producing the narrow profiles at the tops of the CRT battleships. The adoption rate of flat-panel sets has been steep and unprecedented in the domain of television technology, expanding as CRT use plummeted.

precipitous
(prĭ-sĭp´ĭ-təs) *adj.*
When something is *precipitous*, it is very steep, like a cliff.

COLLABORATIVE DISCUSSION When future archaeologists study life in the past—the early twenty-first century—what clues will TV sets provide? Talk about your ideas with other group members.

Analyze Structure: Cause and Effect

ELA RI.7.2, RI.7.5
ELD PI.7.6, PII.7.1

The **structure** of a text is the way it is put together. Authors of informational texts organize their central ideas in paragraphs, and may organize the paragraphs in sections with **headings.** Within the sections, you can identify **patterns of organization,** a particular arrangement of ideas and information. For example, a **cause-and-effect** pattern of organization shows one or more events (causes) leading to one or more other events (effects).

This chart shows a single cause leading to multiple effects, based on details in the first four paragraphs of the section "Television and Daily Life" in the informational text you've just read.

> **CAUSE:** There is at least one TV in 99 percent of U.S. households.

| **EFFECT:** Media broadcast is the main conveyor of culturally shared ideas. | **EFFECT:** Living spaces are organized and designed around a TV set. | **EFFECT:** Oral history and face-to-face conversation are reduced. |

Restate one of these cause-and-effect connections, using the phrase *as a result.*

Cite Evidence

ELA RI.7.1, RI.7.2
ELD PI.7.6

Graphic aids are diagrams, graphs, maps, and other visual tools that are printed, handwritten, or drawn. In informational texts, graphic aids organize, simplify, and summarize information. Here are a few types of graphic aids:

- Line graphs show numerical quantities across time and can indicate trends. The **vertical axis** of a graph indicates frequency. The **horizontal axis** shows the categories being considered.
- Bar graphs use horizontal and vertical bars to show or compare categories of information.
- Picture graphs convey information through symbols instead of lines and bars.

As you read, you can use evidence from both the text and the graphic aids to **draw a conclusion**—make a judgment based on evidence and reasoning.

Reread lines 157–162. Examine the graph on page 227. What conclusion can you draw from the text and the graph about flat-panel TV sets?

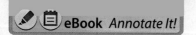

ELA RI.7.1, RI.7.2, RI.7.5,
W.7.2, W.7.7, W.7.8
ELD PI.7.2, PI.7.6,
PI.7.10, PII.7.1

Analyzing the Text

Cite Text Evidence Support your responses with evidence from the text.

1. **Cite Evidence** Reread the first paragraph. What causes more than $50 billion of TV advertising expenditures?

2. **Infer** What information about American families were the archaeologists gathering?

3. **Compare** Reread lines 39–46. According to the author, in what ways is a TV like a hearth?

4. **Summarize** Reread lines 66–99. What are the most important findings in this study of the impacts of TV?

5. **Infer** According to the details in "The Material Legacy of TV" section, during the mid-2000s, 25–27 million American-owned sets were discarded, but only 4–4.5 million were collected in domestic recycling. What might these figures suggest about the purchasing habits of American consumers?

6. **Analyzing Graphics** Of the 32 households represented in the graph on page 223, what number of households own only two TVs? What makes that figure worth noting?

7. **Predict** Look at the graph of battleship curves. How do you think the graph might change in the years ahead?

8. **Draw Conclusions** What do archaeologists look for as they study artifacts, and what does TV have to do with artifacts?

PERFORMANCE TASK

Writing Activity: Informative Essay You've just read that a number of different types of televisions have been available through the years. Find out about a new development in TV technology and write about it in a brief informational essay.

- Use digital or print sources about consumer electronics to research your topic.
- Take notes as you try to answer questions like: Who invented this technology and when? How does it work? How could it change how people watch TVs? Why would consumers want to purchase it?

- Use your notes to create an outline of your ideas.
- Share your completed essay with a partner or group that has written about other new features of TVs. Discuss the different features and consumers' attitudes toward them.

Critical Vocabulary

ELA RI.7.4, L.7.6
ELD PI.7.6, PI.7.12

observation   proliferation   municipal

taper   precipitous

Practice and Apply Complete each sentence to show that you understand the meaning of the bold word.

1. The scientist counted each **observation** of . . .

2. We've recently had a **proliferation** of . . .

3. An example of a **municipal** service is . . .

4. To draw lines that **taper,** you . . .

5. A change that occurs in a **precipitous** way is . . .

Vocabulary Strategy: Domain-Specific Words

The subject areas of *Life at Home in the Twenty-First Century* are sociology and archaeology. Sociology is the study of human societies. Archaeology is the study of the things left behind by past societies. When you read about any area of study, you will encounter **technical language,** terms and phrases used by specialists in a certain field or domain. Note the term *social interactions* in this quotation:

> For all of its influence on the design and organization of space, the TV may as well be a hearth, which until quite recently in human history exerted the most influence on the spatial distribution of *social interactions* and activities inside homes.

One way to figure out the meaning is by looking at its two parts: *social* has something to do with living with other people; *interactions* are the ways people communicate with each other. But often with technical language, you need to use a print or digital dictionary to confirm the meaning. For more highly specialized terms, you might have to use resources specific to the field, such as a manual of nautical terms for language about sailing.

Practice and Apply Compare your ideas with other group members as you find and define these terms: *observational data sets* (line 70); *observations* (line 76); *systemic context* (lines 110–111).

Language Conventions: Eliminate Redundancy

When you write to inform and explain, your goal is to be clear and concise. Watch out for **redundancy,** the use of unnecessary words. Reread your sentences to make sure that every word has a purpose.

This list shows common redundancies; the unnecessary words are underlined.

> - each <u>and every</u> person
> - never before <u>in the past</u>
> - the <u>true</u> facts
> - may <u>possibly</u> exist
>
> - big <u>in size</u>
> - prepared <u>in advance</u>
> - <u>entirely</u> complete
> - connect <u>together</u>

Avoid using words that repeat what you've already said. Compare these two sentences:

> **Television has an impact on our behaviors and actions, affecting everything from what we purchase to what we talk about in our conversations.**

> **Television has an impact on our behaviors, from what we purchase to what we talk about.**

You can tell that the second sentence is stronger because it makes its point in fewer words. In the first sentence, *behaviors* and *actions* are synonyms; *impact* and *affecting* express the same meaning; and *in our conversations* repeats the meaning of *what we talk about.*

Practice and Apply Rewrite each sentence to eliminate the redundancy.

1. Television sets are now essential items in our homes, as basic to our living spaces as refrigerators, stoves, and other necessary appliances.

2. Most American toddlers can turn on the TV without assistance or help from an adult and are also capable of changing a channel from one to another.

3. Although many people hold the belief and opinion that watching TV is a solitary activity, some researchers have evidence that families use the time in front of a TV as a way of spending time together.

4. The TV sets that we discard are enormous in number and will surely provide clues about how we live to archaeologists of the future looking back into the past.

Background *A writer on history, culture, and design,* **Thomas Hine** *coined the word* populuxe *as the title of his first book. The word has become commonly used to describe the enthusiasms of post-World War II America. Hine was born in a small New England town near Boston. He lived in a house that was built in 1770, a very different setting from the modern world he writes about now.*

Always Wanting More
from I WANT THAT!

Informational Text by Thomas Hine

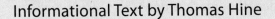

SETTING A PURPOSE What keeps people in our consumer society always wanting more? And when is having more enough? As you read, consider how Thomas Hine answers these questions.

Throughout most of history, few people had more than a couple of possessions, and as a consequence, people were very aware of each object. Life was austere. The ability to be bored by a material surfeit[1] was a rare privilege. There are many stories of kings and emperors who sought a simpler life, if only briefly. Now, that emotion has become widespread, and those who wish to simplify are identified as a distinct market segment. Whole lines of "authentic" products have been created to serve this market, and magazines are published to
10 tell people what they need to buy to achieve a simpler life. In our age of careless abundance, austerity is a luxury, available

---

[1] **surfeit** (sûr′fĭt): an excessive amount.

only to multimillionaires, the occasional monk, and the really smart shopper.

"The standard of life is determined not so much by what a man has to enjoy, as by the rapidity with which he tires of any one pleasure," wrote Simon Patten, the pioneering economist-philosopher of consumption, in 1889. "To have a high standard of life means to enjoy a pleasure intensely and tire of it quickly." Patten's definition of the standard of life was based
20 on **superfluity**: He expected that people would always have more than they need and would never have all they might want. That was a novel idea in Patten's time, and it is one that still makes many people uneasy. In material terms, it seems terribly wasteful, a misuse of the resources of a finite world. And in psychological terms, it seems to trap us in a cycle of false hope and inevitable disappointment. We work in order to consume, and we consume in order to somehow compensate for the emptiness of our lives, including our work. Indeed, there is some evidence that people who feel least fulfilled
30 by their work are the most avid shoppers, while those who love their work find shopping a burden, though they don't necessarily buy less.

Our materialism is oddly abstract, a path toward an ideal. The things we acquire are less important than the act of acquiring, the freedom to choose, and the ability to forget what we have and to keep on choosing. We don't aspire, as people in China did during the 1970s, to "Four Musts": a bicycle, a radio, a watch, and a sewing machine. We aspire instead to such **intangibles** as comfort and modernity,
40 qualities for which standards change so rapidly that the buying can never stop. "Progress is our most important product," Ronald Reagan used to say during his tenure as spokesman for General Electric. And in 1989, after the Berlin Wall fell, multitudes throughout Eastern Europe disappointed intellectuals in the West by behaving as if freedom was the same thing as going shopping. Even China moved on in the 1980s to the "Eight Bigs": a color television, an electric fan, a refrigerator, an audio system, camera, a motorcycle, a furniture suite, and a washing machine. Now China is moving
50 beyond the specific "Bigs" and aspires to more, a quest that will never end. A large super-store chain is opening stores there.

superfluity
(so͞oʹpər-flo͞oʹĭ-tē) *n.*
Superfluity is overabundance or excess.

intangible
(ĭn-tănʹjə-bəl) *n.*
An *intangible* is something that is hard to describe because it cannot be perceived by the senses.

It is amazing to think that from the dawn of time until the time of Adam Smith,[2] a bit more than two centuries ago, people believed that wanting and having things was a drain on wealth, rather than one of its sources. That doesn't mean, however, that they didn't want things or that they didn't, at times, go to great lengths to attain them.

Now, as I move, mildly entranced, behind my cart at a
60 super store, grabbing items I feel for a moment that I need, I am assumed to be increasing the prosperity not merely of my own country, but of the entire world. Indeed, in the wake of the World Trade Center attacks, Americans were **exhorted** not to sacrifice, as is usual in wartime, but to consume.

exhort
(ĭg-zôrt´) *v.* If you *exhort*, you make an urgent appeal to others.

There are those who disagree. Can the massive deficit that the United States runs with other countries, which is driven by our hunger for ever more low-priced goods, be sustained indefinitely? Does our appetite for inexpensive goods from overseas exploit the low-wage workers who make them, or
70 does it give them new opportunities? And more profoundly, are there enough resources in the world to provide everyone with this kind of living standard and still have enough clean air and clean water? How many super-store shoppers can one planet sustain?

---

[2] **Adam Smith:** a Scottish economist who lived in the 18th century.

These are serious questions that need to be addressed, but those who raise such issues have rarely considered the power of objects and the fundamental role that acquiring and using objects has played since prehistoric times. In this story, the big box stores, boutiques, malls, Main Streets, Web sites, and other retailers that constitute the buyosphere[3] represent the fulfillment of an ancient dream. The local super store is a wonder of the world. Never before have so many goods come together from so many places at such low cost. And never before have so many people been able to buy so many things.

Nevertheless, we yawn at a super store rather than marvel at it. That such a store could provoke **apathy** instead of amazement is a perverse tribute to the plenitude of our consumer society and the weakness of the emotional ties that bind us to the many objects in our lives. Never before has so much seemed so dull.

And even if a super store is not the noblest expression of personal liberty or the highest achievement of democracy, we should consider that it does provide a setting for exercising a kind of freedom that has threatened tyrants and autocrats for thousands of years. We go to a super store to acquire things that prove our own power. It is a place where people really do get to choose.

apathy
(ăp´ə-thē) *n. Apathy* is indifference or the lack of interest or concern.

COLLABORATIVE DISCUSSION The author presents ideas about wanting and having things in the past, the present, and the future. What does he say about how wanting and having things change over time? Talk about your ideas with other group members.

---

[3] **buyosphere:** a term the author uses to describe all the places that modern consumers buy things.

Determine Meaning

Often, a written work is a reflection of an author's **style,** a manner of writing that involves how something is said rather than what is said. An author can share ideas or express viewpoints by using stylistic elements like these:

- **Word choice** is an author's use of words. Well-chosen words help an author to express ideas precisely and artistically. Word choice is part of **diction,** which involves the use of vocabulary and word order. An author's word choice can be formal or informal, serious or humorous.
- **Tone** is the author's attitude toward a subject. Like word choice, a tone can convey different feelings. The tone of a work can often be described in one word, such as *playful, serious,* or *determined.*
- **Voice** is an author's unique style of expression. The use of voice can reveal an author's personality, beliefs, or attitudes.

Consider the word choices in this sentence from "Always Wanting More," which describes the author's feelings about being part of a consumer culture:

> **Now, as I move, mildly entranced, behind my cart at a super store, grabbing items I feel for a moment that I need, I am assumed to be increasing the prosperity not merely of my own country, but of the entire world.**

The tone in this sentence could be described as self-mocking, meaning the author is making fun of himself. What word choices are examples of this?

Make Inferences

To grasp an implied or unstated idea in a text, readers can make an **inference**—a logical guess based on facts and a person's own knowledge. The chart shows an inference made from a section of the text you've just read.

Textual Detail	Knowledge	Inference
"And in 1989, after the Berlin Wall fell, multitudes throughout Eastern Europe disappointed intellectuals in the West by behaving as if freedom was the same thing as going shopping."	The Berlin Wall separated East Germany, which was under Communist control, from West Germany, which had a democratic form of government and greater freedom.	The fall of the Berlin Wall signaled freedom for East Germans. They focused on purchasing things that they had not been able to get before.

What inference can you make about the reason "intellectuals in the West" were disappointed?

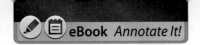
Analyzing the Text

ELA RI.7.1, RI.7.2, RI.7.4, RI.7.5, RI.7.8, SL.7.1 ELD PI.7.1, PI.7.3, PI.7.6, PI.7.8, PI.7.10, PI.7.11

Cite Text Evidence   Support your responses with evidence from the text.

1. **Interpret** A contrast between what is expected and what actually happens is called **irony.** Authors who use irony are often adding a humorous touch in expressing their ideas. In the first paragraph, what words and phrases does the author use to show an ironic tone?

2. **Analyze** An author may express more than one kind of tone in a piece of writing. Reread lines 26–32. What word would you use to describe the author's tone here? What words or phrases contribute to this tone?

3. **Summarize** Reread lines 65–78. How would you summarize the "serious questions" that the author refers to?

4. **Infer** Reread lines 85–90. What point is the author making when he says that we "yawn at a superstore"?

5. **Compare** Reread to compare the ideas in lines 1–13 with the ideas expressed in lines 91–97. What does an ordinary person in modern times now have in common with the kings and emperors of the past?

6. **Analyze** Based on this informational text, what are your impressions of the writing style of Thomas Hine? Explain how the author's word choice, tone, and voice support his style and express his ideas about consumerism.

PERFORMANCE TASK

Speaking Activity: Discussion
In small groups, prepare for a class discussion about the claims, or positions, that Thomas Hine shares about our consumer culture.

- First, identify a list of the claims.
- Consider the following questions: How well does the author support his claims? Are there any I would challenge? How does my own experience as a consumer connect to these claims?

- With your other group members, discuss responses to the questions.
- Participants who disagree with Hine's ideas can present their own views. Be sure to support points with evidence.
- For the class discussion, each small group might choose a reporter to present your responses to the questions.

Critical Vocabulary

ELA L.7.4d, L.7.5b, L.7.6
ELD PI.7.6, PI.7.12

superfluity   **intangible**   **exhort**   **apathy**

Practice and Apply Answer each question with *yes* or *no*. With your group, use examples and reasons to explain your answer.

1. Would you want a **superfluity** of luck?

2. Do **intangibles** bring success?

3. Can advertising **exhort**?

4. Is **apathy** like sympathy?

Vocabulary Strategy: Synonyms and Antonyms

Synonyms are words with similar meanings, such as *chilly* and *cool*. **Antonyms** are words with opposite meanings, such as *chilly* and *warm*. Identifying synonyms and antonyms can help readers understand the meanings of unfamiliar words. Note the synonyms in this sentence from "Always Wanting More":

> We aspire instead to such *intangibles* as comfort and
> modernity, *qualities* for which standards change so
> rapidly that the buying can never stop.

Intangibles are like qualities—both are things that cannot be seen or touched, but still have value.

Note the antonyms in this quotation:

> That such a store could provoke *apathy* instead of *amazement* is
> a perverse tribute to the plenitude of our consumer society . . .

Apathy is the opposite of amazement—apathy is a lack of interest.

Practice and Apply Identify the synonym or antonym for the bold word in each sentence. Use it to make a logical guess about the meaning of the bold word. Verify the meaning in a print or digital dictionary.

1. We live in a **finite** world where resources are limited.

2. The abundance of products makes us forget that we didn't always have such **plenitude.**

3. It is ironic that **austerity** should seem like luxury to wealthy consumers.

4. We were told not to **sacrifice,** as is usual in wartime, but to consume.

5. Individual freedoms have always threatened tyrants and **autocrats.**

Language Conventions: Noun Clauses

A **clause** is a group of words that has a subject and a predicate—the two main parts of a sentence. A **noun clause** is a subordinate clause that is used as a noun; it cannot stand alone and make sense. As the chart shows, the function of noun clauses can vary depending on the specific sentence.

Function	Noun	Noun Clause
subject	Shoppers' choices are amazing.	That shoppers have so many choices is amazing.
direct object	We purchase things.	We purchase whatever we want.
object of preposition	Buy the dress for Mom.	Buy the dress for whoever can wear it.
predicate noun	This place is a superstore.	This place is where we shop.

These pronouns may introduce noun clauses: *that, what, who, whoever, which, whose.* These conjunctions may introduce noun clauses: *how, when, where, why, whether.*

The listed pronouns and conjunctions also introduce other kinds of subordinate clauses. To identify a noun clause, think about how the clause functions in the sentence. Ask: Can I replace the whole clause with a noun or the pronoun *someone* or *something*? If the substituted word fits, you've identified a noun clause.

The noun clause is underlined in this quotation from "Always Wanting More":

> He expected <u>that people would always have more than they need and would never have all they might want.</u>

The noun clause functions as a direct object of the verb *expected.* The pronoun *something* could replace the clause and fit in the sentence: "He expected something."

Practice and Apply Identify the noun clause in each sentence. Tell how you know it is a noun clause.

1. Why we always want more things is an interesting question.

2. We see new products and buy them; this is how we live today.

3. Sometimes we buy more of what we already have.

4. Perhaps we believe that more is better, but we're never content.

5. It's time to step back and think about where all this shopping is leading us.

Background *Writers and poets alike often use their writing to make statements about important topics like consumerism. X. J. Kennedy and Gary Soto each examine our consumer society in their respective poems "Dump" and "How Things Work."*

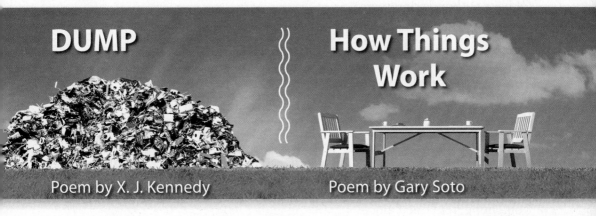

DUMP

Poem by X. J. Kennedy

How Things Work

Poem by Gary Soto

X. J. Kennedy (b. 1929) *has won many awards for his poetry collections, including the Robert Frost Medal. Kennedy has published numerous books for young people, including collections of poetry and novels. Traditional in form, Kennedy's poems often include narrative, wit, and humor, but he also explores themes about serious topics, such as growing up and loss.*

Gary Soto (b. 1952) *never dreamed about writing as a child. But after reading a book of poetry in college, he began to write his own poems and dedicated himself to the craft. While Soto has written poetry and novels for adults, he is probably best known as a writer for young adults and children. From his point of view, he is writing about the feelings and experiences of most American kids.*

SETTING A PURPOSE As you read, think about what each poet is saying about our consumer society and how that society works.

(bg) ©Don Farrall/Getty Images; (tl) ©Ulrich Mueller/Shutterstock; (tr) ©archideaphoto/Shutterstock; (tc) ©caniklgil/Shutterstock; (bc) ©X. J. Kennedy; (b) ©The Associated Press/AP Images

Dump
by X. J. Kennedy

The brink over which we pour
Odd items we can't find
Enough cubic inches to store
In house, in mind,

5 Is come to by a clamber
Up steep unsteady heights
Of beds without a dreamer
And lamps that no hand lights.

Here lie discarded hopes
10 That hard facts had to rout:
Umbrellas—naked spokes
By wind jerked inside-out,

Roof shingles bought on sale
That rotted on their roof,
15 Paintings eternally stale
That, hung, remained aloof,

Pink dolls with foreheads crushed,
Eyes petrified in sleep.
We cast off with a crash
20 What gives us pain to keep.

As we turn now to return
To our lightened living room,
The acrid smell of trash
Arises like perfume.

25 Maneuvering steep stairs
Of bedsprings to our car,
We stumble on homecanned pears
Grown poisonous in their jar

And nearly gash an ankle
30 Against a shard of glass.
Our emptiness may rankle,[1]
But soon it too will pass.

---

[1] **rankle:** to cause constant irritation.

Analyze Poetry: Form

ELA RL.7.5
ELD PII.7.1

The **form** of a poem is its structure, including the arrangement of words and lines. The poem "Dump" has a **fixed,** or **traditional, form** because it follows fixed rules:

- The poem is divided into **stanzas** that include the same number of lines.
- The poem has a pattern of end rhymes, called a **rhyme scheme.** A rhyme scheme is noted by assigning a letter of the alphabet, beginning with *a*, to each line. Lines that rhyme are given the same letter. For example, in the first stanza, the end words are *pour, find, store,* and *mind.* The stanza's rhyme scheme is *abab.*

The **meter** of a poem is the regular pattern of stressed and unstressed syllables. Each **foot,** or unit of meter, includes one stressed syllable. "Dump" has these characteristics of meter:

- Most lines have the same number of feet.
- Each metrical foot is the kind called an iamb—an unstressed syllable followed by a stressed syllable: duh-DAH, duh-DAH.

Because a meter that follows a rigid pattern can sound as singsong as a nursery rhyme, poets often choose to work more loosely with meter. Listen for the meter in stanza 3:

> **Here lie discarded hopes**
> **That hard facts had to rout:**
> **Umbrellas—naked spokes**
> **By wind jerked inside-out,**

Analyzing the Text

ELA RL.7.1, RL.7.4, RL.7.5
ELD PI.7.6, PII.7.1

Cite Text Evidence Support your responses with evidence from the text.

1. **Identify Patterns** How many stanzas does the poem have? How many lines are in each stanza? Why might the poet have chosen to organize the poem this way?

2. **Identify Patterns** Choose and copy a stanza from the poem. Use stress marks to identify the stressed syllables in each line of the stanza.

3. **Analyze** Which stanzas vary from the *abab* rhyme scheme? What impact does this variation have on the poem's meaning?

4. **Analyze** How does the poem's form contribute to its meaning?

How Things Work
by Gary Soto

Today it's going to cost us twenty dollars
To live. Five for a softball. Four for a book,
A handful of ones for coffee and two sweet rolls,
Bus fare, rosin[1] for your mother's violin.
5 We're completing our task. The tip I left
For the waitress filters down
Like rain, wetting the new roots of a child
Perhaps, a belligerent cat that won't let go
Of a balled sock until there's chicken to eat.
10 As far as I can tell, daughter, it works like this:
You buy bread from a grocery, a bag of apples
From a fruit stand, and what coins
Are passed on helps others buy pencils, glue,
Tickets to a movie in which laughter
15 Is thrown into their faces.
If we buy a goldfish, someone tries on a hat.
If we buy crayons, someone walks home with a broom.
A tip, a small purchase here and there,
And things just keep going. I guess.

COLLABORATIVE DISCUSSION Both poems have speakers who
share thoughts about their surroundings or situations. Which
speaker expresses stronger reactions to the situation? What degree
of control does either speaker appear to have over what they
describe? Discuss your responses with other group members.

---

[1] **rosin** (rŏz´ĭn): a sticky substance that comes from tree sap and is used to
increase sliding friction on certain stringed instruments' bows.

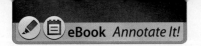

Analyze Poetry: Form

ELA RL.7.5
ELD PI.7.6, PII.7.1

A poem's **form** is its structure and the way its words and lines are arranged. Some forms are also defined by poetic devices, such as rhyme, rhythm, and meter. A poem's form is closely linked to its meaning, which makes the poem's form important to its message.

The poem "How Things Work" is written in a form called **free verse,** which has natural rhythms rather than regular patterns of rhyme, rhythm, meter, or line length. A poet may choose free verse to make the language similar to natural speech.

Still, the sounds of words and the rhythms within lines matter in free verse. The poet has made choices about where to break lines, how to punctuate each line, and which words and phrases will best convey particular sound-meaning connections.

To analyze free verse, ask questions such as the following:

- What ideas is the poet expressing? How does the use of free verse support those ideas?
- What rhythms do the line lengths and the punctuation in the poem create? How do these poetic devices add to my understanding of the poem?

Analyzing the Text

ELA RL.7.1, RL.7.4, RL.7.5
ELD PI.7.6, PI.7.8, PII.7.1

Cite Text Evidence Support your responses with evidence from the text.

1. **Interpret** Reread the first sentence of the poem in lines 1–2. Where would you pause, and what words would you stress to give that sentence meaning and feeling?

2. **Interpret** In lines 5–7, what does the speaker compare to rain, and what does that comparison help readers picture?

3. **Interpret** Reread the last two lines of "How Things Work." Where might be the best places to pause? What words should you stress to help convey the poem's meaning?

4. **Analyze** Review lines 14–19 and examine how the poet arranges the words and lines. Describe the variations in line lengths. What is the poet trying to explain, and how does the form support those ideas?

5. **Analyze** How does the poem's form contribute to its meaning?

Determine Theme

ELA RL.7.2, RL.7.4
ELD PI.7.6

Poems like "Dump" and "How Things Work" often have a **theme,** or a lesson about life or human nature that the poet shares with the reader. A theme usually is developed over the course of a poem, rather than stated directly at the beginning or end. Readers can infer a poem's theme by thinking about the title, the imagery, the form, and the language the poet uses to describe the subject.

Poets might give clues about the poem's theme through the **tone,** or the speaker's attitude toward the subject. One way they may convey the tone is through the use of **irony,** or the use of language to say the opposite of what is meant.

How can you tell that the speaker in "Dump" is using an ironic tone in these lines?

> **The acrid smell of trash**
> **Arises like perfume.**

Pay attention to text details as you dig deeper into the poems. Use text clues to determine the themes in each poem and to analyze how those themes are developed through the tones.

Compare Forms in Poetry

ELA RL.7.2, RL.7.5
ELD PII.7.1

You have read two poems on a shared subject—the things we own. Each poet describes an everyday activity and reflects on it in a unique way. The poem's form is the way the poet organizes ideas, including the arrangement of words and lines.

To compare the forms of these poems, analyze the structure that each poet uses. Use a chart like this to help you make comparisons between the two poems.

Elements to Think About	"Dump"	"How Things Work"
form of poem		
setting		
lines and stanzas		
sensory and figurative language		
tone		
theme		

Analyzing the Text

ELA RL.7.1, RL.7.2, RL.7.4, RL.7.5, W.7.2, W.7.4, W.7.10 **ELD** PI.7.6, PI.7.7, PI.7.8, PI.7.10, PII.7.1

Cite Text Evidence Support your responses with evidence from the poems.

1. **Draw Conclusions** What is the theme of "Dump"?

2. **Draw Conclusions** What is the theme of "How Things Work"?

3. **Compare** In what ways do the poems "Dump" and "How Things Work" seem most alike?

4. **Compare** Reread lines 14–15 of "How Things Work." In what way is the tone similar to the tone in "Dump"?

5. **Compare** Reread the last two lines of each poem. How are the speakers' statements alike, and what message, or theme, do they leave the reader with?

6. **Evaluate** Why might the poet have chosen regular meter and rhyme to express the ideas in "Dump"? Why might the poet have chosen free verse for "How Things Work"?

7. **Connect** Reread lines 1–8 of "Dump." How might those ideas be expressed in language like that in "How Things Work"?

PERFORMANCE TASK

Writing Activity: Literary Analysis Write a one-page analysis of the poems. In your analysis, compare and contrast the views and experiences of consuming expressed in each poem.

- Complete the graphic organizer from the Compare Forms in Poetry section. Use the completed chart to organize your ideas.

- Include words and lines from the poems to support the key points and ideas in your analysis.
- Organize your analysis clearly, using a compare-contrast structure.
- Sum up each speaker's central idea, or theme, and the tone, or attitude toward the subject.

Charles Yu (b. 1976) *wrote his first short story in college, but he didn't write another one until years later after he graduated from law school. During the day, he works as a lawyer for a visual effects company in southern California. He does most of his writing at night, after he has spent time with his family and his children have gone to bed. Yu has written two short story collections and a novel.*

Earth (A Gift Shop)

Short Story by Charles Yu

SETTING A PURPOSE As you read this science fiction story, think about the author's portrayal of Earth's future and how he creates this portrayal.

Come to Earth! Yes, that Earth. A lot of people think we're closed during construction, but we are not! We're still open for business.

Admittedly, it's a little confusing.

First, we were Earth: The Planet. Then life formed, and that was a great and good time.

And then, for a little while, we were Earth: A Bunch of Civilizations!

Until the fossil fuels ran out and all of the nation-states collapsed and a lucky few escaped Earth and went out in search of new worlds to colonize.

Then, for what seemed like forever, we were Earth: Not Much Going On Here Anymore.

And that lasted for a long time. Followed by another pretty long time. Which was then followed by a really long time.

Then, after a while, humans, having semi-successfully established colonies on other planets, started to come back to Earth on vacation. Parents brought their kids, teachers brought their classes on field trips, retirees came in groups of
20 twenty or thirty. They wanted to see where their ancestors had come from. But there was nothing here. Kids and parents and teachers left, disappointed. *That's it?* they would say, or some would even say, *It was okay I guess, but I thought there would be more.*

So, being an **enterprising** species and all, some of us got together and reinvented ourselves as Earth: The Museum, which we thought was a great idea.

We pooled our resources and assembled what we could find. To be sure, there was not a whole lot of good stuff left
30 after the collapse of Earth: A Bunch of Civilizations! One of us had a recording of Maria Callas singing the Violetta aria in *La Traviata*.[1] We all thought it sounded very pretty, so we had that playing in a room in the museum. And I think maybe we had a television playing episodes of *The Tonight Show Starring Johnny Carson*. The main attraction of the museum was the painting we had by some guy of some flowers. No one could remember the name of the guy or the painting, or even the flowers, but we were all pretty sure it was an important painting at some point in the history of paintings and also the
40 history of people, so we put that in the biggest room in the center of everything.

But parents and teachers, being humans (and especially being descendants of the same humans who messed everything up in the first place) thought the whole museum was quite boring, or even *very* boring, and they would say as much, even while we were still within earshot, and we could hear them saying that to each other, about how bored they were. That hurt to hear, but more than that what was hurtful was that no one was coming to Earth anymore, now
50 that it was a small and somewhat eclectic museum. And who could blame them? After the collapse of civilization, school just has never been the same. By the time kids are done with their five years of **mandatory** schooling, they are eight or even nine years old and more than ready to join the leisure force as full-time professional consumers. Humans who went

enterprising
(ĕn´tər-prī´zǐng) *adj.*
An *enterprising* person is someone who accepts challenges and takes initiative.

mandatory
(măn´də-tôr´ē) *adj.*
If something is *mandatory*, it is required.

---

[1] **Violetta aria in *La Traviata*:** a song from the famous opera by Giuseppe Verdi in which the character Violetta sings joyfully about love.

> **After the collapse of civilization, school just has never been the same.**

elsewhere have carried on that tradition from their days on Earth. They are ready to have their credit accounts opened, for their spending to be tracked, to get started in their lifelong loyalty rewards programs. Especially those humans who are

60 rich enough to be tourists coming back here to Earth.

Eventually one of us realized that the most popular part of the museum was the escalator ride. Although you would think interstellar[2] travel would have sort of raised the bar on what was needed to impress people, there was just something about moving diagonally that seemed to amuse the tourists, both kids and adults, and then one of us finally woke up and said, well, why not give them what they want?

So we did some research, in the few books we had left, and on the computer, and the research confirmed our **hypothesis:**

70 Humans love rides.

So Earth: The Museum was shuttered for several years while we reinvented ourselves and developed merchandise and attractions, all of the things we were naturally good at, and after another good long while, we finally were able to reopen as Earth: The Theme Park and Gift Shop, which did okay but it was not too long before we realized the theme park part of it was expensive to operate and kind of a hassle, really, as our engineering was not so good and we kept making people sick or, in a few cases, really **misjudging** g-forces,[3] and word got

80 out among the travel agencies that Earth: The Theme Park and Gift Shop was not so fun and actually quite dangerous, so we really had no choice but to drop the theme park part and that is how we became Earth: The Gift Shop.

Which was all anyone ever wanted anyway. To get a souvenir to take home.

We do have some great souvenirs.

hypothesis
(hī-pŏth´ĭ-sĭs) *n.*
A *hypothesis* is an explanation or theory for something that can be tested for validity.

misjudge
(mĭs-jŭj´) *v.* If you *misjudge* something, you form an incorrect opinion about it.

---

[2] **interstellar:** between stars.

[3] **g-forces:** the amount of force someone experiences when he or she accelerates at the same rate as every unit of his or her mass.

Our top-selling items for the month of October:

1. *History: The Poster!* A 36" × 24" color poster showing all of the major phases of human history. From the Age Before Tools, through the short-lived but exciting Age of Tools, to the (yawn) Age of Learning, and into our current age, the Age After the Age of Learning.

2. *War: The Soundtrack.* A three-minute musical interpretation of the experience of war, with solos for guitar and drums. Comes in an instrumental version (for karaoke lovers).

3. *Art: The Poster!* Beautiful painting of a nature scene. Very realistic-looking, almost like a photograph. Twenty percent off if purchased with History: The Poster!

4. *God, the Oneness: A Mystical 3-D Journey.* 22-minute DVD. Never-before-seen footage. Comes with special glasses for viewing.

5. *Science: The Video Game.* All the science you ever need to bother with! Almost nothing to learn. So easy you really don't have to pay attention. For ages three to ninety-three.

6. *Summer in a Bottle.* Sure, no one can go outside on Earth anymore because it's 170 degrees Fahrenheit, but who needs outside when they have laboratory-synthesized Summer

in a Bottle? Now comes in two odors: "Mist of Nostalgia" or
"Lemony Fresh."

   7. *Happiness: A Skin Lotion*. At last you can be content and
moisturized, at the same time. From the makers of Adventure:
A Body Spray.

   Other strong sellers for the month include Psychologically
Comforting Teddy Bear and Shakespeare: The Fortune
Cookie. All of the items above also come in ring tones,
T-shirts, cups, and key chains.

   And coming for the holidays, get ready for the latest
installment of Earth's greatest artistic work of the last century:
Hero Story: A Hero's Redemption (and Sweet Revenge), a
computer-generated script based on all the key points of the
archetypal[4] story arc that we humans are.

   Which brings us back to our original point. What was our
original point? Oh yeah, Earth: The Gift Shop is still here. Not
just here, but doing great! Okay, maybe not great, but okay,
we're okay. We would be better if you came by and shopped
here. Which is why we sent you this audio catalog, which we
hope you are reading (otherwise we are talking to ourselves).
Earth: The Gift Shop: The Brochure. Some people have said
the name, Earth: The Gift Shop, is a bit confusing because it
makes it seem like this is the official gift shop of some other
attraction here on Earth, when really the attraction is the
gift shop itself. So we are considering changing our name to
Earth (A Gift Shop), which sounds less official but is probably
more accurate. Although if we are going down that road, it
should be pointed out that the most accurate name would
be Earth = A Gift Shop, or even Earth = Merchandise, since
basically, if we are being honest with ourselves, we are a theme
park without the park part, which is to say we are basically
just a theme, whatever that means, although Earth, an Empty
Theme Park would be an even worse name than Earth = A
Gift Shop, so for now we're just going to stick with what we've
got, until something better comes along.

   So, again, we say: Come to Earth! We get millions of
visitors a year, from near and far. Some of you come by
accident. No shame in that! We don't care if you are just
stopping to refuel, or if you lost your way, or even if you just

---

[4] **archetypal:** having the qualities of an original model or prototype. Common
archetypes include the hero, the trickster, the wise old man, and the Earth
mother.

want to rest for a moment and eat a sandwich and drink a cold
bottle of beer. We still have beer! Of course, we prefer if you
150 come here intentionally. Many of you do. Many of you read
about this place in a guidebook, and some of you even go out
of your way and take a detour from your travels to swing by
the gift shop. Maybe you are coming because you just want to
look, or to say you were here. Maybe you are coming to have
a story to tell when you get back. Maybe you just want to be
able to say: I went home. Even if it isn't home, was never your
home, is not anyone's home anymore, maybe you just want to
say, I touched the ground there, breathed the air, looked at the
moon the way people must have done nine or ten or a hundred
160 thousand years ago. So you can say to your friends, if only for
a moment or two: I was a human on Earth. Even if all I did
was shop there.

COLLABORATIVE DISCUSSION In what ways is this a serious
story? In what ways is it not at all serious, and why did the author
choose to do both with his portrayal of Earth's future? Talk about
your ideas with other group members.

Analyze Stories: Science Fiction

ELA RL.7.3
ELD PII.7.1

Written works that come from an author's imagination fall in the broad category called fiction. In **science fiction,** an author explores unexpected possibilities of the past or the future. The author combines knowledge of science and technology with a creative imagination to present a new world. "Earth (A Gift Shop)" has elements found in other science fiction stories:

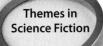

Elements of Science Fiction

- descriptions of how humankind's technologies have altered planet Earth
- colonization of other planets
- impossible events and settings like those in a fantasy story
- a future world with many features and issues common in today's world

Science fiction writers create fantasy worlds, but they often include familiar elements to make these worlds seem believable. Characters usually speak and behave the way real people do. They often have the same goals and motivations as real people, but they pursue them in fantasy worlds set in the future, the past, or a time completely separate from history.

Choose one of the elements in the list and tell how it is shown in "Earth (A Gift Shop)."

Determine Theme

ELA RL.7.2
ELD PI.7.6

A **theme** is a message about life or human nature that the author shares with the reader. In works of fiction, themes are the "big ideas" that readers can infer based on the story the author tells.

While the topic of a science fiction story might be time travel, its theme might be about humans' responsibility for future generations. The following are examples of themes found in science fiction:

Themes in Science Fiction

- Technological advances will make us smarter and happier.
- Technological advances will cause us to lose control over our lives.
- Tampering with biological systems brings ruin.
- Humanity will survive only if we conquer our urge for war.

To identify the theme in a science fiction text, look at the details the author presents. Do certain characters make significant statements about science and technology? Is technology presented as a positive force that benefits mankind, or is it shown as a potentially threatening force? Consider these questions in the context of "Earth (A Gift Shop)."

Analyzing the Text

ELA RL.7.1, RL.7.2, RL.7.3, RL.7.4, W.7.3, W.7.4, W.7.10
ELD PI.7.6, PI.7.7, PI.7.10

Cite Text Evidence   Support your responses with evidence from the text.

1. **Identify** What elements of science fiction does the story "Earth (A Gift Shop)" have?

2. **Infer** To whom might the narrator be referring when using the pronoun *we* throughout the story?

3. **Cite Evidence** In the list of "top-selling items," what are some descriptions that convey ideas about today's consumer culture?

4. **Draw Conclusions** The narrator tells how "Earth: The Planet" has undergone several name changes. What point might the author be making?

5. **Draw Conclusions** What is the theme of this story?

6. **Analyze** How does the narrator's use of language reveal the author's attitude toward the story topic?

PERFORMANCE TASK

Writing Activity: Narrative In the science fiction world of "Earth (A Gift Shop)," humans no longer live on Earth. What would it be like to vacation in that world? How and why might someone have had to escape Earth to find a home on another planet? Pick a part of that plot to expand into a fictional narrative of your own.

- Create an outline of your story, including the narrator, characters, setting, and plot events with a conflict and resolution.
- List the gadgets or technologies that the characters will encounter.
- Include a theme that leaves readers with a message about technology.
- Use your plan to draft and then revise a 2–3-page fictional narrative.

Critical Vocabulary

ELA L.7.4d, L.7.6
ELD PI.7.6

enterprising   **mandatory**   **hypothesis**   **misjudge**

Practice and Apply Use your own knowledge and experiences to answer each question.

1. Who is an **enterprising** person you know? What makes him or her enterprising?

2. What is **mandatory** at your school? Why?

3. What **hypothesis** can you make about human nature? Why is it a hypothesis?

4. When have you **misjudged** someone or something? How did you find out the truth?

Vocabulary Strategy: Verifying Meaning

When you come across an unfamiliar word in a text, there are a number of steps you can take to verify the word's correct meaning.

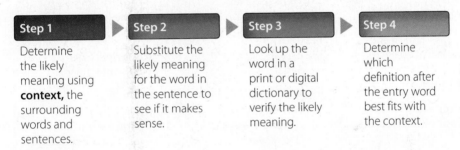

Step 1	Step 2	Step 3	Step 4
Determine the likely meaning using **context,** the surrounding words and sentences.	Substitute the likely meaning for the word in the sentence to see if it makes sense.	Look up the word in a print or digital dictionary to verify the likely meaning.	Determine which definition after the entry word best fits with the context.

Use the steps to consider and verify the meaning of *enterprising* in this sentence from "Earth (A Gift Shop)":

> So, being an *enterprising* species and all, some of us got together and reinvented ourselves as Earth: The Museum, which we thought was a great idea.

The context shows that being enterprising has to do with a great idea and inventing something again, so it might mean "creative" or "cooperative." Both of those meanings make sense in the sentence. The dictionary offers this definition: "Showing initiative and willingness to take on new projects." To be enterprising is to be willing to take on the project Earth: The Museum.

Practice and Apply Find the sentence with the word *eclectic* in line 50 of "Earth (A Gift Shop)." Complete the four steps in the chart to verify the meaning for this context. Then restate the sentence using the dictionary meaning you have identified.

Language Conventions: Spelling

ELA L.7.2b
ELD PI.7.10

When you proofread your writing for accuracy, always check that every word is spelled correctly. If you are using a computer, the spellcheck feature catches most misspellings—but not all. Be especially attentive to **homophones,** words that sound alike but have different meanings and spellings. These descriptions of souvenir items come from "Earth (A Gift Shop)":

> **painting of a nature scene**
> **never-before-seen footage**

The words *scene* ("something to view") and *seen* (a form of the verb *to see*) are homophones. Knowing that a word has one or more homophones helps you check for correct meaning-spelling matches. You can verify the spelling and meaning of a homophone in a digital or print dictionary.

Some commonly misspelled homophones are *threw/through, right/write/ rite, their/there/they're,* and *your/you're.*

This chart shows other commonly misspelled homophones.

affect (to cause a change) **effect** (result)	**cents** (pennies) **scents** (smells) **sense** (feeling; intelligence)	**peace** (calm state) **piece** (part)
aisle (pathway) **I'll** (I will) **isle** (island)	**cereal** (of grain) **serial** (in a series)	**principal** (chief) **principle** (standard; belief)
capital (city; money) **capitol** (lawmakers' building)	**currant** (small raisin) **current** (present time; flow of water)	**rain** (precipitation) **reign** (period of control) **rein** (strap for horse)
cite (quote; summon to court) **sight** (what is seen) **site** (location)	**it's** (it is) **its** (belonging to it)	**wait** (stay) **weight** (heaviness)

Practice and Apply Correct one or more spelling errors in each sentence.

1. Its time for tourists to visit there old planet, Earth.

2. One affect of the collapse of civilizations was the end of national capitols, such as Paris and Washington, D.C.

3. Earth is at piece now, and our principle activity is selling things.

4. Walk through the isles of the gift shop and sniff the sense "Mist of Nostalgia" and "Lemony Fresh."

Interactive Lessons

To help you complete this task, use:
• *Conducting Research*
• *Using Media in a Presentation*

Create a Multimedia Presentation

ELA W.7.2a–f, W.7.4, W.7.5, W.7.6, W.7.7, W.7.8, W.7.10, SL.7.4, SL.7.5, SL.7.6 **ELD** PI.7.4, PI.7.10, PI.7.9, PI.7.12, PII.7.1

This collection focuses on the proliferation of consumerism and how it has affected American culture and our environment. In this activity, you will research a topic related to consumerism. You will draw from *Life at Home in the Twenty-First Century,* other texts in the collection, and your research findings to write an informative essay about the topic you chose. Then you will prepare and give a multimedia presentation on that topic.

A successful multimedia presentation

• uses technology to share information through text, graphics, video, music, and/or sound

• organizes ideas logically in a way that is interesting and appropriate to purpose and audience

• presents findings in a focused manner, with relevant facts, definitions, and examples

• emphasizes salient points from a variety of sources and media

• concludes with a section that summarizes the findings presented

Visit hmhfyi.com to explore your topic and enhance your research.

PLAN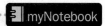

Determine Your Topic Review the texts in the collection. Think about the points each author makes about consumerism. Brainstorm a list of possible topics, such as how TV ads influence consumers or how purchasing behavior in reality TV might affect consumerism. Choose a topic that will interest you and others.

• Transform your topic into a research question you want to answer, such as *What kinds of TV ads influence teenage consumers?* or *How does reality TV change people's attitudes toward and increase consumerism?*

• Make sure your question is open-ended and cannot be answered in a single word.

• Generate further questions that will help you find evidence.

Use the annotation tools in your eBook to find evidence that supports your points. Save each piece of evidence to your notebook.

ACADEMIC VOCABULARY

As you plan and present your presentation, be sure to use the academic vocabulary words.

attitude

consume

goal

purchase

technology

Gather Information In the collection's texts, look for information related to the topic you chose. Take notes on key points, observations, and events that will help you understand your topic, answer your questions, and support your ideas.

Do Research Use print and digital resources to find additional information that addresses your research question.

Interactive Lessons
For help in doing your research, use the following lesson:
· Conducting Research: Taking Notes

- Search for credible sources. Use keywords or subject searching in the library to find books related to your topic. Use a search engine to find Internet sources.

- Take notes on facts, details, and examples that explain and support your main points.

- Identify multimedia components, such as graphics, maps, videos, or sound that could emphasize your main points.

Organize Your Ideas Think about how you will organize your information. Create an outline showing the information you will present in each paragraph. Make sure each idea follows from the previous idea and leads into the next idea.

> **I.** Use Roman numerals for main topics.
>   A. Indent and use capital letters for subtopics.
>   1. Indent and use numbers for supporting facts and details.
>   2. Indent and use numbers for supporting facts and details.
> **II.** Use Roman numerals for main topics.
>   B. Indent and use capital letters for subtopics.
>   1. Indent and use numbers for supporting facts and details.

Consider Your Purpose and Audience Think about your audience as you prepare your presentation. Your goal is to use multimedia to get your points across most effectively to this particular audience.

PRODUCE

Draft an Informative Essay Use your notes and your outline to draft an informative essay that you can use to create your presentation.

Write your rough draft in *my*WriteSmart. Focus on getting your ideas down, rather than on perfecting your choice of language.

- Begin with an attention-grabbing introduction that defines your topic. Include an unusual comment, fact, quote, or story.

- Organize your information into paragraphs of related ideas.

- Include supporting facts, details, and examples.
- Make sure your ideas transition logically.
- Write a conclusion that follows from and supports your main ideas and leaves the reader with a lasting impression.

Prepare Your Presentation Think about what you want your presentation to look like. Choose a presentation tool to create a slideshow.

- Use text from your essay that explains each topic and subtopic. Revise the text to keep your presentation brief and clear.
- Integrate multimedia components that emphasize your main points. Each component should have a clear purpose.
- Check that all text and visuals are large and clear enough that everyone in the audience can see them.

Interactive Lessons
For help in planning your presentation, use the following lesson:
- Using Media in a Presentation: Using Presentation Software

REVISE

✔ my WriteSmart

Have a group of peers review your draft and your multimedia elements in *my*WriteSmart. Ask your reviewers to note any ideas or visuals that are unclear or not in a logical sequence.

Practice Your Presentation Try speaking in front of a mirror, or make a recording of your presentation and listen to it. Then practice your presentation with a partner.

- Speak clearly and loudly.
- Maintain eye contact. Look directly at your audience.
- Use gestures and facial expressions to emphasize ideas.

Evaluate Your Presentation Use the chart on the following page to determine whether your presentation is effective.

- Check that your ideas are clearly and logically presented.
- Verify that your text includes specific and accurate information.
- Examine your audio and visual components to make sure they are relevant and well integrated.

Interactive Lessons
For help in refining your presentation, use:
- Using Media in a Presentation: Building and Practicing Your Presentation

PRESENT

Deliver Your Presentation Finalize your multimedia presentation. Then choose a way to share it with your audience. Consider these options:

- Use your presentation to give a news report about your topic.
- Create and share a video recording of your presentation.

PERFORMANCE TASK RUBRIC
MULTIMEDIA PRESENTATION

	Ideas and Evidence	Organization	Language
4	• The introduction is appealing and informative. • The topic is well developed with relevant facts, concrete details, interesting quotations, and examples from reliable sources. • The conclusion capably summarizes the information presented.	• The organization is effective and logical throughout the essay. • Text, visuals, and sound are combined in a coherent manner. • Transitions successfully connect related ideas.	• The language reflects a formal style. • Sentence beginnings, lengths, and structures vary and have a rhythmic flow. • Grammar, usage, and mechanics are correct.
3	• The introduction could do more to grab the reader's attention; the introduction states the topic. • One or two key points could use more support in the form of relevant facts, concrete details, quotations, and examples from reliable sources. • The concluding section summarizes the information presented.	• The organization is confusing in a few places. • Text, visuals, and sound are mostly combined in a coherent manner. • A few more transitions are needed to connect related ideas.	• The style becomes informal in a few places. • Sentence beginnings, lengths, and structures vary somewhat. • Some grammatical and usage errors are repeated in the presentation.
2	• The introduction is only partly informative; the topic and purpose are unclear. • Most key points need more support in the form of relevant facts, concrete details, quotations, and examples from reliable sources. • The concluding section partially summarizes the information presented.	• The organization is logical in some places but often doesn't follow a pattern. • Text, visuals, and sound are combined in a disorganized way. • More transitions are needed throughout to connect related ideas.	• The style becomes informal in several places. • Sentence structures barely vary, and some fragments or run-on sentences are present. • Grammar and usage are incorrect in several places, but the speaker's ideas are still somewhat clear.
1	• The introduction is missing. • Facts, details, quotations, and examples are from unreliable sources or are missing. • The conclusion is missing.	• A logical organization is not used; information is presented randomly. • Text, visuals, and sound are missing. • Transitions are not used, making the presentation difficult to understand.	• The style is inappropriate for the presentation. • Repetitive sentence structure, fragments, and run-on sentences make the presentation hard to follow. • Several grammatical and usage errors change the meaning of ideas.

Guided by a Cause

❝ The fullness of our heart comes in our actions. ❞

—Mother Teresa

COLLECTION 6

Guided by a Cause

In this collection, you will consider the question: What inspires people to take action to improve their world?

Stream to Start

 fyi hmhfyi.com

1 Channel One News®

COLLECTION

PERFORMANCE TASK Preview

At the end of this collection, you will have the opportunity to:

• research and write an informative essay about a dramatic and deadly fire that destroyed a New York City factory in 1911

• participate in a panel discussion on what commitment to a cause can mean

ACADEMIC VOCABULARY

Study the words and their definitions in the chart below. You will use these words as you discuss and write about the texts in this collection.

Word	Definition	Related Forms
contrast (kən-trăst´) v.	to show differences between two or more things that are being compared	contrasted, contrasting, contrastive
despite (dĭ-spīt´) prep.	in spite of; even though	despiteful
error (ĕr´ər) n.	a mistake	erroneous, erroneously, errorless
inadequate (ĭn-ăd´ĭ-kwĭt) adj.	not enough or sufficient to fulfill a need or meet a requirement	adequate, adequately, inadequacy, inadequately
interact (ĭn´tər-ăkt´) v.	to act upon each other	interaction, interacting, interactive, interactively

Background *An event can be so dramatic and so haunting that it compels the generations that follow it to dissect its details and to trace its impact. A deadly disaster occurred in New York City in 1911 at a company in the ten-story Asch Building. Known today as the Brown Building, it is now a National Historic Landmark. These history writings are detailed accounts of what happened and the long-term effects.*

The Triangle Factory Fire

from Flesh & Blood So Cheap: The Triangle Fire and Its Legacy
History Writing by Albert Marrin

Albert Marrin (b. 1936) *taught social studies in a junior high school and then became a college teacher. But he realized that he missed telling stories as he had as a teacher. That's when Marrin decided to write history for young adults. He has now produced more than thirty nonfiction books, for which he has won numerous awards.*

from The Story of the Triangle Factory Fire
History Writing by Zachary Kent

Zachary Kent *is the author of over fifty books for young readers. He writes primarily about history and has written biographies of various noted figures, including Abraham Lincoln and Charles Lindbergh.*

As you read, mark up the text. Save your work to *my*Notebook.

- Highlight details
- Add notes and questions
- Add new words to *my*WordList

SETTING A PURPOSE As you read, think about how each writer presents information on the same event. How are the pieces similar? How are they different? Write down any questions you have while reading.

(l) ©Photodisc/Getty Images; (r) ©Underwood & Underwood/Corbis

from **Flesh & Blood So Cheap**
by Albert Marrin

The Triangle Waist Company occupied the top three floors of the Asch Building. On the eighth floor, forty cutters,[1] all men, worked at long wooden tables. Nearby, about a hundred women did basting[2] and other tasks. Paper patterns hung from lines of string over the tables. Although cutters wasted as little fabric as possible, there were always scraps, which they threw into bins under the tables. Every two months or so, a rag dealer took away about a ton of scraps, paying about seven cents a pound. He then sold them back to cotton mills to remake into new cloth. The last pickup was in January.

On March 25, the cutters prepared for their next day's work. Since it was Saturday, everyone would leave early, at 4:45 P.M. Workers from other firms had already left; Triangle employees had to stay longer to fill back orders. Carefully, cutters spread "lawn" (from the French word *lingerie*) on their tables 120 layers thick. Lawn was not just *any* cotton fabric. Sheer and lightweight, it was beautiful and comfortable—and burned as easily as gasoline. Each layer was separated from the others by a sheet of equally **flammable** tissue paper.

After cutting, the various pieces would go by freight elevator to the ninth floor for sewing and finishing. There, eight rows of sewing machine tables, holding 288 machines in all, occupied the entire width of the room. Only a narrow aisle separated one row from another; the tables were so close together that chairs touched back to back between the rows. From time to time, workers would take the finished shirtwaists[3] to the tenth floor for inspection, packing, and shipping. This floor also held the showroom and owners' offices.

By 4:40 P.M., the cutters had finished their work. With five minutes to go, they stood around, talking until the quitting bell rang. Although it was against the rules, some lit cigarettes, hiding the smoke by blowing it up their jacket sleeves. On the floor above, workers had begun to walk toward the lockers to

flammable
(flăm'ə-bəl) *adj.*
If something is *flammable*, it is easy for it to catch on fire and burn.

---

[1] **cutters:** people who cut cloth in a clothing factory.
[2] **basting:** stitching.
[3] **shirtwaists:** women's blouses that resemble men's shirts.

get their coats and hats. They looked forward to Sunday and family visits, boyfriends, dances, and nickelodeons.[4] Although they had no inkling of what was about to happen, many had only minutes to live.

We will never know for sure what started the Triangle Fire. Most likely, a cutter flicked a hot ash or tossed a live cigarette butt into a scrap bin. Whatever the cause, survivors said the first sign of trouble was smoke pouring from beneath a cutting table.

Cutters flung buckets of water at the smoking spot, without effect. Flames shot up, igniting the line of hanging paper patterns. "They began to fall on the layers of thin goods underneath them," recalled cutter Max Rothen. "Every time another piece dropped, light scraps of burning fabric began to fly around the room. They came down on the other tables and they fell on the machines. Then the line broke and the whole string of burning patterns fell down." A foreman ran for the hose on the stairway wall. Nothing! No water came. The hose had not been connected to the standpipe.[5] Seconds later, the fire leaped out of control.

Yet help was already on the way. At exactly 4:45 P.M., someone pulled the eighth-floor fire alarm. In less than two minutes, the horse-drawn vehicles of Engine Company 72 arrived from a firehouse six blocks away. The moment they arrived, the firefighters unloaded their equipment and prepared to swing into action. As they did, the area pumping station raised water pressure in the hydrants near the Asch Building. Other units soon arrived from across the Lower East Side with more equipment.

Meanwhile, workers on the eighth floor rang furiously for the two passenger elevators. Safety experts have always advised against using elevators in a fire. Heat can easily damage their machinery, leaving trapped passengers dangling in space, to burn or suffocate. Despite the danger, the operators made several trips, saving scores of workers before heat bent the elevators' tracks and put them out of action.

Those who could not board elevators rushed the stairway door. They caused a pileup, so that those in front could not open the door. Whenever someone tried to get it open, the crowd pinned her against it. "All the girls were falling on me

---

[4] **nickelodeons:** early movie theaters that charged five cents for admission.
[5] **standpipe:** a large pipe into which water is pumped.

and they squeezed me to the door," Ida Willensky recalled. "Three times I said to the girls, 'Please, girls, let me open the door. Please!' But they would not listen to me." Finally, cutter Louis Brown barged through the crowd and forced the
80   door open.

Workers, shouting, crying, and gasping for air, slowly made their way downstairs. There were no lights in the stairway, so they had to grope their way in darkness. A girl fell; others fell on top of her, blocking the stairs until firefighters arrived moments later. Yet everyone who took the stairway from the eighth floor got out alive, exiting through the Washington Place doors. Those on the ninth floor were not so lucky.

New Yorkers say that March comes in like a lion (with
90   cold wind) and leaves like a lamb (with April's warm showers). Now, as fire raged on the eighth floor, the elevator shafts became wind tunnels. Wind gusts made eerie sounds, like the howling of great beasts in pain, while sucking flaming embers upward. On the ninth floor, embers landed on piles of finished shirtwaists and cans of oil used to make the sewing machines run smoothly. Instantly, the air itself seemed to catch fire.

Had there been fire drills, surely more would have survived. Unfortunately, confusion **reigned**. Workers had to make life-and-death decisions in split seconds amid fire,
100   smoke, and panic. It was everyone for themselves. "I was throwing them out of the way," Mary Bucelli said of the women near her. "No matter whether they were in front of me or coming from in back of me, I was pushing them down. I was only looking out for my own life." Mary joined others who ran to the Greene Street stairway. They made it down to the street or up to the tenth floor and the roof, before flames blocked this escape route.

Others headed for the elevators and stairway on the Washington Place side of the building. Forcing open the
110   doors to the elevator shaft, they looked down and saw an elevator starting what would be its last trip from the eighth floor. "I reached out and grabbed the cables, wrapped my legs around them, and started to slide down," recalled Samuel Levine, a sewing machine operator. "While on my way down, as slow as I could let myself drop, the bodies of six girls went falling past me. One of them struck me, and I fell on top of the elevator. I fell on the dead body of a girl. Finally I heard

reign
(rān) *v.* If some things *reign* over something else, it means they dominate it.

Firefighters in a horse-drawn fire engine race to respond to the fire at the Triangle Waist Company.

the firemen cutting their way into the elevator shaft, and they came and let me out."

120   Those who reached the ninth-floor stairway door found it locked. This was not unusual, as employers often locked doors to discourage latecomers and keep out union organizers. "My God, I am lost!" cried Margaret Schwartz as her hair caught fire. Nobody who went to that door survived, nor any who reached the windows.

    With a wave of fire rolling across the room, workers rushed to the windows, only to meet more fire. Hot air expands. Unless it escapes, pressure will keep building, eventually blowing a hole even in a heavy iron container
130 like a boiler. Heat and pressure blew out the eighth-floor windows. Firefighters call the result "lapping in"—that is, sucking flames into open windows above. That is why you see black scorch marks on the wall above the window of a burnt-out room.

    With fire advancing from behind and flames rising before them, people knew they were doomed. Whatever they did meant certain death. By remaining in the room, they chose death by fire or suffocation. Jumping ninety-five feet to the ground meant death on the sidewalk. We cannot know what
140 passed through the minds of those who decided to jump. Yet

their thinking, in those last moments of life, may have gone like this: If I jump, my family will have a body to identify and bury, but if I stay in this room, there will be nothing left.

A girl clung to a window frame until flames from the eighth floor lapped in, burning her face and setting fire to her hair and clothing. She let go. Just then, Frances Perkins reached the scene from her friend's town house on the north side of Washington Square. "Here they come," onlookers shouted as Engine Company 72 reined in their horses. "Don't jump; stay there." Seconds later, Hook and Ladder Company 20 arrived.

Firefighters charged into the building, stretching a hose up the stairways as they went. At the sixth-floor landing, they connected it to the standpipe. Reaching the eighth floor, they crawled into the inferno on their bellies, under the rising smoke, with their hose. Yet nothing they did could save those at the windows. Photos of the **portable** towers show streams of water playing on the three top floors. (A modern high-pressure pumper can send water as high as one thousand feet.) Plenty of water got through the windows, but not those with people standing in them. A burst of water under high pressure would have hurled them backward, into the flames.

Hoping to catch jumpers before they hit the ground, firefighters held up life nets, sturdy ten-foot-square nets made of rope. It was useless. A person falling from the ninth floor struck with a force equal to eleven thousand pounds. Some jumpers bounced off nets, dying when they hit the ground; others tore the nets, crashing through to the pavement. "The force was so great it took men off their feet," said Captain Howard Ruch of Engine Company 18. "Trying to hold the nets, the men turned somersaults. The men's hands were bleeding, the nets were torn and some caught fire" from burning clothing. Officers, fearing their men would be struck by falling bodies, ordered the nets removed. The aerial ladders failed, too, reaching only to the sixth floor. Desperate jumpers tried to grab hold of a rung on the way down, missed, and landed on the sidewalk.

People began to jump singly or in groups of two or three, holding hands as they stepped out the windows. William G. Shepherd, a reporter for United Press, watched the "shower of bodies" in horror.

portable
(pôr′tə-bəl) *adj.*
If something is *portable*, it can be carried or moved easily.

I saw every feature of the tragedy visible from outside the building. I learned a new sound—a more horrible sound than any description can picture. It was the sound of a speeding, living body on a stone sidewalk.

Thud—dead, thud—dead, thud—dead, thud—dead. Sixty-two thud—dead. I call them that, because the sound and the thought of death came to me each time, at the same instant. . . . Down came the bodies in a shower, burning, smoking—flaming bodies, with the disheveled hair trailing upward. . . .

On the sidewalk lay heaps of broken bodies. A policeman later went about with tags, which he fastened with wires to the wrists of the dead girls. . . . The floods of water from the firemen's hose that ran into the gutter was actually stained red with blood.

Onlookers saw many dreadful sights, none more so than the end of a love affair. A young man appeared at a window. Gently, he helped a young woman step onto the windowsill, held her away from the building—and let go. He helped another young woman onto the windowsill. "Those of us who were looking saw her put her arms around him and kiss him," Shepherd wrote. "Then he held her out into space and dropped her. But quick as a flash he was on the windowsill himself. . . . He was brave enough to help the girl he loved to a quicker death, after she had given him a goodbye kiss."

Meanwhile, others managed to reach the fire escape. It had not been designed for a quick exit. FDNY[6] experts later declared that those on the three top floors of the Asch Building could not have made it to the ground in under three hours. In reality, they had only minutes.

People crowded onto the fire escape. As they walked single file, flames lapped at them through broken windows. Worse, the human load became too heavy for the device to bear. Bolts that fastened it to the building became loose. It began to sway, then collapsed at the eighth floor, tumbling dozens into the courtyard. "As the fire-crazed victims were thrown by the collapse of the fire escape, several struck the sharp-tipped palings,"[7] the New York *Herald* reported. "The body of one woman was found with several iron spikes driven

---

[6] **FDNY:** the Fire Department of New York City.
[7] **palings:** fences with stakes.

This is a photograph of the gutted tenth floor of the Asch Building that was taken in the aftermath of the fire.

entirely through it." Others crashed through the skylight into the room below, where they died on the cement floor.

The tenth floor was the best place to be. Those who worked there, or reached it from the floor below, survived by dashing up the stairs to the roof. When they arrived, they found the roof fifteen feet lower than its Washington Place neighbor's, a building shared by New York University and the American Book Company.

Luckily, Professor Frank Sommer was teaching his law
230 class in a room that overlooked the Asch Building. When Sommer realized what was happening, he led his class to the roof of their building. There they found two ladders left by painters during the week. Students lowered the ladders, climbed down, and helped survivors to safety. For some women, said Sommer, "it was necessary to beat out the flames that had caught their clothing, and many of them had blackened faces and singed hair and eyebrows." Yet only one person from the tenth floor died. Seeing flames licking up from the ninth floor, she panicked and jumped out a window.

240 By 5:15 P.M., exactly thirty-five minutes after flames burst from beneath a cutting table, firefighters had brought the blaze under control. An hour later, Chief Croker made his **inspection**. He found that the Asch Building had no damage

inspection
(ĭn-spĕk´shən) *n.*
An *inspection* is an official examination or review.

©Bettmann/Corbis

to its structure. Its walls were in good shape; so were the floors. It had passed the test. It was fireproof.

The woodwork, furniture, cotton goods, and people who worked in it were not. Of the 500 Triangle employees who reported for work that day, 146 died. Of these, sixteen men were identified. The rest were women or bodies and body parts listed as "unidentified." The Triangle Fire was New York's worst workplace disaster up to that time. Only the September 11, 2001, terrorist attacks on the twin towers of the World Trade Center took more (about 2,500) lives.

Chief Croker was no softie; he was used to the horrors that came with his job. But this was different. As he explored the top three floors of the Asch Building, he saw sights "that utterly staggered him," the New York *World* reported. "In the drifting smoke, he had seen bodies burned to bare bones, skeletons bending over sewing machines." Those sights sent him down to the street with quivering lips.

Next morning, March 26, Chief Croker returned for another look. The only creatures he found alive were some half-drowned mice. He picked one up, stroked it gently, and put it in his pocket. The chief would take it home, he said. "It's alive. At least it's alive."

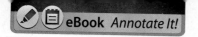
Determine Central Idea and Details

ELA RI.7.2
ELD PI.7.6

The **central idea,** or main idea, in a piece of history writing is the most important idea about the topic. It may be stated explicitly in a sentence, or it may be implied. The main idea is often suggested by smaller key ideas, each developed in a paragraph or a longer section of the work.

Main ideas are supported by **details,** facts and other pieces of information that build upon or clarify the main ideas. When you read history writing, notice the details that answer basic questions, such as, *When and where does the event take place? Who is involved? What are the causes and the immediate and long-term effects?*

As you read, you can keep track of key ideas and details by taking notes in outline form. Restate the main ideas of paragraphs or sections, numbered in Roman numerals. Below each idea, list the supporting details.

> The Triangle Waist Company Fire
> I. The Triangle factory was a dangerous firetrap.
>   A. Paper scraps hung from the rafters.
>   B. There were always scraps under the tables.
>   C.

Once you have completed an outline for the entire text, look to see how all the main ideas and details help to develop the main idea of the entire text. What other details from *Flesh & Blood So Cheap* could you add to this outline?

Analyzing the Text

ELA RI.7.1, RI.7.6
ELD PI.7.6, PI.7.7

Cite Text Evidence   Support your responses with evidence from the text.

1. **Summarize** Review the text to find details about the different floors of the building. What is important to understand about these locations?

2. **Cause/Effect** Reread lines 97–100. Why does the author give a detail about fire drills?

3. **Draw Conclusions** According to the author, why might workers have jumped from the windows?

4. **Cite Evidence** What does the author seem to think of the firefighters' efforts during this disaster?

5. **Evaluate** What is most important to understand about this event?

6. **Connect** Why is the story of the Triangle Fire still being told?

from **The Story of the Triangle Factory Fire**
by Zachary Kent

In the days following the fire, city officials sifted through the charred rubble at the Asch Building and tried to fix the fault for the tragedy. Fire Chief Croker angrily stated, "There wasn't a fire escape anywhere fronting on the street by which these unfortunate girls could escape." Doors that opened inward instead of outward, overcrowding in work areas, and blocked exits also were to blame. Fire Marshal William Beers stunned New Yorkers by soon declaring, "I can show you 150 loft buildings far worse than this one."

10 Lillian D. Wald of the Joint Board of Sanitary Control also reported on the general situation. "The conditions as they now exist are hideous. . . . Our investigators have shown that there are hundreds of buildings which invite disaster just as much as did the Asch structure."

Accused of ignoring their employees' safety, Triangle owners Blanck and Harris were charged with manslaughter. During the three week trial angry citizens packed the courtroom. Outside, in the **corridors**, women screamed, "Murderers! Murderers! Make them suffer for

20 killing our children!" Lawyers argued that Blanck and Harris kept all of the Triangle doors locked during the workday, therefore causing many of the deaths. Weighing the evidence, however, the jury returned a verdict of not guilty. "I cannot see that anyone was responsible for the disaster," explained juror H. Houston Hierst. "It seems to me to have been an act of the Almighty."[1] The New York *Call* viewed the matter differently. "Capital can commit no crime," it angrily declared, "when it is in pursuit of profits."

Furious New Yorkers refused to let the issue rest.

30 In October 1911 the city established a Bureau of Fire Prevention to inspect safety standards in other buildings. Five months earlier the New York State legislature created a special Factory Investigating Commission. Through the

corridor
(kôr´ĭ-dər) *n.*
A *corridor* is a narrow hallway or passageway.

---

[1] **an act of the Almighty:** a term that refers to events or actions that are beyond the control of human beings.

New York City garment workers take part in a May Day parade in 1916.

next four years Commission investigators crawled and pried through the rooms and cellars of factories and tenement houses[2] all across the state. They examined workers' filthy living conditions and witnessed the dangers of crippling machinery and long work hours in dusty, dirty firetraps.

As a result of the Commission's shocking findings,
40 New York State quickly passed thirty-three new labor laws by 1914. These laws formed the foundation of New York

---

[2] **tenement houses:** very run-down city apartments where the poor and immigrants often live.

State's Industrial Code, the finest in the nation. Soon other states followed New York's example and **enacted** protective labor laws.

One Factory Commission investigator had witnessed the fateful Triangle fire. Frances Perkins said, "We heard the fire engines and rushed . . . to see what was going on. . . . We got there just as they started to jump. I shall never forget the frozen horror which came over us as we stood with our hands on our throats watching that horrible sight, knowing that there was no help."

In 1933 President Franklin Roosevelt named Frances Perkins secretary of labor. She and other social reformers dedicated their lives to insuring worker safety throughout the country. "They did not die in vain and we will never forget them," vowed Perkins. From the ashes of the tragic Triangle factory fire came help for millions of United States laborers today.

COLLABORATIVE DISCUSSION You've now read two accounts of a disaster that occurred a century ago. If a similar fire were to start in a garment factory of today, how might the events be the same or different? Talk about your thoughts with other group members.

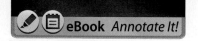
Analyze Structure: Chronological Order

ELA RI.7.5
ELD PII.7.1

A **pattern of organization** is the particular arrangement of ideas and information. Authors of history texts often use the **chronological order** organization to arrange events by their order of occurrence—what happens first, next, then, and finally. When reading history texts, pay attention to dates, times, and words and phrases that signal sequence, such as *before*, *meanwhile*, *later*, and *after that*.

Identify the clues to the chronological organization in this paragraph from *The Story of the Triangle Factory Fire:*

> Furious New Yorkers refused to let the issue rest. In October 1911, the city established a Bureau of Fire Prevention to inspect safety standards in other buildings. Five months earlier the New York State legislature created a special Factory Investigating Commission. Through the next four years Commission investigators crawled and pried through the rooms and cellars of factories and tenement houses all across the state.

Analyzing the Text

ELA RI.7.1, RI.7.2, RI.7.5
ELD PI.7.6, PI.7.10, PII.7.1

Cite Text Evidence   Support your responses with evidence from the selection.

1. **Infer** What was true of factories in New York City before the Triangle fire?

2. **Summarize** What changes occurred in the aftermath of the tragedy? Within what time period did the changes happen?

3. **Compare** Reread lines 15–28. How and why did the jurors' viewpoint differ from that of angry citizens?

4. **Infer** Reread the last sentence. Despite the horror and loss of life caused by the fire, how might it have been a useful experience, according to the author?

Analyze Presentations of Information

History writing is nonfiction that presents events and people of the past. What makes this type of writing interesting is how it presents interactions between people and events. History writing often combines features of a narrative text (a true story with a setting, characters, and a plot) and an informational text (paragraphs of main ideas and factual details).

History writers base their work on factual research. However, two history writers might write about the same event in different ways. How writers shape their presentations of key information can depend on individual points of view. **Author's perspective** is the unique combination of ideas, values, feelings, and beliefs that influence the way a writer looks at a topic.

In comparing the perspectives of two or more authors writing about the same event, look for clues like these in the texts:

Tone	**Tone** is the author's attitude toward his or her subject. Would you describe the writing as serious? Lively? Angry? Notice any emotions the writer expresses while presenting the facts and how the emotions contribute to the overall effect of the writing.
Point of view	Analyze the author's presentation of information to determine his or her point of view. When writing from a **subjective** point of view, an author includes personal opinions, feelings, and beliefs. When writing from an **objective** point of view, the author focuses on factual information and leaves out personal opinions.
Direct statements	Be aware of any statements or comments that seem to come directly from the author. In particular, watch for ideas that may be repeated or restated. What light do these statements shed on the writer's interpretation of facts?
Emphasis	Determine how each author presents his or her ideas about the topic. Do the writers emphasize different evidence? Do they put forth different interpretations of facts?
Portrayals	Pay attention to how the historical figures are portrayed. Think about why that person is included and what makes him or her memorable.

In the excerpt from *Flesh & Blood So Cheap*, read how author Albert Marrin describes Chief Croker (lines 261–265). Next, read the description of Croker by author Zachary Kent in lines 1–7 from *The Story of the Triangle Factory Fire*. Then, compare these two passages. What similarities and differences do you notice in the history writers' descriptions? What do these details reveal about each author's perspective?

Analyzing the Text

ELA RI.7.1, RI.7.2, RI.7.3, RI.7.6, RI.7.9, W.7.2, W.7.6, SL.7.4, SL.7.6 ELD PI.7.6, PI.7.7, PI.7.9

Cite Text Evidence   Support your responses with evidence from the texts.

1. **Cause/Effect** Which of the two texts would you use to research the effects of the Triangle Fire? Why?

2. **Compare** Look back at both texts to find mention of Frances Perkins. Why is she an important person to know about?

3. **Infer** What kinds of sources did both authors use in researching this topic?

4. **Analyze History Writing** Read lines 126–130 from *Flesh & Blood So Cheap*. Are these lines an example of author Albert Marrin's perspective? Explain why or why not.

5. **Analyze Tone** Read lines 36–38 from *The Story of the Triangle Factory Fire*. What clues do you see in these lines to Zachary Kent's attitude about the conditions that are described?

6. **Connect** What idea presented by both authors is most relevant to us today? Why?

7. **Analyze Key Information** The two historical writings cover different aspects of the same event. Briefly review each text for its key details. Then tell what each selection emphasizes.

PERFORMANCE TASK

Speaking Activity: Summary Presentation The Triangle Factory Fire raised issues about inadequate workplace safety, labor rights, and factory jobs. Despite great progress in improving working conditions since 1911, these issues are still in the news. Give a summary presentation about a current event that shares features with the Triangle Factory Fire.

- Use online and print resources to learn about a recent event.

- Use several sources to get varied viewpoints and interpretations of the event.

- Summarize the event by telling what happened, describing the people involved, and discussing any issues surrounding the event.

- End your presentation by telling how this event is similar to and different from the Triangle Factory Fire.

- After rehearsing, deliver your presentation to classmates.

Critical Vocabulary

flammable	**reign**	**portable**
inspection	**corridor**	**enact**

Practice and Apply Complete each sentence to show that you understand the meaning of the bold word.

1. If a cleaning fluid is **flammable,** you should . . .

2. Fear and worry **reign** when . . .

3. A **portable** desk is one that . . .

4. An **inspection** of a restaurant is done to . . .

5. A **corridor** is the same as . . .

6. If a rule is **enacted,** it . . .

Vocabulary Strategy: Latin Roots

A **root** is a word part that came into English from an older language. Roots from the ancient language of Latin appear in many English words. This chart shows three common Latin roots:

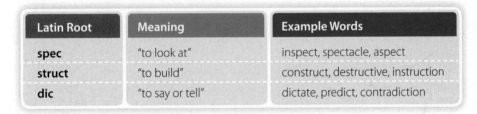

Latin Root	Meaning	Example Words
spec	"to look at"	inspect, spectacle, aspect
struct	"to build"	construct, destructive, instruction
dic	"to say or tell"	dictate, predict, contradiction

Note the words with Latin roots in this sentence from *Flesh & Blood So Cheap*:

> An hour later, Chief Croker made his inspection. He found that the Asch Building had no damage to its structure.

The root meaning of *spec*, "to look at," is in the word *inspection*, "the act of looking closely." The root meaning of *struct*, "to build," is in the word *structure*, "something that is built." Finding a Latin root in an unfamiliar word can help to unlock the word's meaning. A print or digital dictionary can help confirm the meaning.

Practice and Apply Find the words with Latin roots in each sentence. Give a meaning for the word that includes the meaning of the Latin root.

1. Fire obstructed the doorways, so there was no prospect of escape.

2. Nobody could have predicted the destruction caused by the fire.

3. From the perspective of the jurors, their verdict was fair.

Language Conventions: Capitalization

When you proofread your writing, check to see that you have used capital and lowercase letters correctly. This chart shows general rules.

Capitalize	Examples
First words of sentences and quotations	A fire started. One man called, "Everyone out now!"
People and titles	Mayor Sanchez, General Robert E. Lee, Fire Chief Croker
Geographical names such as cities, continents, regions, streets, roads	New York, East River, Fifth Avenue
Organizations and buildings	League of Women Voters, International Monetary Fund, Empire State Building, Eiffel Tower
Time periods such as days, months, holidays, events, and eras (but not seasons)	Friday, May 3; the Fourth of July; the Triangle Factory Fire; the Jurassic Period
Documents and publications	Declaration of Independence, *Harper's Weekly*, *The Boston Globe*
Adjectives formed from proper nouns	North American cities, Japanese food, Mexican folklore

When you're unsure of which capitalization rule applies, a digital or print manual for usage and style can come in very handy to jog your memory of these rules.

Practice and Apply Some capital letters should be lowercase, and some lowercase letters should be capitalized. Find and fix the errors.

1. Most of the workers at the Triangle waist company were young women, including many italian immigrants.

2. The horse-drawn vehicles of engine company 72 arrived from a Firehouse six blocks away.

3. Sewing machine Operator Samuel Levine recalled, "finally I heard the Firemen cutting their way into the elevator shaft, and they came and let me out."

4. on that Saturday in march, Frank Sommer, a Professor of law, was teaching his class in a room that overlooked the Asch building.

5. The new York *world* reported on chief Croker's reaction to viewing the horrible scene.

Margaret Peterson Haddix (b. 1964) *grew up on a farm in Ohio. While her father was a farmer and her mother a nurse, Haddix always wanted to be a writer. Her inspiration was her father, who was always telling her stories. Haddix has now written more than a dozen books for young adults. Asked why she likes writing for young audiences, Haddix replies that teenagers are naturally great characters in books—often more interesting than adults.*

from Uprising

Historical Novel by Margaret Peterson Haddix

SETTING A PURPOSE This fiction excerpt is based on the real-life event of the Triangle Factory Fire. As you read, think about how the author has used facts and her own imagination to make the events of the fire come to life.

Yetta

Yetta was listening for the bell on the time clock, waiting to finish her day. It was a Saturday afternoon in March, and the spring breezes were back. She'd heard them rattling the windows when the machines were shut down for lunch; she knew that as soon as she stepped outside, they'd tease at her hair and tug at her hat. This year, the breezes seemed to carry a slightly different message: *Another year past and what do you have to show for yourself? So you can read English a little bit better, so you handed out a few suffrage[1] flyers—do you*
10 *think that that's enough?*
   What would ever be enough for Yetta?

---
[1] **suffrage:** the right or privilege of voting.

"I think they set the clocks back again," the girl beside her muttered. "It's got to be past quitting time!"

"And that's why we need a strong union, why we need a closed shop," Yetta muttered back.

The girl rolled her eyes at Yetta.

"Don't you ever give up?" she asked over the clatter of the machine.

"No," Yetta said, but she grinned at the girl, and the girl
20 grinned back, and Yetta thought maybe, just maybe, they'd inched just a little closer to the solidarity² Yetta longed for. This girl's name was Jennie, and she was new.

The bell finally rang, and Yetta and Jennie both stood up and stretched, reviving cramped muscles, unhunching rounded shoulders, stamping feet that had gone numb on the sewing machine pedal.

"I'm going dancing tonight," Jennie said, **mischievously** tapping out a rhythm on the floor. "What are you doing?"

"Um . . . I don't know," Yetta said. "I haven't decided yet."
30 Bella and Jane had been nagging her to go visit Rahel and the new baby, a little boy they'd named Benjamin. Bella and Jane had already gone once, but Yetta had had a cold then and only sent her regrets.

Well, really, I wouldn't want the baby getting sick because of me, Yetta told herself. *Maybe I'm not well enough, even yet. . . .*

"I bet that cutter who watches you all the time would take you dancing," Jennie said. "All you have to do is just . . ." She pantomimed cozying up to an invisible man, gazing up adoringly at the invisible man's face, fluttering her eyelashes.
40 Yetta blushed.

"There's not a cutter who watches me all the time," she said, but she couldn't help glancing toward Jacob's table. Jacob hadn't said a word to her about dancing since she'd turned down his invitation, all those months ago. But he did seem to find lots of reasons to walk past her sewing machine, to ride in the same elevator with her, morning and evening. Even halfway across the room, she could instantly pick out his figure in the cluster of cutters standing around laughing and talking and smoking. Jacob was bent over the table, smoothing
50 out the layers of lawn fabric ready to be cut first thing Monday morning. There had to be at least a hundred and twenty layers

mischievous
(mĭs´chə-vəs) *adj.*
If someone is *mischievous*, the person is naughty.

---

² **solidarity:** unity, especially in the case of workers joining together in a union.

of the gauzy fabric spread across the table, each one separated from the others by sheer tissue paper. Jacob handled it all so gently, almost lovingly. Above his head, the tissue-paper patterns dangled from wires, so when he stood up it was like watching someone across a forest, half hidden by hanging moss and low branches.

Suddenly Jacob and the other cutters jumped back. One of the men sprinted over to a shelf on the wall and seized a 60 red fire pail. Jerkily, he raced back and threw the pail of water under one of the tables, at the huge bin of fabric scraps left over from days and days of cutting out shirtwaists.

"Not again! Those cutters and their cigarettes," Yetta said **scornfully**. It was clear what had happened: One of them had dropped a match or a cigarette butt or a still-burning ember into the scrap bin. At least someone was smart enough to keep buckets of water around, if the cutters couldn't be stopped from smoking.

But then there was a flash, and Yetta saw the flame jump, 70 from under the table to the top of it. More men grabbed buckets, desperately pouring water onto the flames, but there'd been only three buckets on that shelf, so they had to run across the room for more.

The water was nothing to the fire. The flames raced the length of the lawn fabric; they sprang up to the dangling paper patterns and danced from one to the next, the patterns writhing[3] down to ash and spitting off more flames. In seconds the fire had gone from being something to scoff at under a table to a voracious beast ready to engulf 80 the entire room.

Beside Yetta, Jennie began to scream.

"Stop it! This is a fireproof building!" Yetta yelled at Jennie.

But we're tinder,[4] she remembered.

Yetta slammed her hands against Jennie's shoulders and screamed, "Go!"

The aisle between the sewing machine tables was narrow, and the wicker baskets where they stacked the shirtwaists kept snagging their skirts. And other girls were blocking the aisle, 90 some screaming and hysterical like Jennie'd been. One girl

scorn
(skôrn) *n. Scorn* is disrespect or disdain.

---

[3] **writhing:** twisting.
[4] **tinder:** material that burns easily.

fainted right at Yetta's feet. Yetta reached down and slapped her, jerked her up.

"No time for that!" Yetta screamed. "You'll die!"

Across the room, Yetta saw a spark land in a woman's hair. In seconds, the woman's whole pompadour[5] was aflame. Everyone was screaming, but Yetta thought she could hear this woman's screams above all the others. The woman lurched across the room, slammed into one of the windows. No— slammed through. She'd thrown herself out the window.

100   *We're on the eighth floor,* Yetta thought numbly, and now it was her turn to freeze in panic and fear. Sparks were flying throughout the room now, landing everywhere. Anyone could be next.

Hands grabbed Yetta from behind.

"Yetta, come on!"

It was Jacob.

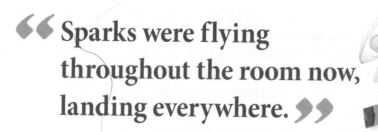

❝ **Sparks were flying throughout the room now, landing everywhere.** ❞

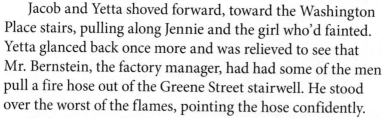

Jacob and Yetta shoved forward, toward the Washington Place stairs, pulling along Jennie and the girl who'd fainted. Yetta glanced back once more and was relieved to see that

110   Mr. Bernstein, the factory manager, had had some of the men pull a fire hose out of the Greene Street stairwell. He stood over the worst of the flames, pointing the hose confidently.

No water came out.

"Turn it on! Turn it on!" Mr. Bernstein was screaming. Yetta wasn't sure if she could hear him or if she was just reading his lips. "Where is the water?" he screamed again.

Not a drop. He flung down the hose and ran.

---

[5] **pompadour:** a woman's hairstyle.

Now Mr. Bernstein was rushing through the crowds of girls, some still heading toward the cloakroom⁶ to get their hats.

"Don't worry about your hats!" he screamed. "Just get out!"

He was slapping and punching the girls, beating them as though he blamed them for the fire. No—he was goading them toward the doors, toward the elevators and the fire escape. He was only slapping the hysterical girls, like Yetta had done with the girl who'd fainted. He was trying to save their lives.

We are on the same side now, Mr. Bernstein and me, Yetta **marveled**.

She shoved against a girl who'd dropped her purse, who'd seen her coins roll under the table.

"Don't stop for that!" Yetta screamed. "It's not worth it! Save your life!"

She and Jacob together pulled the girl up, lifting her past the table, toward the door. There were already dozens of other girls crowded around the door, screaming in Yiddish and English and what Yetta now recognized as Italian. "Open it! Open it!" "Oh, please, for the love of God!" "*Madonna mia, aiutami!*"

But it was locked.

Some of the girls were pounding on the elevator door, too, screaming for the elevator operator to come to them. Miraculously, the elevator door opened, and the crowd surged forward, sobbing and praying and screaming.

"Just wait—just wait—I'll come right back!" the operator hollered.

The doors were closing, but Yetta shoved Jennie forward, shoving her on top of the girls already in the elevator. Saving her, at least.

"*Will* he come back?" Yetta asked Jacob, and Jacob shrugged.

Yetta couldn't just stand there and wait. She wasn't going to stand still while the flames raced toward her, while others pressed their faces against a door that might never open. She grabbed Jacob's hand and pulled him along, circling around the fire. She looked back once and saw that someone had managed to open the door to the Washington Place stairs;

marvel
(mär´vəl) *v.* If you *marvel* at something, you are surprised or astonished by it.

---

⁶ **cloakroom:** a room where coats are hung up.

the door opened in, toward the crowd. Maybe it hadn't been locked after all. Maybe it was just the weight of the crowd pushing forward, pinning it shut.

But it was too late to go back now. Flames were shooting across the path they'd just crossed, speeding across the oiled floor, licking up shirtwaists and fabric scraps and wicker baskets. The air itself seemed to be on fire, the flames living on fabric dust.

"Fire escape," Yetta moaned to Jacob, and it was so hot now that her words felt like flames themselves, painful on her tongue.

"No good," Jacob mumbled back. "Doesn't go all the way to the ground."

So they didn't head for the window near the airshaft, where people were climbing out one at a time, onto the rickety metal railing. What was left?

"Greene Street stairs," Jacob whispered.

Those were back by the table where the fire had started, where it now burned the fiercest. But there was a partition wall blocking off the stairs and the elevator from the rest of the room. On a normal workday that was where the guard sat, inspecting purses and glaring at the girls as if he thought they were all thieves. Today, maybe that partition was enough to keep the fire away from the stairs.

Yetta and Jacob raced on, skirting the flames, still pulling along hysterical, senseless workers who didn't seem to know where to go. They passed a desk where the bookkeeper, Miss Lipshutz, was shouting into the mouthpiece of a telephone, "Please! Somebody listen! Somebody's got to tell the ninth floor! Hello? Somebody—please!"

A spark landed on the sleeve of Yetta's shirtwaist, and she watched in horror as it sputtered and shimmered and burned straight through. She could feel it **singeing** her skin.

Jacob slapped his bare hand onto Yetta's sleeve, starving the flame.

'A *dank*,'[7] Yetta whispered, but there was no time for him to say, "You're welcome," because they were at the doorway to the partition now, shoving their way behind it.

No flames here.

singe
(sĭnj) *v.* If you *singe* something, you slightly burn it.

---
[7] **a dank** (ă dănk): "thank you" in the Yiddish language.

Girls were still standing by the freight elevator door, the only elevator they were normally allowed to use. They were pounding on the closed door like they thought that was their only chance. It was so hot behind the partition that Yetta could barely breathe.

Can people melt? she wondered. In her mind she saw wax dripping down from Sabbath[8] candles. *My life, melting away . . .*

"Stairs!" Jacob screamed at the girls by the elevator door.

He jerked open the stairway door and it opened out, making another obstacle in the tiny vestibule. Yetta and Jacob shoved the girls through the doorway and scrambled in behind them. The stairway was airless and close and still hot, but there were no sparks flying through the air. Through the window in the stairwell, Yetta could see the workers scrambling down the fire escape, teetering precariously on the metal railings, struggling past the metal shutters.

"Hurry!" Yetta screamed at the girls around her. They were sobbing hysterically, clutching the railing, clutching each other. They were yammering away in some language Yetta didn't recognize, or maybe it wasn't a language at all, just witless jabbering.

> **❝ They were sobbing hysterically, clutching the railing, clutching each other. ❞**

"The fire!" one of them managed to say. "What if it's everywhere?"

"There's no smoke coming from down there!" Yetta screamed at them, pointing at the landings below them. "Go down to the ground! You'll be safe! The flames are going up, not down!"

Up.

---

[8] **Sabbath:** the day of worship in the Jewish and other religions.

Yetta glanced up to the landing above her, remembering what the bookkeeper had been screaming into the phone: *Somebody listen! Somebody's got to tell the ninth floor!*

They didn't know. One flight up, on the ninth floor, where two hundred and fifty girls worked, where Yetta had worked before the strike, where Bella worked now—up there, they had no idea there was an inferno raging beneath them, eating up the air, climbing higher and higher and higher.

Almost on their own, Yetta's feet had already started slapping down the stairs, once she finally got the jabbering girls moving. But now she stopped.

Bella, she thought. My other friends. *My sisters. My comrades. My union.*

"What are you doing?" Jacob screamed, already three steps down.

"Somebody has to tell the ninth floor!" she screamed back. "I have to!"

She turned around and began clattering up the stairs.

Jane

"Papa's taking us shopping! Papa's taking us shopping!"
Harriet chanted, bouncing up and down joyously in the
elevator on the way to Mr. Blanck's office at the Triangle
factory.

"Hush. Everybody knows that," Millicent said scornfully.

"She's just excited," Jane said mildly. She patted Harriet's
250 shoulder, trying to calm her down, and gave Millicent and the
elevator operator a sympathetic smile. Harriet's chanting was
a bit maddening. But, as always, it was hard to know the best
way to handle the girls. Miss Milhouse would have scolded
Harriet soundly; she would have taken it as her personal
mission to **stifle** the little girl's exuberant personality. And
she would have praised Millicent to the skies for her tidiness,
her aversion to noise and mess, her ability to sit or stand still
practically forever without squirming or exclaiming.

Personally, Jane thought Millicent was in danger of
260 becoming a priggish bore. And she worried that someday
somebody *would* **stifle** Harriet's exuberance.

"Make it be like a stream," Bella had advised her, when
Jane had asked for help. "You don't want to chop her off—
bam!" She'd slammed the side of her right hand against her
left palm. "But make it go a good way."

"You mean, I should try to channel her enthusiasm into
positive outlets?" Jane asked.

After Jane explained what "channel," "enthusiasm,"
"positive," and "outlets" meant, Bella grinned and nodded:
270 "Yes, yes, exactly! You say what is in my heart for that girl!"

Now, as the elevator zoomed upward, Harriet began
tugging on the elevator operator's jacket.

"Mister, you didn't know we were going shopping, did
you? Papa's taking us as a treat, because our mama went to
Florida for the—what's it called?—social season. And she took
the car with her, on the train, so we had to take a taxi cab to
get here, and the taxi cab's still waiting outside, for us to come
back. Except Madam'selle Michaud's not going shopping with
us, just Papa, and—"
280 "Harriet," Jane said warningly.

"She's okay," the elevator operator said. "You're the Blanck
girls, right? The boss's daughters?"

stifle
(stī'fəl) *v.* If you *stifle*
something, you hold
it back.

"Our papa and Uncle Isaac own the whole factory," Millicent bragged. "They employ more than seven hundred people."

"Millicent!" Jane shot the girl a **reproving** look. *Remember what I've told you about bragging?* she wanted to scold. But she'd always hated Miss Milhouse correcting her in front of other people, so she'd vowed not to do that to Millicent or Harriet. It was just really tempting at times like this. *First thing Monday morning, I need to have a little talk with both girls . . . .*

290

The elevator was gathering speed. Harriet clutched Jane's hand.

"What if the elevator goes all the way through the roof?" she asked.

"Silly, that would never happen," Millicent scoffed.

"Why not?"

"Because—because it wouldn't be proper," Millicent said. She lowered her voice, as if that would keep the elevator operator from hearing. "If we went through the roof, the people below us could see up our skirts."

300

The elevator operator's face turned red, he was trying so hard not to laugh.

Jane sighed.

"There are scientific reasons the elevator would never go through the roof," she said. "Because of how the elevator's made, how it works."

"How does it work?" Harriet asked.

310

Oops. Jane had been afraid she'd ask that. Somehow elevator mechanics had not been in the curriculum at Jane's finishing school.

"Next week we can go to the bookstore and find a book that explains it all," Jane said. "Or maybe you can find one with your papa."

"The elevator runs on a cable," the operator said. "The cable goes up to gears, and those are on the roof. Maybe sometime you can ask your papa to show you the gearbox. But if you want to go to the roof, you have to use the Greene Street stairs. That's the only way to get there."

320

"Thank you," Jane said, smiling gratefully at the operator. He was a pimply boy, maybe a little younger than her. A year ago, he would have been completely invisible to her, but now she wondered about his life. Which country had he come

reprove
(rĭ-prōōv′) *v.* If you *reprove* someone, you express disapproval.

from? Did he bring his family with him, or was he all alone? Was he supporting a widowed mother and a younger brother and sister or two on his salary as an elevator operator? Did Mr. Blanck and Mr. Harris pay him more or less than they paid their sewing machine operators?

330   "Tenth floor," the operator announced, bringing the elevator to a halt and sweeping open the barred door. "Where your papa the boss works."

He had the slightest hint of mockery in his voice, just enough for Jane to hear. He even gave her a conspiratorial wink, which was much too forward, but somehow Jane didn't mind. She winked back, and stepped out onto the polished wood floor of a spacious reception area.

"Miss Mary! Miss Mary!" Harriet cried, running over to one of the desks.

340   "Oh, sweetie, Miss Mary's busy right now," said the short, frazzled-looking woman behind the desk. "The switchboard operator didn't come in today, so Miss Mary has to do all her typing *and* connect every call that comes in. The eighth floor can't even call the ninth floor without my help."

Harriet inspected the telephone switchboard behind the woman's desk, the wires hanging slack.

"So if you plug in this wire here, then—"

"Oh, sweetie, don't touch," Miss Mary said, gently pushing Harriet's hand away. "I really don't have time—I'll explain

350   it to you some other day." She looked up at Jane. "You're the governess, right? You can just take them into Mr. Blanck's office, and then go tell him they're here."

"Where is Mr. Blanck?" Jane asked.

"Oh, he was just down on the ninth floor—no, wait, back in the storeroom? I'm sorry, I'd look for him myself, but—" The harried secretary gestured at the papers strewn across her desk, the bill poking out from her typewriter.

A contraption beside the typewriter buzzed, and Miss Mary looked over at it expectantly.

360   "What's that?" Harriet whispered.

"Oh, it's the new telautograph," Miss Mary said. "'The latest in business machinery,' is how it's advertised. Looks like there's a message coming from the eighth floor. They write something on a pad of paper downstairs, and this pen is supposed to write the same thing on this pad right here."

"Like magic," Harriet breathed.

The pen didn't move.

"It'd be magic if it ever worked right," Miss Mary snorted. "Probably isn't anything anyhow, just the girls downstairs playing with it on their way out the door."

Miss Mary turned back to her typing, and Jane shooed the girls toward Mr. Blanck's office.

"I want to go see the showroom!" Harriet said, skipping down the hall. "Madam'selle Michaud, you'll love it! You can see all the latest fashions before Paris!"

"That's because even Paris doesn't know as much about fashion as our papa," Millicent said, agreeing with her younger sister for once.

"Some other time," Jane said. "Miss Mary said to wait in his office, remember?"

They turned in at a doorway, but the sign on the door said ISAAC HARRIS, not MAX BLANCK.

"Uncle Isaac!" Harriet called.

\A man behind a desk waved, but there was another man with him, a dapper-looking gentleman holding up samples of delicate embroidery.[9]\Jane flashed an apologetic look at Mr. Harris and pulled the girls away.

"Look, you can see into the pressing department from here," Harriet said, pointing past a break in the wall into a vast open space, where rows and rows of weary-looking workers stood over ironing boards. Each one of the irons was connected to the ceiling by an odd array of tubes.

"Is Papa afraid those workers are going to steal his irons?" Harriet asked. "Is that why the irons are tied up?"

Jane didn't have the slightest idea, so she was glad that Millicent answered first.

"No, silly. The gas comes down those tubes and heats the irons," Millicent said. "Papa says we must never ever go in there, because one of those irons could blister our skin in an instant."

And does he care at all about the workers operating the irons? Jane wondered bitterly. *Some of them look no older than Millicent!*

"Quick, now," she told the girls. "Into the office. Wait right there."

---

[9] **embroidery:** decorative needlework in cloth.

> **❝ Papa says we must never ever go in there, because one of those irons could blister our skin in an instant. ❞**

She was infected suddenly with some of Miss Mary's franticness, or maybe she was just tired of hearing the admiring tone in the girls' voices every time they mentioned their papa. Or maybe it was the sight of the **haggard** workers
410 hunched over their irons, girls who looked entirely too young, who would probably look entirely too old after just a year or two on the job. Regardless, Jane was ready to be done working for the day, ready to be out in the fresh air, arm in arm with Bella and Yetta. She was pretty sure that she and Bella had finally convinced Yetta to go with them to visit Rahel and Rahel's new baby. It would probably be a touching family reunion.

Yes, Yetta will be so much happier if she'll just forgive her sister for getting married, Jane thought. *My father and I, on the*
420 *other hand . . .*

She hadn't forgotten her promise to Mr. Corrigan to write her father a letter. She'd written him many, many letters, actually—she'd just torn them all up.

What is there to say?

Jane pulled the door shut on Millicent and Harriet, catching barely a glimpse of Mr. Blanck's imposing mahogany desk, of the lovely arched windows behind the desk. Harriet was scrambling into the huge leather chair.

"Harriet! A young lady would never put her feet up on the
430 desk!" she heard Millicent cry out, in scandalized horror.

Jane decided to let Millicent wage that battle on her own. Secretly, she was thinking, *Oh, Harriet, maybe you should go on being the kind of girl who puts her feet on desks. Better that, than hiding under them . . .*

She scurried down the hall, back to the double elevator doors. She decided to look for Mr. Blanck on the ninth floor first. She knew that was where Bella worked, and it'd be good

haggard
(hăg´ərd) *adj.* If you're *haggard*, you are worn out and exhausted.

if she could warn Bella that she'd be a few minutes late getting
out to the street, especially if it took her a long time to find

440   Mr. Blanck.

     Passing Miss Mary's desk, Jane was surprised to notice
that the woman had vanished, leaving the telephone receiver
hanging off the hook.

     That's odd. She seemed like such a conscientious sort . . . .

     A different elevator operator came up this time, a
swarthily handsome Italian man.

     *If Bella's precious Pietro looks anything like that, no wonder
she can't forget him!* Jane thought. Then she had to hide her
face so he didn't see her giggling at her own wickedness.

450   The elevator buzzed annoyingly. Again and again
and again.

     "Eighth floor's going crazy," the elevator operator growled.
He scowled at the panel of lights that kept flashing at him
as he shut the door behind Jane and the elevator began its
descent. "Hold on a minute! I'm coming! I'm coming!"

     "They've probably all got spring fever," Jane said. "And
it's Saturday."

     "Yeah, yeah," the operator grumbled, letting her out on the
ninth floor. "But do they gotta take it out on me?"

460   The ninth floor was not what Jane expected. After the
cleanliness and elegance of the tenth floor, she wasn't prepared
for this dim, dirty space with the tables and the machines and
the girls packed in so tightly together. The room was huge,
but the tables stretched from one side of the building to the
other. By the windows, there wasn't even space to walk around
the tables. And shirtwaists and shirtwaist parts were piled
everywhere, mountains of fabric by each machine.

     *No wonder Bella felt so overwhelmed, coming here from her
tiny little village in Italy,* Jane thought.

470   Jane herself felt a little overwhelmed.

     "Excuse me. Do you know where I could find Mr. Blanck
or Bella Rossetti?" she asked the girl at the nearest sewing
machine.

     The girl looked up blankly, and said something that might
have been "I don't speak English" in some other language.
Just then a bell sounded, and the machines stopped and
hundreds of girls sprang up from their machines all at once. It
spooked Jane a little, the darkness of the room and the foreign
jabbering and the girls moving like machines, themselves. But

480 then one of the girls stepping out of the cloakroom began to sing, "Ev'ry little movement has a meaning of its own"—one of those popular songs that you heard everywhere, nowadays. Some of the other girls joined in, and they all seemed so light-hearted suddenly. Saturday afternoon and the sun was shining and work was over; these girls looked happier than anyone Jane had ever seen at a formal ball.

Then, two tables away, Jane spotted Bella heading down the aisle between the tables and laughing and talking to the girls around her.

490 "Jane! What are you doing here?" Bella shouted over to her.

" Just then a bell sounded, and the machines stopped and hundreds of girls sprang up from their machines all at once. "

"Looking for you and Mr. Blanck," Jane said.

"Well, we wouldn't be together!" Bella called back merrily.

Jane worked her way through the crowd toward her friend. She explained about Millicent and Harriet and the shopping, and how long it would take her to get down to the sidewalk. Then Bella said, "Oh, wait, you have to meet my friends—this is Annie and Dora and Josie and Essie and Ida. And come here—" She pulled her back down the aisle between the tables.

500 "This is my boss, Signor Carlotti. This is my friend, Jane Wellington, Signor Carlotti, and she knows proper Italian *and* proper English."

"Hello," Signor Carlotti said.

"I am a factory inspector," Jane said, suddenly inspired to lie. "If I were to interview the girls in this factory, would they tell me that you treat them with respect? Are you fair to all your workers?"

At the first word out of her mouth, Signor Carlotti's face changed—first, to awe at her upper-class accent, then to fear.

510   "Oh, er—yes! Yes! Of course!" Signor Carlotti exclaimed.

It was all Jane and Bella could do, not to double over giggling as they walked away.

"Maybe he really will change how he treats you, Monday morning!" Jane whispered.

"Oh, do you think so?" Bella asked **wistfully**.

Across the room, strangely, Jane heard Yetta's voice now. She couldn't make out the words, but Yetta seemed to be calling out in great excitement, from the midst of the crowd of girls getting ready to leave. Maybe she was talking them

520   into another strike. Maybe this one would work—maybe Yetta would get her dearest wish.

"Doesn't Yetta work on the eighth floor?" Jane asked.

Before Bella could answer, screams came suddenly from the back of the room. Screams—and a great burst of light.

wistful
(wĭst´fəl) *adj.* If you're *wistful*, you are thoughtful and longing for something.

Bella

Bella couldn't tell what had happened. It was just like her first day of work, when everyone else was yelling and running and knocking over baskets and trampling shirtwaists they didn't bother to stop and pick up. And, for a moment, just like on that first day, Bella couldn't understand the words everyone
530 else kept saying. The English part of her brain shut off, the Yiddish words in her brain evaporated, even the Italian she heard around her sounded garbled and foreign.

Then she smelled smoke, and the words made sense.

"Fire!"

"*S'brent!*"

"*Fuoco!*"

Jane clutched her shoulders.

"Where do we go? What do we do?" Jane asked. "We always had fire drills at school—where have they told you to
540 go in the event of a fire?"

Bella didn't know what a fire drill was. People were crowded in all around her, shoving and pushing from behind, blocking the way in front of her. The tables on either side of the aisle seemed to be closing in on her. She was penned in, just like a goat or a pig.

No better than an animal, Bella thought, and somehow this seemed all of piece with not being able to read and wanting only food and Signor Carlotti spitting on her and Signor Luciano cheating her. *I bet back home your family
550 slept with goats and chickens in the house,* Signora Luciano had sneered at her once, and Bella hadn't even understood that that was an insult. But now she'd seen how other people lived; she'd seen what Jane and Yetta expected out of life. She refused to think of herself as a hog in a pen waiting to be slaughtered.

"This way!" she said, grabbing Jane's hand and scrambling up on top of the nearest table.

From there, she could see the fire. It was blowing in the back window, one huge ball of flame rolling across the
560 examining tables stacked with shirtwaists. The flames kept dividing, devouring stack after stack of shirtwaists, racing each other down the tables.

Where are they trying to get to? Bella wondered.

The first flame leaped from the examining table to the first row of sewing tables.

"It's coming toward us!" Jane screamed behind her. "Where do we go?"

Bella looked around frantically. Girls were packed in around the doors and elevators. Only a handful seemed to remember that there was another way out.

"The fire escape!" Bella screamed back, grateful for that day so long ago, before the strike, when she'd actually seen where the fire escape was.

The aisles were still crowded. Bella leaped from one table to the next, and somehow Jane managed to follow. Bella leaped again, suddenly surefooted. Except for the smoke burning her eyes and throat, she could have been back in the mountains near Calia, jumping from rock to rock.

"I've got to—make sure—Harriet and Millicent—are—all—right," Jane panted behind her, as they cleared another table. She began coughing, choking on the smoke.

Bella bent down and snatched up a pile of shirtwaist sleeves. She held two over her mouth and handed the others to Jane.

"Here. So you can breathe."

They kept racing across the tables. And it really was a race, because the flames were speeding toward the fire escape window too. Through the smoke, Bella could barely make out the progress of the fire. *The flames are going to get there first— no, we are!—no, look how fast the fire's moving . . . .*

They reached the end of the tables and jumped down to the floor. The flames were reaching for Bella's skirt, so she lifted it up as she ran for the fire escape. She had one leg out the window, balanced on the metal railing, when Jane grabbed for her arm.

"Wait—is that safe?" Jane asked.

She'd actually stopped to peer down at the rickety stairs, at the flames shooting out the eighth-floor window, at the eighth-floor shutters that seemed to be blocking the path of all the other girls already easing their way down.

"Safe?" Bella repeated numbly. Anything seemed safer than where they were now. But she pulled back a little, reconsidering. She shifted her weight back from the foot that was on the fire escape to the knee perched on the windowsill. And in that moment, the fire escape just . . . fell away.

> ## "She'd actually stopped to peer down at the rickety stairs, at the flames shooting out"

"*Madonna mia!*" Bella cried. Jane grabbed her, pulling her back in through the window. "The other girls—"

Jane shook her head, maybe meaning, *Don't ask,* maybe meaning, *I saw it all, them falling, I can't even begin to tell you how awful it was . . . .* Bella tried to remember who'd been ahead of her on the fire escape—Dora? Essie? Ida? All of them? The boot of the girl immediately in front of Bella had had a fancy silver buckle, the kind of thing a girl would have been proud of, the kind of thing she would have gone around showing off, making sure her skirt flounced up to display it as much as possible. Had Bella seen that buckle before?

"Bella! Where's another exit?" Jane cried out.

But Bella couldn't think about anything but a fancy silver buckle.

Suddenly Yetta was there.

"Greene Street stairs!" Yetta was screaming. "Go!"

Bella grabbed her friends' hands and took off running again. But Yetta pulled her hand back.

"You go on!" she screamed. "I still have to—"

The rest of Yetta's words were lost in the crackle of advancing flames.

The smoke rose and fell and shifted. One minute, Bella could see ahead of her, a straight path to the partition by the door. The next minute, she was groping blindly forward, tripping over people who had fallen. She'd dropped the shirtwaist sleeves she'd been using to cover her mouth and nose. She grabbed up another stack, but just before she pressed it to her face she noticed that these shirtwaist sleeves were already burning. She dropped them to the floor, and began to sag toward the floor herself.

But she was still holding Jane's hand. Jane yanked her back up.

"The stairs—" Jane gasped.

They stumbled forward. Bella pulled her wool skirt
640 up over her head, blocking out the smoke and the flames.
Immodest, she thought, an English word she'd just learned.
She didn't care.

Jane grabbed a bucket of water from a nearby shelf and
flung it toward the fire, and some of it splashed back onto
Bella. None of it seemed to reach the fire. Or, if it did, it didn't
make any difference. The flames kept shooting forward. There
were no more buckets left on the shelf, only some tipped over
empty on the floor.

"The girls will be so scared," Jane breathed, and Bella
650 knew she meant Harriet and Millicent, waiting in their
father's office upstairs. "I've got to—"

She stopped, looking down.

"My skirt," she said.

A ring of flames was dancing along the bottom of her
skirt. She stepped forward and the flames flared.

"We'll put it out," Bella said.

Jane began rushing toward a vat by the stairs.

"Water—"

"No, no! That's machine oil, sewing machine oil!" Bella
660 screamed, pulling her back. The dark oil was bubbling over,
running down the sides of the vat. The fire was beginning to
race along the streams of oil. Bella had to jump past it. And
then Jane was on one side of the flames, Bella on the other.

"Jane!" Bella screamed.

"Go on!" Jane screamed back. "Go get the girls! Make sure
they're safe up there!"

"But you—"

"I'll go another way!" Jane said. "I'll meet you later!"

Bella whirled around. The pathway to the stairs was
670 closing in. In a second it would be gone.

Bella ran forward.

COLLABORATIVE DISCUSSION How has the author combined
fact and fiction in this novel excerpt? Talk about your ideas with
other group members.

Analyze Point of View

In a work of fiction, the **narrator** is the voice that tells the story. The author's choice of narrator is called the **point of view**. Authors deliberately choose a point of view in order to give readers a certain perspective on the story. The three types of point of view are shown in this chart.

Point of View in Narratives		
First Person	**Third-Person Limited**	**Third-Person Omniscient ("All-Knowing")**
• Narrator is a story character. • Narrator uses first-person pronouns such as *I, me, mine, we, our.* • Reader sees events and characters through narrator's eyes.	• Narrator is not a character and is outside the story. • Narrator uses third-person pronouns such as *he, she, him, her, their.* • Reader sees events and characters through one character's eyes.	• Narrator is not a character and is outside the story. • Narrator uses third-person pronouns such as *he, she, him, her, their.* • Reader is shown different characters' thoughts and feelings.

In the novel excerpt you've just read, the author has made an unusual choice in point of view. By presenting events through the eyes of multiple characters, the author:

- shows what the characters think of one another as they interact
- shows characters in different places at the same time
- builds suspense by shifting back in time when the reader already knows about the danger to come

Which point of view has the author chosen, and what impact does this have on how the reader experiences the story?

Compare and Contrast: Genres

Historical fiction is set in the past and includes real places and events. The author researches the topic as a nonfiction author does, but uses imagination as well as facts to create imaginary scenes and dialogue between characters. Sometimes the fictional story will depict real people and imaginary characters interacting and experiencing real historical events.

To compare and contrast two forms of writing, notice how the details of real events appear in the fictional story. For example, read lines 15–20 from the nonfiction excerpt *Flesh & Blood So Cheap.* Then read lines 51–57 from the novel *Uprising.* How has the author of the fictional story used factual details differently from the author of the nonfiction selection?

Analyzing the Text

ELA RL.7.2, RL.7.3, RL.7.6, RL.7.9, W.7.3, W.7.4, W.7.5, W.7.9, W.7.10 **ELD** PI.7.2, PI.7.6, PI.7.7, PI.7.10

Cite Text Evidence   Support your responses with evidence from the text.

1. **Summarize** At the end of this novel excerpt, where is each character going and why?

2. **Compare** How does the shifting point of view help you understand the similarities and differences among the three characters?

3. **Cite Evidence** How does the author use the chapter entitled "Jane" to show contrasts between the business owners and the workers?

4. **Analyze** Reread lines 590–618. Then look back to lines 212–222 of the excerpt from *Flesh & Blood So Cheap*. Why might the author of *Uprising* have introduced the fancy silver buckle?

5. **Evaluate** Find a passage in which the author provides facts about the setting. How effectively does the author make this information seem part of a fictional work? Explain.

6. **Synthesize** How is dialogue in this historical novel different from the quotations in the nonfiction excerpt from *The Story of the Triangle Factory Fire*?

PERFORMANCE TASK

Writing Activity: Narrative Suppose that a short chapter follows the three that you have read. In this chapter, the point of view remains third-person limited, but events are seen through the eyes of a different character. Write that new chapter.

- Choose a character already introduced, such as Jacob or Harriet.
- Read closely to learn about the character's likely goals, experiences, and interactions with other characters.

- Reread the nonfiction excerpts about the Triangle Fire to gather more factual details.
- Write a draft of your chapter.
- Read it aloud to a partner, and make revisions based on your listener's suggestions.

Critical Vocabulary

mischievous	scorn	marvel	singe
stifle	reprove	haggard	wistful

Practice and Apply Use each bold word in your answer to the question. Explain your reasoning.

1. Would someone smile with **scorn** or have a **wistful** smile while thinking about an unreachable goal?

2. Would someone have a **haggard** expression while behaving in a **mischievous** way?

3. What might a **reproving** look **stifle**?

4. Would you rather **marvel** at a campfire or have it **singe** you?

Vocabulary Strategy: Analogies

Verbal analogies are comparisons between two pairs of words. The relationship between the first pair of words is the same as the relationship between the second pair. For example, if the first pair of words is *big* and *little*, the second pair might be *tall* and *short*, because both words in each pair are antonyms. The analogy is stated, "*Big* is to *little* as *tall* is to *short*." It is written with colons in this pattern: **big : little :: tall : short**. This chart shows common relationships in verbal analogies.

Relationship	Example
Word : Antonym	heavy : weightless :: troubled : joyful
Word : Synonym	rush : haste :: mistake : error
Part : Whole	finger : hand :: branch : tree
Object : Description	blanket : warm :: sun : bright
Object : Action or Use	ruler : measure :: hammer : pound

Practice and Apply Choose the word that best completes each analogy. Give the reason for your choice.

1. obstacle : barrier :: goal : (achieve, difficulty, destination)

2. basket : wicker :: sweater : (wool, container, jacket)

3. partition : separate :: doorway : (build, enter, elevator)

4. flame : inferno :: snowflake : (fire, blizzard, cooling)

5. respectfully : scornfully :: generously : (selfishly, admiringly, humorously)

Language Conventions: Phrases

A **verbal** is a verb form used as a noun, an adjective, or an adverb. A **participle** is a verbal that functions as an adjective to modify a noun or pronoun.

Verb	Present Participle	Past Participle	Adjective Use
hurry	(is) hurrying	(has) hurried	a hurrying crowd; a hurried job
pay	(is) paying	(has) paid	the paying viewers; a paid bill;
sing	(is) singing	(has) sung	all of us singing; the sung tunes

A **participial phrase** is made of a participle and any other words that complete its meaning. The participial phrase is underlined in each of these sentences. The whole phrase functions as an adjective.

> Yetta listened for the bell <u>signaling the end of work</u>. (participial phrase modifies the noun *bell*)

> <u>Hunched over their machines</u>, the workers grew tired. (participial phrase modifies the noun *workers*)

> <u>Reading this historical novel</u>, we learned about a tragic fire. (participial phrase modifies the pronoun *we*)

A **gerund** is another verbal. It is formed from the present participle of a verb, the form with the ending *-ing*. A gerund functions as a noun in a sentence.

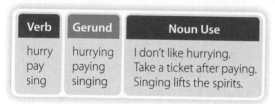

Verb	Gerund	Noun Use
hurry	hurrying	I don't like hurrying.
pay	paying	Take a ticket after paying.
sing	singing	Singing lifts the spirits.

A **gerund phrase** is made of a gerund and any other words that complete its meaning. The gerund phrases are underlined in this sentence. Each whole phrase functions as a noun.

> The factory workers began <u>screaming in fear</u> and <u>running for their lives</u>, but <u>escaping the flames</u> was not possible.

Practice and Apply Identify the verbal phrase in each sentence. Tell how you know it is a gerund phrase or a participial phrase.

1. Men grabbed buckets and started pouring water onto the flames.

2. Blinded by the smoke, workers could not find their way.

3. The fire was like a wild beast, attacking everything in its path.

4. Some people met their death by leaping out a window.

Background *In 1995, when* **Craig Kielburger** (b. 1982) *was only twelve years old, he founded Free the Children, an international organization whose goal is to help young people achieve their fullest potential. Almost two million youths are now involved in education and development programs in 45 countries. Kielburger has received wide recognition, recently becoming one of the youngest recipients of the Order of Canada.*

Craig Kielburger Reflects on Working Toward Peace

Personal Essay by Craig Kielburger

SETTING A PURPOSE In this essay, Kielburger calls for a fairer, more just world. As you read, pay attention to how he describes his experiences as a young activist.

When I was very young I dreamed of being Superman, soaring high above the clouds and swooping down to snatch up all of the bad people seeking to destroy our planet. I would spend hours flying across the park, stopping momentarily to kick a soccer ball in my path or to pat my dog, Muffin, who ran faithfully at my heels.

One day, when I was twelve years old and getting ready for school, I reached for the newspaper comics. On the front page was a picture of another twelve-year-old boy from Pakistan, with a bright red vest and his fist held high. According to the article, he had been sold into bondage[1] as a weaver and forced to work twelve hours a day tying tiny knots to make carpets. He had lost his freedom to laugh and to play. He had lost his

10

---

[1] **bondage:** the state of being held as a slave.

(t) ©David Livingston/Getty Images; (c) ©Katrina Brown/Shutterstock

Craig Kielburger Reflects on Working Toward Peace **307**

freedom to go to school. Then, when he was twelve years old, the same age as me, he was murdered.

I had never heard of child labor and wasn't certain where Pakistan was—but that day changed my life forever. I gathered a group of friends to form an organization called Free the Children.

Over the past four years, in my travels for Free the Children, I have had the opportunity to meet many children around the world—children like Jeffrey, who spends his days in a Manila garbage dump, alongside rats and maggots, where he sifts through decaying food and trash, trying to salvage a few valuable items to help his family survive. He dreams of leaving the garbage dump one day.

I have met children like eight-year-old Muniannal, in India, with a pretty ribbon in her hair, but no shoes or gloves, who squats on the floor every day separating used **syringes** gathered from hospitals and the streets for their plastics. When she pricks herself, she dips her hand into a bucket of dirty water. She dreams of being a teacher.

I have met children in the sugarcane fields of Brazil who wield huge machetes close to their small limbs. The cane they cut sweetens the cereal on our kitchen tables each morning. They dream of easing the hunger pains in their stomachs.

Poverty is the biggest killer of children. More than 1.3 billion people—one-quarter of the world's population— live in absolute poverty, struggling to survive on less than one dollar a day. Seventy percent of them are women and children. I dream of a day when people learn how to share, so that children do not have to die.

Every year, the world spends $800 billion on the military, $400 billion on cigarettes, $160 billion on beer, and $40 billion playing golf. It would only cost an extra $7 billion a year to put every child in school by the year 2010, giving them hope for a better life. This is less money than Americans spend on cosmetics in one year; it is less than Europeans spend on ice cream. People say, "We can't end world poverty; it just can't be done." The 1997 United Nations Development Report carries a clear message that poverty can be ended, if we make it our goal. The document states that the world has the materials and natural resources, the know-how, and the people to make a poverty-free world a reality in less than one generation.

syringe
(sə-rĭnj´) n. A *syringe* is a medical instrument used to inject fluids into the body.

Gandhi[2] once said that if there is to be peace in the world it must begin with children. I have learned my best lessons from other children—children like the girls I encountered in India who carried their friend from place to place because she had no legs—and children like José.

I met José in the streets of San Salvador, Brazil, where he lived with a group of street children between the ages of eight and fourteen. José and his friends showed me the old abandoned bus shelter where they slept under cardboard boxes. They had to be careful, he said, because the police might beat or shoot them if they found their secret hideout. I spent the day playing soccer on the streets with José and his friends—soccer with an old plastic bottle they had found in the garbage. They were too poor to own a real soccer ball.

> **Gandhi once said that if there is to be peace in the world it must begin with children.**

We had great fun, until one of the children fell on the bottle and broke it into several pieces, thus ending the game. It was getting late and time for me to leave. José knew I was returning to Canada and wanted to give me a gift to remember him by. But he had nothing—no home, no food, no toys, no **possessions**. So he took the shirt off his back and handed it to me. José didn't stop to think that he had no other shirt to wear or that he would be cold that night. He gave me the most precious thing he owned: the jersey of his favorite soccer team. Of course, I told José that I could never accept his shirt, but he insisted. So I removed the plain white T-shirt I was wearing and gave it to him. Although José's shirt was dirty and had a few small holes, it was a colorful soccer shirt

possession
(pə-zĕsh´ən) *n.*
A *possession* is
something you own.

[2] **Gandhi:** Mohandas Karamchand Gandhi (more commonly called Mahatma Gandhi), an Indian leader whose belief in justice inspired many people around the world.

and certainly much nicer than mine. José grinned from ear to ear when I put it on.

I will never forget José, because he taught me more about sharing that day than anyone I have ever known. He may have been a poor street child, but I saw more goodness in him than all of the world leaders I have ever met. If more people had the heart of a street child, like José, and were willing to share, there would be no more poverty and a lot less suffering in this world. Sometimes young people find life today too depressing. It all seems so hopeless. They would rather escape, go dancing or listen to their favorite music, play video games or hang out with their friends. They dream of true love, a home of their own, or having a good time at the next party. At sixteen, I also like to dance, have fun, and dream for the future. But I have discovered that it takes more than material things to find real happiness and meaning in life.

One day I was the guest on a popular television talk show in Canada. I shared the interview with another young person involved in cancer research. Several times during the program this young man, who was twenty years old, told the host that he was "gifted," as indicated by a test he had taken in third grade. Turning my way, the host **inquired** whether I, too, was gifted. Never having been tested for the gifted program, I answered that I was not.

inquire
(ĭn-kwīr´) v. If you *inquire* about something, you ask about it.

When I returned home my mother asked me, "Are you certain you aren't gifted?" I realized that I had given the wrong answer. I was gifted, and the more I reflected, the more I concluded that I had never met a person who was not special or talented in some way.

Some people are gifted with their hands and can produce marvelous creations in their **capacity** as carpenters, artists, or builders. Others have a kind heart, are compassionate, understanding, or are special peacemakers; others, again, are humorous and bring joy into our lives. We have all met individuals who are gifted in science or sports, have great organizational skills or a healing touch. And, of course, some people are very talented at making money. Indeed, even the most physically or mentally challenged person teaches all of us about the value and worth of human life.

capacity
(kə-păs´ĭ-tē) n. A person's *capacity* is his or her role or position.

I think that God, in fact, played a trick on us. He gave each and every person special talents or gifts, but he made no one gifted in all areas.

Collectively, we have all it takes to create a just and peaceful world, but we must work together and share our talents. We all need one another to find happiness within ourselves and within the world.

I realize, now, that each of us has the power to be Superman and to help rid the world of its worst evils—
140 poverty, loneliness, and **exploitation**. I dream of the day when Jeffrey leaves the garbage dump, when Muniannal no longer has to separate used syringes and can go to school, and when all children, regardless of place of birth or economic circumstance, are free to be children. I dream of the day when we all have José's courage to share.

exploitation
(ĕk´sploi-tā´shən) *n.*
Exploitation is the unfair treatment or use of something or someone for selfish reasons.

COLLABORATIVE DISCUSSION What is Craig Kielburger's purpose in describing the particular children he has met? Talk about your ideas with other group members.

Analyze Text: Personal Essay

A **personal essay,** like "Craig Kielburger Reflects on Working Toward Peace," is a nonfiction essay in which an author expresses an opinion or provides some insight based on personal experiences. Authors have different purposes for writing a personal essay. Often it is to make others aware of an important issue or topic by connecting the topic to the author's own life.

Personal essays often include the following elements:
- descriptions of personal experiences in which the author gained significant insight or learned a lesson
- first-person point of view, using the pronouns *I* and *we*
- a mixture of storytelling, personality, facts, and wisdom
- casual language that seems like a conversation with the reader

Review Kielburger's personal essay, and find an example of each element.

Determine Author's Point of View

The author of a personal essay has a **perspective,** the unique combination of ideas, values, feelings, and beliefs that influence the way he or she looks at a topic. In his essay, Kielburger shows how he looks at himself, others, and his role in the world. To understand an author's perspective, note these features in the essay:
- statements of the author's **opinions**—personal ideas that cannot be proven true
- details and examples from the author's experiences
- words and descriptions that have emotional impact
- the writer's **tone,** or attitude toward a subject, such as humorous or serious

As you read personal essays, you can figure out the author's perspective by completing a chart such as this one.

Statement, Detail, or Tone	What It Reveals About Kielburger
"that day changed my life forever" (line 17)	He is affected by the stories and hardships of others.

Reread lines 20–41. What does the last sentence of each paragraph reveal about Kielburger's perspective?

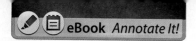

ELA RI.7.1, RI.7.2, RI.7.3, RI.7.5, RI.7.6, RI.7.8, W.7.1, SL.7.4a, SL.7.6
ELD PI.7.3, PI.7.4, PI.7.6, PI.7.7, PI.7.9, PI.7.11, PII.7.1

Analyzing the Text

Cite Text Evidence Support your responses with evidence from the text.

1. **Cause/Effect** Why did the story about the murdered boy have such a strong impact on Kielburger?

2. **Infer** What words would you use to describe Kielburger, and why are those descriptions fitting?

3. **Analyze** Reread lines 37–54. Why does Kielburger provide this information? What effect might he hope this section has on the reader?

4. **Draw Conclusions** What is Kielburger's purpose in saying that he is gifted?

5. **Analyze** How does Kielburger connect the introduction and conclusion of his essay?

6. **Evaluate** Reread lines 94–108. Is Kielburger's statement about "the heart of a street child" valid? Why do you think that?

PERFORMANCE TASK

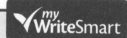

Speaking Activity: Argument Has this essay persuaded you that global poverty can be ended? Why or why not? Present an oral argument in which you give your opinion of Craig Kielburger's essay.

- Consider questions such as, *Does Kielburger do enough to convince you? Does his choice of evidence effectively support his point of view? If not, why is it inadequate and what additional evidence might he have included?*

- Take notes on the evidence that Kielburger uses to support his claim about ending poverty.
- As you draft your speech, be sure to include an interesting introduction that clearly states your claim.
- Use the evidence you found in the text to support your claim.
- Include a conclusion that summarizes your opinion.
- Practice your speech aloud, using appropriate eye contact, adequate volume, and clear pronunciation.
- Deliver your speech and have a group of peers evaluate it.

Critical Vocabulary

syringe	possession	inquire
capacity	exploitation	

Practice and Apply Identify the vocabulary word that is tied in meaning to the italicized word in each question. Give your reasons.

1. Which word goes with *needle*?

2. Which word goes with *answer*?

3. Which word goes with *underpaid*?

4. Which word goes with *ownership*?

5. Which word goes with *skill*?

Vocabulary Strategy: Multiple Meanings

The definition of a word often depends on its **context,** the words and sentences that surround it. Note the word *capacity* in these two sentences:

> **A. The only tickets left were "Standing Room Only" because the theater was filled to capacity.**

> **B. Some people are gifted with their hands and can produce marvelous creations in their capacity as carpenters, artists, or builders.**

To figure out the meaning in each sentence, first use context to make a logical guess. Then you can use a print or digital dictionary to look up and choose the appropriate definition.

The word *capacity* has many meanings. The context helps you make a logical guess about which one fits in each sentence. In sentence A, *capacity* means "a maximum number." In sentence B, from Kielburger's essay, *capacity* means "a position or role." These meanings can be confirmed in a dictionary.

Practice and Apply Use context to give a likely meaning for the italicized word in each sentence. Check your idea in a print or digital dictionary.

1. A. Kielburger read an *article* in the newspaper.
   B. Remember to put the correct *article* before a noun.

2. A. Kielburger met children at work in fields of *cane*.
   B. The man tapped the *cane* on the sidewalk as he walked.

3. A. The United Nations published a *document* about ending poverty.
   B. Students learn to *document* their sources when doing research.

Language Conventions: Dangling Modifiers

A **modifier** is a word or a group of words that changes, or modifies, the meaning of another word in a sentence. Some modifiers are phrases used as adjectives and adverbs to describe or give more detail. A **dangling modifier** is a modifier that modifies a word not clearly stated in the sentence. It often appears at the start of a sentence.

In the following examples, take note of the sentences with a dangling modifier and their corrected versions.

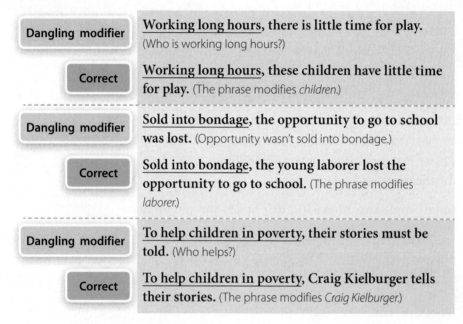

Dangling modifier	<u>Working long hours</u>, there is little time for play. (Who is working long hours?)
Correct	<u>Working long hours</u>, these children have little time for play. (The phrase modifies *children*.)
Dangling modifier	<u>Sold into bondage</u>, the opportunity to go to school was lost. (Opportunity wasn't sold into bondage.)
Correct	<u>Sold into bondage</u>, the young laborer lost the opportunity to go to school. (The phrase modifies *laborer*.)
Dangling modifier	<u>To help children in poverty</u>, their stories must be told. (Who helps?)
Correct	<u>To help children in poverty</u>, Craig Kielburger tells their stories. (The phrase modifies *Craig Kielburger*.)

Practice and Apply Identify the correctly written sentences. Fix the sentences with dangling modifiers.

1. Shocked by the article about a murdered child weaver, Kielburger felt a strong desire to make a change.

2. To bring attention to child poverty, the first step was forming an organization.

3. To support his family, one boy hunts for items in a garbage dump.

4. Separating used syringes for plastic parts, harm to the little girl's health is likely.

5. Sharing their few possessions, generous hearts are found among the poor.

6. Finding poverty everywhere in the world, it's hard to imagine ending the problem.

Background *When child activist Craig Kielburger was twelve years old, he became interested in the plight of child laborers. Inspired by the story of twelve-year-old Iqbal, a child labor activist who had been murdered in South Asia, Kielburger realized that a child could make a difference in the world. Kielburger then traveled to South Asia to see child labor first hand. With the help of a film crew, he documented his journey so that the world could see what he himself had witnessed.*

MEDIA ANALYSIS

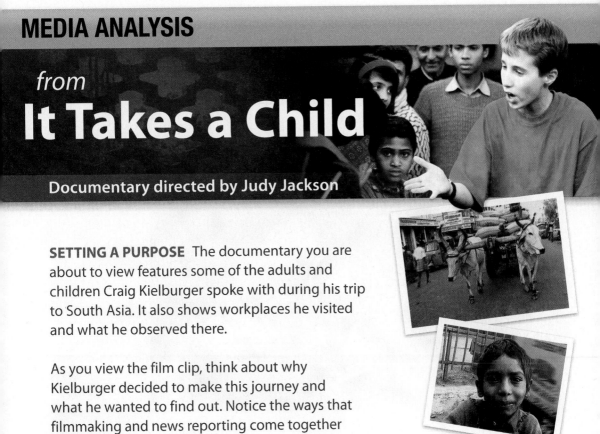

from It Takes a Child

Documentary directed by Judy Jackson

SETTING A PURPOSE The documentary you are about to view features some of the adults and children Craig Kielburger spoke with during his trip to South Asia. It also shows workplaces he visited and what he observed there.

As you view the film clip, think about why Kielburger decided to make this journey and what he wanted to find out. Notice the ways that filmmaking and news reporting come together to help you understand Kielburger's reasons for traveling to South Asia. Write down any questions you have during viewing.

Format: Documentary

Running Time: 2:54 minutes

AS YOU VIEW Documentary filmmakers gather factual material about their subjects, much like news reporters do, and use film to tell a true story about their subjects. The filmmakers then use various techniques to convey the information in a way that will have an impact on the viewers.

As you view the documentary clip, consider how the director's choice of scenes affects the impact of the words spoken in the interviews. As needed, pause the video and write notes about what impresses you and about ideas you might want to talk about later. Replay or rewind the video so that you can clarify anything you do not understand.

COLLABORATIVE DISCUSSION With a partner, discuss how the film presents an inside view into child labor conditions. Which of the interviews and images had the most impact? Why? Discuss the concepts the film conveys and how it conveys them. Cite specific evidence from the documentary to support your ideas.

Analyze Media

A **documentary** is a nonfiction film that gives viewers information about important people, major events, significant discoveries, or historical places. Documentaries use features to help viewers understand the information.

Features of a Documentary	Strategies for Viewing
Interviews are usually filmed specifically for a documentary. Filmmakers may interview: • experts on the subject • people who knew the person • people who were involved in an event	Think about why the filmmaker chose this person for an interview. Does the person: • have special knowledge about the subject? • present another side of the story?
Footage is filmed material that gives information about a subject. Documentary filmmakers combine different types of footage to tell their subject's story. Footage can include film clips, news reports, photographs, and interviews about a subject.	Think about why the particular footage was chosen. Does it: • show details of a historical time? • create an emotional response? • reveal the filmmaker's perspective or point of view?
Voice-over narration is the voice of an unseen speaker that is heard on a documentary. The voice-over can provide important facts about the subject. It can also help explain the footage.	Listen to the voice-over narration for additional information about the footage. Does the voice-over change from one speaker to another? What points made by voice-overs seem most important to the subject?
Sound effects can be used for a variety of purposes.	Follow the music cues. Do they signal a change in the documentary's setting or mood? Listen for sound effects, such as screeching tires or bombs exploding. Do they help you better understand what is happening? Listen to the dialogue. Does it help you better understand the subjects?

Think about how these features interact with each other in the clip from *It Takes a Child* to tell the story of Craig Kielburger's commitment to the cause of exposing the injustices of child labor.

Analyzing the Media

ELA RI.7.6, RI.7.7, SL.7.2, SL.7.3, SL.7.4, SL.7.5
ELD PI.7.6, PI.7.7, PI.7.9

Cite Text Evidence   Support your responses with evidence from the media.

1. **Infer and Summarize** What is the **central idea,** or most important idea about a topic, that the documentary presents? Describe the scenes that take place in the film and how those scenes support the central idea.

2. **Analyze** Identify the filmmaker's purpose or purposes in making the documentary. What key parts of the film convey the purpose or purposes?

3. **Infer** Think about the features the filmmaker uses in the documentary. Fill out a chart like this one and tell how they clarify the issues presented.

Feature	How It Clarifies Issues

4. **Analyze** How does the opening introduce the setting? What combination of features work together in the opening to present a sense of the place Kielburger is visiting and to help you understand the setting?

5. **Compare** Compare and contrast the information in the narrator voice-over and in the interviews. What information does each feature contribute?

6. **Evaluate** Think about your reading of the personal essay by Craig Kielburger in this collection. How do the ideas presented in the documentary help clarify the points made in the essay, and how do both relate to the collection topic, "Guided by a Cause"?

PERFORMANCE TASK

Media Activity: Photo Documentary
What does it take to be committed to a cause despite great obstacles? Let people know about a person in your school or community who works on an important social cause. Create a photo documentary to tell that person's story.

- Take photos of the person involved in his or her work, or use photos that already exist.

- Choose some of the documentary features you learned about to help you create your documentary.

- Interview your subject and include quotations in your documentary or record a soundtrack of the interview with music.

- Present your documentary to a group of classmates. Then discuss their reactions to it.

Nikki Giovanni (b. 1943) *has been one of the best-known American poets since publishing her first book of poetry in 1968. Giovanni grew up in the racially segregated South. When Giovanni attended college, she became a part of a movement of African American writers who were finding new ways to express pride in their distinct culture. In addition to her poetry collections, Giovanni is also an award-winning children's author.*

A Poem for My Librarian, Mrs. Long

(YOU NEVER KNOW WHAT TROUBLED LITTLE GIRL NEEDS A BOOK)

Poem by Nikki Giovanni

AS YOU READ In the poem, Nikki Giovanni looks back at her childhood and the people who most influenced her. As you read, think about how Giovanni's childhood experiences shaped her dreams and her writing.

At a time when there was no tv before 3:00 P.M.
And on Sunday none until 5:00
We sat on front porches watching
The jfg[1] sign go on and off greeting
5 The neighbors, discussing the political
Situation congratulating the preacher
On his sermon

---

[1] **jfg:** a brand of coffee that was popular in Knoxville, Tennessee; an old
electrically lit sign for the coffee is a famous landmark in Knoxville, Tennessee.

There was always radio which brought us
Songs from wlac in nashville and what we would now call
10 Easy listening or smooth jazz but when I listened
Late at night with my portable (that I was so proud of)
Tucked under my pillow
I heard nat king cole and matt dennis, june christy and
      ella fitzgerald
15 And sometimes sarah vaughan sing black coffee
Which I now drink
It was just called music

There was a bookstore uptown on gay street
Which I visited and inhaled that wonderful odor
20 Of new books
Even today I read hardcover as a preference paperback only
As a last resort

And up the hill on vine street
(The main black corridor) sat our carnegie library[2]
25 Mrs. Long always glad to see you
The stereoscope[3] always ready to show you faraway
Places to dream about

Mrs. Long asking what are you looking for today
When I wanted *Leaves of Grass* or alfred north whitehead
30 She would go to the big library uptown and I now know
Hat in hand to ask to borrow so that I might borrow
Probably they said something humiliating since southern
Whites like to humiliate southern blacks

But she nonetheless brought the books
35 Back and I held them to my chest
Close to my heart
And happily skipped back to grandmother's house
Where I would sit on the front porch
In a gray glider and dream of a world
40 Far away

---

[2] **carnegie library:** a library built with money donated by the businessman
   Andrew Carnegie.

[3] **stereoscope:** an optical instrument with two eyepieces used to create a three-
   dimensional effect when looking at two photographs of the same scene.

I love the world where I was
I was safe and warm and grandmother gave me neck kisses
When I was on my way to bed

But there was a world
45 Somewhere
Out there
And Mrs. Long opened that wardrobe
But no lions or witches[4] scared me
I went through
50 Knowing there would be
Spring

COLLABORATIVE DISCUSSION Notice how the poet talks about
familiar and faraway places. How does the poem itself travel
to a faraway place? How does it keep the reader grounded in
familiarity? Talk about your ideas with other group members.

---

[4] **wardrobe . . . lions or witches:** refers to *The Lion, the Witch and the Wardrobe*
by C. S. Lewis; in the book, the characters visit a make-believe land, called
Narnia, via the wardrobe, or closet, in a spare room.

Determine Meaning: Style

ELA RL.7.4, RL.7.5
ELD PI.7.8

Style is the particular way in which a poet or author writes—not *what* is said but *how* it is said. It is made up of many elements, including word choice, stanza and line length, figurative language, sound devices, and form. Style can be described with words such as *formal, whimsical, flowery,* and *plain*.

By making careful use of word choices and techniques, a poet can craft poetry with a signature style. For example, "A Poem for My Librarian, Mrs. Long," written by Nikki Giovanni in the form of **free verse,** presents irregular rhythm and rhyme and language that flows like everyday speech. The poet conveys meaning through a variety of stylistic techniques, including:

Punctuation/ Capitalization	Poets might use these in unconventional ways to draw attention or prompt readers to look at something differently.
Stanza and Line Length	In free verse, poets can vary the lengths of stanzas or lines to suit the stylistic effects the poet wants to achieve.
Figurative Language	Using simile and metaphor allows a poet to play creatively with language.
Sound Devices	Along with rhythm and rhyme, a poet can choose from a range of devices, often to create a mood or convey certain meanings.

Read lines 8–17 of "A Poem for My Librarian, Mrs. Long." Identify the stylistic technique you see.

Determine Theme

ELA RL.7.2
ELD PI.7.6

A **theme** is a message about life or human nature that a writer or poet shares with the reader. In poetry, themes are not always stated directly. The reader of a poem can infer a theme by thinking about the poem as a whole and looking at what is said, what is suggested, and how the words, sounds, and ideas come together.

In the poem you've just read, the poet is also the speaker, reflecting on her childhood experiences. After giving details about everyday activities, she turns her attention to her love of books. The poem is dedicated to Mrs. Long, the librarian who likely endured adversity so that the young girl could have access to the books she wanted.

What seems most important to understand about the poet's relationship with Mrs. Long?

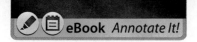

Analyzing the Text

ELA RL.7.1, RL.7.2, RL.7.4, RL.7.5,
W.7.3, W.7.4, W.7.10
ELD PI.7.6, PI.7.7, PI.7.8, PI.7.10

Cite Text Evidence   Support your responses with evidence from the text.

1. **Cite Evidence** What words would you use to describe the poet as a child? Why would those words fit?

2. **Infer** Reread lines 28–33. What does the poet now understand about Mrs. Long?

3. **Interpret** An **allusion** is a reference to a famous person, place, event, or work of literature. The final stanza of this poem makes an allusion to C. S. Lewis's famous fantasy novel *The Lion, the Witch and the Wardrobe*, in which young characters help end a witch's curse of endless winter. Why might the poet have ended the poem with this allusion?

4. **Analyze** How does the poet's use of punctuation and capitalization contribute to the poem's meaning?

5. **Evaluate** The **tone** of a poem expresses the poet's attitude toward a subject. These are some words that can be used to describe tone: *awed, ironic, thoughtful, grateful, hopeful, angry*. Do any of those words seem to fit this poem? Choose one word, or think of another, that describes the poem's tone, and tell why that word fits the poem.

6. **Analyze** How would you describe Nikki Giovanni's style based on the stylistic techniques she employs in "A Poem for My Librarian, Mrs. Long"?

7. **Draw Conclusions** What could be the theme of this poem?

PERFORMANCE TASK

Writing Activity: Poem Mrs. Long acted generously to a child, and that child never forgot it. Think back to an experience or a connection with someone who acted generously to you. Free-write about your memory— noting phrases, sentences, quotations, and anything else that comes to mind.

Use your written ideas to write a poem in free verse form. Look back at the poem you've just read for ideas about how to:

- convey the sights, sounds, and smells you remember
- portray the person you remember
- tell about your feelings then and now

Language Conventions: Combining Sentences with Phrases

ELA L.7.1a, L.7.1c
ELD PII.7.7

By using phrases to combine sentences, you can vary the length of your sentences and make your writing sound mature. The following are types of phrases you can use to combine sentences.

- A **prepositional phrase** begins with a preposition, such as *at, about, for, from, in,* or *of.*
- An **infinitive phrase** begins with an infinitive verb (*to* + verb).
- A **participial phrase** begins with the past or present participle of a verb, such as *walked* or *walking.*
- A **gerund phrase** begins with a gerund, or *-ing* word. A gerund phrase always functions as a noun, rather than an adjective or an adverb.

The chart below provides an example for how to use each phrase type to combine sentences.

Phrase Type	Two Sentences	Combined Sentence
Prepositional phrase	The poet remembers her childhood. She has vivid memories.	The poet has vivid memories of her childhood.
Infinitive phrase	The stereoscope showed pictures of faraway places. The girl dreamed about the places.	The stereoscope showed the girl pictures of faraway places to dream about.
Participial phrase	The girl held borrowed books close to her heart. She skipped home with them.	Holding her borrowed books close to her heart, the girl skipped home.
Gerund phrase	The poet remembers her librarian. She feels grateful for the librarian's help.	Remembering her librarian's help makes the poet feel grateful.

Practice and Apply Combine the two sentences with a phrase of your choice.

1. Families sat on their front porches. They greeted their neighbors.

2. The young girl visited the bookstore. New books smelled wonderful.

3. The library was located in the black neighborhood. It was on Vine Street.

4. The girl loved poetry. She asked the librarian for *Leaves of Grass.*

5. Mrs. Long borrowed the book from the uptown library. She probably faced prejudice there.

6. The poet says that Mrs. Long opened a wardrobe. Mrs. Long helped a child enter a new world.

Background *In the late 1800s, social reformers in the United States believed they could help move Native Americans into mainstream society by re-educating Native American children away from their families. Author* **D'Arcy McNickle** *(1904–1977) was forced to go to a boarding school. McNickle went on to college where he became interested in literature and writing. In his stories, he gained a reputation for vivid descriptions of how the larger mainstream culture affected traditional Native American ways.*

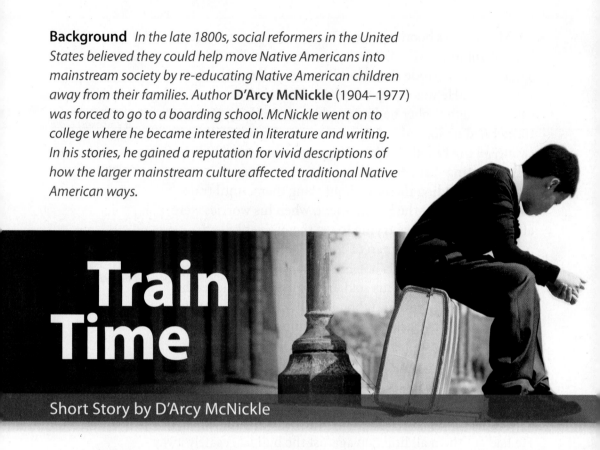

Train Time

Short Story by D'Arcy McNickle

SETTING A PURPOSE As you read, think about the moral problem that the main character is faced with. What is that problem, and how does he deal with it?

On the depot platform everybody stood waiting, listening. The train has just whistled, somebody said. They stood listening and gazing eastward, where railroad tracks and creek emerged together from a tree-choked canyon.

Twenty-five boys, five girls, Major Miles—all stood waiting and gazing eastward. Was it true that the train had whistled?

"That was no train!" a boy's voice explained.

"It was a steer bellowing."

10   "It was the train!"

Girls crowded backward against the station building, heads hanging, tears starting; boys pushed forward to the edge of the platform. An older boy with a voice already turning heavy stepped off the weather-shredded boardwalk and stood wide-legged in the middle of the track. He was the doubter. He had heard no train.

Major Miles boomed, "You! What's your name? Get back here! Want to get killed! All of you, stand back!"

The Major strode about, soldierlike, and waved
20 commands. He was **exasperated**. He was tired. A man driving cattle through timber had it easy, he was thinking. An animal trainer had no idea of trouble. Let anyone try corralling twenty to thirty Indian kids, dragging them out of hiding places, getting them away from relatives and together in one place, then holding them, without tying them, until train time! Even now, at the last moment, when his worries were almost over, they were trying to get themselves killed!

Major Miles was a man of **conscience**. Whatever he did, he did earnestly. On this hot end-of-summer day he perspired
30 and frowned and wore his soldier bearing. He removed his hat from his wet brow and thoughtfully passed his hand from the hair line backward. Words tumbled about in his mind. Somehow, he realized, he had to vivify¹ the moment. These children were about to go out from the Reservation and get a new start. Life would change. They ought to realize it, somehow—

"Boys—and girls—" there were five girls he remembered. He had got them all lined up against the building, safely away from the edge of the platform. The air was stifling with end-
40 of-summer heat. It was time to say something, never mind the heat. Yes, he would have to make the moment real. He stood soldierlike and thought that.

"Boys and girls—" The train whistled, dully, but unmistakably. Then it repeated more clearly. The rails came to life, something was running through them and making them sing.

Just then the Major's eye fell upon little Eneas and his sure voice faltered. He knew about little Eneas. Most of the boys and girls were mere names; he had seen them around
50 the Agency with their parents, or had caught sight of them scurrying behind tipis and barns when he visited their homes. But little Eneas he knew. With him before his eyes, he paused.

He remembered so clearly the winter day, six months ago, when he first saw Eneas. It was the boy's grandfather, Michel Lamartine, he had gone to see. Michel had contracted to cut wood for the Agency but had not started work. The Major had gone to discover why not.

---

¹ **vivify:** to make more lively.

exasperate
(ĭg-zăs′pə-rāt′) v.
If you *exasperate* someone, you make the person very angry.

conscience
(kŏn′shəns) n.
Conscience is the conforming to or living up to one's own sense of what is right.

It was the coldest day of the winter, late in February, and
the cabin, sheltered as it was among the pine and cottonwood
60   of a creek bottom, was shot through by frosty drafts. There
was wood all about them. Lamartine was a woodcutter
besides, yet there was no wood in the house. The fire in
the flat-topped cast-iron stove burned weakly. The reason
was apparent. The Major had but to look at the bed where
Lamartine lay, twisted and shrunken by rheumatism.[2] Only
his black eyes burned with life. He tried to wave a hand as the
Major entered.

   "You see how I am!" the gesture indicated. Then a nerve-
strung voice faltered. "We have it bad here. My old woman,
70   she's not much good."

   Clearly she wasn't, not for wood-chopping. She sat close by
the fire, trying with a good-natured grin to lift her **ponderous**
body from a low seated rocking chair. The Major had to
motion her back to her ease. She breathed with an asthmatic[3]
roar. Wood-chopping was not within her range. With only a
squaw's hatchet[4] to work with, she could scarcely have come
within striking distance of a stick of wood. Two blows, if she
had struck them, might have put a stop to her laboring heart.

   "You see how it is," Lamartine's eyes flashed.

80   The Major saw clearly. Sitting there in the frosty cabin,
he pondered their plight and at the same time wondered if he
would get away without coming down with pneumonia.[5] A
stream of wind seemed to be hitting him in the back of the
neck. Of course, there was nothing to do. One saw too many
such situations. If one undertook to provide **sustenance** out
of one's own pocket there would be no end to the demands.
Government salaries were small, resources were limited.
He could do no more than shake his head sadly, offer some
vague hope, some small sympathy. He would have to get away
90   at once.

   Then a hand fumbled at the door; it opened. After a
moment's struggle, little Eneas appeared, staggering under a
full armload of pine limbs hacked into short lengths. The boy
was no taller than an ax handle, his nose was running, and

ponderous
(pŏn´dər-əs) *adj.*
If something is
ponderous, it is very
heavy.

sustenance
(sŭs´tə-nəns) *n.*
Sustenance is the food
needed to live.

---

[2] **rheumatism** (rōō´mə-tĭz´əm): a disease causing stiffness in the joints and
muscles.
[3] **asthmatic** (ăz´măt´ĭk): characterized by labored breathing and coughing.
[4] **squaw's hatchet:** a small hand ax used by Native American women to cut small
things.
[5] **pneumonia** (nŏō-mōn´yə): a disease causing inflammation of the lungs.

he had a croupy cough.[6] He dropped the wood into the empty box near the old woman's chair, then straightened himself.

A soft chuckling came from the bed. Lamartine was full of pride. "A good boy, that. He keeps the old folks warm."

Something about the boy made the Major forget his determination to depart. Perhaps it was his wordlessness, his uncomplaining wordlessness. Or possibly it was his loyalty to the old people. Something drew his eyes to the boy and set him to thinking. Eneas was handing sticks of wood to the old woman and she was feeding them into the stove. When the firebox was full a good part of the boy's armload was gone. He would have to cut more, and more, to keep the old people warm.

The Major heard himself saying suddenly: "Sonny, show me your woodpile. Let's cut a lot of wood for the old folks."

It happened just like that, **inexplicably**. He went even farther. Not only did he cut enough wood to last through several days, but when he had finished he put the boy in the Agency car and drove him to town, five miles there and back. Against his own principles, he bought a week's store of groceries, and excused himself by telling the boy, as they drove homeward, "Your grandfather won't be able to get to town for a few days yet. Tell him to come see me when he gets well."

That was the beginning of the Major's interest in Eneas. He had decided that day that he would help the boy in any way possible, because he was a boy of quality. You would be shirking your duty if you failed to recognize and to help a boy of his sort. The only question was, how to help?

When he saw the boy again, some weeks later, his mind saw the problem clearly. "Eneas," he said, "I'm going to help you. I'll see that the old folks are taken care of, so you won't have to think about them. Maybe the old man won't have rheumatism next year, anyhow. If he does, I'll find a family where he and the old lady can move in and be looked after. Don't worry about them. Just think about yourself and what I'm going to do for you. Eneas, when it comes school time, I'm going to send you away. How do you like that?" The Major smiled at his own happy idea.

inexplicable
(ĭn-ĕk´splĭ-kə-bəl) *adj.* If something is *inexplicable*, it is difficult to understand.

---

[6] **croupy cough:** an illness that causes a loud barking cough.

> ## He had decided that day that he would help the boy in any way possible.

There was silence. No shy smiling, no look of gratitude, only silence. Probably he had not understood.

"You understand, Eneas? Your grandparents will be taken care of. You'll go away and learn things. You'll go on a train."

The boy looked here and there and scratched at the ground with his foot. "Why do I have to go away?"

"You don't have to, Eneas. Nobody will make you. I thought you'd like to. I thought—" The Major paused, confused.

"You won't make me go away, will you?" There was fear in the voice, tears threatened.

"Why, no Eneas. If you don't want to go. I thought—"

The Major dropped the subject. He didn't see the boy again through spring and summer, but he thought of him. In fact, he couldn't forget the picture he had of him that first day. He couldn't forget either that he wanted to help him. Whether the boy understood what was good for him or not, he meant to see to it that the right thing was done. And that was why, when he made up a quota[7] of children to be sent to the school in Oregon, the name of Eneas Lamartine was included. The Major did not discuss it with him again but he set the wheels in motion. The boy would go with the others. In time to come, he would understand. Possibly he would be grateful.

Thirty children were included in the quota, and of them all Eneas was the only one the Major had actual knowledge of, the only one in whom he was personally interested. With each of them, it was true, he had had difficulties. None had wanted to go. They said they "liked it at home," or they were "afraid" to go away, or they would "get sick" in a strange country; and the parents were no help. They, too, were frightened and uneasy. It was a tiresome, hard kind of duty, but the Major knew what was required of him and never hesitated.

---

[7] **quota:** a predetermined, fixed amount of something or people.

The difference was, that in the cases of all these others, the problem was routine. He met it, and passed over it. But in the case of Eneas, he was bothered. He wanted to make clear what this moment of going away meant. It was a breaking
170 away from fear and doubt and **ignorance**. Here began the new. Mark it, remember it.

His eyes lingered on Eneas. There he stood, drooping, his nose running as on that first day, his stockings coming down, his jacket in need of buttons. But under that shabbiness, the Major knew, was real quality. There was a boy who, with the right help, would blossom and grow strong. It was important that he should not go away hurt and resentful.

The Major called back his straying thoughts and cleared his throat. The moment was important.
180 "Boys and girls—"

The train was pounding near. Already it had emerged from the canyon, and momentarily the headlong flying locomotive loomed blacker and larger. A white plume flew upward—*Whoo-oo, whoo-oo.*

The Major realized in sudden sharp remorse that he had waited too long. The vital moment had come, and he had paused, looked for words, and lost it. The roar of rolling steel was upon them.

Lifting his voice in desperate haste, his eyes fastened on
190 Eneas, he bellowed: "Boys and girls—be good—"

That was all anyone heard.

ignorance
(ĭg′nər-əns) *n.*
Ignorance is the condition of being uneducated or uninformed.

COLLABORATIVE DISCUSSION What has the Major succeeded in doing? What has he failed to do? Talk about your ideas with other group members.

Analyze Stories: Character Development

The **characters** in a work of fiction are the people, animals, or imaginary creatures who take part in the action. The way that the author creates and develops the characters is called **characterization**. Authors use four basic methods of characterization:

Methods of Characterization

- making direct comments about a character through the voice of the narrator
- describing the character's physical appearance
- presenting the character's speech, thoughts, and actions
- presenting information about the character through the thoughts, speech, and actions of other characters

With these methods, the author helps readers identify **character traits,** which are the qualities of appearance and personality that make a character seem real. Readers can infer character traits from the character's words, actions, thoughts, appearance, and interactions with other characters.

Reread lines 53–118 of "Train Time," the paragraphs in which the Major first meets Eneas. Tell how the author uses each of the four listed methods of characterization to show Eneas to readers and to develop his character.

Analyze Stories: Flashback

ELA RL.7.3
ELD PI.7.6

In a literary work, a **flashback** is an interruption of the action to show events that took place at an earlier time. A flashback provides information to help readers understand a character's current situation. To follow a narrative, readers pay attention to language that signals shifts in time. For example:

the author shifts back in time, using flashback	**"Stanley thought back to last month, when he first saw his new home."**
the author ends the flashback, shifting ahead to the present time of the story	**"Now, just one month later, Stanley felt as if he had never lived anywhere else."**

In which sentence of "Train Time" does the author first lead readers back in time?

ELA RL.7.1, RL.7.2, RL.7.3, RL.7.6,
W.7.1, W.7.4, W.7.9a, W.7.10
ELD PI.7.6, PI.7.7, PI.7.10

Analyzing the Text

Cite Text Evidence   Support your responses with evidence from the text.

1. **Predict** What is going to happen to the children waiting for the train?

2. **Cite Evidence** Reread lines 17–27. What does this section tell you about Major Miles? What method(s) of characterization was used to convey that information?

3. **Infer** How does the Major's point of view differ from the other characters' points of view?

4. **Analyze** What section of the story is told as a flashback? What does the flashback reveal about the plot and characters?

5. **Analyze** What might the reader understand about the situation that the Major appears not to understand?

6. **Connect** How does the **setting**—the time and place of the action— affect the reader's understanding of the characters?

7. **Draw Conclusions** Why might the author have decided to end the story as he did?

PERFORMANCE TASK

Writing Activity: Character Analysis
In "Train Time," the Major does not think he is doing anything wrong—or does he? Write two or three paragraphs to describe the character of the Major.

- Answer these questions to help organize your ideas: What does the Major value? What actions does he take? How does the Major seem to feel about Reservation Indians?

- Include quotations from the story to support your ideas about the Major.

- Discuss the different ways the author reveals the Major's character traits.

Critical Vocabulary

ELA L.7.4c, L.7.6
ELD PI.7.6

| exasperate | conscience | ponderous |
| sustenance | inexplicable | ignorance |

Practice and Apply Answer each question with *yes* or *no*. With your group, use examples and reasons to explain your answer.

1. If someone was **exasperated,** could you tell?

2. Should you trust a person of **conscience**?

3. Could an action be **ponderous**?

4. Is **sustenance** unnecessary?

5. Could a person behave in an **inexplicable** way?

6. Is **ignorance** the same as ignoring someone?

Vocabulary Strategy: Using a Dictionary

When you find an unknown word in a text, you can first use **context,** or the words and sentences around the word, to try to determine its meaning. Note the word *conscience* in this sentence from "Train Time": *Major Miles was a man of* conscience. There are no helpful context clues to the meaning of *conscience*. If you look it up in a dictionary, you might find these definitions:

> **1a.** An awareness of morality in regard to one's behavior; a sense of right and wrong that urges one to act morally: *Let your conscience be your guide.* **b.** A source of moral or ethical judgment or pronouncement: *a document that serves as the nation's conscience.* **c.** Conformity to one's own sense of right conduct: *a person of unflagging conscience.*

Definition **1c** best matches the meaning of *conscience* in the sentence.

A dictionary entry has additional information about a word, including a word's **pronunciation** and **part of speech**. The letters and symbols in parentheses show the word's pronunciation, followed by an italicized abbreviation of the part of speech. The pronunciation key in a dictionary can help you determine how to pronounce a word.

Practice and Apply Find these words in "Train Time": *bearing* (line 30), *tipis* (line 51), *gesture* (line 88). Use a print or digital dictionary to identify the definition that matches the context and the part of speech. Then use the pronunciation key to say the word.

Language Conventions: Misplaced Modifiers

A **modifier** is a word or a group of words that changes, or modifies, the meaning of another word in a sentence. A **misplaced modifier** is in the wrong place in a sentence and can confuse a reader. As you review your writing, follow these steps to identify and fix misplaced modifiers.

- Find the modifier.
- Identify what word the modifier was intended to modify.
- Place the modifier as close as possible to the word, phrase, or clause it is supposed to describe.

In the following examples, note the underlined modifier and the word or phrase it was intended to modify.

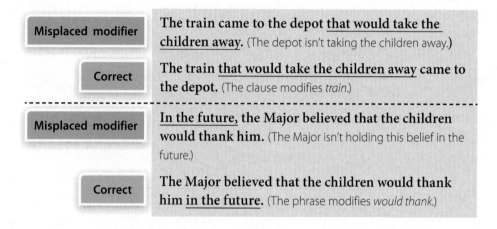

Misplaced modifier	The train came to the depot <u>that would take the children away.</u> (The depot isn't taking the children away.)
Correct	The train <u>that would take the children away</u> came to the depot. (The clause modifies *train*.)
Misplaced modifier	<u>In the future,</u> the Major believed that the children would thank him. (The Major isn't holding this belief in the future.)
Correct	The Major believed that the children would thank him <u>in the future</u>. (The phrase modifies *would thank*.)

Practice and Apply Each sentence has a misplaced modifier. Find and fix the error.

1. Major Miles made a list of thirty children's names fulfilling his duty.

2. Little Eneas was the only one of all the children the Major knew.

3. Leaving the Reservation, Major Miles was sure that the children would have better lives.

4. The children had tears and fearful faces who were leaving their families.

5. Eneas would give up the only culture he had known at the school in Oregon.

6. The train was coming down the tracks that would change the children's lives forever.

COLLECTION 6
PERFORMANCE TASK A

Write an Informative Essay

ELA W.7.2a–f, W.7.4, W.7.5, W.7.6, W.7.7, W.7.8, W.7.10
ELD PI.7.4, PI.7.10, PII.7.1, PII.7.7

This collection focuses on important social causes. In the selections about the Triangle Factory Fire, you learned how a great tragedy led to public outcry to improve workplace conditions. In this activity, you will do additional research about a topic or person related to this fire. You will draw from the texts in the collection and your research findings to write an informative essay.

A successful informative essay

- clearly states the topic in a strong thesis statement
- organizes ideas and concepts logically
- supports central ideas with details from credible sources
- uses appropriate transitions to link ideas
- establishes and maintains a formal style
- provides a conclusion that follows from and supports the information presented

Visit hmhfyi.com to explore your topic and enhance your research.

Mentor Text The opening phrases of these sentences help readers to follow the order of events in this passage from *Flesh & Blood So Cheap.*

> " At exactly 4:45 P.M., someone pulled the eighth-floor fire alarm. In less than two minutes, the horse-drawn vehicles of Engine Company 72 arrived from a firehouse six blocks away. The moment they arrived, the firefighters unloaded their equipment and prepared to swing into action. "

myNotebook

Use the annotation tools in your eBook to record details from the selections that support your topic. Save each detail to your notebook.

PLAN

Determine Your Topic Review the excerpts from *The Story of the Triangle Factory Fire, Flesh & Blood So Cheap,* and *Uprising.* Brainstorm a list of possible topics or people to research, such as the trial following the fire, the new labor laws, Frances Perkins, or Fire Chief Croker. Choose the topic that most interests you.

- Transform your topic into a research question you want to answer, such as *How did the fire impact workplace safety, and what was Frances Perkins' role in that? Why were fire precautions so inadequate during that time?*

ACADEMIC VOCABULARY

As you plan and draft your essay, be sure to use the academic vocabulary words.

contrast

despite

error

inadequate

interact

- Make sure your question is open-ended.
- Generate further questions that will help you find specific evidence.

Gather Information Look for information in the selections that relates to your topic. Take notes on key points, observations, and events that will help you gain a better understanding of your topic, answer your questions, and support your main points.

Do Research Use print and digital sources to find additional information that addresses your research question.

- Use keywords or subject searching in the library to find print sources. Find credible Internet sources.
- Use evidence to explain and support your main points.
- Check that the information you find is supported by the information you read in the collection.

Interactive Lessons
For help in doing your research, use
- Conducting Research: Types of Sources

Organize Your Ideas Organize your essay by creating an outline showing the information you will present in each paragraph. Make sure each idea follows logically from the previous idea and leads into the next idea.

Consider Your Purpose and Audience What does the audience already know? What background information will they need? Keep this in mind as you prepare to write.

PRODUCE

✓*my*WriteSmart
Write your rough draft in *my*WriteSmart. Focus on getting your ideas down, rather than on perfecting your choice of language.

Write Your Essay Use your notes and your outline as you begin your draft.

- Begin with an attention-grabbing introduction.
- Organize your information into paragraphs of related ideas.
- Include facts, concrete details, definitions, and examples.
- Transition from one logical point to another, using words and phrases such as *because, despite, therefore,* and *as a result of.*
- Use a formal tone.
- Write a conclusion that supports your explanation.

Interactive Lessons
For help in drafting your essay, use
- Writing Informative Texts: Elaboration

Language Conventions: Condensing Ideas

The more precisely worded the sentence, the more ideas a piece of writing can convey. For example, read this passage from *Flesh & Blood So Cheap.*

> "Workers, shouting, crying, and gasping for air, slowly made their way downstairs. "

The passage might have read, "Workers slowly made their way downstairs. The workers were shouting. The workers were crying. The workers were gasping for air." Instead, the actions are condensed into a participial phrase, making it more precise.

REVISE

Evaluate Your Draft Use the chart to evaluate your essay.

Have a group of peers review your draft in *my*WriteSmart. Ask your reviewers to note any facts, details, or examples that do not support your thesis.

Questions	Tips	Revision Techniques
Is my thesis statement, or controlling idea, clear?	**Underline** the thesis statement.	**Revise** your thesis statement to explain what the essay will explore.
Is the essay organized by order of importance or in the order that key elements appear?	**Highlight** the key details. **Decide** whether they reflect a logical order.	**Rearrange** details in a logical order. **Use** transitions to connect the details.
Are my facts and details credible?	**Underline** the facts and details. **Check** that the evidence is from reliable sources.	**Add** facts and details from reliable sources.
Is the style of my essay formal?	**Highlight** any contractions and use of casual wording.	**Change** contractions. **Revise** any slang or casual expressions.
Does the conclusion restate my thesis?	**Underline** the restatement.	**Add** a sentence restating the thesis, if you need to. **Check** that it summarizes the main points.

PRESENT

Create a Finished Copy Post your essay as a blog on a personal or school website. Consider these additional options:

- Deliver your essay as a speech to the class.
- Organize a group discussion to share your ideas.
- Circulate a video recording of your essay.

PERFORMANCE TASK A RUBRIC
INFORMATIVE ESSAY

Ideas and Evidence	Organization	Language
4 • The introduction is appealing and informative; a thesis statement clearly identifies the topic in an engaging way. • The topic is well developed with relevant examples, concrete details, and interesting facts from the selections and other credible sources. • The concluding section capably summarizes the information presented.	• The organization is effective and logical throughout the essay. • Transitions successfully connect related ideas.	• The writing reflects a formal style, with strong, precise language. • Sentence beginnings, lengths, and structures vary and have a rhythmic flow. • Spelling, capitalization, and punctuation are correct. • Grammar and usage are correct.
3 • The introduction could do more to grab the reader's attention; the thesis statement identifies the topic. • One or two key points could be better supported with more relevant examples, concrete details, and facts from the selections and other credible sources. • The concluding section summarizes the information presented.	• The organization is confusing in a few places. • A few more transitions are needed to connect related ideas.	• The style is informal in a few places. • Language is too general in some places. • Sentence beginnings, lengths, and structures vary somewhat. • A few spelling, capitalization, and punctuation mistakes occur. • Some grammatical and usage errors are repeated in the essay.
2 • The introduction is only partly informative; the thesis statement only hints at a topic. • Most key points need more support in the form of relevant examples, concrete details, and facts. • The concluding section partially summarizes the information presented.	• The organization is logical in some places but often doesn't follow a pattern. • More transitions are needed throughout to connect related ideas.	• The style becomes informal in several places. • Overly general language is used in several places. • Sentence structures barely vary, with some fragments or run-on sentences present. • Spelling, capitalization, and punctuation are often incorrect. • Grammar and usage are incorrect in several places.
1 • The introduction is missing. • Examples, details, and facts are missing. • The essay lacks a concluding section.	• A logical organization is not used; information is presented randomly. • Transitions are not used, making the essay difficult to understand.	• The style is inappropriate for the essay. • Language is too general to convey the information. • Repetitive sentence structure, fragments, and run-on sentences make the writing difficult to follow. • Spelling, capitalization, and punctuation are incorrect throughout. • Several grammatical and usage errors change the meaning of the writer's ideas.

Interactive Lessons

To help you complete this task, use *Participating in Collaborative Discussions.*

Participate in a Panel Discussion

ELA W.7.2a–f, W.7.4, W.7.5, W.7.10, SL.7.1a–d
ELD PI.7.3, PI.7.4, PI.7.5, PI.7.9, PI.7.10, PI.7.12

In this collection, you read about problems in the world that inspire people to take action to solve those problems. In this activity, you will draw from the selections you read to take part in a panel discussion about what commitment to a cause can mean.

A successful participant in a panel discussion

- makes a clear, logical generalization about the value of committing to a cause
- uses quotations and specific examples to illustrate ideas
- responds politely to the moderator and other group members
- evaluates other group members' contributions
- summarizes the discussion by synthesizing ideas

PLAN

Get Organized Work with your classmates to prepare for the discussion.

- Form a small group and choose three texts from this collection, including "Craig Kielburger Reflects on Working Toward Peace," for the discussion of the importance of causes.
- Select one student to be the moderator. The rest of your classmates will be the audience when you hold the panel discussion.
- Set up a format for your discussion—a schedule that shows the order in which members will speak and for how long. The moderator will make sure members follow the schedule.
- Develop rules for the appropriate times for either the moderator or the audience to ask panel members questions.

Gather Evidence Work individually to analyze "Craig Kielburger Reflects on Working Toward Peace" and two other texts from the collection. Gather evidence about what it means to commit to a cause. Note specific details, examples, or quotations that illustrate your views. Then think about your own experiences. Ask yourself questions as you take notes.

ACADEMIC VOCABULARY

As you plan and draft your discussion points, be sure to use the academic vocabulary words.

contrast

despite

error

inadequate

interact

- What sorts of problems motivate people to take action?
- What degree of positive change might one person or a group hope to accomplish?
- Are good intentions enough? How knowledgeable does a person need to be in order to take on an issue?
- What are the benefits or drawbacks of committing to a cause?
- How can working for change build character?

Interactive Lessons
For help in gathering evidence, use
· Preparing for Discussion

Use the annotation tools in your eBook to find evidence from the text to support your generalization. Save your evidence to *my*Notebook, in a folder titled *Collection 6 Performance Task.*

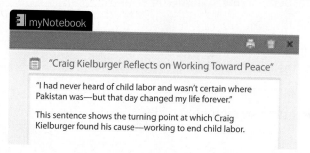

myNotebook

"Craig Kielburger Reflects on Working Toward Peace"

"I had never heard of child labor and wasn't certain where Pakistan was—but that day changed my life forever."

This sentence shows the turning point at which Craig Kielburger found his cause—working to end child labor.

During this time, the moderator should make a list of relevant questions to be asked during the panel discussion.

PRODUCE

my WriteSmart

Write and Practice Work individually to outline your ideas. Then practice with your group.

- State a clear generalization about the ways people in your assigned texts respond to a social problem.
- Write several central ideas that support your generalization.
- Match each piece of evidence with the idea it best supports.
- Prepare to "think on your feet" as you present your ideas to your group. The moderator will ask questions about your ideas and examples in order to prepare you for the real discussion.
- If you are the moderator, decide how to introduce and conclude the discussion. Write a statement telling the audience the topic and format. Write notes for a concluding statement. Be ready to alter your remarks if new ideas emerge in the discussion.

Write your outline in *my*WriteSmart. Focus on getting your ideas down, rather than on perfecting your choice of language.

Interactive Lessons
For help in planning and practicing the discussion, use
· Establishing and Following Procedure
· Speaking Constructively

REVISE

Reinforce Your Ideas Based on the practice session and the rubric on the following page, make changes to your written response to the texts. Consider the following questions:

- Were you able to defend your generalization? If not, revise your response so that it better reflects your textual evidence and your central ideas.

- Were you able to answer the moderator's questions clearly and without hesitation? If not, you may need to adjust your response to find the information you need more easily.

- Did the moderator's questions help you see your text in a new light? If so, add new evidence to your response that you can share during the real discussion.

PRESENT

Have the Discussion Now it's time to present your panel discussion before the rest of the class. Have your outline at hand for reference during the discussion.

- Begin by having the moderator introduce the topic, the panelists, and the basic format for the discussion. The moderator will then ask the first question and continue to facilitate the discussion in the agreed-upon format.

- Speak directly to the panel and audience. Refer to your notes as a reminder of your main points. Don't just read from them.

- Listen closely to all speakers so that you can respond fully.

- Maintain a respectful tone toward your fellow panel members, even when you disagree with their ideas.

- When all the panelists have made their statements and discussed ideas among themselves, the moderator should invite panelists and audience members to ask questions.

- Conclude by having the moderator summarize the discussion and thank the panelists for their participation.

Summarize Write a summary of the main points from the discussion. Then explain whether the discussion caused you to rethink your generalization, and why.

PERFORMANCE TASK B RUBRIC
PANEL DISCUSSION

	Ideas and Evidence	Organization	Language
4	• The panelist clearly states a valid generalization and supports it with strong, relevant ideas and well-chosen evidence from the texts. • The panel member carefully evaluates others' evidence and reasoning and responds with insightful comments and questions. • The panelist synthesizes the analysis of the texts to help listeners understand the generalization.	• The panelist's remarks are based on a well-organized outline that clearly identifies the generalization and the supporting ideas and evidence. • The panelist concludes with a statement that reinforces the generalization and includes the ideas that have emerged from the discussion.	• The panelist adapts speech to the context of the discussion, using appropriately formal English to discuss the texts and ideas. • The panelist consistently quotes accurately from the texts to support ideas. • The panel member consistently maintains a polite and thoughtful tone throughout the discussion.
3	• The panelist states a generalization and supports it with relevant ideas and evidence from the texts. • The panel member evaluates others' evidence and reasoning and responds with appropriate comments and questions. • The panelist synthesizes some ideas and links to the generalization.	• The panelist's remarks are based on an outline that identifies the generalization, supporting ideas, and evidence. • The panelist concludes with a statement that reinforces the generalization.	• The panelist mostly uses formal English to discuss texts and ideas. • The panelist mostly quotes accurately from the texts to support ideas. • The panel member maintains a polite and thoughtful tone throughout most of the discussion.
2	• The panelist states a reasonably clear generalization and supports it with some ideas and evidence. • The panel member's response to others' comments shows limited evaluation of the evidence and reasoning. • The panelist does not synthesize ideas but simply repeats the generalization in a vague way.	• The panelist's remarks reflect an outline that may identify the generalization but does not organize ideas and evidence very effectively. • The panelist makes a weak concluding statement that does little to reinforce the generalization.	• The panelist uses some formal and some informal English to discuss the texts and ideas. • The panelist's quotations and examples sometimes do not accurately reflect the texts. • The panel member occasionally forgets to maintain a polite tone when responding to others' comments and questions.
1	• The panelist's generalization is unclear; ideas and evidence are not coherent. • The panel member does not evaluate others' evidence and reasoning. • The panelist does not synthesize ideas.	• The panelist does not follow an outline that organizes ideas and evidence. • The panelist's remarks lack any kind of conclusion or summary.	• The panelist uses informal English and/or slang, resulting in a lack of clarity. • The panelist's quotations and examples do not accurately reflect the texts. • The panel member does not maintain a polite tone when responding to others' comments and questions.

Writing an Argument

ELA W.7.1a–e, W.7.4
ELD PI.7.3, PI.7.4, PI.7.7, PI.7.10, PI.7.11, PII.7.1, PII.7.2

Many of the Performance Tasks in this book ask you to craft an argument in which you support your ideas with text evidence. Any argument you write should include the following sections and characteristics.

Introduction

Clearly state your **claim**—the point your argument makes. As needed, provide context or background information to help readers understand your position. Note the most common opposing views as a way to distinguish and clarify your ideas. From the very beginning, make it clear for readers why your claim is strong; consider providing an overview of your reasons or a quotation that emphasizes your view in your introduction.

EXAMPLES

vague claim: Dogs need places to play.	**precise claim:** The city should create a large designated dog park.
not distinguished from opposing view: There are plenty of people who are afraid of dogs.	**distinguished from opposing view:** While some people consider it dangerous for dogs to run free, the facts show that dog parks are safe.
confusing relationship of ideas: Bored dogs get sick. Dog parks have lots of space.	**clear relationship of ideas:** By providing a large, safe area for dogs to run off-leash and play, dog owners throughout the city would also benefit.

Development of Claims

The body of your argument must provide strong, logical reasons for your claim and must support those reasons with relevant evidence. A **reason** tells why your claim is valid; **evidence** provides specific examples that illustrate a reason. In the process of developing your claim you should also refute **counterclaims,** or opposing views, with equally strong reasons and evidence. To demonstrate that you have thoroughly considered your view, provide a well-rounded look at both the strengths and limitations of your claim and opposing claims. The goal is not to undercut your argument, but rather to answer your readers' potential objections to it. Be sure, too, to consider how much your audience may already know about your topic in order to avoid boring or confusing readers.

EXAMPLES

claim lacking reasons: A dog park would be a good thing because dogs would enjoy it and it would help the community.	**claim developed by reasons:** Among the benefits of a dog park are not only potentially healthier dogs and more well-adjusted pets, but also a stronger sense of community among dog owners.
omission of limitations: People who hate dogs and are opposed to this idea see no problems or safety issues, they just think the park is a waste of money.	**fair discussion of limitations:** We should not dismiss safety concerns. Planning for the park should include posted signs with rules of behavior, first aid facilities, and ongoing maintenance.
inattention to audience's knowledge: Socialization skills can't be taught in isolation, but issues of dominance are possible to teach with other dogs.	**awareness of audience's knowledge:** Readers unfamiliar with dog behavior may be surprised to learn that most injuries involving dogs happen in homes and on the street, not in well-planned dog parks.

Links Among Ideas

Even the strongest reasons and evidence will fail to sway readers if it is unclear how the reasons relate to the central claim of an argument. Make the connections clear for your readers, using not only transitional words and phrases, but also using clauses and even entire sentences as a bridge between ideas you have already discussed and ideas you are introducing.

EXAMPLES

transitional word linking claim and reason: The entire community will benefit from a dog park. First, dogs who are freed from always walking outside on leashes become better adjusted and better behaved, resulting in less aggressive behavior.

transitional phrase linking reason and evidence: A dog park must be large enough for dogs to run and not be crowded. In fact, evidence shows crowding can result in fights.

transitional clause linking claim and counter-claim: The benefits of the park are clear. Those opposed to the park plan, though, would say otherwise: They feel that there is too much potential for injuries to both people and pets.

Appropriate Style and Tone

An effective argument is most often written in a direct and formal style. The style and tone you choose in an argument should not be an afterthought—the way you express your argument can either drive home your ideas or detract from them. Even as you argue in favor of your viewpoint, take care to remain objective in tone—avoid using loaded language when discussing opposing claims.

EXAMPLES

informal style: The park will help dog owners all over the city, so the city should put out the cash.	**formal style:** Because the benefits of the park would reach dog owners throughout the city, it is logical for the city to provide the funding for the project.

continued

biased tone: It would be ridiculous to be against this plan.	**objective tone:** Arguments opposing the dog park plan have been refuted by statistics from reliable sources.
inattention to conventions: Let's make this park happen!	**attention to conventions:** This proposal, which will help provide humane treatment of pets at little cost, deserves City Council attention.

Conclusion

Your conclusion may range from a sentence to a full paragraph, but it must wrap up your argument in a satisfying way; a conclusion that sounds tacked-on helps your argument no more than providing no conclusion at all. A strong conclusion is a logical extension of the argument you have presented. It carries forth your ideas through an inference, question, quotation, or challenge.

EXAMPLES

inference: Humane treatment of dogs begins with community support.

question: Who doesn't want to live in a community that cares for its dogs humanely?

quotation: As our city's animal control warden says, "Dogs who run freely and play companionably are far less likely to be aggressive and cause injury to themselves or others."

challenge: Facilities of this type make the difference between a city that treats its dogs humanely and a city that ignores dogs' needs.

Writing an Informative Essay

ELA W.7.2a–f, W.7.4
ELD PI.7.4, PI.7.8, PI.7.9, PI.7.10, PI.7.12, PII.7.1, PII.7.2

Most of the Performance Tasks in this book ask you to write informational or explanatory texts in which you present a topic and examine it thoughtfully through a well-organized analysis of relevant content. Any informative or explanatory text that you create should include the following parts and features.

Introduction

Develop a strong **thesis statement.** That is, clearly state your **topic** and the **organizational framework** through which you will **connect** or **distinguish** elements of your topic. For example, you might state that your text will compare ideas, examine causes and effects, or explore a problem and its solutions.

EXAMPLE

Topic: street lighting		
Sample Thesis Statements		
Compare-contrast: To decide whether to install brighter street lamps or keep dimmer lights, consider the costs and the benefits of each type.		
Cause-effect: While the causes of poor night-time visibility on city streets isn't difficult to guess, the effects can be many and devastating.		
Problem-solution: Our town's poor nighttime visibility creates a growing problem with accidents, but through community action we can manage the issue.		

Clarifying the organizational framework up front will help you organize the body of your text, suggest **headings** you can use to guide your readers, and help you identify **graphics** that you may need to clarify information. For example, if you compare and contrast the costs and benefits of installing brighter street lamps, you might create a chart like the one here to guide your writing. You could include the same chart in your paper as a graphic for readers. The row or column headings serve as natural paragraph headings.

	low lighting	bright lighting
Costs	Minimal maintenance of existing lights	Investment in all-new fixtures
Benefits	Old-fashioned charm	Increased visibility for motorists and pedestrians

Development of the Topic

In the body of your text, flesh out the organizational framework you established in your introduction with strong supporting paragraphs. Include only support directly relevant to your topic. Don't rely on a single source, and make sure the sources you do use are reputable and current. The table below illustrates types of support you might use to develop aspects of your topic. It also shows how transitions link text sections, create cohesion, and clarify the relationships among ideas.

Types of Support in Explanatory/ Informative Texts	Uses of Transitions in Explanatory/ Informative Texts
Facts and examples: One cause of poor lighting is inappropriate placement of lights; *for example, most pedestrian crosswalks currently have no extra lighting, increasing the risk to pedestrians from motor vehicles.*	*One cause* signals the shift from the introduction to the body text in a cause-and-effect essay. *For example* introduces the support for the cause being cited.

continued

Types of Support in Explanatory/ Informative Texts	Uses of Transitions in Explanatory/ Informative Texts
Concrete details: On the other hand, if residents want to preserve the surrounding darkness of night, they may want to explore other sources of lighting for pedestrian safety. *Hand-held flashlights, arm band lights, shoe reflectors, and strap-on head lighting are options.*	*On the other hand* transitions the reader from one point of comparison to another in a compare-contrast essay.
Statistics: Turn to the city's accident statistics for evidence of pedestrian accidents that occur after dark: 54 accidents in the prior year.	The entire transitional sentence introduces the part of a problem-solution essay that demonstrates the existence of a problem.

You can't always include all of the information you'd like to in a short essay, but you can plan to point readers directly to useful **multimedia links** either in the body of or at the end of your essay.

Style and Tone

Use formal English to establish your credibility as a source of information. To project authority, use the language of the domain, or field, that you are writing about. However, be sure to define unfamiliar terms to avoid using jargon your audience may not know. Provide extended definitions when your audience is likely to have limited knowledge of the topic.

Using quotations from reputable sources can also give your text authority; be sure to credit the source of quoted material. In general, keep the tone objective, avoiding slangy or biased expressions.

Informal, jargon-filled, biased language: People who think that navigating our city's streets as a pedestrian is a walk in the park obviously don't walk much. They have never had an SUV brush them off the crosswalk.

Extended definition in formal style and objective tone: Pedestrian safety refers to a variety of precautions. According to our city's official website, pedestrians can follow several tips for safe walking in low-light situations such as dusk, dawn, and night. Michael Keen, our city's safety expert, advises that as a pedestrian you should wear light clothing after dark, use a flashlight to light the walking path and to alert drivers, and never assume a car's driver will see you and stop for you, even if you have the Walk sign.

Conclusion

Wrap up your essay with a concluding statement or section that sums up or extends the information in your essay.

EXAMPLES

Articulate implications: Fifty-four pedestrian accidents in a year is an unacceptable number. If the city and its citizens can work together to provide necessary safety precautions and learn more about specific actions to encourage safety, we can significantly reduce the number of pedestrian accidents each year.

Emphasize significance: Pedestrian safety is everyone's responsibility. Safety islands, well-lit crosswalks, driver and pedestrian safety-awareness programs, and adequate street lighting are the city's responsibility. Pedestrians too have a responsibility—to dress so they are visible, to always look out for themselves, and to never assume a driver sees them. By working together toward awareness, we can significantly reduce pedestrian accidents in our city.

Writing a Narrative

ELA W.7.3a–e, W.7.4
ELD PI.7.4, PI.7.8, PI.7.10, PII.7.1

When you are writing a fictional tale, an autobiographical incident, or a firsthand biography, you write in the narrative mode. That means telling a story with a beginning, a climax, and a conclusion. Though there are important differences between fictional and nonfiction narratives, you use similar processes to develop both kinds.

Identify a Problem, Situation, or Observation

For a nonfiction narrative, dig into your memory bank for a problem you dealt with or an observation you've made about your life. For fiction, try to invent a problem or situation that can unfold in interesting ways.

EXAMPLES

Problem (nonfiction)	Our family needed to train our newly chosen four-month-old West Highland White Terrier.
Situation (fiction)	One day, George, a nervous worrier, receives a mysterious gift in the mail.

Establish a Point of View

Decide who will tell your story. If you are writing a reflective essay about an important experience or person in your own life, you will be the narrator of the events you relate. If you are writing a work of fiction, you can choose to create a first-person narrator or to tell the story from the third-person point of view. The narrator can focus on one character or reveal the thoughts and feelings of all the characters. The examples below show the differences between a first- and third-person narrator.

First-person narrator (nonfiction)	Seven hundred fifty dollars: That's what it would cost me to go on the class trip to Washington, D.C. But it might as well have been a million dollars.

Third-person narrator (fiction)	Peter's fingers froze over the "What's new with you" prompt of his status page. The box was already filled out, waiting for him to press the Update key. "My mom found a new job!" said the box. Peter hadn't written those words. And, as far as he knew, his mother had stopped looking for work months ago.

Gather Details

To make real or imaginary experiences come alive on the page, you will need to use narrative techniques like description and dialogue. The questions in the left column in the chart below can help you search your memory or imagination for the details that will form the basis of your narrative. You don't have to respond in full sentences, but try to capture the sights, sounds, and feelings that bring your narrative to life.

Who, What, When, Where?	Narrative Techniques
People: Who are the people or characters involved in the experience? What did they look like? What did they do? What did they say?	**Description:** George, a friend I've known for as long as I can remember, is outgoing and loves being with people. But George has one quality that I find hard to understand. Even though he has no allergies, he is terribly afraid of certain foods and of getting sick from them. When we go out to eat together, he'll only eat fruit or a slice of meat. He'll never eat a sauce or any food like it. He'll say something like, "I don't know what's in their spaghetti sauce. It might not be good for me."

continued

Who, What, When, Where?	Narrative Techniques
Experience: What led up to or caused the event? What is the main event in the experience? What happened as a result of the event?	**Description:** The next morning my brother and I ventured outside with Maggie. It was February and freezing cold. Maggie didn't like the wind and snow. She balked, stopping with a jerk when we walked. An hour later, our fingers and toes numb, our noses red and raw, Maggie cooperated. She had learned something, and we did too—we had a stubborn dog to train.
Places: When and where did the events take place? What were the sights, sounds, and smells of this place?	**Description:** In December, the air crisp but not yet bitingly cold, I thought ahead to winter break delights— sledding swiftly down the steepest hill, the smell of peppermint cookies, the crunch of ice when we skated.

Sequence Events

Before you write, list key events of the experience or story in chronological, or time, order. Place a star next to the point of highest tension—for example, the point at which a key decision determines the outcome. In fiction, this point is called the climax, but a nonfiction narrative can also have a climactic event.

To build suspense—the uncertainty a reader feels about what will happen next—you'll want to think about the pacing or rhythm of your narrative. Consider disrupting the chronological order of events by beginning at the end, then starting over. Or interrupt the forward flow of events with a flashback, which takes the reader to an earlier point in the narrative.

Another way to build suspense is with multiple plot lines. For example, the story about George's fear of foods involves a second plot line in which the narrator's aunt discovers what happened to her holiday fruitcake. Both plot lines intersect when the narrator shovels snow for a week, and as a result raises money for the class trip.

Use Vivid Language

As you revise, make an effort to use vivid language. Use precise words and phrases to describe feelings and action. Use telling details to show, rather than directly state, what a character is like. Use sensory language that lets readers see, feel, hear, smell, and taste what you or your characters experienced.

First Draft	Revision
My aunt usually sends a fruitcake to us, and I can't stand fruitcake.	Suddenly I thought of my aunt's usual holiday present—the dreaded fruitcake. [telling details]
I remembered my friend George and his dislike for certain foods.	My friend George and his fear of foods with mixed ingredients came to mind. I began to concoct a delicious scheme. [precise words and phrases]
George was afraid when he opened the box and saw a weird-looking cake.	George felt the heavy box from the unknown sender and shrieked when he saw the sticky mixture of dried fruit. [sensory details]

Conclusion

At the conclusion of the narrative, you or your narrator will reflect on the meaning of the events. The conclusion should follow logically from the climactic moment of the narrative. The narrator of a personal narrative usually reflects on the significance of the experience—the lessons learned or the legacy left.

EXAMPLE

Puppy class and its grueling weekly sessions with 12 yipping puppies had ended long ago. Maggie's performance wasn't stellar—she'd had to repeat the whole class to pass. But as I remembered the chill of that first morning walk in sub-zero winds, and the feeling of my numbed fingers, I thought what a smart dog she was after all. After repeated efforts, many crunchy biscuit treats, and lots of warm hugs, Maggie was trained. I proudly stroked her fur as she looked up at me with her knowing eyes.

Conducting Research

ELA W.7.7, W.7.8
ELD PI.7.10, PI.7.11

The Performance Tasks in this book will require you to complete research projects related to the texts you've read in the collections. Whether the topic is stated in a Performance Task or is one you generate, the following information will guide you through your research project.

Focus Your Research and Formulate a Question

Some topics for a research project can be effectively covered in three pages; others require an entire book for a thorough treatment. Begin by developing a topic that is neither too narrow nor too broad for the time frame of the assignment. Also check your school and local libraries and databases to help you determine how to choose your topic. If there's too little information, you'll need to broaden your focus; if there's too much, you'll need to limit it.

With a topic in hand, formulate a research question; it will keep you on track as you conduct your research. A good research question cannot be answered in a single word. It should be open-ended. It should require investigation. You can also develop related research questions to explore your topic in more depth.

EXAMPLES

Possible topics	Sailing—too broad Navigating waves—too narrow Sailing—in fair and foul weather
Possible research question	What is involved in learning to sail in all kinds of weather?
Related questions	What sailing equipment and techniques are essential? What knowledge of weather patterns is critical?

Locate and Evaluate Sources

To find answers to your research question, you'll need to investigate primary and secondary sources, whether in print or digital formats. **Primary sources** contain original, firsthand information, such as diaries, autobiographies, interviews, speeches, and eyewitness accounts. **Secondary sources** provide other people's versions of primary sources in encyclopedias, newspaper and magazine articles, biographies, and documentaries.

Your search for sources begins at the library and on the World Wide Web. Use **advanced search features** to help you find things quickly. Add a minus sign (–) before a word that should not appear in your results. Use an asterisk (*) in place of unknown words. List the name and location of each possible source, adding comments about its potential usefulness. Assessing, or evaluating, your sources is an important step in the research process. Your goal is to use sources that are credible, or reliable and trustworthy.

Criteria for Assessing Sources	
Relevance: It covers the target aspect of my topic.	• How will the source be useful in answering my research question?
Accuracy: It includes information that can be verified by more than one authoritative source.	• Is the information up-to-date? Are the facts accurate? How can I verify them? • What qualifies the author to write about this topic? Is he or she an authority?
Objectivity: It presents multiple viewpoints on the topic.	• What, if any, biases can I detect? Does the writer favor one view of the topic?

Incorporate and Cite Source Material

When you draft your research project, you'll need to include material from your sources. This material can be **direct quotations, summaries,** or **paraphrases** of the original source material. Two well-known **style manuals** provide information on how to cite a range of print and digital sources: the *MLA Handbook for Writers of Research Papers* (published by the Modern Language Association) and Kate L. Turabian's *A Manual for Writers* (published by The University of Chicago Press). Both style manuals provide a wealth of information about conducting, formatting, drafting, and presenting your research, including guidelines for citing sources within the text (called parenthetical citations) and preparing the list of Works Cited, as well as correct use of the mechanics of writing. Your teacher will indicate which style manual you should use. The following examples use the format in the *MLA Handbook*.

Any material from sources must be completely documented, or you will commit **plagiarism,** the unauthorized use of someone else's words or ideas. Plagiarism is not honest. As you take notes for your research project, be sure to keep complete information about your sources so that you can cite them correctly in the body of your paper. This applies to all sources, whether print or digital. Having complete information will also enable you to prepare the list of Works Cited. The list of Works Cited, which concludes your research project, provides author, title, and publication information for both print and digital sources. The following pages show the *MLA Handbook's* Works Cited citation formats for a variety of sources.

EXAMPLES

Direct quotation [The writer is citing a sailing manual.]	In high winds, you need to know how to tack into the wind. This is an essential skill. [Woods, 120]
Summary [The writer is summarizing the experiences of a sailing expert.]	Johnson fought winds so stiff that if he hadn't had an expert sailor with him to assist with the boom, he would have definitely capsized. [Johnson, 94]
Paraphrase [The writer is paraphrasing, or stating in her own words, material from page 48 of Gloria Schott's book.]	Learning key sailing terminology is essential. For example, as Schott explains, knowing what the preventer is and how to rig it can prevent the boom from swinging around and knocking someone overboard. [Schott, 48]

MLA Citation Guidelines

Today, you can find free websites that generate ready-made citations for research papers, using the information you provide. Such sites have some time-saving advantages when you're developing a Works Cited list. However, you should always check your citations carefully before you turn in your final paper. If you are following MLA style, use these guidelines to evaluate and finalize your work.

Books

One author

Lastname, Firstname. *Title of Book*. City of Publication: Publisher, Year of Publication. Medium of Publication.

Two authors or editors

Lastname, Firstname, and Firstname Lastname. *Title of Book*. City of Publication: Publisher, Year of Publication. Medium of Publication.

Three authors

Lastname, Firstname, Firstname Lastname, and Firstname Lastname. *Title of Book*. City of Publication: Publisher, Year of Publication. Medium of Publication.

Four or more authors

The abbreviation *et al*. means "and others." Use et al. instead of listing all the authors.

Lastname, Firstname, et al. *Title of Book*. City of Publication: Publisher, Year of Publication. Medium of Publication.

No author given

Title of Book. City of Publication: Publisher, Year of Publication. Medium of Publication.

An author and a translator

Lastname, Firstname. *Title of Book*. Trans. Firstname Lastname. City of Publication: Publisher, Year of Publication. Medium of Publication.

An author, a translator, and an editor

Lastname, Firstname. *Title of Book*. Trans. Firstname Lastname. Ed. Firstname Lastname. City of Publication: Publisher, Year of Publication. Medium of Publication.

Parts of Books

An introduction, a preface, a foreword, or an afterword written by someone other than the author(s) of a work

Lastname, Firstname. Part of Book. *Title of Book*. By Author of book's Firstname Lastname. City of Publication: Publisher, Year of Publication. Page span. Medium of Publication.

A poem, a short story, an essay, or a chapter in a collection of works by one author

Lastname, Firstname. "Title of Piece." *Title of Book*. Ed. Firstname Lastname. City of Publication: Publisher, Year of Publication. Page span. Medium of Publication.

A poem, a short story, an essay, or a chapter in an anthology of works by several authors

Lastname, Firstname. "Title of Piece." *Title of Book*. Ed. Firstname Lastname. City of Publication: Publisher, Year of Publication. Page range. Medium of Publication.

Magazines, Newspapers, and Encyclopedias

An article in a newspaper

Lastname, Firstname. "Title of Article." *Title of Book Periodical* Day Month Year: pages. Medium of Publication.

An article in a magazine

Lastname, Firstname. "Title of Article." *Title of Book Periodical* Day Month Year: pages. Medium of Publication.

An article in an encyclopedia

"Title of Article." *Title of Encyclopedia*. Year ed. Medium of Publication.

Miscellaneous Nonprint Sources

An interview

Lastname, Firstname. Personal interview. Day Month Year.

A video recording

Title of Recording. Producer, Year. Medium of Publication.

Electronic Publications

A CD-ROM

"Title of Piece." *Title of CD*. Year ed. City of Publication: Publisher, Year of Publication. CD-ROM.

A document from an Internet site

Entries for online source should contain as much information as available.

Lastname, Firstname. "*Title of Piece*." Information on what the site is. Year. Web. Day Month Year (when accessed).

Participating in a Collaborative Discussion

ELA SL.7.1a–d
ELD PI.7.1, PI.7.3, PI.7.4, PI.7.5, PI.7.7, PI.7.8

Often, class activities, including the Performance Tasks in this book, will require you to work collaboratively with classmates. Whether your group will analyze a work of literature or try to solve a community problem, use the following guidelines to ensure a productive discussion.

Prepare for the Discussion

A productive discussion is one in which all the participants bring useful information and ideas to share. If your group will discuss a short story the class read, first re-read and annotate a copy of the story. Your annotations will help you quickly locate evidence to support your points. Participants in a discussion about an important issue should first research the issue and bring notes or information sources that will help guide the group. If you disagree with a point made by another group member, your case will be stronger if you back it up with specific evidence from your sources.

EXAMPLES

disagreeing without evidence: I don't think physical art is relevant today because nobody goes to museums.

providing evidence for disagreement: I disagree that physical art is relevant today because so few people go to museums. For example, every large museum, such as the Metropolitan Museum of Art in New York, the Art Institute of Chicago, and the San Francisco Museum of Modern Art, has a website where the public can view art online. Current exhibitions are shown and previous exhibitions are archived for viewing. Why would someone need to go to a dark museum when images are so easy to view online? Even artists such as Julian Beever, who creates physical public art, have websites for the public to view their art. We can clearly view and compare multiple images of Beever's chalk art by clicking on his online gallery.

Set Ground Rules

The rules your group needs will depend on what your group is expected to accomplish. A discussion of themes in a poem will be unlikely to produce a single consensus; however, a discussion aimed at developing a solution to a problem should result in one strong proposal that all group members support. Answer the following questions to set ground rules that fit your group's purpose:

- What will this group produce? A range of ideas, a single decision, a plan of action, or something else?
- How much time is available? How much of that time should be allotted to each part of our discussion (presenting ideas, summarizing or voting on final ideas, creating a product such as a written analysis or speech)?
- What roles need to be assigned within the group? Do we need a leader, a note-taker, a timekeeper, or other specific roles?
- What is the best way to synthesize our group's ideas? Should we take a vote, list group members as "for" or "against" in a chart, or use some other method to reach a consensus or sum up the results of the discussion?

Move the Discussion Forward

Everyone in the group should be actively involved in synthesizing ideas. To make sure this happens, ask questions that draw out ideas, especially from less-talkative members of the group. If an idea or statement is confusing, try to paraphrase it, or ask the speaker to explain more about it. If you disagree with a statement, say so politely and explain in detail why you disagree.

SAMPLE DISCUSSION

JACK: How about you, Ella? Do you think physical art is relevant to people today? The rest of us say it is.	*Question draws out quiet member*
ELLA: Well, I don't know. We took a field trip to an art museum once to learn about the importance of art and the time periods of art, but none of the people I know go to museums otherwise. We also read about art and artists, like Julian Beever, but we can see his art online too.	*Response relates discussion to larger ideas*
JOSHUA: But don't we have the option of going to see physical art? I mean, we can go to a public space that has public art or to a museum and experience the art in person, right?	*Question challenges Ella's conclusion*
ELLA: Sure, but think of the possibilities for comparing images online versus in person. Someone can view and compare images by the same artist that are displayed in different museums by clicking online. How could they do that in person?	*Response elaborates on ideas*
VIVIAN: So you mean that people can view and compare more art online and the experience and the quantity is significant and worthwhile? I can see that, but is it more worthwhile than being physically present to view the actual work of art? There are things we can see and experience by examining the real object—things like texture in a painting or drawing—that might not be seen as well in an on-screen image.	*Paraphrases idea and challenges it further based on evidence*

Respond to Ideas

In a diverse group, everyone may have a different perspective on the topic of discussion, and that's a good thing. Consider what everyone has to say, and don't resist changing your view if other group members provide convincing evidence for theirs. If, instead, you feel more strongly than ever about your view, don't hesitate to say so and provide reasons related to what those with opposing views have said. Before wrapping up the discussion, try to sum up the points on which your group agrees and disagrees.

SAMPLE DISCUSSION

VIVIAN: OK, we just have a few more minutes. Do we want to take a vote?	*Vivian and Jack try to summarize points of agreement*
JACK: Sure. I think the three positions are NO, YES, and YES, BUT. . . . Does that sound right?	
JOSHUA: Yeah, let's make a chart of these. I still say YES, physical art is relevant today. No BUT about it, because physical elements and experience are at the core.	*Joshua maintains his position*
ELLA: And I say YES, BUT. You've convinced me that physical art offers some experiences and close viewing possibilities, but I still think that easy, quick, universal access to online images removes barriers for viewing art for a lot of people today.	*Ella and Jack qualify their views based on what they have heard*
JACK: That makes sense. I'm changing my position from solid YES to YES, BUT. I think quick and easy access is important, though not always more important than slow and careful scrutiny of physical art and actually being there—like walking alongside sidewalk art.	
VIVIAN: I'm with Joshua. I think being able to move around a work of art literally adds a whole new dimension to understanding art.	*Vivian supports her position by making a new connection*

Debating an Issue

ELA SL.7.3a, SL.7.4
ELD PI.7.1, PI.7.3, PI.7.4, PI.7.5, PI.7.9, PI.7.10, PI.7.11

The selection and collection Performance Tasks in this text will direct you to engage in debates about issues relating to the selections you are reading. Use the guidelines that follow to have a productive and balanced argument about both sides of an issue.

The Structure of a Formal Debate

In a debate, two teams compete to win the support of the audience about an issue. In a **formal debate,** two teams, each with two members, present their arguments on a given proposition or policy statement. One team argues for the proposition or statement and the other team argues against it. Each debater must consider the proposition closely and must research both sides of it. To argue convincingly either for or against a proposition, a debater must be familiar with both sides of the issue.

Plan the Debate

The purpose of a debate is to allow participants and audience members to consider both sides of an issue. Use these planning suggestions to hold a balanced and productive debate:

- **Identify Debate Teams** Form groups of six members based on the issues that the Performance Tasks include. Three members of the team will argue for the affirmative side of the issue—that is, they support the issue. The other three members will argue for the negative side of the issue—that is, they do not support the issue.
- **Appoint a Moderator** The moderator will present the topic and goals of the debate, keep track of the time, and introduce and thank the participants.
- **Research and Prepare Notes** Search texts you've read as well as print and online sources for valid reasons and evidence to support your team's claim. As with argument, be sure to anticipate possible opposing claims and compile evidence to counter those claims. You will use notes from your research during the debate.

- **Assign Debate Roles** One team member will introduce the team's claim and supporting evidence. Another team member will respond to questions and opposing claims in an exchange with a member of the opposing team. The last member will present a strong closing argument.

Hold the Debate

A formal debate is not a shouting match—rather, a well-run debate is an excellent forum for participants to express their viewpoints, build on others' ideas, and have a thoughtful, well-reasoned exchange of ideas. The moderator will begin by stating the topic or issue and introducing the participants. Participants should follow the moderator's instructions concerning whose turn it is to speak and how much time each speaker has.

Formal Debate Format

Speaker	Role	Time
Affirmative Speaker 1	Present the claim and supporting evidence for the affirmative ("pro") side of the argument.	5 minutes
Negative Speaker 1	Ask probing questions that will prompt the other team to address flaws in the argument.	3 minutes
Affirmative Speaker 2	Respond to the questions posed by the opposing team and counter any concerns.	3 minutes

continued

Speaker	Role	Time
Negative Speaker 2	Present the claim and supporting evidence for the negative ("con") side of the argument.	5 minutes
Affirmative Speaker 3	Summarize the claim and evidence for the affirmative side and explain why your reasoning is more valid.	3 minutes
Negative Speaker 3	Summarize the claim and evidence for the negative side and explain why your reasoning is more valid.	3 minutes

Evaluate the Debate

Use the following guidelines to evaluate a team in a debate:

- Did the team prove that the issue is significant? How thorough was the analysis?
- How did the team members effectively argue that you should support their affirmative or negative side of the proposition or issue?
- How effectively did the team present reasons and evidence, including evidence from the texts, to support the proposition?
- How effectively did the team rebut, or respond to, arguments made by the opposing team?
- Did the speakers maintain eye contact and speak at an appropriate rate and volume?
- Did the speakers observe proper debate etiquette—that is, did they follow the moderator's instructions, stay within their allotted time limits, and treat their opponents respectfully?

Reading Informational Texts: Patterns of Organization

ELA RI.7.2, RI.7.5
ELD PII.7.1, PII.7.2

Reading any type of writing is easier once you recognize how it is organized. Writers usually arrange ideas and information in ways that best help readers see how they are related. There are several common patterns of organization.

- main idea and supporting details
- chronological order
- cause-effect organization
- compare-and-contrast organization

1. Main Idea and Supporting Details

Main idea and supporting details is a basic pattern of organization in which a central idea about a topic is supported by details. The **main idea** is the most important idea about a topic that a particular text or paragraph conveys. **Supporting details** are words, phrases, or sentences that tell more about the main idea. The main idea may be directly stated at the beginning and then followed by supporting details, or it may be merely implied by the supporting details. It may also be stated after it has been implied by supporting details.

Sometimes you will come across a main idea that is a **factual claim**—a statement that can be verified by observation, a reliable source, or an expert's view. In some cases the main idea may be stated as a **commonplace assertion**—a statement that many people assume to be true, but is not necessarily so. In both cases, the details should support the statements.

Strategies for Reading

- To find a stated main idea in a paragraph, identify the paragraph's topic. The topic is what the paragraph is about and can usually be summed up in one or two words. The word, or synonyms of it, will usually appear throughout the paragraph. Headings and subheadings are also clues to the topics of paragraphs.
- Ask: What is the topic sentence? The topic sentence states the most important idea, message, or information the paragraph conveys about this topic. It is often the first sentence in a paragraph; however, it may appear at the end.
- To find an implied main idea, ask yourself: Whom or what did I just read about? What do the details suggest about the topic?
- Formulate a sentence stating this idea and add it to the paragraph. Does your sentence convey the main idea?

Notice how the main idea is expressed in each of the following models.

Model:
Main Idea as the First Sentence

When the nomads of Africa began using camels around AD 300, trade across the Sahara became easier. [Main idea] The donkeys, horses, and oxen that had been used previously could not travel far without stopping for food and water. Camels, on the other hand, could cover 25 miles in a day and often go for two weeks without water. [Supporting details]

Model:
Main Idea as the Last Sentence

The new trade routes passed through lands occupied by the Soninke people. These farming people referred to their chief as ghana. Soon the land came to be known as the kingdom of Ghana. The tribal chiefs taxed the goods that traveled across their territory. [Supporting details] By the eighth century, trade had made Ghana a rich kingdom. [Main idea]

Model:
Implied Main Idea

The West African savannas and forests south of the savanna were rich in gold. No salt was available there, though. In the Sahara, on the other hand, there was abundant salt but no gold. Traders brought salt south through the desert and traded it for gold mined from the forests.

> **Implied main idea:** Gold and salt were two important items that were traded in West Africa.

Practice and Apply

Read each paragraph, and then do the following:

1. Identify the main idea in the paragraph, using one of the strategies discussed on the previous page.
2. Identify whether the main idea is stated or implied in the paragraph.

Every day we are surrounded by technology and computerized devices. We sit at our computers for hours for all kinds of purposes—writing and researching topics for our assignments, watching movies, posting messages on our social network pages, listening to music, and more. We call friends on our mobile devices. We tweet. But what we do most frequently is text. E-mail used to be important for messages. Now, it's not fast enough to compete with texting.

When we view a news article or any other text, our eyes see the words, and we begin to read. The eye is the organ of vision, and its job is to send signals about visuals to the brain. Once the eyes transmit the words to the brain, the real actions involved in reading begin to happen. Many areas of the brain work together to decipher the written word, and signals travel with amazing speed to all those areas.

2. Chronological Order

Chronological order is the arrangement of events in the order in which they happen. This type of organization is used in short stories and novels, historical writing, biographies, and autobiographies. To show the order of events, writers use order words such as *before, after, next,* and *later* and time words and phrases that identify specific times of day, days of the week, and dates, such as *the next morning, Tuesday,* and *on July 4, 1776.*

Strategies for Reading

- Look in the text for headings and subheadings that may indicate a chronological pattern of organization.
- Look for words and phrases that identify times, such as *in a year, three hours earlier, in 202 BC,* and *the next day.*
- Look for words that signal order, such as *first, afterward, then, during,* and *finally,* to see how events or steps are related.
- Note that a paragraph or passage in which ideas and information are arranged chronologically will have several words or phrases that indicate time order, not just one.
- Ask yourself: Are the events in the paragraph or passage presented in time order?

Notice the words and phrases that signal time order in the first two paragraphs of the following model.

Model

A Butterfly Gets Its Wings

How does a butterfly get its wings? During its life, the butterfly goes through different growth stages. There are four main stages altogether: 1) the egg, 2) the caterpillar, 3) the pupa, and 4) the adult. The ancient Greeks called this whole process *metamorphosis,* a word we still use today.

> **Events**

At first, the butterfly is a single slimy egg, no larger than a fingertip. The baby insect grows within the egg until it is ready to hatch. For most types of butterflies, this first stage lasts about ten days. When the egg cracks open, a caterpillar crawls out.

> **Order words and phrases**

> **Time words and phrases**

In the second stage, the caterpillar spends most of its time eating and growing. As the caterpillar becomes bigger, it sheds its spiky or fuzzy skin. This process is called *molting.* A caterpillar molts several times during its life. Once the caterpillar has shed its skin for the last time, it becomes a pupa.

In the third stage, the pupa immediately grows a hard shell called a *chrysalis*. Then, inside the chrysalis, the pupa goes through the changes that will make it a butterfly. The pupa's hormones turn its body into wings, antennas, and other butterfly parts. After all the changes are complete, the shell splits open. A butterfly is ready to make its entrance.

Finally, the adult butterfly breaks from the chrysalis. Its body, however, doesn't look quite right. It's all soft and wrinkly. As air and blood are pumped through the butterfly's body, it starts to look more like its usual self. In a short time, the butterfly is ready to try out its new wings. With a few flutters, it's off and away!

Practice and Apply

Refer to the preceding model to do the following:

1. List at least six words in the last three paragraphs that indicate time or order.
2. What does the writer call the four main parts in the life of a butterfly?
3. In what form does a butterfly begin its life?

3. Cause-Effect Organization

Cause-effect organization is a pattern of organization that shows causal relationships between events, ideas, and trends. Cause-effect relationships may be directly stated or merely implied by the order in which the information is presented. Writers often use the cause-effect pattern in historical and scientific writing. Cause-effect relationships may have several forms.

One cause with one effect

One cause with multiple effects

Multiple causes with a single effect

A chain of causes and effects

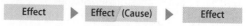

Strategies for Reading

- Look for headings and subheadings that indicate a cause-effect pattern of organization, such as "Effects of Food Allergies."
- To find the effect or effects, read to answer the question, What happened?
- To find the cause or causes, read to answer the question, Why did it happen?
- Look for words and phrases that help you identify specific relationships between events, such as *because, since, had the effect of, led to, as a result, resulted in, for that reason, due to, therefore, if . . . then,* and *consequently.*
- Look closely at each cause-effect relationship. Do not assume that because one event happened before another, the first event caused the second event.
- Use graphic organizers like the diagrams shown to record cause-effect relationships as you read.

Notice the words that signal causes and effects in the following model.

Model

How a Tsunami Forms

Tsunami is a word that brings fear to people who live near the sea. Also known in English as a tidal wave, a tsunami is a huge ocean wave caused by an underwater volcanic eruption or earthquake.

An earthquake or the explosion of a volcano on the ocean floor creates massive waves of energy. These energy waves spread out in widening circles, like waves from a pebble dropped into a pond.

As the tsunami nears the shore, it begins to scrape along the ocean bottom. This friction causes the waves in the front to slow down. As a result, the waves traveling behind begin piling up and growing higher. This increase in height can happen very quickly—by as much as 90 feet in 10 or 15 minutes.

The effects of a tsunami can include the death of many people and the destruction of ships, buildings, and land along the shore. An especially dangerous situation may occur when the first part of a tsunami to hit the shore is the trough, or low point, rather than the crest of a wave. This trough sucks all the water away from the shore and may attract curious people on the beach. Within a few minutes, however, the crest of the wave will hit and may drown the onlookers. The most destructive tsunami ever recorded struck the Indonesian island of Sumatra, in 2004. It left more than 200,000 people dead.

Margin labels:
- Effect
- Signal words
- Cause
- Cause
- Effect

Practice and Apply

1. Use the pattern of a chain of causes and effects, illustrated on page R18, to make a graphic organizer showing the causes and effects described in the text.
2. List three words that the writer uses to signal cause and effect in the last two paragraphs.

4. Compare-and-Contrast Organization

Compare-and-contrast organization is a pattern of organization that provides a way to look at similarities and differences in two or more subjects. A writer may use this pattern of organization to compare the important points or characteristics of two or more subjects. These points or characteristics are called **points of comparison.** The compare-and-contrast pattern of organization may be developed in either of two ways:

Point-by-point organization—The writer discusses one point of comparison for both subjects, then goes on to the next point.

Subject-by-subject organization—The writer covers all points of comparison for one subject and then all points of comparison for the next subject.

Strategies for Reading

- Look in the text for headings, subheadings, and sentences that may suggest a compare-and-contrast pattern of organization, such as "Plants Share Many Characteristics," to help you identify where similarities and differences are addressed.
- To find similarities, look for words and phrases such as *like, similarly, both, all, every, also,* and *in the same way.*
- To find differences, look for words and phrases such as *unlike, but, on the other hand, more, less, in contrast,* and *however.*
- Use a graphic organizer, such as a Venn diagram or a compare-and-contrast chart, to record points of comparison and similarities and differences.

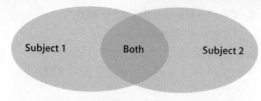

	Subject 1	Subject 2
Point 1		
Point 2		
Point 3		

Read the following models. As you read, use the signal words and phrases to identify the similarities and differences between the subjects and how the details are organized in each text.

Model 1

Living in Outer Space

Ten . . . nine . . . eight . . . The date is December 21, 1968.

Seven . . . six . . . five . . . alongside a launch gantry at Cape Kennedy, Florida, a huge Saturn V rocket stands fueled and ready for blastoff, hydrogen vapor steaming from its rocket motors.

Four . . . three . . . two . . . at the top of the rocket sits the *Apollo 8* command module, the capsule that will ferry astronauts Frank Borman, James A. Lovell Jr., and William A. Anders to the moon and back.

One . . . zero . . . Liftoff! The Saturn's powerful engines roar to life, and another exciting chapter in the history of the United States space program begins.

Today, that same *Apollo 8* command module is one of the most popular attractions at the Henry Crown Space Center at the Museum of Science and Industry in Chicago. For six days in 1968, this cone-shaped capsule was home to the first humans to leave the security of earth's orbit and venture out to visit another heavenly body.

Museum visitors, especially young people accustomed to space travel in the shuttle era, are often amazed at the cramped quarters within the capsule, and they wonder just how three adults lived for six days in such a compact environment. Space travel has come a long way since those pioneering days of the 1960s. Some of the main similarities and differences relate to living quarters and food.

Today's shuttle crews have both a flight deck and a lower crew-quarters deck in which to move around. The *Apollo* crews, however, were pretty much confined to their metal-and-fabric flight couches, although there was a little stretching room beneath the couches and around the hatch area that led to the lunar Excursion Module.

Mealtime is a highlight of anyone's day, including every astronaut's. Early space travelers were limited to puréed foods squeezed out of toothpaste tubes and juices in plastic bags. Shuttle crews, on the other hand, enjoy a much more appetizing diet. It's still not exactly fine dining, but at least the food is served on trays, is eaten with utensils, and includes healthy snacks, like fresh fruit.

At the end of a working "day" in space, all astronauts are ready for some rest. In *Apollo*, the crew simply drifted off to sleep on their couches. Aboard the shuttle, crew members sleep in special sleep restraints. Some sleep horizontally, while others opt for a vertical snooze. In zero gravity, position doesn't matter!

The United States has continued to develop the space program. The lessons learned during the first three decades of space flight are making life in the alien environment beyond earth's atmosphere much more pleasant for a new generation of space explorers.

Comparison words and phrases

Contrast words and phrases

Subjects

Model 2

To compare the two types of energy, we must first understand what energy is. Energy is the ability to do work. That doesn't just mean work as in homework or yard work. Energy comes in many forms, such as a rock falling off a cliff, a moving bicycle, or the stored energy in food. With all these forms, there are only two main types of energy, potential and kinetic. These are the energies of rest and motion. `Subjects`

Potential energy is the energy an object has stored up based on how high up it is or how much it weighs. For instance, suppose two kids weigh the same and climb a tree. If they are on different branches, the kid on the higher branch has more potential energy than the kid on the lower branch. However, if one kid weighs more than the other, and they both sit at the same height, the heavier kid has more potential energy than the lighter kid. `Comparison words and phrases` `Contrast words and phrases`

If the kids jump out of the tree, their potential energy becomes kinetic energy. This kind comes from the motion of an object. Kinetic energy increases with the speed of an object. When the kids jump, their speed increases as they fall. They have more kinetic energy when they are falling faster than they do when they first jump and are falling more slowly. Also, the more mass an object has, the more kinetic energy it has. Even if both kids jump at the exact same time, the one with more mass will always have more kinetic energy.

These two kids probably knew they were using a lot of energy, but they would probably be surprised to know how much work they had been doing.

Practice and Apply

Refer to the preceding models to answer the following questions:

1. Which model is organized by subject? Which model is organized by points of comparison?
2. Identify two words or phrases in each model that signal a compare-and-contrast pattern of organization.
3. List two points that the writer of each model compares and contrasts.
4. Use a Venn diagram or a compare-and-contrast chart to identify two or more points of comparison and the similarities and differences shown in one of the two models.

5. Problem-Solution Order

Problem-solution order is a pattern of organization in which a problem is stated and analyzed and then one or more solutions are proposed and examined. This pattern of organization is often used in persuasive writing, such as editorials or proposals.

Strategies for Reading

- Look for an explanation of the problem in the first or second paragraph.
- Look for words, such as *problem* and *reason*, that may signal an explanation of the problem.
- To find the solution, ask: What suggestion does the writer offer to solve the problem?
- Look for words, such as *propose, conclude,* and *answer,* that may signal a solution.

Model

I love baseball, but I won't be going to any major-league games, and I won't be rooting for the local major-league team. The reason is simple. There is no local major-league team in North Dakota. There's none in South Dakota or in Montana or even in Wyoming. The closest major-league team is the Minnesota Twins, and that's over 240 miles away!

The problem is that getting a major-league team costs money. Any city that wants a team has to have enough money to build a stadium. The city also has to have a big enough population to support the team. Fargo is the biggest city in North Dakota, and it only has about 91,484 people. That's not enough to support a major-league franchise. Sports stadiums often hold more people than Fargo has!

Even though the towns around here aren't exactly huge, there are a lot of die-hard baseball fans like my friends and me. So here's my plan. Why couldn't a couple of towns get together to build a stadium and start a team? For example, Moorhead, Minnesota, is right next to Fargo. They already share the same airport, and the metropolitan area has about 174,367 people. That might be enough to support a team. If it's not, then maybe Grand Forks, or even Aberdeen, could join in too.

People might say that there would be a problem naming a team that is supported by cities in two or three different states. I think baseball fans would be so happy to have a team, they wouldn't really care what it was called.

If enough people wrote to the Fargo and Moorhead city governments, maybe the idea could be put on the ballot. Major-league baseball is supposed to be our national pastime. Shouldn't we be a part of it too?

Practice and Apply

Reread the model and then answer the following questions:

1. According to the model, what is the cause of the problem?
2. What solution does the writer offer? What words are a clue?

ELA RI.7.2, RI.7.4, RI.7.5, RI.7.6, RI.7.8
ELD PI.7.7, PI.7.8, PI.7.10, PI.7.11,
PII.7.1, PII.7.2

Reading Arguments

1. Analyzing an Argument

An **argument** expresses a position on an issue or problem and supports it with reasons and evidence. Being able to analyze and evaluate arguments will help you distinguish between claims you should accept and those you should not. A sound argument should appeal strictly to reason. However, arguments are often used in texts that also contain other types of persuasive devices. An argument includes the following elements:

- A **claim** is the writer's position on an issue or problem.
- **Support** is any material that serves to prove a claim. In an argument, support usually consists of reasons and evidence.
- **Reasons** are declarations made to justify an action, decision, or belief—for example, "My reason for thinking we will be late is that the drive takes longer than five minutes."
- **Evidence** can be the specific references, quotations, facts, examples, and opinions that support a claim. Evidence may also consist of statistics, reports of personal experience, or the views of experts.
- A **counterargument** is an argument made to oppose another argument. A good argument anticipates the opposition's objections and provides counterarguments to disprove or answer them.

Claim	I think I should be allowed more time online.

Reason	The Internet can provide opportunities for learning and enjoyment.

Evidence	The Internet can take you to faraway places and can bring art, music, and science right into your home.

Counter-argument	Some people think the Internet is bad for kids, but those people are looking at only the worst part of the Internet, not the best.

Practice and Apply

Read the following editorial and use a chart like the one shown to identify the claim, reason, evidence, and counterargument.

Important Hours by Gina Maraini

"The Golden Years." That is what some people call old age. They think it is a time of peace and relaxation. But many old people spend time alone. Some cannot get out of their homes because of illness. "What can I do?" you ask. You can do more than you think to make an important contribution to an older person's life. Even spending an hour a week can mean a lot to an older neighbor who lives alone.

Some kids might say that they can only do good for an older person if they have lots of time and lots of patience. It's easy to talk yourself out of volunteering your time by saying, "I only have an hour a week. What good would that do?" Never underestimate just how much good you can do even in a little bit of time.

Sometimes things happen that seem unimportant to a kid but can really be a problem to an old person. If a small object like a pen or pencil slides under furniture, an older person often is not able to stoop down and pick it up. But they feel embarrassed to ask for help. So, the pen stays there. Sometimes it gets forgotten about and becomes lost. You can help that older person find these things. and by helping, you are reminding that person that he or she is not forgotten about either.

Sometimes it is hard for an older person to reach up high. Putting things away, like groceries, becomes a problem. Often the older person gets tired and gives up. You can help to put groceries and other heavy objects away. And by doing that, you are helping that older person feel like he or she can still keep up with life's challenges.

One of the most important things you can do for a senior citizen who lives alone is to give that person someone to talk to. Old people, who have lived long lives and had many experiences, have stories to tell that you can learn a lot from. And it is important for you to say so, too. That way, you can show the older person that he or she is contributing to your life.

You can make a real contribution to an older person's life. Even if you only have an hour to spend, you can help an older person feel cared about and important. Find ways to reach out, whether through volunteer organizations or just by being aware of who is alone in your neighborhood. And always remember: as much as you give, you get back so much more, simply by knowing the difference that you have made.

2. Recognizing Persuasive Techniques

Persuasive texts typically rely on more than just the **logical appeal** of an argument to be convincing. They also rely on ethical and emotional appeals and other **persuasive techniques**—devices that can convince you to adopt a position or take an action.

Ethical appeals establish a writer's credibility and trustworthiness with an audience. When a writer links a claim to a widely accepted value, the writer not only gains moral support for that claim but also establishes a connection with readers. For example, with the following appeal, the writer reminds readers of a value they should accept and links a claim to it: "Most of us agree that we should protect our natural resources, but we don't invest a lot of time or money to preserve them."

The chart shown here explains several other means by which a writer may attempt to sway you to adopt his or her position. Learn to recognize these techniques, and you are less likely to be influenced by them.

Persuasive Technique	Example
Appeals by Association	
Bandwagon appeal Suggests that a person should believe or do something because "everyone else" does	Every day more buyers are enjoying the conveniences of Internet shopping.
Testimonial Relies on endorsements from well-known people or satisfied customers	Todd Marshall, star of stage and screen, buys his shoes at Fine Footwear. Shouldn't you?
Snob appeal Taps into people's desire to be special or part of an elite group	Be among the first to enjoy the upgraded facilities at Spring Lake Fitness Center.
Appeal to loyalty Relies on people's affiliation with a particular group	Say *Yes!* to your community— support the campaign to build a new library!
Emotional Appeals	
Appeals to pity, fear, or vanity Use strong feelings, rather than facts, to persuade	We need to keep the homeless shelter open— think how you would feel if you had no place to go.
Word Choice	
Glittering generality A generalization that includes a word or phrase with positive connotations, to promote a product, person, or idea.	Buying handmade jewelry from the Hang Up helps support small-town America.

Practice and Apply

Identify the persuasive techniques used in this model.

Vote for Velazquez!

Whom do you want to represent you in congress—a dinosaur who's stuck in the past or someone who's courageously facing the future? Why settle for Jill Jolsen, who hasn't lifted a finger to help this community? Don't let her slick ads fool you. Instead, join the leaders in the community and many of your neighbors who have already put their support behind Victor Velazquez. Local businesswoman Janice Wu is behind Velazquez all the way—she says he will bring new jobs and fresh ideas that will really work. Don't miss this once-in-a-lifetime chance to change this town. Vote for Velazquez!

3. Analyzing Logic and Reasoning

While persuasive techniques may sway you to side with a writer, they should not be enough to convince you that an argument is sound. To determine the soundness of an argument, you really need to examine the argument's claim and support and the logic or reasoning that links them. To do this, it is helpful to identify the writer's mode of reasoning.

The Inductive Mode of Reasoning

When a person uses specific evidence to arrive at a **general principle,** or generalization, that person is using **inductive reasoning.** Similarly, when a writer presents specific evidence first and then offers a generalization drawn from that evidence, the writer is making an **inductive argument.** Here is an example of inductive reasoning.

Specific Facts

Fact 1 Turtles are the only reptiles that have a shell.

Fact 2 The green turtle, a sea turtle, can swim almost 20 miles an hour.

Fact 3 Snapping turtles have powerful, sharp-edged jaws and are aggressive when attacked.

Generalization

Turtles have a variety of protective strategies.

There are several types of inductive reasoning.

- **argument by cause and effect:** In this type of argument, the writer or speaker attempts to persuade by showing the causes that would lead to a desired or an undesired effect. **Example:** *If we don't see the movie today, we won't be able to see it on the weekend because the theater will be too crowded.*
- **argument by analogy:** In this type of argument, the writer or speaker compares familiar events and things to those that are unfamiliar in an attempt to persuade the audience to accept the new situation. **Example:** *You'll like this new movie because it has a plot that is similar to others you've seen.*
- **argument by authority:** In this type of

argument, the writer or speaker attempts to persuade by using an authoritative and reliable source as evidence. **Example:** *The movie critic gave the new movie three stars, so we should go see it.*

Strategies for Determining the Soundness of Inductive Arguments

Ask yourself the following questions to evaluate an inductive argument:

- **Is the evidence valid and sufficient support for the conclusion?** Inaccurate facts lead to inaccurate conclusions.
- **Does the conclusion follow logically from the evidence?** From the facts listed above, the conclusion that *all* turtles have a wide variety of protective strategies would be too broad a generalization.
- **Is the evidence drawn from a large enough sample?** Even though there are only three facts listed above, the sample is large enough to support the claim. If you wanted to support the conclusion that only turtles have a variety of protective strategies, the sample is not large enough.

The Deductive Mode of Reasoning

When a person uses a **general principle,** or generalization, to form a conclusion about a particular situation or problem, that person is using **deductive reasoning.** For example,

Being exposed to loud noise over a long period will damage a person's hearing.	General principle or generalization
▼	
I listen to my stereo at its highest setting for hours every day.	The situation being observed or considered
▼	
I will have some hearing loss.	Conclusion (also considered a deduction)

Similarly, a writer is making a **deductive argument** when he or she begins the argument with a claim that is based on a general principle and then presents evidence to support the claim. For example, a writer might begin a deductive argument with the claim "Many people have some hearing loss."

Strategies for Determining the Soundness of Deductive Arguments

Ask yourself the following questions to evaluate a deductive argument.

- **Is the general principle actually stated, or is it implied?** Note that writers often use deductive reasoning in arguments without stating the general principles. They assume that readers will recognize and agree with the principles. Be sure to identify the general principle for yourself.
- **Is the general principle sound?** Don't just assume the general principle is sound. Ask yourself whether it is really true.
- **Is the conclusion valid?** To be valid, a conclusion in a deductive argument must follow logically from the general principle and the specific situation.

The following chart shows two conclusions drawn from the same general principle.

All seventh-graders are going to the zoo next week.	
Accurate Deduction	**Inaccurate Deduction**
Laura is in the seventh grade; therefore, Laura is going to the zoo next week.	Laura is going to the zoo next week; therefore, Laura is in the seventh grade.

Laura may be going to the zoo with her family or friends.

Practice and Apply

Identify whether inductive or deductive reasoning is used in the following paragraph. If the mode of reasoning used is inductive, tell whether the paragraph uses argument by cause and effect, analogy, or authority.

In science class, I learned what different substances do for the human body. Protein aids growth and repairs muscles. Fruits and vegetables provide critical vitamins, and calcium strengthens bones. Carbohydrates supply energy to the body. Clearly, a balanced diet is important for good health.

Identifying Faulty Reasoning

Sometimes an argument at first appears to make sense but isn't valid because it is based on a fallacy. A **rhetorical fallacy** is a false or misleading statement. Learn to recognize these rhetorical fallacies.

Type of Fallacy	Definition	Example
Circular reasoning	Supporting a statement by simply repeating it in different words	I'm tired because **I don't have any energy.**
Either/or fallacy	A statement that suggests that there are only two choices available in a situation that really offers more than two options	**Either** we raise taxes, **or** we close the parks.
Oversimplification	An explanation of a complex situation or problem as if it were much simpler than it is	Getting a good grade in Mrs. Raimi's class depends on **whether she likes you.**
Overgeneralization	A generalization that is too broad. You can often recognize overgeneralizations by the use of words such as *all, everyone, every time, anything, no one,* and *none.*	You **never** get me anything I want.
Hasty generalization	A conclusion drawn from too little evidence or from evidence that is biased	She left after fifteen minutes. **She must not like us.**
Stereotyping	A dangerous type of overgeneralization. Stereotypes are broad statements about people on the basis of their gender, ethnicity, race, or political, social, professional, or religious group	**All rock stars** are self-centered.
Ad hominem or attacking the person	An attempt to discredit an idea by attacking the person or group associated with it. Candidates often engage in name-calling during political campaigns.	The **narrow-minded** senator opposes recycling.
Evading the issue	Responding to an objection with arguments and evidence that do not address its central point	Yes, I broke my campaign promise not to raise taxes, **but higher taxes have led to increases in police patrols and paved highways.**
False cause	The mistake of assuming that because one event occurred after another event in time, the first event caused the second one to occur	John didn't get his homework done because he had to take the dog for a walk.

Look for examples of logical fallacies in the following argument. Identify each one and explain why you identified it as such.

Dear Editors:

There has been a lot of talk about students' lack of concern for the appearance of our school. Nobody gets rid of his or her trash properly and everyone writes graffiti on the walls. But if the school seemed more worth caring about, students would take better care of it. Most of the school is very old. The halls are dark and the walls are dingy because the maintenance staff has been on strike for several weeks. The old-fashioned school board said that an entirely new building wasn't needed. So only a new gym was added. It is clean and bright because students have kept it that way. Either we build a new school, or it will be destroyed in three years.

4. Evaluating Persuasive Texts

Learning how to evaluate persuasive texts and identify bias will help you become more selective when doing research and also help you improve your own reasoning and arguing skills. **Bias** is an inclination for or against a particular opinion or viewpoint. A writer may reveal a strongly positive or negative bias on an issue by

- **presenting only one way** of looking at it
- **overlooking key information**
- **stacking more evidence on one side** of the argument than the other
- **using unfairly weighted evidence,** which is weak or unproven evidence that a writer treats as if it is more important than it really is
- **using loaded language,** which consists of words with strongly positive or negative connotations

EXAMPLE:

Barbara Larsen is the best choice for student council president because she has fresh ideas and fantastic people skills. (*Fresh* and *fantastic* have very positive connotations.)

Propaganda is any form of communication that is so distorted that it conveys false or misleading information. Some politicians create and distribute propaganda. Many logical fallacies, such as name-calling, the either/or fallacy, and false causes, are often used in propaganda. The following example shows an oversimplification. The writer uses one fact to support a particular point of view but does not reveal another fact that does not support that viewpoint.

EXAMPLE:

Since the new park opened, vandalism in the area has increased by 10 percent. Clearly, the park has had a negative impact on the area. (The writer does not include the fact that the vandalism was caused by people who were not drawn into the area by the park.)

Strategies for Assessing Evidence

It is important to have a set of standards by which you can evaluate persuasive texts. Use the questions below to help you assess the adequacy, accuracy, and appropriateness of facts and opinions that are presented as evidence.

- **Are the facts accurate?** Facts can be proved by eyewitness accounts, authoritative sources such as encyclopedias and experts, or research.
- **Are the opinions well informed?** Any opinions offered should be supported by facts, be based on research or eyewitness accounts, or come from experts on the topic.
- **Is the evidence sufficient?** Thorough, or sufficient, evidence leaves no reasonable question unanswered. If a choice is offered to the reader, enough evidence for making the choice should be given. If taking a side is called for, all sides of the issue should be presented.
- **Is the evidence biased?** Be alert to evidence that contains loaded language or other signs of bias.
- **Is the evidence relevant?** The evidence needs to apply to the topic and come from people, groups, or organizations that have important knowledge of, or credentials relating to, the topic.

- **Is it important that the evidence be current?** Where timeliness is crucial, as in the areas of medicine and technology, the evidence should reflect the latest developments in the areas.

Read the argument below. Identify the facts, opinion, and elements of bias.

Let your voice be heard. The students' league is hosting a demonstration against U.S. Representative Sharon Bullhorn on Saturday. Just last week, Representative Bullhorn voted against raising the minimum wage. Obviously Representative Bullhorn doesn't care about young people. If she did, she would have helped pass the much-needed minimum wage increase, so that preteens and teens could earn the money they deserve.

Strategies for Determining a Strong Argument

Make sure that all or most of the following statements are true:

- The argument presents a claim or thesis.
- The claim is connected to its support by a general principle that most readers would readily agree with. Valid general principle: *It is the job of a school to provide a well-rounded physical education program.* Invalid general principle: *It is the job of a school to produce healthy, physically fit people.*
- The reasons make sense.
- The reasons are presented in a logical and effective order.
- The claim and all reasons are adequately supported by sound evidence.
- The evidence is sufficient, accurate, and relevant.
- The logic is sound. There are no instances of faulty reasoning.
- The argument adequately anticipates and addresses reader concerns and counterclaims with counterarguments.

Use the preceding criteria to evaluate the strength of the following proposal.

Summary of Proposal

I propose that our school install video cameras in halls, lunchrooms, and other public areas to monitor students' activities.

Need

The halls and public areas of our school are not well supervised because of a shortage of security staff. Last month, three students were hurt in fights on school property.

Proposed Solution

Installing video monitors in the halls and public areas of the school will create a safe environment for students at a reasonable cost.

There is good evidence that video monitoring works. Westview School has monitored its students for over a year. In that time there has not been one incident of fighting or damage to property

People who are against video monitoring don't agree. They say that monitoring violates students' rights to privacy.

In my opinion, junior high students need to act like responsible adults. We need guidelines and monitoring to show us where the limits are and to help us learn to act responsibly on our own.

Not only does video monitoring work, but installing the equipment can lower supervisory costs in the long run. Only eight cameras would be needed, installed in the two main hallways, the lunchroom, and the auditorium. The total cost would be around $16,000. I believe the money can be found in the general school budget.

What idiot would not support video monitoring of students?

It would be a crime not to have video monitoring.

Most school officials only care about their jobs and not what's good for students. I say to those school officials who do care: Either install video cameras or wait for more students to be injured.

Grammar

ELA L.7.1a–c, L.7.2a–b, L.7.3
ELD PII.7.3, PII.7.4, PII.7.5, PII.7.6, PII.7.7

Writing that has a lot of mistakes can confuse or even annoy a reader. A business letter with a punctuation error might lead to a miscommunication and delay a reply. Or a sentence fragment might lower your grade on an essay. Paying attention to grammar, punctuation, and capitalization rules can make your writing clearer and easier to read.

Quick Reference: Parts of Speech

Part of Speech	Function	Examples
Noun	names a person, a place, a thing, an idea, a quality, or an action	
Common	serves as a general name, or a name common to an entire group	poet, novel, love, journey
Proper	names a specific, one-of-a-kind person, place, or thing	Jackson, Pleasant Street, Statue of Liberty
Singular	refers to a single person, place, thing, or idea	shark, planet, flower, truth
Plural	refers to more than one person, place, thing, or idea	sharks, planets, flowers, truths
Concrete	names something that can be perceived by the senses	snake, path, Philadelphia, damage
Abstract	names something that cannot be perceived by the senses	intelligence, fear, joy, loneliness
Compound	expresses a single idea through a combination of two or more words	girlfriend, father-in-law, Christmas Eve
Collective	refers to a group of people or things	army, flock, class, species
Possessive	shows who or what owns something	Strafford's, Bess's, children's, witnesses'
Pronoun	takes the place of a noun or another pronoun	
Personal	refers to the person making a statement, the person(s) being addressed, or the person(s) or thing(s) the statement is about	I, me, my, mine, we, us, our, ours, you, your, yours, she, he, it, her, him, hers, his, its, they, them, their, theirs
Reflexive	follows a verb or preposition and refers to a preceding noun or pronoun	myself, yourself, herself, himself, itself, ourselves, yourselves, themselves
Intensive	emphasizes a noun or another pronoun	(same as reflexives)
Demonstrative	points to one or more specific persons or things	this, that, these, those

Part of Speech	Function	Examples
Interrogative	signals a question	who, whom, whose, which, what
Indefinite	refers to one or more persons or things not specifically mentioned	both, all, most, many, anyone, everybody, several, none, some
Relative	introduces an adjective clause by relating it to a word in the clause	who, whom, whose, which, that
Verb	expresses an action, a condition, or a state of being	
Action	tells what the subject does or did, physically or mentally	run, reaches, listened, consider, decides, dreamed
Linking	connects the subject to something that identifies or describes it	am, is, are, was, were, sound, taste, appear, feel, become, remain, seem
Auxiliary	precedes the main verb in a verb phrase	be, have, do, can, could, will, would, may, might
Transitive	directs the action toward someone or something; always has an object	The storm **sank** the ship.
Intransitive	does not direct the action toward someone or something; does not have an object	The ship **sank.**
Adjective	modifies a noun or pronoun	**strong** women, **two** epics, **enough** time
Adverb	modifies a verb, an adjective, or another adverb	walked **out, really** funny, **far** away
Preposition	relates one word to another word	at, by, for, from, in, of, on, to, with
Conjunction	joins words or word groups	
Coordinating	joins words or word groups used the same way	and, but, or, for, so, yet, nor
Correlative	used as a pair to join words or word groups used the same way	both . . . and, either . . . or, neither . . . nor
Subordinating	introduces a clause that cannot stand by itself as a complete sentence	although, after, as, before, because, since, when, if, unless
Interjection	expresses emotion	wow, ouch, hurrah

Quick Reference: The Sentence and Its Parts

The diagrams that follow will give you a brief review of the essentials of a sentence and some of its parts.

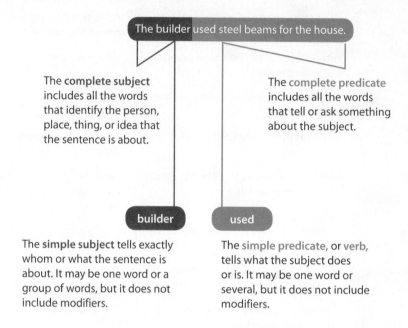

The builder used steel beams for the house.

The **complete subject** includes all the words that identify the person, place, thing, or idea that the sentence is about.

The **complete predicate** includes all the words that tell or ask something about the subject.

builder

The **simple subject** tells exactly whom or what the sentence is about. It may be one word or a group of words, but it does not include modifiers.

used

The **simple predicate**, or **verb**, tells what the subject does or is. It may be one word or several, but it does not include modifiers.

Every word in a sentence is part of a complete subject or a complete predicate.

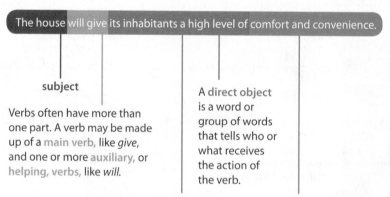

The house will give its inhabitants a high level of comfort and convenience.

subject

Verbs often have more than one part. A verb may be made up of a **main verb,** like *give*, and one or more **auxiliary,** or **helping, verbs,** like *will.*

A **direct object** is a word or group of words that tells who or what receives the action of the verb.

An **indirect object** is a word or group of words that tells to whom or for whom or to what or for what the verb's action is performed. A sentence can have an indirect object only if it has a direct object. The indirect object always comes before the direct object.

A **prepositional phrase** consists of a preposition, its object, and any modifiers of the object. In this phrase, *of* is the preposition and *comfort and convenience* is its object.

Quick Reference: Punctuation

Mark	Function	Examples
End Marks period, question mark, exclamation point	ends a sentence	We can start now. When would you like to leave? What a fantastic hit!
period	follows an initial or abbreviation **Exception:** postal abbreviations of states	Mrs. Dorothy Parker C. P. Cavafy, P.M., A.D., lb., oz., Blvd., Dr. NE (Nebraska), NV (Nevada)
period	follows a number or letter in an outline	I. Volcanoes A. Central-vent 1. Shield
Comma	separates part of a compound sentence	I had never disliked poetry, but now I really love it.
	separates items in a series	She is brave, loyal, and kind.
	separates adjectives of equal rank that modify the same noun	The slow, easy route is best.
	sets off a term of address	Maria, how can I help you? You must do something, soldier.
	sets off a parenthetical expression	Hard workers, as you know, don't quit. I'm not a quitter, believe me.
	sets off an introductory word, phrase, or dependent clause	Yes, I forgot my key. At the beginning of the day, I feel fresh. While she was out, I was here. Having finished my chores, I went out.
	sets off a nonessential phrase or clause	Ed Pawn, the captain of the chess team, won. Ed Pawn, who is the captain, won. The two leading runners, sprinting toward the finish line, finished in a tie.
	sets off parts of dates and addresses	Mail it by May 14, 2010, to the Hauptman Company, 321 Market Street, Memphis, Tennessee.
	follows the salutation and closing of a letter	Dear Jim, Sincerely yours,

Mark	Function	Examples
	separates words to avoid confusion	By noon, time had run out. What the minister does, does matter. While cooking, Jim burned his hand.
Semicolon	separates items that contain commas in a series	We spent the first week of summer vacation in Chicago, Illinois; the second week in St. Louis, Missouri; and the third week in Albany, New York.
	separates parts of a compound sentence that are not joined by a coordinating conjunction	The last shall be first; the first shall be last. I read the Bible; however, I have not memorized it.
	separates parts of a compound sentence when the parts contain commas	After I ran out of money, I called my parents; but only my sister was home, unfortunately.
Colon	introduces a list	The names we wrote were the following: Dana, John, and Will.
	introduces a long quotation	Abraham Lincoln wrote: "Four score and seven years ago, our fathers brought forth on this continent a new nation. . . ."
	follows the salutation of a business letter	To Whom It May Concern: Dear Leonard Atole:
	separates certain numbers	1:28 P.M., Genesis 2:5
Dash	indicates an abrupt break in thought	I was thinking of my mother—who is arriving tomorrow—just as you walked in.
Parentheses	enclose less important material	It was so unlike him (John is always on time) that I began to worry. The last World Series game (did you see it?) was fun.

continued

Mark	Function	Examples
Hyphen	joins parts of a compound adjective before a noun	The not-so-rich taxpayer won't stand for this!
	joins parts of a compound with *all-, ex-, self-,* or *-elect*	The ex-firefighter helped rescue him. Our president-elect is self-conscious.
	joins parts of a compound number (to ninety-nine)	Today, I turned twenty-one.
	joins parts of a fraction	My cup is one-third full.
	joins a prefix to a word beginning with a capital letter	Which Pre-Raphaelite painter do you like best? It snowed in mid-October.
	indicates that a word is divided at the end of a line	How could you have any reasonable expectations of getting a new computer?
Apostrophe	used with *s* to form the possessive of a noun or an indefinite pronoun	my friend's book, my friends' books, anyone's guess, somebody else's problem
	replaces one or more omitted letters in a contraction or numbers in a date	don't (omitted *o*), he'd (omitted *woul*), the class of '99 (omitted *19*)
	used with *s* to form the plural of a letter	I had two A's on my report card.
Quotation Marks	set off a speaker's exact words	Sara said, "I'm finally ready." "I'm ready," Sara said, "finally." Did Sara say, "I'm ready"? Sara said, "I'm ready!"
	set off the title of a story, an article, a short poem, an essay, a song, or a chapter	I like Doctorow's "Another Place, Another Time" and Giovanni's "A Poem for My Librarian, Mrs. Long." I like Douglas Fox's essay "Big Rocks' Balancing Acts."
Ellipses	replace material omitted from a quotation	"When in the course of human events ... and to assume among the powers of the earth. . . ."
Italics	indicate the title of a book, a play, a magazine, a long poem, an opera, a film, or a TV series, or the name of a ship	*Mississippi Solo, Sorry, Wrong Number, Newsweek,* the *Odyssey, Madame Butterfly, Gone with the Wind, Seinfeld, Titanic*
Brackets	indicate a word or phrase that has been added to a quotation to make it clearer	"Spreading awareness [of the hurricane's damage] is an important part of our work."

Quick Reference: Capitalization

Category	Examples
People and Titles	
Names and initials of people	Amy Tan, W. H. Auden
Titles used before a name	Professor Holmes, Senator Long
Deities and members of religious groups	Jesus, Allah, Buddha, Zeus, Baptists, Roman Catholics
Names of ethnic and national groups	Hispanics, Jews, African Americans
Geographical Names	
Cities, states, countries, continents	Philadelphia, Kansas, Japan, Europe
Regions, bodies of water, mountains	the South, Lake Baikal, Mount Everest
Geographic features, parks	Great Basin, Yellowstone National Park
Streets and roads, planets	318 East Sutton Drive, Charles Court, Jupiter, Pluto
Organizations, Events, Etc.	
Companies, organizations, teams	Ford Motor Company, Boy Scouts of America, St. Louis Cardinals
Buildings, bridges, monuments	Empire State Building, Eads Bridge, Washington Monument
Documents, awards	Declaration of Independence, Stanley Cup
Special named events	Mardi Gras, World Series
Government bodies, historical periods and events	U.S. Senate, House of Representatives, Middle Ages, Vietnam War
Days and months, holidays	Thursday, March, Thanksgiving, Labor Day
Specific cars, boats, trains, planes	Porsche, *Carpathia*, *Southwest Chief*, Concorde
Proper Adjectives	
Adjectives formed from proper nouns	French cooking, Spanish omelet, Edwardian age, Western movie
First Words and the Pronoun *I*	
First word in a sentence or quotation	This is it. He said, "Let's go."
First word of a sentence in parentheses that is not within another sentence	The spelling rules are covered in another section. (Consult that section for more information.)
First words in the salutation and closing of a letter	Dear Madam, Very truly yours,
First word, last word, and all important words in a title	*The Call of the Wild*, "Take Me Out to the Ball Game"

1 Nouns

A **noun** is a word used to name a person, a place, a thing, an idea, a quality, or an action. Nouns can be classified in several ways.

For more information on different types of nouns, see **Quick Reference: Parts of Speech, page R30.**

1.1 COMMON NOUNS

Common nouns are general names, common to entire groups.

1.2 PROPER NOUNS

Proper nouns name specific, one-of-a-kind people, places, and things.

Common	Proper
leader, park, forest, mountain	Sequoya, Sierra Nevada, Giant Forest, Mount Whitney

For more information, see **Quick Reference: Capitalization,** page R36.

1.3 SINGULAR AND PLURAL NOUNS

A noun may take a singular or a plural form, depending on whether it names a single person, place, thing, or idea or more than one. Make sure you use appropriate spellings when forming plurals.

Singular	Plural
tourist, city, mouse	tourists, cities, mice

For more information, see **Forming Plural Nouns,** page R61.

1.4 POSSESSIVE NOUNS

A **possessive noun** shows who or what owns something.

For more information, see **Forming Possessives,** page R62.

2 Pronouns

A **pronoun** is a word that is used in place of a noun or another pronoun. The word or word group to which the pronoun refers is called its **antecedent.**

2.1 PERSONAL PRONOUNS

Personal pronouns change their form to express person, number, gender, and case. The forms of these pronouns are shown in the following chart.

	Nominative	Objective	Possessive
Singular			
First person	I	me	my, mine
Second person	you	you	your, yours
Third person	she, he, it	her, him, it	her, hers, his, its
Plural			
First person	we	us	our, ours
Second person	you	you	your, yours
Third person	they	them	their, theirs

2.2 AGREEMENT WITH ANTECEDENT

Pronouns should agree with their antecedents in number, gender, and person.

If an antecedent is singular, use a singular pronoun.

> EXAMPLE: *Rachel wrote a **detective story**. It has a surprise ending.*

If an antecedent is plural, use a plural pronoun.

> EXAMPLES: ***The characters** have their motives for murder.*
> *Javier loves **mysteries** and reads them all the time.*

The gender of a pronoun must be the same as the gender of its antecedent.

> EXAMPLE: *The **man** has to use all his wits to stay alive and solve the crime.*

The person of the pronoun must be the same as the person of its antecedent. As the chart in Section 2.1 shows, a pronoun can be in first-person, second-person, or third-person form.

> EXAMPLE: ***You** want a story to grab your attention.*

Grammar Practice

Rewrite each sentence so that the underlined pronoun agrees with its antecedent.

1. Our class created a blog that tells about the books they've read.
2. When classmates write to us, we answer him.
3. If I find a comment from my teacher, I always answer them.
4. Every day there are more comments, and it is hard to ignore.
5. When you view the blog, we might enjoy the comments posted there.

2.3 PRONOUN FORMS

Personal pronouns change form to show how they function in sentences. The three forms are the subject form, the object form, and the possessive form. For examples of these pronouns, see the chart in Section 2.1.

A **subject pronoun** is used as a subject in a sentence.

> EXAMPLE: *All of my friends like our family dog. He is so friendly.*

Also use the subject form when the pronoun follows a linking verb.

> EXAMPLE: *The first puppy we chose was he.*

An **object pronoun** is used as a direct object, an indirect object, or the object of a preposition.

SUBJECT OBJECT
He will lead them to us.
OBJECT OF PREPOSITION

A **possessive pronoun** shows ownership. The pronouns *mine, yours, hers, his, its, ours,* and *theirs* can be used in place of nouns.

> EXAMPLE: *This money is mine.*

The pronouns *my, your, her, his, its, our,* and *their* are used before nouns.

> EXAMPLE: *We thanked the neighbors for their help.*

WATCH OUT! Many spelling errors can be avoided if you watch out for *its* and *their.* Don't confuse the possessive pronoun *its* with the contraction *it's,* meaning "it is" or "it has." The homonyms *they're* (a contraction of *they are*) and *there* ("in that place" or an expletive) are often mistakenly used for *their.*

TIP To decide which pronoun to use in a comparison such as "He tells better tales than (*I* or *me*)," fill in the missing word(s): *He tells better tales than I tell.*

Grammar Practice

Write the correct pronoun form to complete each sentence.

1. William Butler Yeats wrote the poem "The Song of Wandering Aengus," and it was published when (he, him) was in his early 30s.
2. This poem of (him, his) was published in 1899 in the collection *The Wind Among the Reeds*.
3. This collection contains 37 poems. All of (they, them) are written in Yeats's early style.
4. Yeats wrote many other poems. All of (their, his) dates of publication can be found by searching reputable online sources.
5. Yeats won the Nobel Prize in Literature in 1923 for (his, its) literary contributions.

2.4 REFLEXIVE AND INTENSIVE PRONOUNS

These pronouns are formed by adding *-self* or *-selves* to certain personal pronouns. Their forms are the same, and they differ only in how they are used.

A **reflexive pronoun** follows a verb or preposition and reflects back on an earlier noun or pronoun.

> EXAMPLES: *He likes himself too much. She is now herself again.*

Intensive pronouns intensify or emphasize the nouns or pronouns to which they refer.

> EXAMPLES: *They themselves will educate their children. You did it yourself.*

WATCH OUT! Avoid using *hisself* or *theirselves.* Standard English does not include these forms.

> NONSTANDARD: *Alex dedicated hisself to learning the magician's secrets.*
> STANDARD: *Alex dedicated himself to learning the magician's secrets.*

2.5 DEMONSTRATIVE PRONOUNS

Demonstrative pronouns point out things and persons near and far.

	Singular	Plural
Near	this	these
Far	that	those

2.6 INDEFINITE PRONOUNS

Indefinite pronouns do not refer to specific persons or things and usually have no antecedents. The chart shows some commonly used indefinite pronouns.

Singular	Plural	Singular or Plural	
another	both	all	none
anybody	few	any	some
no one	many	more	most
neither			

TIP Indefinite pronouns that end in *one, body,* or *thing* are always singular.

> INCORRECT: *Did everybody play their part well?*

If the indefinite pronoun might refer to either a male or a female, *his or her* may be used to refer to it, or the sentence may be rewritten.

> CORRECT: *Did everybody play his or her part well?*
> *Did all the students play their parts well?*

2.7 INTERROGATIVE PRONOUNS

An **interrogative pronoun** tells a reader or listener that a question is coming. The interrogative pronouns are *who, whom, whose, which,* and *what.*

> EXAMPLES: *Who is going to rehearse with you?*
> *From whom did you receive the script?*

TIP *Who* is used as a subject; *whom* is used as an object. To find out which pronoun you need to use in a question, change the question to a statement.

> QUESTION: *(Who/Whom) did you meet there?*

> STATEMENT: *You met (?) there.*

Since the verb has a subject (*you*), the needed word must be the object form, *whom.*

> EXAMPLE: *Whom did you meet there?*

WATCH OUT! A special problem arises when you use an interrupter, such as *do you think,* within a question.

> EXAMPLE: *(Who/Whom) do you think will win?*

If you eliminate the interrupter, it is clear that the word you need is *who.*

2.8 RELATIVE PRONOUNS

Relative pronouns relate, or connect, adjective clauses to the words they modify in sentences. The noun or pronoun that a relative clause modifies is the antecedent of the relative pronoun. Here are the relative pronouns and their uses.

	Subject	Object	Possessive
Person	who	whom	whose
Thing	which	which	whose
Thing/Person	that	that	whose

Often, short sentences with related ideas can be combined by using a relative pronoun to create a more effective sentence.

> SHORT SENTENCE: *Yeats wrote "The Song of Wandering Aengus."*

> RELATED SENTENCE: *"The Song of Wandering Aengus" is a well-known poem in literature.*

> COMBINED SENTENCE: *Yeats wrote "The Song of Wandering Aengus," which is a well-known poem in literature.*

Grammar Practice

Write the correct form of each incorrect pronoun.

1. Whom has read or studied how the brain works?
2. Individuals whom study the brain understand more about how we learn and think.
3. Nobody knows everything they can about the brain.
4. Each person's brain develops and forms new connections, but they aren't aware of these changes.
5. Scientists theyselves often can't tell how their own brains change over time.

2.9 PRONOUN REFERENCE PROBLEMS

The referent of a pronoun should always be clear. Avoid problems by rewriting sentences.

An **indefinite reference** occurs when the pronoun *it, you,* or *they* does not clearly refer to a specific antecedent.

> UNCLEAR: *My aunt hugged me in front of my friends, and it was embarrassing.*

> CLEAR: *My aunt hugged me in front of my friends, and I was embarrassed.*

A **general reference** occurs when the pronoun *it, this, that, which,* or *such* is used to refer to a general idea rather than a specific antecedent.

> UNCLEAR: *Jenna takes acting lessons. This has improved her chances of getting a part in the school play.*

> CLEAR: *Jenna takes acting lessons. The lessons have improved her chances of getting a part in the school play.*

Ambiguous means "having more than one possible meaning." An **ambiguous reference** occurs when a pronoun could refer to two or more antecedents.

> UNCLEAR: *Tony talked to Fred and said that he could meet us later.*

> CLEAR: *Tony talked to Fred and said that Fred could meet us later.*

Grammar Practice

Rewrite the following sentences to correct indefinite, ambiguous, and general pronoun references.

1. When computer networks were first developed in the late 1950s and early 1960s, they didn't know how it would change worldwide communications.
2. Early networks were created for special purposes, and airlines and the U.S. Department of Defense used it.
3. Today people all around the world can use the Internet. This makes immediate communication possible.
4. With the Internet and wireless access, it can connect almost anyone anywhere.

3 Verbs

A **verb** is a word that expresses an action, a condition, or a state of being.

For more information, see Quick Reference: Parts of Speech, page R30.

3.1 ACTION VERBS

Action verbs express mental or physical activity.

> EXAMPLE: *Mr. Cho slept with the window open.*

3.2 LINKING VERBS

Linking verbs join subjects with words or phrases that rename or describe them.

> EXAMPLE: *When he awoke the next morning, his bed was wet from the rain.*

3.3 PRINCIPAL PARTS

Action and linking verbs typically have four principal parts, which are used to form verb tenses. The principal parts are the **present**, the **present participle**, the **past**, and the **past participle**.

Action verbs and some linking verbs also fall into two categories: regular and irregular. A **regular verb** is a verb that forms its past and past participle by adding *-ed* or *-d* to the present form.

Present	Present Participle	Past	Past Participle
jump	(is) jumping	jumped	(has) jumped
solve	(is) solving	solved	(has) solved
grab	(is) grabbing	grabbed	(has) grabbed
carry	(is) carrying	carried	(has) carried

An **irregular verb** is a verb that forms its past and past participle in some other way than by adding *-ed* or *-d* to the present form.

Present	Present Participle	Past	Past Participle
begin	(is) beginning	began	(has) begun
break	(is) breaking	broke	(has) broken
go	(is) going	went	(has) gone

3.4 VERB TENSE

The **tense** of a verb indicates the time of the action or the state of being. An action or state of being can occur in the present, the past, or the future. There are six tenses, each expressing a different range of time.

The **present tense** expresses an action or state that is happening at the present time, occurs regularly, or is constant or generally true. Use the present part.

NOW: *That snow looks deep.*

REGULAR: *It snows every day.*

GENERAL: *Snow falls.*

The **past tense** expresses an action that began and ended in the past. Use the past part.

EXAMPLE: *The storyteller finished his tale.*

The **future tense** expresses an action or state that will occur. Use *shall* or *will* with the present part.

EXAMPLE: *They will attend the next festival.*

The **present perfect** tense expresses an action or state that (1) was completed at an indefinite time in the past or (2) began in the past and continues into the present. Use *have* or *has* with the past participle.

EXAMPLE: *Poetry has inspired many readers.*

The **past perfect tense** expresses an action in the past that came before another action in the past. Use *had* with the past participle.

EXAMPLE: *He had built a fire before the dog ran away.*

The **future perfect tense** expresses an action in the future that will be completed before another action in the future. Use *shall have* or *will have* with the past participle.

EXAMPLE: *They will have read the novel before they see the movie version of the tale.*

TIP A past-tense form of an irregular verb is not used with an auxiliary verb, but a past-participle main irregular verb is always used with an auxiliary verb.

INCORRECT: *I have saw her somewhere before.* (*Saw* is the past-tense form of an irregular verb and shouldn't be used with *have*.)

CORRECT: *I have seen her somewhere before.*

INCORRECT: *I seen her somewhere before.* (*Seen* is the past participle of an irregular verb and shouldn't be used without an auxiliary verb.)

3.5 PROGRESSIVE FORMS

The progressive forms of the six tenses show ongoing actions. Use forms of **be** with the present participles of verbs.

PRESENT PROGRESSIVE: *She is rehearsing her lines.*

PAST PROGRESSIVE: *She was rehearsing her lines.*

FUTURE PROGRESSIVE: *She will be rehearsing her lines.*

PRESENT PERFECT PROGRESSIVE: *She has been rehearsing her lines.*

PAST PERFECT PROGRESSIVE: *She had been rehearsing her lines.*

FUTURE PERFECT PROGRESSIVE: *She will have been rehearsing her lines.*

WATCH OUT! Do not shift from tense to tense needlessly. Watch out for the following special cases.

• In most compound sentences and in sentences with compound predicates, keep the tenses the same.

INCORRECT: *His boots freeze, and he shook with cold.*

CORRECT: *His boots freeze, and he shakes with cold.*

• If one past action happens before another, do shift tenses.

INCORRECT: *They wished they started earlier.*

CORRECT: *They wished they had started earlier.*

Rewrite each sentence using a form of the verb(s) in parentheses. Identify each form that you use.

1. Some medical developments (begin) with the space age—for example, laparoscopy and robotics.
2. Both of these areas (grow) and (advance) the field of surgery.
3. In the 1990s "robotic assistants" (help) in surgery.
4. People (come) to expect simpler procedures because of these new techniques.
5. Some day other procedures that avoid cutting into tissue (develop).

Rewrite each sentence to correct an error in tense.

1. I seen a movie about the cobra and its natural enemy, the mongoose.
2. Most snakes hide and avoided people.
3. The cobra raised its head when it seeks out its next victim.
4. Both the male and female protected their eggs and will attack an approaching intruder.
5. The venom of a cobra was deadly and kills a human being within a few hours.

3.6 ACTIVE AND PASSIVE VOICE

The voice of a verb tells whether its subject performs or receives the action expressed by the verb. When the subject performs the action, the verb is in the **active voice.** When the subject is the receiver of the action, the verb is in the **passive voice.**

Compare these two sentences:

ACTIVE: *Virginia Hamilton wrote "The People Could Fly."*

PASSIVE: *"The People Could Fly" was written by Virginia Hamilton.*

To form the passive voice, use a form of **be** with the past participle of the verb.

WATCH OUT! Use the passive voice sparingly. It can make writing awkward and less direct.

AWKWARD: *"The People Could Fly" is a folk tale that was written by Virginia Hamilton.*

BETTER: *Virginia Hamilton wrote the tale "The People Could Fly."*

There are occasions when you will choose to use the passive voice because:

- you want to emphasize the receiver: **The king was shot.**
- the doer is unknown: **My books were stolen.**
- the doer is unimportant: **French is spoken here.**

4 Modifiers

Modifiers are words or groups of words that change or limit the meanings of other words. Adjectives and adverbs are common modifiers.

4.1 ADJECTIVES

Adjectives modify nouns and pronouns by telling which one, what kind, how many, or how much.

WHICH ONE: *this, that, these, those*

EXAMPLE: *That bird is a scarlet ibis.*

WHAT KIND: *small, sick, courageous, black*

EXAMPLE: *The sick bird sways on the branch.*

HOW MANY: *some, few, ten, none, both, each*

EXAMPLE: *Both brothers stared at the bird.*

HOW MUCH: *more, less, enough*

EXAMPLE: *The bird did not have enough strength to remain perched.*

4.2 PREDICATE ADJECTIVES

Most adjectives come before the nouns they modify, as in the examples above. A **predicate adjective,** however, follows a linking verb and describes the subject.

EXAMPLE: *My friends are very intelligent.*

Be especially careful to use adjectives (not adverbs) after such linking verbs as **look, feel, grow, taste,** and **smell.**

EXAMPLE: *The bread smells wonderful.*

4.3 ADVERBS

Adverbs modify verbs, adjectives, and other adverbs by telling where, when, how, or to what extent.

WHERE: *The children played outside.*

WHEN: *The author spoke yesterday.*

HOW: *We walked slowly behind the leader.*

TO WHAT EXTENT: *He worked very hard.*

Adverbs may occur in many places in sentences, both before and after the words they modify.

EXAMPLES: *Suddenly the wind shifted.*
The wind suddenly shifted.
The wind shifted suddenly.

4.4 ADJECTIVE OR ADVERB?

Many adverbs are formed by adding *-ly* to adjectives.

EXAMPLES: *sweet, sweetly; gentle, gently*

However, *-ly* added to a noun will usually yield an adjective.

EXAMPLES: *friend, friendly; woman, womanly*

4.5 COMPARISON OF MODIFIERS

Modifiers can be used to compare two or more things. The form of a modifier shows the degree of comparison. Both adjectives and adverbs have **comparative** and **superlative** forms.

The **comparative form** is used to compare two things, groups, or actions.

EXAMPLES: *His father's hands were stronger than his own.*
His father was more courageous than the other man.

The **superlative form** is used to compare more than two things, groups, or actions.

EXAMPLES: *His father's hands were the strongest in the family.*
His father was the most courageous of them all.

4.6 REGULAR COMPARISONS

Most one-syllable and some two-syllable adjectives and adverbs form comparatives and superlatives by adding *-er* and

-est. All three-syllable and most two-syllable modifiers have comparatives and superlatives formed with *more* or *most.*

Modifier	Comparative	Superlative
small	smaller	smallest
thin	thinner	thinnest
sleepy	sleepier	sleepiest
useless	more useless	most useless
precisely	more precisely	most precisely

WATCH OUT! Note that spelling changes must sometimes be made to form the comparatives and superlatives of modifiers.

EXAMPLES: *friendly, friendlier* (Change *y* to *i* and add the ending.)
sad, sadder (Double the final consonant and add the ending.)

4.7 IRREGULAR COMPARISONS

Some commonly used modifiers have irregular comparative and superlative forms. They are listed in the following chart. You may wish to memorize them.

Modifier	Comparative	Superlative
good	better	best
bad	worse	worst
far	farther *or* further	farthest *or* furthest
little	less *or* lesser	least
many	more	most
well	better	best
much	more	most

4.8 PROBLEMS WITH MODIFIERS

Study the tips that follow to avoid common mistakes.

Farther* and *Further Use *farther* for distances; use *further* for everything else.

Double Comparisons Make a comparison by using *-er/-est* or by using *more/most*. Using *-er* with *more* or using *-est* with *most* is incorrect.

INCORRECT: *I like her more better than she likes me.*

CORRECT: *I like her better than she likes me.*

Illogical Comparisons An illogical or confusing comparison results when two unrelated things are compared or when something is compared with itself. The word *other* or the word *else* should be used when comparing an individual member to the rest of a group.

ILLOGICAL: *The narrator was more curious about the war than any student in his class.* (implies that the narrator isn't a student in the class)

LOGICAL: *The narrator was more curious about the war than any other student in his class.* (identifies that the narrator is a student)

Bad vs. Badly *Bad,* always an adjective, is used before a noun or after a linking verb. *Badly,* always an adverb, never modifies a noun. Be sure to use the right form after a linking verb.

INCORRECT: *Ed felt badly after his team lost.*

CORRECT: *Ed felt bad after his team lost.*

Good vs. Well *Good* is always an adjective. It is used before a noun or after a linking verb. *Well* is often an adverb meaning "expertly" or "properly." *Well* can also be used as an adjective after a linking verb when it means "in good health."

INCORRECT: *Helen writes very good.*

CORRECT: *Helen writes very well.*

CORRECT: *Yesterday I felt bad; today I feel well.*

Double Negatives If you add a negative word to a sentence that is already negative, the result will be an error known as a double negative. When using *not* or *-n't* with a verb, use *any-* words, such as *anybody* or *anything,* rather than *no-* words, such as *nobody* or *nothing,* later in the sentence.

INCORRECT: *We haven't seen nobody.*

CORRECT: *We haven't seen anybody.*

Using *hardly, barely,* or *scarcely* after a negative word is also incorrect.

INCORRECT: *They couldn't barely see two feet ahead.*

CORRECT: *They could barely see two feet ahead.*

Misplaced Modifiers Sometimes a modifier is placed so far away from the word it modifies that the intended meaning of the sentence is unclear. Prepositional phrases and participial phrases are often misplaced. Place modifiers as close as possible to the words they modify.

MISPLACED: *We found the child in the park who was missing.*

CLEARER: *We found the child who was missing in the park.* (The child was missing, not the park.)

Dangling Modifiers Sometimes a modifier doesn't appear to modify any word in a sentence. Most dangling modifiers are participial phrases or infinitive phrases.

DANGLING: *Looking out the window, his brother was seen driving by.*

CLEARER: *Looking out the window, Josh saw his brother driving by.*

Grammar Practice

Choose the correct word or words from each pair in parentheses.

1. When Ellis Island opened, it was the (larger, largest) port of entry to the United States.
2. In the 1980s, the facility underwent the (greatest, most greatest) restoration ever performed.
3. The restoration project (bad, badly) needed funds.
4. The project didn't have (no, any) funding until fundraising efforts began in 1982.
5. In 1990, the (grandly, grand) reopening was received (good, well).

5 The Sentence and Its Parts

A **sentence** is a group of words used to express a complete thought. A complete sentence has a subject and a predicate.

For more information, see **Quick Reference: The Sentence and Its Parts,** page R32.

5.1 KINDS OF SENTENCES

There are four basic types of sentences.

Type	Definition	Example
Declarative	states a fact, a wish, an intent, or a feeling	Charles Yu understands science fiction.
Interrogative	asks a question	Did you read "Earth (A Gift Shop)"?
Imperative	gives a command or direction	Read the story.
Exclamatory	expresses strong feeling or excitement	The story is great!

5.2 COMPOUND SUBJECTS AND PREDICATES

A compound subject consists of two or more subjects that share the same verb. They are typically joined by the coordinating conjunction *and* or *or*.

> EXAMPLE: *A short story or novel will keep you engaged.*

A compound predicate consists of two or more predicates that share the same subject. They too are usually joined by a coordinating conjunction such as *and, but,* or *or.*

> EXAMPLE: *The class finished all the poetry but did not read the short stories.*

5.3 COMPLEMENTS

A **complement** is a word or group of words that completes the meaning of the sentence. Some sentences contain only a subject and a verb. Most sentences, however, require additional words placed after the verb to complete the meaning of the sentence. There are three kinds of complements: direct objects, indirect objects, and subject complements.

Direct objects are words or word groups that receive the action of action verbs. A direct object answers the question *what* or *whom.*

> EXAMPLES: *The students asked many questions.* (Asked what?)
> *The teacher quickly answered the students.* (Answered whom?)

Indirect objects tell to whom or what or for whom or what the actions of verbs are performed. Indirect objects come before direct objects. In the examples that follow, the indirect objects are highlighted.

> EXAMPLES: *My sister usually gave her friends good advice.* (Gave to whom?)
> *Her brother sent the store a heavy package.* (Sent to what?)

Subject complements come after linking verbs and identify or describe the subjects. A subject complement that names or identifies a subject is called a **predicate nominative.** Predicate nominatives include **predicate nouns** and **predicate pronouns.**

>EXAMPLES: *My friends are very hard workers.*
>*The best writer in the class is she.*

A subject complement that describes a subject is called a **predicate adjective.**

>EXAMPLE: *The pianist appeared very energetic.*

6 Phrases

A **phrase** is a group of related words that does not contain a subject and a predicate but functions in a sentence as a single part of speech.

6.1 PREPOSITIONAL PHRASES

A **prepositional phrase** is a phrase that consists of a preposition, its object, and any modifiers of the object. Prepositional phrases that modify nouns or pronouns are called **adjective phrases.** Prepositional phrases that modify verbs, adjectives, or adverbs are **adverb phrases.**

>ADJECTIVE PHRASE: *The central character of the story is a villain.*

>ADVERB PHRASE: *He reveals his nature in the first scene.*

6.2 APPOSITIVES AND APPOSITIVE PHRASES

An **appositive** is a noun or pronoun that identifies or renames another noun or pronoun. An **appositive phrase** includes an appositive and modifiers of it. An appositive usually follows the noun or pronoun it identifies.

An appositive can be either **essential** or **nonessential.** An **essential appositive** provides information that is needed to identify what is referred to by the preceding noun or pronoun.

>EXAMPLE: *The book is about the author Naomi Shihab Nye.*

A **nonessential appositive** adds extra information about a noun or pronoun whose meaning is already clear.

Nonessential appositives and appositive phrases are set off with commas.

>EXAMPLE: *The book, an autobiography, tells how she began writing.*

7 Verbals and Verbal Phrases

A **verbal** is a verb form that is used as a noun, an adjective, or an adverb. A **verbal phrase** consists of a verbal along with its modifiers and complements. There are three kinds of verbals: **infinitives, participles,** and **gerunds.**

7.1 INFINITIVES AND INFINITIVE PHRASES

An **infinitive** is a verb form that usually begins with *to* and functions as a noun, an adjective, or an adverb. An **infinitive phrase** consists of an infinitive plus its modifiers and complements.

>NOUN: *To know her is my only desire.* (subject)
>*I'm planning to walk with you.* (direct object)
>*Her goal was to promote women's rights.* (predicate nominative)

>ADJECTIVE: *We saw his need to be loved.* (adjective modifying *need*)

>ADVERB: *She wrote to voice her opinions.* (adverb modifying *wrote*)

Because *to,* the sign of the infinitive, precedes infinitives, it is usually easy to recognize them. However, sometimes *to* may be omitted.

>EXAMPLE: *Let no one dare [to] enter this shrine.*

7.2 PARTICIPLES AND PARTICIPIAL PHRASES

A **participle** is a verb form that functions as an adjective. Like adjectives, participles modify nouns and pronouns. Most participles are present-participle forms, ending in *-ing,* or past-participle forms ending in *-ed* or *-en.* In the examples below, the participles are highlighted.

>MODIFYING A NOUN: *The dying man had a smile on his face.*

MODIFYING A PRONOUN: *Frustrated, everyone abandoned the cause.*

Participial phrases are participles with all their modifiers and complements.

MODIFYING A NOUN: *The dogs searching for survivors are well trained.*

MODIFYING A PRONOUN: *Having approved your proposal, we are ready to act.*

7.3 DANGLING AND MISPLACED PARTICIPLES

A participle or participial phrase should be placed as close as possible to the word that it modifies. Otherwise the meaning of the sentence may not be clear.

MISPLACED: *The boys were looking for squirrels searching the trees.*

CLEARER: *The boys searching the trees were looking for squirrels.*

A participle or participial phrase that does not clearly modify anything in a sentence is called a **dangling participle.** A dangling participle causes confusion because it appears to modify a word that it cannot sensibly modify. Correct a dangling participle by providing a word for the participle to modify.

DANGLING: *Running like the wind, my hat fell off.* (The hat wasn't running.)

CLEARER: *Running like the wind, I lost my hat.*

7.4 GERUNDS AND GERUND PHRASES

A **gerund** is a verb form ending in *-ing* that functions as a noun. Gerunds may perform any function nouns perform.

SUBJECT: *Running is my favorite pastime.*

DIRECT OBJECT: *I truly love running.*

INDIRECT OBJECT: *You should give running a try.*

SUBJECT COMPLEMENT: *My deepest passion is running.*

OBJECT OF PREPOSITION: *Her love of running keeps her strong.*

Gerund phrases are gerunds with all their modifiers and complements.

SUBJECT: *Wishing on a star never got me far.*

OBJECT OF PREPOSITION: *I will finish before leaving the office.*

APPOSITIVE: *Her avocation, flying airplanes, finally led to full-time employment.*

Grammar Practice

Rewrite each sentence, adding the type of phrase shown in parentheses.

1. I read Jackie Robinson's autobiography. (infinitive phrase)
2. Robinson was the first major league African American baseball player in the United States. (participial phrase)
3. Robinson played his entire major league career with the same team. (appositive phrase)
4. Robinson went on to become one of the most popular Dodger players. (gerund phrase)
5. Today Robinson is famous worldwide. (prepositional phrase)

8 Clauses

A **clause** is a group of words that contains a subject and a predicate. There are two kinds of clauses: independent, or main, clauses and subordinate clauses.

8.1 MAIN AND SUBORDINATE CLAUSES

A **main (independent) clause** can stand alone as a sentence.

MAIN CLAUSE: *I read "Train Time."*

A sentence may contain more than one main clause.

EXAMPLE: *I finished dinner, and I read the story.*

In the preceding example, the coordinating conjunction **and** joins two main clauses.

For more information, see **Coordinating Conjunction,** page R31.

A **subordinate (dependent) clause** cannot stand alone as a sentence. It is subordinate to, or dependent on, a main clause.

EXAMPLE: *After I finished dinner, I read "Train Time."*

The highlighted clause cannot stand by itself. Note that a comma is added to the end of a dependent clause when it comes before a main clause.

8.2 ADJECTIVE CLAUSES

An **adjective clause** is a subordinate clause used as an adjective. It usually follows the noun or pronoun it modifies.

EXAMPLE: *Antonio and I are the actors who play the lead characters in our school's play.*

Adjective clauses are typically introduced by the relative pronouns *who, whom, whose, which,* and *that.*

For more information, see **Relative Pronouns,** page R40.

EXAMPLE: *The production, which is our school's big theatrical event, will take place in May.*

An adjective clause can be either essential or nonessential. An **essential adjective clause** provides information that is necessary to identify the preceding noun or pronoun.

EXAMPLE: *The drama club had to make a decision that three performances would be sufficient.*

A **nonessential adjective clause** adds additional information about a noun or pronoun whose meaning is already clear. Nonessential clauses are set off with commas.

EXAMPLE: *The club members, who had been discussing it for a long time, needed to come to an agreement about performance times and dates.*

8.3 ADVERB CLAUSES

An **adverb clause** is a subordinate clause that is used to modify a verb, an adjective, or an adverb. It is introduced by a subordinating conjunction.

For examples of subordinating conjunctions, see **Noun Clauses,** page R49.

Adverb clauses typically occur at the beginning or end of sentences.

MODIFYING A VERB: *When we need you, we will call.*

MODIFYING AN ADVERB: *I'll stay here where there is shelter from the rain.*

MODIFYING AN ADJECTIVE: *Roman felt as good as he had ever felt.*

TIP An adverb clause should be followed by a comma when it comes before a main clause. When an adverb clause comes after a main clause, a comma may not be needed.

8.4 NOUN CLAUSES

A **noun clause** is a subordinate clause that is used as a noun. A noun clause may be used as a subject, a direct object, an indirect object, a predicate nominative, or the object of a preposition. Noun clauses are introduced either by pronouns, such as *that, what, who, whoever, which,* and *whose,* or by subordinating conjunctions, such as *how, when, where, why,* and *whether.*

For more subordinating conjunctions, see **Quick Reference: Parts of Speech,** page R30.

TIP Because the same words may introduce adjective and noun clauses, you need to consider how a clause functions within its sentence. To determine if a clause is a noun clause, try substituting *something* or *someone* for the clause. If you can do it, it is probably a noun clause.

EXAMPLE: *I know whose woods these are.* ("I know *something.*" The clause is a noun clause, a direct object of the verb *know.*) *Give a copy to whoever wants one.* ("Give a copy to *someone.*" The clause is a noun clause, an object of the preposition *to.*)

Add descriptive details to each sentence by writing the type of clause indicated in parentheses.

1. Some students volunteer at animal shelters. (adjective clause)
2. They help take care of dogs and cats. (adverb clause)
3. The veterinarian tries to explain to the students. (noun clause)
4. Many people appreciate the students. (adjective clause)
5. I plan to work at the shelter. (adverb clause)

9 The Structure of Sentences

When classified by their structure, there are four kinds of sentences: simple, compound, complex, and compound-complex.

9.1 SIMPLE SENTENCES

A **simple sentence** is a sentence that has one main clause and no subordinate clauses.

> EXAMPLE: *Sam ran to the theater.*
> *Max waited in front of the theater.*

A simple sentence may contain a compound subject or a compound verb.

> EXAMPLE: *Sam and Max went to the movie.* (compound subject)
> *They clapped and cheered at their favorite parts.* (compound verb)

9.2 COMPOUND SENTENCES

A **compound sentence** consists of two or more main clauses. The clauses in compound sentences are joined with commas and coordinating conjunctions (*and, but, or, nor, yet, for, so*) or with semicolons. Like simple sentences, compound sentences do not contain any subordinate clauses.

> EXAMPLES: *Sam likes action movies, but Max prefers comedies.*
> *The actor jumped from one building to another; he barely made the final leap.*

WATCH OUT! Do not confuse compound sentences with simple sentences that have compound parts.

> EXAMPLE: *The actor knew all the lines but didn't play the part well.*
> (Here *but* joins parts of a compound predicate, not a compound sentence.)

9.3 COMPLEX SENTENCES

A **complex sentence** consists of one main clause and one or more subordinate clauses.

> EXAMPLE: *One should not complain unless one has a better solution.*
> *Mr. Neiman, who is an artist, sketched pictures until the sun went down.*

9.4 COMPOUND-COMPLEX SENTENCES

A **compound-complex sentence** contains two or more main clauses and one or more subordinate clauses. Compound-complex sentences are, simply, both compound and complex. If you start with a compound sentence, all you need to do to form a compound-complex sentence is add a subordinate clause.

> COMPOUND: *All the students knew the answer, yet they were too shy to volunteer.*

> COMPOUND-COMPLEX: *All the students knew the answer that their teacher expected, yet they were too shy to volunteer.*

9.5 PARALLEL STRUCTURE

When you write sentences, make sure that coordinate parts are equivalent, or **parallel,** in structure.

> NOT PARALLEL: *Erin loved basketball and to play hockey.* (*Basketball* is a noun; *to play hockey* is a phrase.)

> PARALLEL: *Erin loved basketball and hockey.* (*Basketball* and *hockey* are both nouns.)

> NOT PARALLEL: *He wanted to rent an apartment, a new car, and traveling around the country.* (*To rent* is an infinitive, *car* is a noun, and *traveling* is a gerund.)

PARALLEL: *He wanted to rent an apartment, to drive a new car, and to travel around the country.*
(*To rent, to drive,* and *to travel* are all infinitives.)

10 Writing Complete Sentences

Remember, a sentence is a group of words that expresses a complete thought. In writing that you wish to share with a reader, try to avoid both sentence fragments and run-on sentences.

10.1 CORRECTING FRAGMENTS

A **sentence fragment** is a group of words that is only part of a sentence. It does not express a complete thought and may be confusing to a reader or listener. A sentence fragment may be lacking a subject, a predicate, or both.

FRAGMENT: *Waited for the boat to arrive.* (no subject)

CORRECTED: *We waited for the boat to arrive.*

FRAGMENT: *People of various races, ages, and creeds.* (no predicate)

CORRECTED: *People of various races, ages, and creeds gathered together.*

FRAGMENT: *Near the old cottage.* (neither subject nor predicate)

CORRECTED: *The burial ground is near the old cottage.*

In your writing, fragments may be a result of haste or incorrect punctuation. Sometimes fixing a fragment is a matter of attaching it to a preceding or following sentence.

FRAGMENT: *We saw the two girls. Waiting for the bus to arrive.*

CORRECTED: *We saw the two girls waiting for the bus to arrive.*

10.2 CORRECTING RUN-ON SENTENCES

A **run-on sentence** is made up of two or more sentences written as though they were one. Some run-ons have no punctuation within them. Others may have only commas where conjunctions or

stronger punctuation marks are necessary. Use your judgment in correcting run-on sentences, as you have choices. You can change a run-on to two sentences if the thoughts are not closely connected. If the thoughts are closely related, you can keep the run-on as one sentence by adding a semicolon or a conjunction.

RUN-ON: *We found a place for the picnic by a small pond it was three miles from the village.*

MAKE TWO SENTENCES: *We found a place for the picnic by a small pond. It was three miles from the village.*

RUN-ON: *We found a place for the picnic by a small pond it was perfect.*

USE A SEMICOLON: *We found a place for the picnic by a small pond; it was perfect.*

ADD A CONJUNCTION: *We found a place for the picnic by a small pond, and it was perfect.*

WATCH OUT! When you form compound sentences, make sure you use appropriate punctuation: a comma before a coordinating conjunction, a semicolon when there is no coordinating conjunction, and a semicolon before a conjunctive adverb and a comma after it. A very common mistake is to use a comma alone instead of a comma and a conjunction. This error is called a **comma splice.**

INCORRECT: *He finished the job, he left the village.*

CORRECT: *He finished the job, and he left the village.*

11 Subject-Verb Agreement

The subject and verb in a clause must agree in number. Agreement means that if the subject is singular, the verb is also singular, and if the subject is plural, the verb is also plural.

11.1 BASIC AGREEMENT

Fortunately, agreement between subjects and verbs in English is simple. Most verbs show the difference between singular and plural only in the third person of the present tense. In the present tense, the third-person singular form ends in -s.

Present-Tense Verb Forms	
Singular	**Plural**
I sleep	we sleep
you sleep	you sleep
she, he, it sleeps	they sleep

11.2 AGREEMENT WITH *BE*

The verb *be* presents special problems in agreement, because this verb does not follow the usual verb patterns.

Forms of *Be*			
Present Tense		**Past Tense**	
Singular	**Plural**	**Singular**	**Plural**
I am	we are	I was	we were
you are	you are	you were	you were
she, he, it is	they are	she, he, it was	they were

11.3 WORDS BETWEEN SUBJECT AND VERB

A verb agrees only with its subject. When a prepositional phrase or other words come between a subject and a verb, ignore them when considering proper agreement. Identify the subject, and make sure the verb agrees with it.

> EXAMPLES: *A story in the newspapers tells about the 1890s.*
> *Dad as well as Mom reads the paper daily.*

11.4 AGREEMENT WITH COMPOUND SUBJECTS

Use plural verbs with most compound subjects joined by the word *and.*

> EXAMPLE: *My father and his friends play chess every day.*

To confirm that you need a plural verb, you could substitute the plural pronoun *they* for *my father and his friends.*

If a compound subject is thought of as a unit, use a singular verb. Test this by substituting the singular pronoun *it.*

> EXAMPLE: *Peanut butter and jelly [it] is my brother's favorite sandwich.*

Use a singular verb with a compound subject that is preceded by *each, every,* or *many a.*

> EXAMPLE: *Each novel and short story seems grounded in personal experience.*

When the parts of a compound subject are joined by *or, nor,* or the correlative conjunctions *either . . . or* or *neither . . . nor,* make the verb agree with the noun or pronoun nearest the verb.

> EXAMPLES: *Cookies or ice cream is my favorite dessert.*
> *Either Cheryl or her friends are being invited.*
> *Neither ice storms nor snow is predicted today.*

11.5 PERSONAL PRONOUNS AS SUBJECTS

When using a personal pronoun as a subject, make sure to match it with the correct form of the verb *be.* (See the chart in Section 11.2.) Note especially that the pronoun *you* takes the forms *are* and *were,* regardless of whether it is singular or plural.

WATCH OUT! *You is* and *you was* are nonstandard forms and should be avoided in writing and speaking. *We was* and *they was* are also forms to be avoided.

> INCORRECT: *You was a good student.*
> CORRECT: *You were a good student.*
> INCORRECT: *They was starting a new school.*
> CORRECT: *They were starting a new school.*

11.6 INDEFINITE PRONOUNS AS SUBJECTS

Some indefinite pronouns are always singular; some are always plural.

Singular Indefinite Pronouns			
another	either	neither	one
anybody	everybody	nobody	somebody
anyone	everyone	no one	someone
anything	everything	nothing	something
each	much		

EXAMPLES: *Each of the writers was given an award.*
Somebody in the room upstairs is sleeping.

Plural Indefinite Pronouns			
both	few	many	several

EXAMPLES: *Many of the books in our library are not in circulation.*
Few have been returned recently.

Still other indefinite pronouns may be either singular or plural.

Singular or Plural Indefinite Pronouns		
all	more	none
any	most	some

The number of the indefinite pronoun *any* or *none* often depends on the intended meaning.

EXAMPLES: *Any of these topics has potential for a good article.* (any one topic)
Any of these topics have potential for good articles. (all of the many topics)

The indefinite pronouns *all, some, more, most,* and *none* are singular when they refer to quantities or parts of things. They are plural when they refer to numbers of individual things. Context will usually give a clue.

EXAMPLES: *All of the flour is gone.* (referring to a quantity)
All of the flowers are gone. (referring to individual items)

11.7 INVERTED SENTENCES

A sentence in which the subject follows the verb is called an **inverted sentence.** A subject can follow a verb or part of a verb phrase in a question; a sentence beginning with *here* or *there*; or a sentence in which an adjective, an adverb, or a phrase is placed first.

EXAMPLES: *There clearly are far too many cooks in this kitchen.*
What is the correct ingredient for this stew?
Far from the embroiled cooks stands the master chef.

TIP To check subject-verb agreement in some inverted sentences, place the subject before the verb. For example, change ***There are many people*** to ***Many people are there.***

11.8 SENTENCES WITH PREDICATE NOMINATIVES

In a sentence containing a predicate noun (nominative), the verb should agree with the subject, not the predicate noun.

EXAMPLES: *The speeches of Martin Luther King Jr. are a landmark in American civil rights history.* (*Speeches* is the subject— not *landmark*—and it takes the plural verb *are.*)
One landmark in American civil rights history is the speeches of Martin Luther King Jr. (The subject is *landmark*—not *speeches*—and it takes the singular verb *is.*)

11.9 *DON'T* AND *DOESN'T* AS AUXILIARY VERBS

The auxiliary verb *doesn't* is used with singular subjects and with the personal pronouns *she, he,* and *it.* The auxiliary verb *don't* is used with plural subjects and with the personal pronouns *I, we, you,* and *they.*

SINGULAR: *She doesn't know Martin Luther King Jr.'s famous "I Have a Dream" speech.*
Doesn't the young woman read very much?

PLURAL: *We don't have the speech memorized.*
Don't speakers usually memorize their speeches?

11.10 COLLECTIVE NOUNS AS SUBJECTS

Collective nouns are singular nouns that name groups of persons or things. *Team,* for example, is the collective name of a group of individuals. A collective noun takes a singular verb when the group acts as a single unit. It takes a plural verb when the members of the group act separately

> EXAMPLES: *Our team usually wins.* (The team as a whole wins.)
> *Our team vote differently on most issues.* (The individual members vote.)

11.11 RELATIVE PRONOUNS AS SUBJECTS

When the relative pronoun *who, which,* or *that* is used as a subject in an adjective clause, the verb in the clause must agree in number with the antecedent of the pronoun.

> SINGULAR: *I didn't read the* **poem** *about fireflies that was assigned.*

The antecedent of the relative pronoun *that* is the singular *poem*; therefore, *that* is singular and must take the singular verb *was.*

> PLURAL: *Mary Oliver and Pat Moran, who are very different from each other, are both outstanding poets.*

The antecedent of the relative pronoun *who* is the plural compound subject *Mary Oliver and Pat Moran.* Therefore *who* is plural, and it takes the plural verb *are.*

Locate the subject of each verb in parentheses in the sentences below. Then choose the correct verb form.

1. In our school, students have a chance to (learn, learns) many techniques and media for making art.

2. Our art program (offer, offers) many different types of classes throughout the year.

3. Many of the students (think, thinks) that the summer is a good time for taking art class.

4. Some (go, goes) to camp, work part-time jobs, or take classes during the summer months, while others just (hang, hangs) around.

5. For those who (go, goes) to school for art class, the experience will be worth the time.

6. Everyone (has, have) a chance to try new techniques, such as printmaking or computer manipulation of photo-graphs and drawings.

7. Does anyone (want, wants) to discover creative ideas in art class?

8. Found objects, such as discarded wire or consumer by-products (is, are) useful for creating art with an environ-mental message.

9. There (is, are) many beautiful objects made from old things.

10. Each of the students (leave, leaves) art class having learned something special.

Vocabulary and Spelling

ELA L.7.2b, L.7.4a–d, L.7.5a–c, L.7.6
ELD PI.7.6, PI.7.8, PI.7.12

The key to becoming an independent reader is to develop a tool kit of vocabulary strategies. By learning and practicing the strategies, you'll know what to do when you encounter unfamiliar words while reading. You'll also know how to refine the words you use for different situations—personal, school, and work.

Being a good speller is important when communicating your ideas in writing. Learning basic spelling rules and checking your spelling in a dictionary will help you spell words that you may not use frequently.

1 Using Context Clues

The context of a word is made up of the punctuation marks, words, sentences, and paragraphs that surround the word. A word's context can give you important clues about its meaning.

1.1 GENERAL CONTEXT

Sometimes you need to determine the meaning of an unfamiliar word by reading all the information in a passage.

> *The sweater was of inferior quality. It was torn and had several buttons missing.*

You can figure out from the context that *inferior* means "poor or low."

1.2 SPECIFIC CONTEXT CLUES

Sometimes writers help you understand the meanings of words by providing specific clues such as those shown in the chart.

1.3 IDIOMS, SLANG, AND FIGURATIVE LANGUAGE

An **idiom** is an expression whose overall meaning is different from the meaning of the individual words. **Slang** is informal language in which madeup words and ordinary words are used to mean something different from their meanings in formal English. **Figurative language** is language that communicates meaning beyond the literal meaning of the words. Use context clues to figure out the meanings of idioms, slang, and figurative language.

Button your lip about the party. (idiom; means "keep quiet")

That's a really bad jacket; I want one. (slang; means "good-looking, excellent")

My brother had tried to make dinner. The kitchen was a battleground of dirty dishes, stains, spills, and potato peels. (figurative language; battleground, dirty dishes, stains, spills, and potato peels represent a messy scene)

Specific Context Clues		
Type of Clue	**Key Words/ Phrases**	**Example**
Definition or restate-ment of the meaning of the word	or, which is, that is, in other words, also known as, also called	Most chemicals are *toxic*, or **poisonous.**
Example following an unfamiliar word	such as, like, as if, for example, espe-cially, including	*Amphibians,* such as **frogs and salaman-ders,** live in the pond by our house.
Comparison with a more familiar word or concept	as, like, also, similar to, in the same way, likewise	Like the rest of my *frugal* family, I always **save** most of the money I earn.

continued

Contrast with a familiar word or experience	unlike, but, however, although, on the other hand, on the contrary	I wish I had more *ingenuity* in making money instead of simply relying on the **same old** babysitting jobs.
Cause-and-effect relationship in which one term is familiar	because, since, when, consequently, as a result, therefore	Because the chemicals are *flammable,* the scientists wear special **fire-resistant** clothing.

2 Analyzing Word Structure

Many words can be broken into smaller parts. These word parts include base words, roots, prefixes, and suffixes.

2.1 BASE WORDS

A **base word** is a word part that by itself is also a word. Other words or word parts can be added to base words to form new words.

2.2 ROOTS

A **root** is a word part that contains the core meaning of the word. Many English words contain roots that come from older languages such as Greek, Latin, Old English (Anglo-Saxon), and Norse. Knowing the meaning of the word's root can help you determine the word's meaning.

Root	Meaning	Example
photo (Greek)	light	photography
therm (Greek)	heat	thermometer
cred (Latin)	believe	credit

continued

mot (Latin)	move	motion
hēadfod (Old English)	head, top	headfirst

2.3 PREFIXES

A **prefix** is a word part attached to the beginning of a word. Most prefixes come from Greek, Latin, or Old English.

Prefix	Meaning	Example
mal-	bad or wrong	**mal**function
micro-	small or short	**micro**scope
semi-	half	**semi**circle

2.4 SUFFIXES

A **suffix** is a word part that appears at the end of a root or base word to form a new word. Some suffixes do not change word meaning. These suffixes are:

- added to nouns to change the number of persons or objects
- added to verbs to change the tense
- added to modifiers to change the degree of comparison

Suffix	Meaning	Example
-s, -es	to change the number of a noun	lock + s = locks
-d, -ed, -ing	to change verb tense	stew + ed = stewed
-er, -est	to indicate comparison in modifiers	mild + er = milder soft + est = softest

Other suffixes can be added to the root or base to change the word's meaning. These suffixes can also determine a word's part of speech.

Suffix	Meaning	Example
-er	one who does	teacher
-able	capable of	readable
-ly	in what manner	slowly

2.5 CONTENT-AREA VOCABULARY

Knowing the meaning of Greek, Latin, and Anglo-Saxon word parts can help you figure out the meaning of content-area vocabulary.

Word Part	Meaning	Example
derm	skin	dermatologist
logy	study of	astrology
bio	life	biography
hydr	water	hydrant
hypo	below, beneath	hypodermic
vid/vis	to see	visual
fract	to break	fraction

Strategies for Understanding Unfamiliar Words

- Look for any prefixes or suffixes. Remove them so that you can concentrate on the base word or the root.
- See if you recognize any elements—prefix, suffix, root, or base—of the word. You may be able to guess its meaning by analyzing one or two elements.
- Think about the way the word is used in the sentence. Use the context and the word parts to make a logical guess about the word's meaning.
- Look in a dictionary to see whether you are correct.

Practice and Apply

Use the strategies in this section and the vocabulary lessons in this book to help you figure out the meanings of the following content-area words.

forefathers	vision	microfilm
biology	fracture	import
auditory	ecology	hypothermia

3 Understanding Word Origins

3.1 ETYMOLOGIES

Etymologies show the origin and historical development of a word. When you study a word's history and origin, you can find out when, where, and how the word came to be.

ge•om•e•try (jē-ŏmˊĭ-trē) *n.*, pl. **-tries**
1. The mathematics of the properties, measurement, and relationships of points, lines, angles, surfaces, and solids. **2.** Arrangement. **3.** A physical arrangement suggesting geometric lines and shapes. [from Greek *geōmetriā*, from *geōmetrein*, to measure land].

3.2 WORD FAMILIES

Words that have the same root make up a word family and have related meanings. The following chart shows a common Greek root and a common Latin root. Notice how the meanings of the example words are related to the meanings of their roots.

Latin Root	sens: "sense or feel"
English	**sensory** relating to the senses
	sensitive responsive to sensations
	sensation a perception or feeling

continued

Greek Root	*ast(e)r: "star"*
English	**asteroid** a small object in outer space **asterisk** a star-shaped punctuation mark **astronomy** the study of outer space

3.3 FOREIGN WORDS

The English language includes words from diverse languages, such as French, Dutch, Spanish, Italian, and Chinese. Many words have stayed the way they were in their original languages.

French	Dutch	Spanish	Italian
ballet	boss	canyon	diva
vague	caboose	rodeo	cupola
mirage	dock	bronco	spaghetti

4 Synonyms and Antonyms

4.1 SYNONYMS

A **synonym** is a word with a meaning similar to that of another word. You can find synonyms in a thesaurus or a dictionary. In a dictionary, synonyms are often given as part of the definition of the word. The following word pairs are synonyms:

satisfy/please   occasionally/sometimes

rob/steal   schedule/agenda

4.2 ANTONYMS

An **antonym** is a word with a meaning opposite that of another word. The following word pairs are antonyms:

accurate/incorrect   similar/different

fresh/stale   unusual/ordinary

5 Denotation and Connotation

5.1 DENOTATION

A word's dictionary meaning is called its **denotation.** For example, the denotation of the word *thin* is "having little flesh; spare; lean."

5.2 CONNOTATION

The images or feelings you connect to a word add a finer shade of meaning, called **connotation.** The connotation of a word goes beyond its basic dictionary definition. Writers use connotations of words to communicate positive or negative feelings.

Positive	Negative
slender	scrawny
thrifty	cheap
young	immature

Make sure you understand the denotation and connotation of a word when you read it or use it.

6 Analogies

An **analogy** is a comparison based on similarities between some things. Analogies can be used to explain unfamiliar words, subjects, or ideas in terms of familiar ones. An **analogy problem** shows a relationship between pairs of words. The relationship between the first pair of words is the same as the relationship between the second pair. Two relationships that analogy problems can express are part to whole and whole to part.

Part to Whole

handle : mug :: hilt : _____

a. hammer   **b.** jewelry   **c.** plate   **d.** sword

*Read this analogy as "handle **is to** mug as hilt **is to** _____."*

What is the relationship between a *handle* and a *mug*? (A *handle* is the part designed for holding a *mug.*)

A *hilt* is part of which item? (A *hilt* is the handle of a *sword*.)

Whole to Part

horse : mane :: pheasant : _____

a. bird **b.** feather **c.** paw **d.** animal

What is the relationship between a *horse* and a *mane*? (A *horse* has a *mane,* the long hair along the top and sides of its neck.)

Which item is part of a *pheasant*? (The bird called a *pheasant* has a *feather* covering.)

7 Homonyms, Homographs, and Homophones

7.1 HOMONYMS

Homonyms are words that have the same spelling and sound but have different meanings.

> *The snake shed its skin in the shed behind the house.*

Shed can mean "to lose by natural process," but an identically spelled word means "a small structure."

If only one of the meanings of a homonym is familiar to you, use context clues to help you define the word if it is used in an unfamiliar way.

7.2 HOMOGRAPHS

Homographs are words that are spelled the same but have different meanings and origins. Some are also pronounced differently, as in these examples.

> *Please close the door. (klōz)*
>
> *That was a close call. (klōs)*

If you see a word used in a way that is unfamiliar to you, check a dictionary to see if it is a homograph.

7.3 HOMOPHONES

Homophones are words that sound alike but have different meanings and spellings. The following homophones are frequently misused:

it's/its   they're/their/there

to/too/two   stationary/stationery

Many misused homophones are pronouns and contractions. Whenever you are unsure whether to write *your* or *you're* and *who's* or *whose,* ask yourself if you mean *you are* and *who is/has.* If you do, write the contraction. For other homophones, such as *fair* and *fare,* use the meaning of the word to help you decide which one to use.

8 Words with Multiple Meanings

Some words have acquired additional meanings over time that are based on the original meaning.

> *I had to be replaced in the cast of the play because of the cast on my arm.*

The word *cast* has two meanings here, but both have the same origin. All of the meanings of *cast* are listed in one entry in the dictionary.

9 Specialized Vocabulary

Specialized vocabulary refers to terms used in a particular field of study or work. For example, science and mathematics each has its own technical or specialized vocabulary. You can use context clues, dictionaries on specific subjects, atlases, or manuals to help you define these terms.

10 Using Reference Sources

10.1 DICTIONARIES

A **general dictionary** will tell you a word's definitions, spelling, syllables, pronunciation, parts of speech, and history and origin.

tan·gi·ble (tăn´jə-bəl) *adj.* **1a.** Discernible by the touch; palpable. **b.** Possible to touch. **c.** Possible to be treated as fact; real or concrete. **2.** Possible to understand or realize. **3.** *Law* Relating to or being property, such as land, objects, and goods. [Late Latin *tangibilis,* from Latin *tangere,* to touch.]

① Entry word syllabication
② Pronunciation
③ Part of speech
④ Definitions
⑤ Etymology

A **specialized dictionary** focuses on terms related to a particular field of study or work.

10.2 THESAURI

A **thesaurus** (plural, *thesauri*) is a dictionary of synonyms. A thesaurus can be especially helpful when you find yourself using the same modifiers over and over again.

10.3 SYNONYM FINDERS

A **synonym finder** is often included in word processing software. It enables you to highlight a word and be shown a display of its synonyms.

10.4 GLOSSARIES

A **glossary** is a list of specialized terms, their definitions, and sometimes their pronunciations. Many textbooks contain glossaries, which are found at the back of the book. In fact, this text has three glossaries: the **Glossary of Literary and Informational Terms,** the **Glossary of Academic Vocabulary,** and the **Glossary of Critical Vocabulary.** Use these glossaries to help you understand how terms are used in this textbook. You can find electronic versions of many reference sources on the Internet, or in software programs at your school or library.

11 Spelling Rules

11.1 WORDS ENDING IN A SILENT *E*

Before adding a suffix beginning with a vowel or *y* to a word ending in a silent *e,* drop the *e* (with some exceptions).

amaze + -ing = amazing

love + -able = lovable

create + -ed = created

nerve + -ous = nervous

Exceptions: *change* + *-able* = *changeable; courage* + *-ous* = *courageous*

When adding a suffix beginning with a consonant to a word ending in a silent *e,* keep the *e* (with some exceptions).

late + -ly = lately

spite + -ful = spiteful

noise + -less = noiseless

state + -ment = statement

Exceptions: *truly, argument, ninth, wholly, awful,* and others

When a suffix beginning with *a* or *o* is added to a word with a final silent *e,* the final *e* is usually retained if it is preceded by a soft *c* or a soft *g.*

bridge + -able = bridgeable

peace + -able = peaceable

outrage + -ous = outrageous

advantage + -ous = advantageous

When a suffix beginning with a vowel is added to words ending in *ee* or *oe,* the final, silent *e* is retained.

agree + -ing = agreeing free + -ing = freeing

hoe + -ing = hoeing see + -ing = seeing

11.2 WORDS ENDING IN Y

Before adding most suffixes to a word that ends in *y* preceded by a consonant, change the *y* to *i.*

easy + -est = easiest

crazy + -est = craziest

silly + -ness = silliness

marry + -age = marriage

Exceptions: *dryness, shyness,* and *slyness*

However, when you add *-ing,* the *y* does not change.

empty + -ed = emptied but

empty + -ing = emptying

When adding a suffix to a word that ends in *y* preceded by a vowel, the *y* usually does not change.

play + -er = player

employ + -ed = employed

coy + -ness = coyness

pay + -able = payable

11.3 WORDS ENDING IN A CONSONANT

In **one-syllable** words that end in one consonant preceded by one short vowel, double the final consonant before adding a suffix beginning with a vowel, such as

-ed or *-ing.* These are sometimes called 1+1+1 words.

dip + -ed = dipped   **set + -ing = setting**

slim + -est = slimmest   **fit + -er = fitter**

The rule does not apply to words of one syllable that end in a consonant preceded by two vowels.

feel + -ing = feeling   **peel + -ed = peeled**

reap + -ed = reaped   **loot + -ed = looted**

In words of more than one syllable, double the final consonant when (1) the word ends with one consonant preceded by one vowel and (2) when the word is accented on the last syllable.

be•gin′   per•mit′   re•fer′

In the following examples, note that in the new words formed with suffixes, the accent remains on the same syllable:

be•gin′ + -ing = be•gin′ning = beginning

per•mit′ + -ed = per•mit′ted = permitted

Exceptions: In some words with more than one syllable, though the accent remains on the same syllable when a suffix is added, the final consonant is nevertheless not doubled, as in the following examples:

tra′vel + er = tra′vel•er = traveler

mar′ket + er = mar′ket•er = marketer

In the following examples, the accent does not remain on the same syllable; thus, the final consonant is not doubled:

re•fer′ + -ence = ref′er•ence = reference

con•fer′ + -ence = con′fer•ence = conference

11.4 PREFIXES AND SUFFIXES

When adding a prefix to a word, do not change the spelling of the base word. When a prefix creates a double letter, keep both letters.

dis- + approve = disapprove

re- + build = rebuild

ir- + regular = irregular

mis- + spell = misspell

anti- + trust = antitrust

il- + logical = illogical

When adding *-ly* to a word ending in *l,* keep both *l*'s. When adding *-ness* to a word ending in *n,* keep both *n*'s.

careful + -ly = carefully

sudden + -ness = suddenness

final + -ly = finally

thin + -ness = thinness

11.5 FORMING PLURAL NOUNS

To form the plural of most nouns, just add *-s.*

prizes   dreams   circles   stations

For most singular nouns ending in *o,* add *-s.*

solos   halos   studios   photos   pianos

For a few nouns ending in *o,* add *-es.*

heroes   tomatoes   potatoes   echoes

When the singular noun ends in *s, sh, ch, x,* or *z,* add *-es.*

waitresses   brushes   ditches

axes   buzzes

When a singular noun ends in *y* with a consonant before it, change the *y* to *i* and add *-es.*

army—armies   **candy—candies**

baby—babies   **diary—diaries**

ferry—ferries   **conspiracy—conspiracies**

When a vowel (*a, e, i, o, u*) comes before the *y,* just add *-s.*

boy—boys   **way—ways**

array—arrays   **alloy—alloys**

weekday —weekdays   **jockey—jockeys**

For most nouns ending in *f* or *fe,* change the *f* to *v* and add *-es* or *-s.*

life—lives   **thief—thieves**

calf—calves   **shelf—shelves**

knife—knives   **loaf—loaves**

For some nouns ending in *f,* add *-s* to make the plural.

roofs   chiefs   reefs   beliefs

Some nouns have the same form for both singular and plural.

deer   sheep   moose   salmon   trout

For some nouns, the plural is formed in a special way.

man—men

goose—geese

ox—oxen

woman—women

mouse—mice

child—children

For a compound noun written as one word, form the plural by changing the last word in the compound to its plural form.

stepchild—stepchildren   firefly—fireflies

If a compound noun is written as a hyphenated word or as two separate words, change the most important word to the plural form.

brother-in-law—brothers-in-law

life jacket—life jackets

11.6 FORMING POSSESSIVES

If a noun is singular, add 's.

mother—my mother's car

Ross—Ross's desk

Exception: The s after the apostrophe is dropped after *Jesus', Moses',* and certain names in classical mythology (*Zeus'*). These possessive forms can thus be pronounced easily.

If a noun is plural and ends with **s,** add an apostrophe.

parents—my parents' car

the Santinis—the Santinis' house

If a noun is plural but does not end in **s,** add 's.

people—the people's choice

women—the women's coats

11.7 SPECIAL SPELLING PROBLEMS

Only one English word ends in *-sede: supersede.* Three words end in *-ceed: exceed, proceed,* and *succeed.* All other verbs ending in the sound "seed" are spelled with *-cede.*

concede   precede   recede   secede

In words with **ie** or **ei,** when the sound is long *e* (as in *she*), the word is spelled *ie* except after *c* (with some exceptions).

i before *e*	thief	relieve	field
	piece	grieve	pier
except after *c*	conceit	perceive	ceiling
	receive	receipt	
Exceptions:	either	neither	weird
	leisure	seize	

12 Commonly Confused Words

Words	Definitions	Examples
accept/ except	The verb *accept* means "to receive or believe"; *except* is usually a preposition meaning "excluding."	Did the teacher **accept** your report? Everyone smiled for the photographer **except** Jody.
advice/ advise	*Advise* is a verb; *advice* is a noun naming that which an *adviser* gives.	I **advise** you to take that job. Whom should I ask for **advice**?
affect/ effect	As a verb, *affect* means "to influence." *Effect* as a verb means "to cause." If you want a noun, you will almost always want *effect.*	How deeply did the news **affect** him? The students tried to **effect** a change in school policy. What **effect** did the acidic soil produce in the plants?
all ready/ already	*All ready* is an adjective meaning "fully ready." *Already* is an adverb meaning "before or by this time."	He was **all ready** to go at noon. I have **already** seen that movie.

continued

Words	Definitions	Examples
desert/dessert	*Desert* (dĕz´ərt) means "a dry, sandy, barren region." *Desert* (dĭ-zûrt´) means "to abandon." *Dessert* (dĭ-zûrt´) is a sweet, such as cake.	The Sahara, in North Africa, is the world's largest **desert.** The night guard did not **desert** his post. Alison's favorite **dessert** is chocolate cake.
among/between	*Between* is used when you are speaking of only two things. *Among* is used for three or more.	**Between** ice cream and sherbet, I prefer the latter. Gary Soto is **among** my favorite authors.
bring/take	*Bring* is used to denote motion toward a speaker or place. *Take* is used to denote motion away from such a person or place.	**Bring** the books over here, and I will **take** them to the library.
fewer/less	*Fewer* refers to the number of separate, countable units. *Less* refers to bulk quantity.	We have **less** literature and **fewer** selections in this year's curriculum.
leave/let	*Leave* means "to allow something to remain behind." *Let* means "to permit."	The librarian will **leave** some books on display but will not **let** us borrow any.
lie/lay	To *lie* is "to rest or recline." It does not take an object. *Lay* always takes an object.	Rover loves to **lie** in the sun. We always **lay** some bones next to him.
loose/lose	*Loose* (lo͞os) means "free, not restrained"; *lose* (lo͞oz) means "to misplace or fail to find."	Who turned the horses **loose**? I hope we won't **lose** any of them.
passed/past	*Passed* is the past tense of *pass* and means "went by." *Past* is an adjective that means "of a former time." *Past* is also a noun that means "time gone by."	We **passed** through the Florida Keys during our vacation. My **past** experiences have taught me to set my alarm. Ebenezer Scrooge is a character who relives his **past.**
than/then	Use *than* in making comparisons. Use *then* on all other occasions.	Ramon is stronger **than** Mark. Cut the grass and **then** trim the hedges.
two/too/to	*Two* is the number. *Too* is an adverb meaning "also" or "very." Use *to* before a verb or as a preposition.	Meg had **to** go to town, **too.** We had **too** much reading **to** do. **Two** chapters is **too** many.
their/there/they're	*Their* means "belonging to them." *There* means "in that place." *They're* is the contraction for "they are."	**There** is a movie playing at 9 P.M. **They're** going to see it with me. Sakara and Jessica drove away in **their** car after the movie.

Glossary of Literary and Informational Terms

Act An act is a major division within a play, similar to a chapter in a book. Each act may be further divided into smaller sections, called scenes. Plays can have as many as five acts or as few as one.

Adventure Story An adventure story is a literary work in which action is the main element. An **adventure novel** usually focuses on a main character who is on a mission and is facing many challenges and choices.

Alliteration Alliteration is the repetition of consonant sounds at the beginning of words. Note the repetition of the **b** sound in this line: The **b**oy's dog **b**egan **b**egging for **b**iscuits.

Allusion An allusion is a reference to a famous person, place, event, or work of literature.

Analogy An analogy is a point-by-point comparison between two things that are alike in some respect. Often, writers use analogies in nonfiction to explain unfamiliar subjects or ideas in terms of familiar ones.
See also Extended Metaphor; Metaphor; Simile.

Anecdote An anecdote is a short account of an event that is usually intended to entertain or make a point.

Antagonist The antagonist is a force working against the protagonist, or main character, in a story, play, or novel. The antagonist is usually another character but can be a force of nature, society itself, or an internal force within the main character.
See also Protagonist.

Argument An argument is speaking or writing that expresses a position on a problem and supports it with reasons and evidence. An argument often takes into account other points of view, anticipating and answering objections that opponents might raise.
See also Claim; Counterargument; Evidence.

Assonance Assonance is the repetition of vowel sounds within nonrhyming words. An example of assonance is the repetition of the *i* sound in the following line: Into the ink-filled jar she inserted the brush.

Assumption An assumption is an opinion or belief that is taken for granted. It can be about a specific situation, a person, or the world in general. Assumptions are often unstated.

Author's Message An author's message is the main idea or theme of a particular work.
See also Main Idea; Theme.

Author's Perspective An author's perspective is the unique combination of ideas, values, feelings, and beliefs that influences the way the writer looks at a topic. Tone, or attitude, often reveals an author's perspective.
See also Author's Purpose; Tone.

Author's Position An author's position is his or her opinion on an issue or topic.
See also Claim; Writer's Point of View.

Author's Purpose A writer usually writes for one or more of these purposes: to express thoughts or feelings, to inform or explain, to persuade, and to entertain.
See also Author's Perspective; Writer's Point of View.

Autobiography An autobiography is a writer's account of his or her own life. In almost every case, it is told from the first-person point of view. Generally, an autobiography focuses on the most significant events and people in the writer's life over a period of time.
See also Memoir.

Ballad A ballad is a type of narrative poem that tells a story and was originally meant to be sung or recited. Because it tells a story, a ballad has a setting, a plot, and characters. **Folk ballads** were composed orally and handed down by word of mouth from generation to generation.

Bias In a piece of writing, the author's bias is the side of an issue that he or she favors. Words with extremely positive or negative connotations are often a signal of an author's bias.

Biography A biography is the true account of a person's life, written by another person.

As such, biographies are usually told from a third-person point of view. The writer of a biography usually researches his or her subject in order to present accurate information. The best biographers strive for honesty and balance in their accounts of their subjects' lives.

Bibliography A bibliography is a list of related books and other materials used to write a text. Bibliographies can be good sources for further study on a subject.

See also Works Consulted.

Career Development Documents These documents include written business communications such as business letters, e-mails, and memos. In general, business correspondence is brief, to the point, clear, courteous, and professional.

Cast of Characters In the script of a play, a cast of characters is a list of all the characters in the play, usually in order of appearance. It may include a brief description of each character.

Cause and Effect Two events are related by cause and effect when one event brings about, or causes, the other. The event that happens first is the **cause**; the one that follows is the **effect.** Cause and effect is also a way of organizing an entire piece of writing. It helps writers show the relationships between events or ideas.

Character Characters are the people, animals, or imaginary creatures who take part in the action of a work of literature. Like real people, characters display certain qualities, or **character traits,** that develop and change over time, and they usually have **motivations,** or reasons, for their behaviors.

  Central character: Central or main characters are the most important characters in literary works. Generally, the plot of a short story focuses on one main character, but a novel may have several main characters.

  Minor characters: The less important characters in a literary work are known as minor characters. The story is not centered on them, but they help carry out the action of the story and help the reader learn more about the main character.

Dynamic character: A dynamic character is one who undergoes important changes as a plot unfolds. The changes occur because of the character's actions and experiences in the story. The changes are usually internal and may be good or bad. Main characters are usually, though not always, dynamic.

Static character: A static character is one who remains the same throughout a story. The character may experience events and have interactions with other characters, but he or she is not changed because of them.

See also Characterization; Character Traits.

Characterization The way a writer creates and develops characters is known as characterization. There are four basic methods of characterization.

  • The writer may make direct comments about a character through the voice of the narrator.
  • The writer may describe the character's physical appearance.
  • The writer may present the character's own thoughts, speech, and actions.
  • The writer may present thoughts, speech, and actions of other characters.

See also Character; Character Traits.

Character Traits Character traits are the qualities shown by a character. Traits may be physical (brown eyes) or expressions of personality (shyness). Writers reveal the traits of their characters through methods of characterization. Sometimes writers directly state a character's traits, but more often readers need to infer traits from a character's words, actions, thoughts, appearance, and relationships. Examples of words that describe traits include *courageous, humble, generous,* and *wild.*

Chronological Order Chronological order is the arrangement of events by their order of occurrence. This type of organization is used in fictional narratives and in historical writing, biography, and autobiography.

Claim In an argument, a claim is the writer's position on an issue or problem. Although an argument focuses on supporting one claim, a writer may make more than one claim in a text.

Clarify Clarifying is a reading strategy that helps readers understand or make clear what they are reading. Readers usually clarify by rereading, reading aloud, or discussing.

Classification Classification is a pattern of organization in which objects, ideas, and/or information are presented in groups, or classes, based on common characteristics.

Cliché A cliché is an overused expression. "Better late than never" and "hard as nails" are common examples. Good writers generally avoid clichés unless they are using them in dialogue to indicate something about a character's personality.

Climax The climax stage is the point of greatest interest in a story or play. The climax usually occurs toward the end of a story, after the reader has understood the **conflict** and become emotionally involved with the characters. At the climax, the conflict is resolved and the outcome of the plot usually becomes clear.

See also Plot.

Comedy A comedy is a dramatic work that is light and often humorous in tone, usually ending happily with a peaceful resolution of the main conflict.

Compare and Contrast To compare and contrast is to identify the similarities and differences of two or more subjects. Compare and contrast is also a pattern of organizing an entire piece of writing.

Conclusion A conclusion is a statement of belief based on evidence, experience, and reasoning. A valid conclusion is one that logically follows from the facts or statements upon which it is based.

Conflict A conflict is a struggle between opposing forces. Almost every story has a main conflict—a conflict that is the story's focus. An **external conflict** involves a character who struggles against a force outside him- or herself, such as nature, a physical obstacle, or another character. An **internal conflict** is one that occurs within a character.

See also Plot.

Connect Connecting is a reader's process of relating the content of a text to his or her own knowledge and experience.

Connotation A word's connotations are the ideas and feelings associated with the word, as opposed to its dictionary definition. For example, the word *mother,* in addition to its basic meaning ("a female parent"), has connotations of love, warmth, and security.

Consumer Documents Consumer documents are printed materials that accompany products and services. They usually provide information about the use, care, operation, or assembly of the product or service they accompany. Some common consumer documents are applications, contracts, warranties, manuals, instructions, labels, brochures, and schedules.

Context Clues When you encounter an unfamiliar word, you can often use context clues to understand it. Context clues are the words or phrases surrounding the word that provide hints about the word's meaning.

Counterargument A counterargument is an argument made to oppose another argument. A good argument anticipates opposing viewpoints and provides counterarguments to disprove them.

Couplet A couplet is a rhymed pair of lines. A couplet may be written in any rhythmic pattern: Follow your heart's desire/And good things may transpire.

See also Stanza.

Credibility Credibility is the believability or trustworthiness of a source and the information it provides.

Critical Essay *See* Essay.

Critical Review A critical review is an evaluation or critique by a reviewer, or critic. Types of reviews include film reviews, book reviews, music reviews, and art show reviews.

Database A database is a collection of information that can be quickly and easily accessed and searched and from which information can be easily retrieved. It is frequently presented in an electronic format.

Debate A debate is basically an argument—but a very structured one that requires a good deal of preparation. In school settings, debate usually is a formal contest in which two opposing teams defend and attack a proposition.

See also Argument.

Deductive Reasoning Deductive reasoning is a way of thinking that begins with a generalization, presents a specific situation, and then moves forward with facts and evidence toward a logical conclusion. The following passage has a deductive argument embedded in it: "All students in the math class must take the quiz on Friday. Since Lana is in the class, she had better show up." This deductive argument can be broken down as follows: generalization—All students in the math class must take the quiz on Friday; specific situation—Lana is a student who is in the math class; conclusion—Therefore, Lana must take the math quiz.

Denotation A word's denotation is its dictionary definition.

See also Connotation.

Description Description is writing that helps a reader to picture events, objects, and characters. To create descriptions, writers often use **imagery**—words and phrases that appeal to the reader's senses.

Dialect A dialect is a form of a language that is spoken in a particular place or by a particular group of people. Dialects may feature unique pronunciations, vocabulary, and grammar.

Dialogue Dialogue is written conversation between two or more characters. Writers use dialogue to bring characters to life and to give readers insights into the characters' qualities, traits, and reactions to other characters. In fiction, dialogue is usually set off with quotation marks. In drama, stories are told primarily through dialogue.

Diary A diary is a daily record of a writer's thoughts, experiences, and feelings. As such, it is a type of autobiographical writing. The terms *diary* and *journal* are often used synonymously.

Dictionary *See* Reference Works.

Drama A drama, or play, is a form of literature meant to be performed by actors in front of an audience. In a drama, the characters' dialogue and actions tell the story. The written form of a play is known as a script. A script usually includes dialogue, a cast of characters, and stage directions that give instructions about performing the drama. The person who writes the drama is known as the playwright or dramatist.

Draw Conclusions To draw a conclusion is to make a judgment or arrive at a belief based on evidence, experience, and reasoning.

Dynamic Character *See* Character.

Editorial An editorial is an opinion piece that usually appears on the editorial page of a newspaper or as part of a news broadcast. The editorial section of the newspaper presents opinions rather than objective news reports.

See also Op/Ed Piece.

Either/Or Fallacy An either/or fallacy is a statement that suggests that there are only two choices available in a situation when in fact there are more than two.

Emotional Appeals Emotional appeals are messages that create strong feelings to make a point. An appeal to fear is a message that taps into people's fear of losing their safety or security. An appeal to pity is a message that taps into people's sympathy and compassion for others to build support for an idea, a cause, or a proposed action. An appeal to vanity is a message that attempts to persuade by tapping into people's desire to feel good about themselves.

Encyclopedia *See* Reference Works.

Epic Poem An epic poem is a long narrative poem about the adventures of a hero whose actions reflect the ideals and values of a nation or a group of people.

Essay An essay is a short work of nonfiction that deals with a single subject. There are many types of essays. An **expository essay** presents or explains information and ideas. A **personal essay** usually reflects the writer's experiences, feelings, and personality. A **persuasive essay** attempts to convince the reader to adopt a certain viewpoint. A **critical essay** evaluates a situation or a work of art.

Evaluate To evaluate is to examine something carefully and to judge its value or worth. Evaluating is an important skill. A reader can evaluate the actions of a particular character, for example. A reader can also form opinions about the value of an entire work.

Evidence Evidence is a specific piece of information that supports a claim. Evidence can take the form of a fact, a quotation, an example, a statistic, or a personal experience, among other things.

Exaggeration An extreme overstatement of an idea is called an exaggeration. It is often used for purposes of emphasis or humor.

Exposition Exposition is the first stage of a typical story plot. The exposition provides important background information and introduces the setting and the important characters. The conflict the characters face may also be introduced in the exposition, or it may be introduced later, in the rising action.

See also Plot.

Expository Essay *See* Essay.

Extended Metaphor An extended metaphor is a figure of speech that compares two essentially unlike things at some length and in several ways. It does not contain the words *like* or *as.*

See also Metaphor.

External Conflict *See* Conflict.

Fable A fable is a brief tale told to illustrate a moral or teach a lesson. Often the moral of a fable appears in a distinct and memorable statement near the tale's beginning or end.

See also Moral.

Fact Versus Opinion A fact is a statement that can be proved, or verified. An opinion, on the other hand, is a statement that cannot be proved because it expresses a person's beliefs, feelings, or thoughts.

See also Generalization; Inference.

Fallacy A fallacy is an error—usually in reasoning. Typically, a fallacy is based on an incorrect inference or a misuse of evidence.

See also Either/Or Fallacy; Logical Appeal; Overgeneralization.

Falling Action The falling action is the stage of the plot in which the story begins to draw to a close. The falling action comes after the climax and before the resolution. Events in the falling action show the results of the important decision or action that happened at the climax. Tension eases as the falling action begins; however, the final outcome of the story is not yet fully worked out at this stage.

See also Climax; Plot.

Fantasy Fantasy is a type of fiction that is highly imaginative and portrays events, settings, or characters that are unrealistic. The setting might be a nonexistent world, the plot might involve magic or the supernatural, and the characters might have superhuman powers.

Farce Farce is a type of exaggerated comedy that features an absurd plot, ridiculous situations, and humorous dialogue. The main purpose of a farce is to keep an audience laughing. Comic devices typically used in farces include mistaken identity, wordplay (such as puns and double meanings), and exaggeration.

Faulty Reasoning *See* Fallacy.

Feature Article A feature article is a main article in a newspaper or a cover story in a magazine.

Fiction Fiction is prose writing that tells an imaginary story. The writer of a fictional work might invent all the events and characters or might base parts of the story on real people and events. The basic elements of fiction are plot, character, setting, and theme. Fiction includes short stories, novellas, and novels.

See also Novel; Novella; Short Story.

Figurative Language In figurative language, words are used in an imaginative way to express ideas that are not literally true. "Tasha's money is burning a hole in her pocket" is an example of figurative language. The sentence does not really mean that Tasha's pocket is on fire.

Instead, it means that Tasha is anxious to spend her money. Figurative language is used for comparison, emphasis, and emotional effect.

See also Metaphor; Onomatopoeia; Personification; Simile.

First-Person Point of View *See* Point of View.

Flashback In a literary work, a flashback is an interruption of the action to present events that took place at an earlier time. A flashback provides information that can help a reader better understand a character's current situation.

Foil A foil is a character who provides a striking contrast to another character. By using a foil, a writer can call attention to certain traits possessed by a main character or simply enhance a character by contrast.

Folklore The traditions, customs, and stories that are passed down within a culture are known as its folklore. Folklore includes various types of literature, such as legends, folk tales, myths, trickster tales, and fables.

See Fable; Folk Tale; Myth.

Folk Tale A folk tale is a story that has been passed from generation to generation by word of mouth. Folk tales may be set in the distant past and involve supernatural events. The characters in them may be animals, people, or superhuman beings.

Foreshadowing Foreshadowing occurs when a writer provides hints that suggest future events in a story. Foreshadowing creates suspense and makes readers eager to find out what will happen.

Form The structure or organization of a work of writing is often called its form. The form of a poem includes the arrangement of its words and lines on the page.

Free Verse Poetry without regular patterns of rhyme and rhythm is called free verse. Some poets use free verse to capture the sounds and rhythms of ordinary speech.

See also Rhyme.

Generalization A generalization is a broad statement about a class or category of people, ideas, or things based on a study of, or a belief about, some of its members.

See also Overgeneralization; Stereotyping.

Genre The term *genre* refers to a category in which a work of literature is classified. The major genres in literature are fiction, nonfiction, poetry, and drama.

Government Publications Government publications are documents produced by government organizations. Pamphlets, brochures, and reports are just some of the many forms these publications take. Government publications can be good resources for a wide variety of topics.

Graphic Aid A graphic aid is a text feature that is printed, handwritten, or drawn. Charts, diagrams, graphs, photographs, maps, and captions are examples of graphic aids.

Graphic Organizer A graphic organizer is a "word picture"—a visual illustration of a verbal statement—that helps a reader understand a text. Charts, tables, webs, and diagrams can all be graphic organizers. Graphic organizers and graphic aids can look the same. However, graphic organizers and graphic aids do differ in how they are used. Graphic aids help deliver important information to students using a text. Graphic organizers are actually created by students themselves. They help students understand the text or organize information.

Haiku Haiku is a form of Japanese poetry in which 17 syllables are arranged in three lines of 5, 7, and 5 syllables. The rules of haiku are strict. In addition to following the syllabic count, the poet must create a clear picture that will evoke a strong emotional response in the reader. Nature is a particularly important source of inspiration for Japanese haiku poets, and details from nature are often the subjects of their poems.

Hero A hero is a main character or protagonist in a story. In older literary works, heroes tend to be better than ordinary humans. They are typically courageous, strong, honorable, and intelligent. They are protectors of society who hold back the forces of evil and fight to make the world a better place. In modern literature, a hero may simply be the most important character in a story. Such a hero is often an ordinary person with ordinary problems.

Historical Documents Historical documents are writings that have played a significant role in human events. The Declaration of Independence, for example, is a historical document.

Historical Dramas Historical dramas are plays that take place in the past and are based on real events. In many of these plays, the characters are also based on real historical figures. The dialogue and the action, however, are mostly created by the playwright.

Historical Fiction A short story or a novel can be called historical fiction when it is set in the past and includes real places and real events of historical importance.

How-To Book A how-to book explains how to do something—usually an activity, a sport, or a household project.

Humor Humor is a quality that provokes laughter or amusement. Writers create humor through exaggeration, amusing descriptions, irony, and witty and insightful dialogue.

Hyperbole Hyperbole is a figure of speech in which the truth is exaggerated for emphasis or humorous effect.

Idiom An idiom is an expression that has a meaning different from the meaning of its individual words. For example, "to go to the dogs" is an idiom meaning "to go to ruin."

Imagery Imagery consists of words and phrases that appeal to a reader's five senses. Writers use sensory details to help the reader imagine how things look, feel, smell, sound, and taste.

Implied Main Idea *See* Main Idea.

Index The index of a book is an alphabetized list of important topics covered in the book and the page numbers on which they can be found. An index can be used to quickly find specific information about a topic.

Inductive Reasoning Inductive reasoning is the process of logical reasoning that starts with observations, examples, and facts and moves on to a general conclusion or principle.

Inference An inference is a logical guess that is made based on facts and one's own knowledge and experience.

Informational Text Informational text is writing that provides factual information. Examples include news reports, a science textbook, manuals, lab reports, and signs. Informational text also includes literary nonfiction, such as personal essays, opinion pieces, speeches, biographies, and historical accounts.

Internal Conflict *See* Conflict.

Internet The Internet is a global, interconnected system of computer networks that allows for communication through e-mail, listservs, and the World Wide Web. The Internet connects computers and computer users throughout the world.

Interview An interview is a conversation conducted by a writer or reporter in which facts or statements are elicited from another person, recorded, and then broadcast or published.

Journal A journal is a periodical publication issued by a legal, medical, or other professional organization. The term may also be used to refer to a diary or daily record.

Legend A legend is a story handed down from the past about a specific person, usually someone of heroic accomplishments. Legends usually have some basis in historical fact.

Limerick A limerick is a short, humorous poem composed of five lines. It usually has the rhyme scheme *aabba,* created by two rhyming couplets followed by a fifth line that rhymes with the first couplet. A limerick typically has a sing-song rhythm.

Loaded Language Loaded language consists of words with strongly positive or negative connotations intended to influence a reader's or listener's attitude.

Logical Appeal A logical appeal is a way of writing or speaking that relies on logic and facts. It appeals to people's reasoning or intellect rather than to their values or emotions. Flawed logical appeals—that is, errors in reasoning—are called logical fallacies.

See also Fallacy.

Logical Argument A logical argument is an argument in which the logical relationship between the support and claim is sound.

Lyric Poetry Lyric poetry is poetry that presents the personal thoughts and feelings of a single speaker. Most poems, other than narrative poems, are lyric poems. Lyric poetry can be in a variety of forms and cover many subjects, from love and death to everyday experiences.

Main Idea The main idea, or central idea, is the most important idea about a topic that a writer or speaker conveys. It can be the central idea of an entire work or of just a paragraph. Often, the main idea of a paragraph is expressed in a topic sentence. However, a main idea may just be implied, or suggested, by details. A main idea is typically supported by details.

Make Inferences *See* Inference.

Memoir A memoir is a form of autobiographical writing in which a writer shares his or her personal experiences and observations of significant events or people. Often informal or even intimate in tone, memoirs usually give readers insight into the impact of historical events on people's lives.

See also Autobiography.

Metaphor A metaphor is a comparison of two things that are basically unlike but have some qualities in common. Unlike a simile, a metaphor does not contain the words *like* or *as*.

See also Extended Metaphor; Figurative Language; Simile.

Meter In poetry, meter is the regular pattern of stressed (´) and unstressed (˘) syllables. Although poems have rhythm, not all poems have regular meter. Each unit of meter is known as a **foot** and is made up of one stressed syllable and one or two unstressed syllables.

See also Rhythm.

Minor Character *See* Character.

Monitor Monitoring is the strategy of checking your comprehension as you read and modifying the strategies you are using to suit your needs. Monitoring often includes the following strategies: questioning, clarifying, visualizing, predicting, connecting, and rereading.

Mood Mood is the feeling or atmosphere that a writer creates for the reader. Descriptive words, imagery, and figurative language all influence the mood of a work.

See also Tone.

Moral A moral is a lesson that a story teaches. A moral is often stated at the end of a fable.

See also Fable.

Motivation *See* Character.

Myth A myth is a traditional story that attempts to answer basic questions about human nature, origins of the world, mysteries of nature, and social customs.

Narrative Nonfiction Narrative nonfiction is writing that reads much like fiction, except that the characters, setting, and plot are real rather than imaginary. Narrative nonfiction includes autobiographies, biographies, and memoirs.

Narrative Poetry Poetry that tells a story is called narrative poetry. Like fiction, a narrative poem contains characters, a setting, and a plot. It might also contain such elements of poetry as rhyme, rhythm, imagery, and figurative language.

Narrator The narrator is the voice that tells a story. Sometimes the narrator is a character in the story. At other times, the narrator is an outside voice created by the writer. The narrator is not the same as the writer.

An **unreliable narrator** is one who tells a story or interprets events in a way that makes readers doubt what he or she is saying. An unreliable narrator is usually a character in the story. The narrator may be unreliable for a number of different reasons. For example, the narrator may not have all the facts or may be too young to understand the situation.

See also Point of View.

News Article A news article is writing that reports on a recent event. In newspapers, news articles are usually brief and to the point, presenting the most important facts first, followed by more detailed information.

Nonfiction Nonfiction is writing that tells about real people, places, and events. Unlike fiction, nonfiction is mainly written to convey factual information. Nonfiction includes a wide range of writing—newspaper articles, textbooks, instructional manuals, letters, essays, biographies, movie reviews, speeches, true-life adventure stories, advertising, and more.

Novel A novel is a long work of fiction. Like a short story, a novel is the product of a writer's imagination. Because a novel is considerably longer than a short story, a novelist can develop the characters and story line more thoroughly.

See also Fiction.

Novella A novella is a short prose tale, or short novel. It is longer than a short story and often teaches a moral, or satirizes a subject.

See also Short Story; Novel.

Ode An ode is a type of lyric poem that deals with serious themes, such as justice, truth, or beauty.

Onomatopoeia Onomatopoeia is the use of words whose sounds echo their meanings, such as *buzz, whisper, gargle,* and *murmur.*

Op/Ed Piece An op/ed piece is an opinion piece that typically appears opposite ("op") the editorial page of a newspaper. Unlike editorials, op/ed pieces are written and submitted by readers.

Oral Literature Oral literature consists of stories that have been passed down by word of mouth from generation to generation. Oral literature includes folk tales, legends, and myths. In more recent times, some examples of oral literature have been written down or recorded so that the stories can be preserved.

Organization *See* Pattern of Organization.

Overgeneralization An overgeneralization is a generalization that is too broad. You can often recognize overgeneralizations by the appearance of words and phrases such as *all, everyone, every time, any, anything, no one,* or *none.* An example is "None of the city's workers

really cares about keeping the environment clean." In all probability, there are many exceptions. The writer can't possibly know the feelings of every city worker.

Overview An overview is a short summary of a story, a speech, or an essay.

Paraphrase Paraphrasing is the restating of information in one's own words.

See also Summarize.

Pattern of Organization The term *pattern of organization* refers to the way ideas and information are arranged and organized. Patterns of organization include cause and effect, chronological, compare and contrast, classification, and problem-solution, among others.

See also Cause and Effect; Chronological Order; Classification; Compare and Contrast; Problem-Solution Order; Sequential Order.

Periodical A periodical is a magazine or another type of publication that is issued on a regular basis.

Personal Essay *See* Essay.

Personification The giving of human qualities to an animal, object, or idea is known as personification. For example, animals are personified when they have conversations with each other as if they were human.

See also Figurative Language.

Persuasion Persuasion is the art of swaying others' feelings, beliefs, or actions. Persuasion normally appeals to both the minds and the emotions of readers.

See also Emotional Appeals; Loaded Language; Logical Appeal.

Persuasive Essay *See* Essay.

Play *See* Drama.

Playwright *See* Drama.

Plot The series of events in a story is called the plot. The plot usually centers on a **conflict,** or struggle, faced by the main character. The action that the characters take to solve the problem builds toward a climax in the story. At this point, or shortly afterward, the problem is solved and the story ends. Most story plots have five stages: exposition, rising action, climax, falling action, and resolution.

See also Climax; Conflict; Exposition; Falling Action; Rising Action.

Poetry Poetry is a type of literature in which words are carefully chosen and arranged to create certain effects. Poets use a variety of sound devices, imagery, and figurative language to express emotions and ideas.

See also Alliteration; Assonance; Ballad; Free Verse; Imagery; Meter; Narrative Poetry; Rhyme; Rhythm; Stanza.

Point of View Point of view refers to how a writer chooses to narrate a story. When a story is told from the **first-person** point of view, the narrator is a character in the story and uses first-person pronouns, such as *I, me,* and *we.* In a story told from the **third-person** point of view, the narrator is not a character. Third-person narration makes use of pronouns such as *he, she, it,* and *they.* A writer's choice of narrator affects the information readers receive.

It is also important to consider whether a writer is writing from a **subjective** or an **objective** point of view. When writing from a subjective point of view, the writer includes personal opinions, feelings, and beliefs. When writing from an objective point of view, the writer leaves out personal opinions and instead presents information in a straightforward, unbiased way.

See also Narrator.

Predict Predicting is a reading strategy that involves using text clues to make a reasonable guess about what will happen next in a story.

Primary Source *See* Sources.

Prior Knowledge Prior knowledge is the knowledge a reader already possesses about a topic. This information might come from personal experiences, expert accounts, books, films, and other sources.

Problem-Solution Order Problem-solution order is a pattern of organization in which a problem is stated and analyzed and then one or more solutions are proposed and examined.

Prop The word *prop,* originally an abbreviation of the word *property,* refers to any physical object that is used in a drama.

Propaganda Propaganda is a form of communication that may use false or misleading information.

Prose The word *prose* refers to all forms of writing that are not in verse form. The term may be used to describe very different forms of writing—short stories as well as essays, for example.

Protagonist A protagonist is the main character in a story, play, or novel. The protagonist is involved in the main conflict of the story. Usually, the protagonist undergoes changes as the plot runs its course.

Public Documents Public documents are documents that were written for the public to provide information that is of public interest or concern. They include government documents, speeches, signs, and rules and regulations. Most public documents use text features, such as graphics, headers, or captions, to make sure readers can easily understand the information they communicate.

See also Government Publications.

Radio Play A radio play is a drama that is written specifically to be broadcast over the radio. Because the audience is not meant to see a radio play, sound effects are often used to help listeners imagine the setting and the action. The stage directions in the play's script indicate the sound effects.

Recurring Theme *See* Theme.

Reference Works Reference works are sources that contain facts and background information on a wide range of subjects. Most reference works are good sources of reliable information because they have been reviewed by experts. The following are some common reference works: encyclopedias, dictionaries, thesauri, almanacs, atlases, and directories.

Refrain A refrain is one or more lines repeated in each stanza of a poem.

See also Stanza.

Repetition Repetition is a technique in which a sound, word, phrase, or line is repeated for emphasis or unity. Repetition helps to reinforce meaning and create an appealing rhythm.

See also Alliteration; Sound Devices.

Resolution *See* Falling Action.

Review *See* Critical Review.

Rhetorical Questions Rhetorical questions are those that have such obvious answers that they do not require a reply. Writers often use them to suggest that their claim is so obvious that everyone should agree with it.

Rhyme Rhyme is the repetition of sounds at the end of words. Words rhyme when their accented vowels and the letters that follow have identical sounds. *Cat* and *hat* rhyme, as do *feather* and *leather.* The most common type of rhyme in poetry is called **end rhyme,** in which rhyming words come at the ends of lines. Rhyme that occurs within a line of poetry is called **internal rhyme.**

Rhyme Scheme A rhyme scheme is a pattern of end rhymes in a poem. A rhyme scheme is noted by assigning a letter of the alphabet, beginning with *a,* to each line. Lines that rhyme are given the same letter.

Rhythm Rhythm is a pattern of stressed and unstressed syllables in a line of poetry. Poets use rhythm to bring out the musical quality of language, to emphasize ideas, and to create moods. Devices such as alliteration, rhyme, assonance, and consonance often contribute to creating rhythm.

See also Meter.

Rising Action The rising action is the stage of the plot that develops the **conflict,** or struggle. During this stage, events occur that make the conflict more complicated. The events in the rising action build toward a **climax,** or turning point.

See also Plot.

Scanning Scanning is the process used to search through a text for a particular fact or piece of information. When you scan, you sweep your eyes across a page, looking for key words that may lead you to the information you want.

Scene In drama, the action is often divided into acts and scenes. Each scene presents an episode of the play's plot and typically occurs at a single place and time.

See also Act.

Scenery Scenery is a painted backdrop or other structures used to create the setting for a play.

Science Fiction Science fiction is fiction in which a writer explores unexpected possibilities of the past or the future, using known scientific data and theories as well as his or her creative imagination. Most science fiction writers create believable worlds, although some create fantasy worlds that have familiar elements.

See also Fantasy.

Screenplay A screenplay is a play written for film.

Script The text of a play, film, or broadcast is called a script.

Secondary Source *See* Sources.

Sensory Details Sensory details are words and phrases that appeal to the reader's senses of sight, sound, touch, smell, and taste. Note the sensory details in the following line. The morning sun shone brightly as a light breeze gently blew and rustled the poplar leaves. These details appeal to the senses of touch and smell.

See also Imagery.

Sequential Order Sequential order is a pattern of organization that shows the order of steps or stages in a process.

Setting The setting of a story, poem, or play is the time and place of the action. Sometimes the setting is clear and well defined. At other times, it is left to the reader's imagination. Elements of setting include geographic location, historical period (past, present, or future), season, time of day, and culture.

Setting a Purpose The process of establishing specific reasons for reading a text is called setting a purpose. Readers can look at a text's title, headings, and illustrations to guess what it might be about. They can then use these guesses to figure out what they want to learn from reading the text.

Short Story A short story is a work of fiction that centers on a single idea and can be read in one sitting. Generally, a short story has one main conflict that involves the characters and keeps the story moving.

See also Fiction.

Sidebar A sidebar is additional information set in a box alongside or within an article. Popular magazines often make use of sidebars.

Signal Words In a text, signal words are words and phrases that help show how events or ideas are related. Some common examples of signal words are *and, but, however, nevertheless, therefore,* and *in addition.*

Simile A simile is a figure of speech that makes a comparison between two unlike things using the words *like* or *as*: The calm lake was smooth as glass.

See also Figurative Language; Metaphor.

Sonnet A sonnet is a poem that has a formal structure, containing 14 lines and a specific rhyme scheme and meter. The sonnet, which means "little song," can be used for a variety of topics.

See also Rhyme Scheme.

Sound Devices Sound devices are ways of using words for the sound qualities they create. Sound devices can help convey meaning and mood in a writer's work. Some common sound devices include **alliteration, assonance, meter, onomatopoeia, repetition, rhyme,** and **rhythm.**

See also Alliteration; Assonance; Meter; Onomatopoeia; Repetition; Rhyme; Rhythm.

Sources A source is anything that supplies information. **Primary sources** are materials written by people who witnessed or took part in an event. Letters, diaries, autobiographies, and speeches are primary sources. Unlike primary sources, **secondary sources** are made by people who were not directly involved in an event or present when it occurred. Encyclopedias, textbooks, biographies, and most newspaper and magazine articles are examples of secondary sources.

Speaker In poetry the speaker is the voice that "talks" to the reader, similar to the narrator in fiction. The speaker is not necessarily the poet.

Speech A speech is a talk or public address. The purpose of a speech may be to entertain, to explain, to persuade, to inspire, or any combination of these purposes.

Stage Directions In the script of a play, the instructions to the actors, director, and stage crew are called the stage directions. Stage directions might suggest scenery, lighting, sound effects, and ways for actors to move and speak. Stage directions often appear in parentheses and in italic type.

Stanza A stanza is a group of two or more lines that form a unit in a poem. Each stanza may have the same number of lines, or the number of lines may vary.

See also Couplet; Form; Poetry.

Static Character *See* Character.

Stereotype In literature, characters who are defined by a single trait are known as stereotypes. Such characters do not usually demonstrate the complexities of real people. Familiar stereotypes in popular literature include the absent-minded professor and the busybody.

Stereotyping Stereotyping is a dangerous type of overgeneralization. It can lead to unfair judgments of people based on their ethnic background, beliefs, practices, or physical appearance.

Structure The structure of a work of literature is the way in which it is put together. In poetry, structure involves the arrangement of words and lines to produce a desired effect. One structural unit in poetry is the stanza. In prose, structure involves the arrangement of such elements as sentences, paragraphs, and events.

Style A style is a manner of writing. It involves how something is said rather than what is said.

Summarize To summarize is to briefly retell the main ideas of a piece of writing in one's own words.

See also Paraphrase.

Support Support is any information that helps to prove a claim.

Supporting Detail *See* Main Idea.

Surprise Ending A surprise ending is an unexpected plot twist at the end of a story. The surprise may be a sudden turn in the action or a piece of information that gives a different perspective to the entire story.

Suspense Suspense is a feeling of growing tension and excitement experienced by a reader. Suspense makes a reader curious about the outcome of a story or an event within a story. A writer creates suspense by raising questions in the reader's mind. The use of **foreshadowing** is one way that writers create suspense.

See also Foreshadowing.

Symbol A symbol is a person, a place, an object, an animal, or an activity that stands for something beyond itself. For example, a flag is a colored piece of cloth that stands for a country. A white dove is a bird that represents peace.

Synthesize To synthesize information means to take individual pieces of information and combine them in order to gain a better understanding of a subject.

Tall Tale A tall tale is a humorously exaggerated story about impossible events, often involving the supernatural abilities of the main character.

Teleplay A teleplay is a play written for television. In a teleplay, scenes can change quickly and dramatically. The camera can focus the viewer's attention on specific actions. The camera directions in teleplays are much like the stage directions in stage plays.

Text Features Text features are elements of a text, such as boldface type, headers, and subheadings, that help organize and call attention to important information. Italic type, bulleted or numbered lists, sidebars, captions, and graphic aids such as charts, tables, timelines, illustrations, and photographs are also considered text features.

Theme A theme is a message about life or human nature that the writer shares with the reader. In many cases, readers must infer what the writer's message is. One way of figuring out a theme is to apply the lessons learned by the main characters to people in real life.

> **Recurring themes:** Themes found in a variety of works. For example, authors from different backgrounds might express similar themes having to do with the importance of family values.

> **Universal themes:** Themes that are found throughout the literature of all time periods.

See also Moral.

Thesaurus *See* Reference Works.

Thesis Statement A thesis statement, or controlling idea, is the main proposition that a writer attempts to support in a piece of writing.

Third-Person Point of View *See* Point of View.

Title The title of a piece of writing is the name that is attached to it. A title often refers to an important aspect of the work.

Tone The tone of a literary work expresses the writer's attitude toward his or her subject. Words such as *angry, sad,* and *humorous* can be used to describe different tones.

See also Author's Perspective; Mood.

Topic Sentence The topic sentence of a paragraph states the paragraph's main idea; all other sentences in the paragraph provide supporting details.

Tragedy A tragedy is a dramatic work that presents the downfall of a dignified character or characters who are involved in historically or socially significant events. The events in a tragic plot are set in motion by a decision that is often an error in judgment on the part of the hero. Succeeding events are linked in a cause-and-effect relationship and lead inevitably to a disastrous conclusion, usually death. William Shakespeare's *Romeo and Juliet* is a famous tragedy.

Traits *See* Character.

Treatment The way a topic is handled in a work is referred to as its treatment. Treatment includes the form the writing takes as well as the writer's purpose and tone.

Turning Point *See* Climax.

Understatement Understatement is a technique of creating emphasis by saying less than is actually or literally true. It is the opposite of **hyperbole,** or exaggeration. Understatement is often used to create a humorous effect.

Universal Theme *See* Theme.

Unreliable Narrator *See* Narrator.

Visualize Visualizing is the process of forming a mental picture based on written or spoken information.

Voice The term *voice* refers to a writer's unique use of language that allows a reader to "hear" a human personality in the writer's work. Elements of style that contribute to a writer's voice can reveal much about the author's personality, beliefs, and attitudes.

Website A website is a collection of "pages" on the World Wide Web, usually devoted to one specific subject. Pages are linked together and accessed by clicking hyperlinks or menus, which send the user from page to page within a website. Websites are created by companies, organizations, educational institutions, branches of the government, the military, and individuals.

Word Choice The success of any writing depends on the writer's choice of words. Words not only communicate ideas but also help describe events, characters, settings, and so on. Word choice can make a writer's work sound formal or informal, serious or humorous. A writer must choose words carefully depending on the goal of the piece of writing. For example, a writer working on a science article would probably use technical, formal words; a writer trying to establish the setting in a short story would probably use more descriptive words.

See also Style.

Workplace Documents Workplace documents are materials that are produced or used within a work setting, usually to aid in the functioning of the workplace. They include job applications, office memos, training manuals, job descriptions, and sales reports. Effective workplace documents include text features, such as graphics, headers, and captions, to help communicate information clearly.

Works Cited The term *works cited* refers to a list of all the works a writer has referred to in his or her text. This list often includes not only books and articles but also Internet sources.

Works Consulted The term *works consulted* refers to a list of all the works a writer consulted in order to create his or her text. It is not limited just to those cited in the text.

See also Bibliography.

Writer's Point of View A writer's point of view is the writer's opinion about a topic.

Using the Glossary

This glossary is an alphabetical list of vocabulary words found in the selections in this book. Use this glossary just as you would a dictionary—to determine the meanings, parts of speech, pronunciation, and syllabication of words. (Some technical, foreign, and more obscure words in this book are not listed here but are defined for you in the footnotes that accompany many of the selections.)

Many words in the English language have more than one meaning. This glossary gives the meanings that apply to the words as they are used in the selections in this book. Words closely related in form and meaning are listed together in one entry (for instance, *consumption* and *consume*), and the definition is given for the first form.

The following abbreviations are used to identify parts of speech of words:

adj. adjective   *adv.* adverb   *n.* noun   *v.* verb

Each word's pronunciation is given in parentheses. A guide to the pronunciation symbols appears in the Pronunciation Key below. The stress marks in the Pronunciation Key are used to indicate the force given to each syllable in a word. They can also help you determine where words are divided into syllables.

For more information about the words in this glossary or for information about words not listed here, consult a dictionary.

Pronunciation Key

Symbol	Examples	Symbol	Examples		
ă	pat	m	mum	ûr	urge, term, firm, word, heard
ā	pay	n	no, sudden* (sud'n)	**Symbol**	**Examples**
ä	father	ng	thing	v	valve
âr	care	ŏ	pot	w	with
b	bib	ō	toe	y	yes
ch	church	ô	caught, paw	z	zebra, xylem
d	deed, milled	oi	noise	zh	vision, pleasure, garage
ě	pet	ŏŏ	took	ə	about, item, edible, gallop, circus
ē	bee	ōō	boot		
f	fife, phase, rough	ŏŏr	lure	ər	butter
g	gag	ôr	core		
h	hat	ou	out		
hw	which	p	pop	**Sounds in Foreign Words**	
ĭ	pit	r	roar	KH	German ich, ach; Scottish loch
ī	pie, by	s	sauce	N	French, (bôn) bon
îr	pier	sh	ship, dish	œ	French feu, œuf; German schön
j	judge	t	tight, stopped		
k	kick, cat, pique	th	thin	ü	French tu; German über
l	lid, needle* (nēd'l)	th	this		
		ŭ	cut		

* In English the consonants *l* and *n* often constitute complete syllables by themselves.

Stress Marks

The relevant emphasis with which the syllables of a word or phrase are spoken, called stress, is indicated in three different ways. The strongest, or primary, stress is marked with a bold mark ('). An intermediate, or secondary, level of stress is marked with a similar but lighter mark ('). The weakest stress is unmarked. Words of one syllable show no stress mark.

Glossary of Academic Vocabulary

abnormal (ăb-nôr′məl) *adj.* not typical, usual, or regular; not normal

affect (ə-fĕkt′) *v.* to have an influence on or effect a change in something

aspect (ăs′pĕkt) *n.* a characteristic or feature of something

attitude (ăt′ĭ-tōōd′) *n.* a way of thinking or feeling about something or someone

complex (kŏm′plĕks′) *adj.* consisting of many interwoven parts that make something difficult to understand

consume (kən sōōm′) *v.* to buy things for your own use or ownership

contrast (kən-trăst′) *v.* to show differences between two or more things that are being compared

cultural (kul′chər-əl′) *adj.* of or relating to culture or cultivation

despite (dĭ-spīt′) *prep.* in spite of; even though

element (ĕl′ə-mənt) *n.* a part or aspect of something

ensure (ĕn-shōŏr′) *v.* to make sure or certain

error (ĕr′ər) *n.* a mistake

evaluate (ĭ-văl′yoo-āt′) *tr.v.* to examine something carefully to judge its value or worth

feature (fē′chər) *n.* a prominent or distinctive part, quality, or characteristic

focus (fō′kəs) *v.* to direct toward a specific point or purpose

goal (gōl) *n.* the object toward which your work and planning is directed; a purpose

inadequate (ĭn-ăd′ĭ-kwĭt) *adj.* not enough or sufficient to fulfill a need or meet a requirement

interact (ĭn′tər-ăkt′) *v.* to act upon each other

participate (pär-tĭs′ə-pāt′) *v.* to be active and involved in something or to share in something

perceive (pər-sēv′) *v.* to become aware of something directly through any of the senses

potential (pə-tĕn′shəl) *adj.* capable of doing or being something; having possibility

purchase (pûr′chĭs) *v.* to buy

rely (rĭ-lī′) *v.* to depend on something or someone for support, help, or supply

resource (rē′-sors′) *n.* something that can be used for support or help

specify (spĕs′ə-fī′) *v.* to state exactly or in detail what you want or need

stress (strĕs) *v.* to put emphasis on something

task (tăsk) *n.* an assignment or work done as part of one's duties

technology (tĕk-nŏl′ə-jē) *n.* the application of science and engineering as part of a commercial or industrial undertaking

text (tĕkst) *n.* a literary work that is regarded as an object of critical analysis

valid (văl′ĭd) *adj.* convincing or having a sound reason for something

Glossary of Critical Vocabulary

addiction (ə-dĭk´shən) *n*. An *addiction* is a habit one is dependent on.

anxiety (ăng-zī´ĭ-tē) *n*. *Anxiety* is an uneasy, worried feeling.

apathy (ăp´ə-thē) *n*. *Apathy* is indifference or the lack of interest or concern.

arboretum (är´bə-rē´təm) *n*. An *arboretum* is a place where many trees are grown for educational or viewing purposes.

avalanche (ăv´ə-lănch) *n*. An *avalanche* is a large mass of snow, ice, dirt, or rocks falling quickly down the side of a mountain.

bedrock (bĕd´rŏk´) *n*. *Bedrock* is the solid rock that lies under sand, soil, clay, and gravel.

cache (kăsh) *n*. A *cache* is an amount of something that has been hidden away.

capacity (kə-păs´ĭ-tē) *n*. A person's *capacity* is his or her role or position.

coincidence (kō-ĭn´sĭ-dəns) *n*. A *coincidence* is a sequence of events that although accidental seems to have been planned.

conscience (kŏn´shəns) *n*. *Conscience* is the conforming to or living up to one's own sense of what is right.

corridor (kôr´ĭ-dər) *n*. A *corridor* is a narrow hallway or passageway.

croon (krōōn) *v*. When someone *croons,* that person hums or sings softly.

cynic (sĭn´ĭk) *n*. A *cynic* is a person who has negative opinions about other people and what they do.

deck (dĕk) *n*. The *deck* is the platform on a ship or boat where people stand.

decompose (dē´kəm-pōz´) *v*. When things *decompose,* they decay and break down into their basic parts.

diplomat (dĭp´lə-măt´) *n*. A *diplomat* is a person appointed by a government to interact with other governments.

eloquence (ĕl´ə-kwəns) *n*. If someone behaves or speaks with *eloquence,* she uses persuasive, powerful expression.

enact (ĕn-ăkt´) *v*. If you *enact* something, you make it into a law.

enterprising (ĕn´tər-prī´zĭng) *adj*. An *enterprising* person is someone who accepts challenges and takes initiative.

ethereal (ĭ-thîr´ē-əl) *adj*. If something is *ethereal*, it is light and airy.

exasperate (ĭg-zăs´pə-rāt´) *v*. If you *exasperate* someone, you make the person very angry.

exhibition (ĕk´sə-bĭsh´ən) *n*. An *exhibition* is an organized presentation or show.

exhort (ĭg-zôrt´) *v*. If you *exhort,* you make an urgent appeal to others.

exploit (ĭk-sploit´) *v*. If you *exploit* something, you use it selfishly.

exploitation (ĕk´sploi-tā´shən) *n*. *Exploitation* is the unfair treatment or use of something or someone for selfish reasons.

flammable (flăm´ə-bəl) *adj*. If something is *flammable*, it is easy for it to catch on fire and burn.

frantic (frăn´tik) *adj*. If you do something in a *frantic* way, you do it quickly and nervously.

geyser (gī´zər) *n*. A *geyser* is a natural hot spring that shoots hot water and steam into the air.

gradual (grăj´ōō-əl) *adj*. If something is *gradual*, it advances little by little.

gully (gŭl´ē) *n*. A *gully* is a deep ditch cut in the earth by running water.

haggard (hăg´ərd) *adj*. If you're *haggard,* you are worn out and exhausted.

hypothesis (hī-pŏth´ĭ-sĭs) *n*. A *hypothesis* is an explanation or theory for something that can be tested for validity.

ignorance (ĭg´nər-əns) *n*. *Ignorance* is the condition of being uneducated or uninformed.

impairment (ĭm-pâr´mənt) *n*. An *impairment* is an injury or weakness.

impetus (ĭm´pĭ-təs) *n.* The *impetus* is the driving force or motivation behind an action.

inexplicable (ĭn-ĕk´splĭ-kə-bəl) *adj.* If something is *inexplicable*, it is difficult to understand.

inquire (ĭn-kwīr´) *v.* If you *inquire* about something, you ask about it.

inspection (ĭn-spĕk´shən) *n.* An *inspection* is an official examination or review.

insulate (ĭn´sə-lāt´) *v.* When you *insulate* something, you prevent the passage of heat through it.

intangible (ĭn-tăn´jə-bəl) *n.* An *intangible* is something that is hard to describe because it cannot be perceived by the senses.

inundate (ĭn´ŭndāt´) *v.* To *inundate* is to give a huge amount of something.

judicious (jōō-dĭsh´əs) *adj.* If you are *judicious*, you have good judgment.

mandatory (măn´də-tôr´ē) *adj.* If something is *mandatory*, it is required.

maroon (mə-rōōn´) *v.* To *maroon* is to abandon or leave someone in a place that is hard to get away from.

marvel (mär´vəl) *v.* If you *marvel* at something, you are surprised or astonished by it.

meager (mē´gər) *adj.* If something is *meager*, it is small or deficient in quantity.

median (mē´dē-ən) *n.* A *median* is a dividing area between opposing lanes of traffic on a highway or road.

metabolism (mĭ-tăb´ə-lĭz´əm) *n.* The *metabolism* of a living thing is all the processes that allow for growth and life.

mischievous (mĭs´chə-vəs) *adj.* If someone is *mischievous*, the person is naughty.

misjudge (mĭs-jŭj´) *v.* If you *misjudge* something, you form an incorrect opinion about it.

moderate (mŏd´ər-ĭt) *adj.* When something is kept *moderate*, it is kept within a certain limit.

municipal (myōō-nĭs´ə-pəl) *adj.* If something is *municipal*, it relates to a city or town.

navigation (năv´ĭ-gā´shən) *n.* The *navigation* of a ship or boat is the act of guiding it along a planned course.

neural (nŏŏr´əl) *adj.* Anything that is *neural* is related to the nervous system.

neuron (nŏŏr´ŏn´) *n.* A *neuron* is a cell in the nervous system that carries messages between the brain and other body parts.

neuroscience (nŏŏr´ō-sī´əns) *n. Neuroscience* is any of the sciences that study the nervous system.

neuroscientist (nŏŏr´ō-sī´ən-tĭst) *n.* A *neuroscientist* is a person who studies the brain and the nervous system.

obituary (ō-bĭch´ōō-ĕr´ē) *n.* An *obituary* is a public notice of a death.

observation (ŏb´zər-vā´shən) *n.* An *observation* is the act of watching something.

plantation (plăn-tā´shən) *n.* A *plantation* is a large farm or estate on which crops are raised.

ponderous (pŏn´dər-əs) *adj.* If something is *ponderous*, it is very heavy.

portable (pôr´tə-bəl) *adj.* If something is *portable*, it can be carried or moved easily.

porthole (pŏrt´hōl) *n.* A *porthole* is a circular window on a boat or ship.

possession (pə-zĕsh´ən) *n.* A *possession* is something you own.

precarious (prĭ-kâr´ē-əs) *adj.* If something is *precarious*, it is dangerous and unstable.

precaution (prĭ-kô´shən) *n.* A *precaution* is an action taken to avoid possible danger.

precipitous (prĭ-sĭp´ĭ-təs) *adj.* When something is *precipitous*, it is very steep, like a cliff.

proliferation (prə-lĭf´ər-rā´shən) *n.* A *proliferation* is the fast growth of something.

prowess (prou´ĭs) *n. Prowess* is the strength and courage someone has.

reign (rān) *v.* If some things *reign* over something else, it means they dominate it.

reprove (rĭ-prōōv´) *v.* If you *reprove* someone, you express disapproval.

restrictive (rĭ-strĭk´tĭv) *adj.* When something is *restrictive*, it is limiting in some way.

scorn (skôrn) *n. Scorn* is disrespect or disdain.

sextant (sĕk´stənt) *n.* A *sextant* is an instrument used to determine location by measuring the position of the stars and sun.

shuffle (shuf´əl) *v.* When you *shuffle*, you move with short sliding steps.

singe (sĭnj) *v.* If you *singe* something, you slightly burn it.

snag (snăg) *v.* If you *snag* something, you catch it quickly and unexpectedly.

splinter (splĭn´tər) *v.* To *splinter* means to break up into sharp, thin pieces.

spyglass (spī´glăs´) *n.* A *spyglass* is a small telescope.

steward (stōō´ərd) *n.* A *steward* is a person who supervises or manages something.

stifle (stī´fəl) *v.* If you *stifle* something, you hold it back.

submerge (səb-mûrj´) *v.* When something *submerges,* it becomes covered by water.

superfluity (sōō´pər-flōō´ĭ-tē) *n. Superfluity* is overabundance or excess.

sustain (sə-stān´) *v.* If things *sustain,* they remain in existence.

sustenance (sŭs´tə-nəns) *n. Sustenance* is the food needed to live.

swell (swĕl) *n.* A *swell* is a long, unbroken wave.

syringe (sə-rĭnj´) *n.* A *syringe* is a medical instrument used to inject fluids into the body.

taper (tā´pər) *v.* When things *taper,* they gradually get thinner.

tectonic (tĕk-tŏn´ĭk) *adj.* If something is *tectonic,* it relates to the deformation of Earth's rocky crust.

tedious (tē´dē-əs) *adj.* Something that is *tedious* is boring.

wistful (wĭst´fəl) *adj.* If you're *wistful,* you are thoughtful and longing for something.

Index of Skills

A

abstract nouns, R30

Academic Vocabulary, 2, 53, 57, 62, 127, 131, 136, 175, 179, 184, 215, 220, 259, 264, 337, 341, R79. *See also* Glossary of Academic Vocabulary

act, of a play, R64. *See also* scenes

active voice, 55, R43

ad hominem, R27

adjective clauses, 200, R49, R50, R54

adjective phrases, R47

adjectives, 38, 200, R31, R43

  comparative forms of, R44

  compound, R35

  coordinate, 38

  gerund phrases as, 326

  infinitives as, R47

  as modifiers, 38, 88, 200, 306, 316, R43, R44, R47

  participial phrases as, 306, R48

  predicate, R43

  prepositional phrases as, R47

  proper, 110, R36

  superlative forms of, R44

  verbals as, 212, 306, R47

adventure story, R64

adverb clauses, 88, R49

adverb phrases, R47

adverbs, 88, R31, R44

  comparative forms of, R44

  conjunctive, R51

  gerund phrases as, 326

  infinitive phrases as, 212, R47

  as modifiers, 88, 316, R44

  superlative forms of, R44

  verbals as, 212, 306, R47

alliteration, 41, R64

allusion, 143, 325, R64

almanacs, R73

analogies, 305, R58, R64. *See also* metaphors; simile

analogy problem, R58

analyzing, 142, 214, 248. *See also* Analyzing the Text; media analysis; poetry analysis; structural analysis

arguments, R23–R24

  presenting, 57–60, 215–218, 314

  writing, 127–130, 154, 210

  author's style, 141, 153, 237, 324, R5, R75

  character, 35, 126, 153, 334

  details, 107

  form, 41, 75, 125, 147, 171, 173, 244, 246

  free verse, 246

  language, 147

logic, R25–R26

point of view, 303

reasons/reasoning, R23, R25–R26

stories, 15, 35, 68, 107, 255, 333

symbols, 107

text, 141, 279, 313

Analyzing the Media, 23, 27, 29, 92, 320

Analyzing the Text, 16, 36, 42, 50, 69, 73, 75, 76, 86, 108, 126, 142, 148, 154, 166, 171, 173, 174, 190, 198, 210, 214, 230, 238, 244, 248, 256, 274, 278, 280, 304, 314, 325

anecdote, 23, 132, R64

Annotate It!, 16, 23, 27, 36, 42, 50, 69, 73, 75, 86, 108, 126, 142, 148, 154, 166, 171, 174, 190, 198, 210, 214, 230, 238, 244, 246, 256, 274, 278, 280, 304, 314, 325, 334

antagonist, R64. *See also* protagonist

antecedents, R37–R38

antonyms, 239, 305, R58

apostrophe, R35, R62

appeals, R24

appositives, R47–R48

arguments, 189, R64. *See also* claims; debates; evidence

  analysis of, R23

  claims in, 27, 197, R2, R23, R65

  conclusion in, R3

  counterarguments, 27, 189, 197, R23, R29, R66

  in debates, R14–R15, R67

  deductive, R25–R26, R67

  editorials as, 27

  elements of, 197, R2–R3

  evaluating, 27, 189

  evidence for, 27, 197, 216, R23, R29

  facts in, 27

  inductive, R25

  introduction in, R2

  logical, R71

  opinions in, 27

  persuasion in, 189, 197, R23–R29

  point of view of, R73

  reasons/reasoning in, 27, 189, 197, R23

  support for, 189, R23–R24

  tracing, 27, 189

  writing, R2–R3

artist's perspective, 92

assonance, R64, R74

As You Read, 321

As You View, 28, 90, 91, 318

audience

  for argument, 57–59, 127–129, 215–217

  for fictional narrative, 54–55

for informative essay, 338

for multimedia presentation, 259–261

for personal narrative, 176–177

for poetry analysis, 180–181

for public art, 92

author's perspective, 279, 313

author's purpose, 49, 73, 92, R64

autobiography, 141, R65. *See also* memoirs

auxiliary verbs, R31, R32, R53

B

ballad, R64

base words, R56

bias, R28, R64

bibliography, R65. *See also* works cited; works consulted

biography, R64–R65

blank verse, 147

blog, 30

boldface type, 85, R76

brainstorming, 53, 176, 259, 337

C

capitalization, 192, 282

  of first words, R36

  of geographical names, 110, R36

  of organizations, 192, R36

  of personal titles, 110

  in poems/poetry, 324

  of pronouns, R36

  of proper adjectives, R36

  of proper names, 110, R36

  of proper nouns, 192

  quick references for, R36

  in quotations, 282

  rules for, 192, 282, R30

career development documents, R65

cast of characters, 125, R65

cause-and-effect relationships, 209

cause-effect organization, 165, 229, R4, R18–R19

central ideas, 23, 165, 209, 274, 320. *See also* main ideas

characterization, 333, R65

character analysis, 108

characters, 107, R65. *See also* characterization

  action of, 107, 333

  analysis of, 35, 126, 153, 334

  antagonists, R64

  cast of, 125, R65

  central, R65

  development of, 333

  dialogue of, 125, 303, R67

  dynamic, R65

  foil as, R69

slang, R5, R55
soliloquy, 147–148
sonnets, 75, R75. *See also* rhyme
    scheme
sound devices, 324, R73, R75. *See also*
    alliteration; assonance; meter;
    onomatopoeia; repetition;
    rhyme; rhythm
sound reasons/reasoning, 197
sounds effects, 319
sources, R75. *See also* references
    primary, R8, R73, R75
    reference, R59–R60
    for research, R8
    secondary, R8, R74–R75
spatial order, 165
speaker, 214, R75
    in argument, 60, 189, 218, R25
    claim by, 189, 218
    debates by, R14–R15
    in lyric poem, 173
    theme of, 247, 324
    voice-over narration of, 319
speaking activity
    argument, 314
    demonstration, 86
    discussion, 76, 238
    dramatic reading, 69, 148
    informal debate, 198
    oral presentation, 280
    oral report, 166
    response to literature, 42
specialized dictionaries, R60
specialized vocabulary, R59
specific context clues, R55
speech, 215–218, 335, R30–R31, R75
spell correctly, 110
spelling, 110, 258, R55–R63
stage directions, 125, R75
stanza, 41, 244, 324, R75. *See also*
    couplet; form
statements
    commonplace assertions as, R16
    concluding, 217, R5, R66
    direct, 279
    either-or fallacies as, 197, R27, R67
    facts as, 27, R68
    factual claims as, R16
    false, R27
    misleading, R27
    opinions as, 27
    paradoxes as, 75
    policy, R14
    thesis, R4, R76
static character, R65
stereotype/stereotyping, R27, R75
Stream to Start, 2, 62, 136, 184,
    220, 264
structural analysis
    cause-and-effect, 229
    chronological order, 278
    essays, 165

news reports, 23
organizational patterns, 209
sound reasoning, 197
text, 85
TV news interviews, 29
words, R56–R57
style, 141, 153, 237, 324, R5, R75
style manuals, R9
subheading, 85, R16–R17, R76
subject-by-subject organization, R19
subject complements, R46
subject pronouns, R38
subject-verb agreement, R51–R54
subordinate clauses, 52, 88, 156, 240,
    R48–R50
subordinating conjunction, 52, 88,
    156, R31, R48, R51
suffixes, 37, 70, R56, R61
summary/summarizing, 68, 85, 229,
    R9, R75. *See also* paraphrase/
    paraphrasing
summary presentation, 131–134,
    166, 280
superlative forms, R44
superlative modifiers, R44
support, 189, R23, R75
supporting conclusions, 49
supporting details, 23, 165, 274, R16,
    R75. *See also* main ideas
surprise ending, R38, R76
suspense, 15, 53–55, R7, R76. *See also*
    foreshadowing
symbols, 107, R76
synonym finder, R60
synonyms, 109, 239, R58
synthesizing, R12, R76

T

tall tale, R76
technical language, 85
telling details, R7
tenses, R42
text analysis, 141, 279, 313. *See also*
    Analyzing the Text
textual evidence. *See* Cite Text
    Evidence
theme, 35, 153, 214, 247, 255, 324,
    R76. *See also* moral
    recurring, R73, R76
    universal, R76–R77
thesaurus, 109, R60, R76
thesis statements, 180, 337, R4, R76
third-person limited, 303
third-person omniscient, 303
third-person point of view, 303, R73,
    R76
title, 85, R76
tone, 132, 197, 237, 279, 313, 325, 342,
    R76
    of arguments, 58–59, 128,
        216–217, R3
    formal, 132, 342

in informative essays, 132, 339
of informative text, R5
in memoirs, R71
objective, 279, R3, R5
in personal essay, 176
in poetry, 247
subjective, 279, R73
topic sentence, R16, R71, R76
tracing arguments, 27, 189
traditional form (poem), 244
tragedy, 337, R76
traits. *See* characters
transitional clause, R3
transitional phrases, R3
transitional word, R3
transitioning action, 54
transitive verbs, R31
treatment, R8, R76
turning point, R74, R76. *See also*
    climax
TV news interview, 29–30
-ty, 36

U

understatement, R76
unfamiliar words, R55
universal theme, R76–R77
unreliable narrator, R71, R77

V

vague claims, R2
verbal analogies, 305
verbal phrases, 212, 306, R47
verbs, R31, R41
    action, R31, R41
    auxiliary, R31–R32, R53
    helping, R32
    intransitive, R31
    irregular, R41
    linking, R31, R41
    main, R32
    as modifiers, 88, R44
    in prepositional phrases, R52
    principal parts of, R41
    regular, R41
    simple, R32
    tense of, R42
    transitive, R31
vertical axis, 229
visualizing, R71, R77
visuals, 29, 58–59, 216–217, 261
vivid language, 144, R7
vocabulary, R55–R63
    Academic, 2, 62, 131, 136, 184, 220,
        259, 264, R79
    Critical, 17, 37, 51, 70, 87, 109, 143,
        155, 167, 191, 199, 211, 231, 239,
        257, 281, 305, 315, 335, R80
    specialized, R59
Vocabulary and Spelling
    analogies, R58

Index of Titles and Authors

Acknowledgments

"Allied with Green" from *There is No Long Distance Now: Very Short Stories* by Naomi Shihab Nye. Text copyright © 2011 by Naomi Shihab Nye. Reprinted by permission of HarperCollins Publishers.

"Always Wanting More" from *I Want That: How We All Became Shoppers* by Thomas Hine. Text copyright © 2002 by Thomas Hine. Reprinted by permission of HarperCollins Publishers.

Excerpt from *The American Heritage Dictionary of the English Language, Fifth Edition*. Text copyright © 2011 by Houghton Mifflin Harcourt. Adapted and reprinted by permission of Houghton Mifflin Harcourt Publishing Company.

"Another Place, Another Time" by Cory Doctorow from *The Chronicles of Harris Burdick* by Chris Van Allsburg. Text copyright © 2011 by Cory Doctorow. Illustrations copyright © 1984 by Chris Van Allsburg. Reprinted by permission of Houghton Mifflin Harcourt Publishing Company.

"Big Rocks' Balancing Acts" by Douglas Fox from *Science News for Kids,* October 19, 2011. Text copyright © 2011 by the Society for Science and the Public. Reprinted by permission of Science News for Kids.

"Dump" from *In a Prominent Bar in Secaucus: New and Selected Poems, 1955-2007* by X. J. Kennedy. Text copyright © 2007 by X. J. Kennedy. Reprinted by permission of Johns Hopkins University Press.

"Earth (A Gift Shop)" by Charles Yu from *Shadow Show*, edited by Sam Weller and Mort Castle. Text copyright © 2012 by Charles Yu. Reprinted by permission of Signature Literary Agency on behalf of the author.

Excerpt from *Flesh & Blood So Cheap: The Triangle Fire and Its Legacy* by Albert Marrin. Text copyright © 2011 by Albert Marrin. Reprinted by permission of Alfred A. Knopf, a division of Random House, Inc. Any third party use of this material, outside of this publication, is prohibited. Interested parties must apply directly to Random House, Inc. for permission.

"The Flight of Icarus" from *Stories of the Gods and Heroes* by Sally Benson. Text copyright 1940, renewed © 1968 by Sally Benson. Reprinted by permission of Dial Books for Young Readers, a division of Penguin Group (USA) Inc.

"How Things Work" from *A Fire in My Hand: Poems* by Gary Soto. Text copyright © 2006, 1999 by Gary Soto. Reprinted by permission of Houghton Mifflin Harcourt Publishing Company and BookStop Literary Agency, LLC, on behalf of the author. All rights reserved.

"Icarus's Flight" from *Mystery, So Long* by Stephen Dobyns. Text copyright © 2006 by Stephen Dobyns. Originally published by Penguin. Reprinted by permission of the author.

Excerpt from *julianbeever.net*. Text copyright © by Julian Beever. Reprinted by permission of Julian Beever.

Excerpt from *Life at Home in the 21st Century: 32 Families Open Their Doors* by Jeanne E. Arnold, Anthony P. Graesch, Enzo Ragazzini and Elinor Ochs. Text copyright © 2012 by the Regents of the University of California. Reprinted by permission of the Regents of the University of California, Cotsen Institute and Jeanne Arnold. All rights reserved.

"Living in the Dark" by Cheryl Bardoe from *Muse*, Vol. 16, No. 2. Text copyright © 2012 by Cheryl Bardoe. Reprinted by permission of Cricket Magazine Group, a division of Carus Publishing Company.

"Magic and the Brain" by Susana Martinez-Conde and Stephen L. Macknik, from *Scientific American*, December 2008. Text copyright © 2008 by Scientific American, Inc. Reprinted by permission of Scientific American, Inc.

Excerpt from *Mississippi Solo* by Eddy Harris. Text copyright © 1988 by Eddy Harris. Reprinted by permission of Globe Pequot Press.

"Ode to Enchanted Light" from *Odes to Opposites* compiled by Ferris Cook. Originally published in Spanish as "Oda a la luz encantada" by Pablo Neruda, translated by Ken Krabbenhoft. Translation copyright © 1995 by Ken Krabbenhoft. Text copyright © 1995 by Pablo Neruda and Fundación Pablo Neruda. Text compilation copyright © 1995 by Ferris Cook. Reprinted by permission of Bullfinch and Agencia Literaria Carmen Balcells S.A. All rights reserved.

"Parents of rescued teenage sailor Abby Sunderland accused of risking her life" by Paul Harris from *The Observer*, June 13, 2010. Text copyright © 2012 Guardian News and Media Limited or its affiliated companies. Reprinted by permission of Guardian News Media.

Excerpt from *The People Could Fly: American Black Folktales* by Virginia Hamilton. Text copyright © 1985 by Virginia Hamilton. Reprinted by permission of Alfred A. Knopf, an imprint of Random House Children's Books, a division of Random House, Inc. Any third party use of this material, outside of this publication, is prohibited. Interested parties must apply directly to Random House, Inc. for permission.

"Poem for My Librarian, Mrs. Long" from *Acolytes* by Nikki Giovanni. Text copyright © 2007 by Nikki Giovanni. Reprinted by permission of HarperCollins Publishers.

"Reflections on Working Toward Peace" by Craig Kielburger from *Architects of Peace: Visions of Hope in Words and Images*, edited by Michael Collopy and Jason Gardner. Text copyright © 2000 by Michael Collopy. Reprinted by permission of New World Library.

"Rogue Wave" from *Rogue Wave and Other Red-Blooded Sea Stories* by Theodore Taylor. Text copyright © 1996 by Theodore Taylor. Reprinted by permission of the Theodore Taylor Estate and the Watkins/Loomis Agency.

"Ship of Fools" by Joanna Weiss from *The Boston Globe*, June 15, 2010. Text copyright © 2010 by Globe Newspaper Company. Reprinted by permission of PARS International on behalf of The Boston Globe. All rights reserved.

"Sleeping in the Forest" from *Twelve Moons* by Mary Oliver. Text copyright © 1972, 1973, 1974, 1976, 1977, 1978, 1979 by Mary Oliver. Reprinted by permission of Little, Brown and Company and Charlotte Sheedy Literary Agency on behalf of the author.

"The Song of Wandering Aengus" from *The Wind in the Reeds* by William Butler Yeats. Text copyright © The Estate of the Late William Butler Yeats. Reprinted by permission of United Agents, LLP, on behalf of The Estate of the Late William Butler Yeats.

"Sorry, Wrong Number" by Lucille Fletcher. Text copyright © 1948 by Lucille Fletcher. Reprinted by permission of William Morris Endeavor Entertainment, LLC.

Excerpt from *The Story of the Triangle Factory Fire* by Zachary Kent. Text copyright © 1989 by Children's Press, Inc. Reprinted by permission of Children's Press, an imprint of Scholastic Library Publishing, Inc. All rights reserved.

Excerpt from *Uprising* by Margaret Peterson Haddix. Text copyright © 2007 by Margaret Peterson Haddix. Reprinted by permission of Simon & Schuster Books for Young Readers, an imprint of Simon & Schuster's Children's Publishing Division and Adams Literary.

"Why Exploring the Ocean is Mankind's Next Giant Leap" by Phillippe Cousteau from *Light Years Blog*, March 13, 2012. Text copyright © Philippe Cousteau. Reprinted by permission of Philippe Cousteau.

Excerpt from "Women in Aviation" from *Red-Tail Angels* by Fredrick and Patricia McKissack. Text copyright © 1995 by Fredrick and Patricia McKissack. Reprinted by permission of Walker & Co.

"Your World" from *Share My World* by Georgia Douglas Johnson. Text copyright © 1962 by Georgia Douglas Johnson. Reprinted by permission of the Moorland-Spingarn Research Center, Howard University.

California Department of Education
English Language Development Standards for Grade 7

Section 1: Goal, Critical Principles, and Overview

Goal: English learners read, analyze, interpret, and create a variety of literary and informational text types. They develop an understanding of how language is a complex, dynamic, and social resource for making meaning, as well as how content is organized in different text types and across disciplines using text structure, language features, and vocabulary depending on purpose and audience. They are aware that different languages and variations of English exist, and they recognize their home languages and cultures as resources to value in their own right and also to draw upon in order to build proficiency in English. English learners contribute actively to class and group discussions, asking questions, responding appropriately, and providing useful feedback. They demonstrate knowledge of content through oral presentations, writing, collaborative conversations, and multimedia. They develop proficiency in shifting language use based on task, purpose, audience, and text type.

Critical Principles for Developing Language and Cognition in Academic Contexts: While advancing along the continuum of English language development levels, English learners at all levels engage in intellectually challenging literacy, disciplinary, and disciplinary literacy tasks. They use language in meaningful and relevant ways appropriate to grade level, content area, topic, purpose, audience, and text type in English language arts, mathematics, science, social studies, and the arts. Specifically, they use language to gain and exchange information and ideas in three communicative modes (collaborative, interpretive, and productive), and they apply knowledge of language to academic tasks via three cross-mode language processes (structuring cohesive texts, expanding and enriching ideas, and connecting and condensing ideas) using various linguistic resources.

PART I: Interacting in Meaningful Ways

A. COLLABORATIVE

	Corresponding Common Core State Standards for English Language Arts*
1. Exchanging information and ideas with others through oral collaborative discussions on a range of social and academic topics	SL.7.1,6; L.7.3,6
2. Interacting with others in written English in various communicative forms (print, communicative technology, and multimedia)	W.7.6; WHST.7.6; SL.7.2; L.7.3,6
3. Offering and justifying opinions, negotiating with and persuading others in communicative exchanges	W.7.1; WHST.7.1; SL.7.1,4,6; L.7.3,6
4. Adapting language choices to various contexts (based on task, purpose, audience, and text type)	W.7.4–5; WHST.7.4–5; SL.7.6; L.7.1,3,6

B. INTERPRETIVE

5. Listening actively to spoken English in a range of social and academic context	SL.7.1,3,6; L.7.1,3,6
6. Reading closely literary and informational texts and viewing multimedia to determine how meaning is conveyed explicitly and implicitly through language	RL.7.1–7,9–10; RI.7.1–10; RH.7.1–10; RST.7.1–10; SL.7.2; L.7.1,3,6
7. Evaluating how well writers and speakers use language to support ideas and arguments with details or evidence depending on modality, text type, purpose, audience, topic, and content area	RL.7.4–5; RI.7.4,6,8; RH.7.4–6,8; RST.7.4–6,8; SL.7.3; L.7.3,5–6
8. Analyzing how writers and speakers use vocabulary and other language resources for specific purposes (to explain, persuade, entertain, etc.) depending on modality, text type, purpose, audience, topic, and content area	RL.7.4–5; RI.7.4–5; RH.7.4–5; RST.7.4–5; SL.7.3; L.7.3,5–6

C. PRODUCTIVE

9. Expressing information and ideas in formal oral presentations on academic topics	SL.7.4–6; L.7.1,3
10. Writing literary and informational texts to present, describe, and explain ideas and information, using appropriate technology	W.7.1–10; WHST.7.1–2,4–10; L.7.1–6
11. Justifying own arguments and evaluating others' arguments in writing	W.7.1,8–9; WHST.7.1,8–9; L.7.1–3,6
12. Selecting and applying varied and precise vocabulary and language structures to effectively convey ideas	W.7.4–5; WHST.7.4–5; SL.7.4,6; L.7.1,3,5–6

PART II: Learning About How English Works

	Corresponding Common Core State Standards for English Language Arts*
A. STRUCTURING COHESIVE TEXTS	
1. Understanding text structure	**RL.7.5; RI.7.5; RH.7.5; RST.7.5; W.7.1-5,10; WHST.7.1-2,4-5,10; SL.7.4**
2. Understanding cohesion	**RI.7.5; RH.7.5; RST.7.5; W.7.1-5,10; WHST.7.1-2,4-5,10; L.7.1,3-6**
B. EXPANDING & ENRICHING IDEAS	
3. Using verbs and verb phrases	**W.7.5; WHST.7.5; SL.7.6; L.7.1,3-6**
4. Using nouns and noun phrases	**W.7.5; WHST.7.5; SL.7.6; L.7.1,3-6**
5. Modifying to add ideas	**W.7.4-5; WHST.7.4-5; SL.7.6; L.7.1,3-6**
C. CONNECTING & CONDENSING IDEAS	
6. Connecting ideas	**W.7.1-5; WHST.7.1-2,4-5; SL.7.4,6; L.7.1,3-6**
7. Condensing ideas	**W.7.1-5; WHST.7.1-2,4-5; SL.7.4,6; L.7.1,3-6**

PART III: Using Foundational Literacy Skills

	RF.K-1.1-4; RF.2-5.3-4 (as appropriate)

* The California English Language Development Standards correspond to California's Common Core State Standards for English Language Arts (ELA) and, for grades 6–12, Literacy in History/Social Studies, Science, and Technical Subjects. English learners should have full access to and opportunities to learn ELA, mathematics, science, history/social studies, and other content at the same time they are progressing toward full proficiency in English.

Note: **Examples** provided in specific standards *are offered only as illustrative possibilities* and should not be misinterpreted as the only objectives of instruction or as the only types of language English learners might or should be able to understand or produce.

Section 2: Elaboration on Critical Principles for Developing Language & Cognition in Academic Contexts

PART I: Interacting in Meaningful Ways

Texts and Discourse in Context	English Language Development Level Continuum		
	A. COLLABORATIVE		
	Emerging	**Expanding**	**Bridging**
Part I, strands 1–4 Corresponding Common Core State Standards for English Language Arts 1. **SL.7.1,6; L.7.3,6** 2. **W.7.6; WHST.7.6; SL.7.2; L.7.3,6** 3. **W.7.1; WHST.7.1; SL.7.1,4,6; L.7.3,6** 4. **W.7.4-5; WHST.7.4-5; SL.7.6; L.7.1,3,6** **Purposes for using language include:** describing, entertaining, informing, interpreting, analyzing, recounting, explaining, persuading, negotiating, justifying, evaluating **Text types include:** **Informational text types include:** descriptions or accounts (e.g., scientific, historical, economic, technical), recounts (e.g., biography, memoir), information reports, explanations (e.g., causal, factorial), expositions (e.g., speeches, opinion pieces, argument, debate), responses (e.g., literary analysis), etc. **Literary text types include:** stories (e.g., historical fiction, myths, graphic novels), poetry, drama, etc. **Audiences include:** Peers (one-to-one), Small group (one-to-group), Whole group (one-to-many)	1. *Exchanging information/ideas* Engage in conversational exchanges and express ideas on familiar topics by asking and answering *yes-no* and *wh-* questions and responding using simple phrases. 2. *Interacting via written English* Engage in short written exchanges with peers and collaborate on simple written texts on familiar topics, using technology when appropriate. 3. *Supporting opinions and persuading others* Negotiate with or persuade others in conversations (e.g., to gain and hold the floor or ask for clarification) using basic learned phrases (e.g., *I think . . . , Would you please repeat that?*), as well as open responses. 4. *Adapting language choices* Adjust language choices according to social setting (e.g., classroom, break time) and audience (e.g., peers, teacher).	1. *Exchanging information/ideas* Contribute to class, group, and partner discussions by following turn-taking rules, asking relevant questions, affirming others, adding relevant information, and paraphrasing key ideas. 2. *Interacting via written English* Engage in longer written exchanges with peers and collaborate on more detailed written texts on a variety of topics, using technology when appropriate. 3. *Supporting opinions and persuading others* Negotiate with or persuade others in conversations (e.g., to provide counter-arguments) using an expanded set of learned phrases (*I agree with X, but . . .*), as well as open responses. 4. *Adapting language choices* Adjust language choices according to purpose (e.g., explaining, persuading, entertaining), task, and audience.	1. *Exchanging information/ideas* Contribute to class, group, and partner discussions by following turn-taking rules, asking relevant questions, affirming others, adding relevant information and evidence, paraphrasing key ideas, building on responses, and providing useful feedback. 2. *Interacting via written English* Engage in extended written exchanges with peers and collaborate on complex written texts on a variety of topics, using technology when appropriate. 3. *Supporting opinions and persuading others* Negotiate with or persuade others in conversations using appropriate register (e.g., to acknowledge new information) using a variety of learned phrases, indirect reported speech (e.g., *I heard you say X, and I haven't thought about that before*), and open responses. 4. *Adapting language choices* Adjust language choices according to task (e.g., facilitating a science experiment, providing peer feedback on a writing assignment), purpose, task, and audience.

Texts and Discourse in Context

English Language Development Level Continuum

B. INTERPRETIVE

Part I, strands 5–7 Corresponding Common Core State Standards for English Language Arts

5. SL.7.1,3,6; L.7.1,3,6
6. RL.7.1-7,9-10; RI.7.1-10; RH.7.1-10; RST.7.1-10; SL.7.2; L.7.1,3,6
7. RL.7.4-5; RI.7.4,6,8; RH.7.4-6,8; RST.7.4-6,8; SL.7.3; L.7.3,5-6

Purposes for using language include: describing, entertaining, informing, interpreting, analyzing, recounting, explaining, persuading, negotiating, justifying, evaluating

Text types include:
Informational text types include: descriptions or accounts (e.g., scientific, historical, economic, technical), recounts (e.g., biography, memoir), information reports, explanations (e.g., causal, factorial), expositions (e.g., speeches, opinion pieces, argument, debate), responses (e.g., literary analysis), etc.

Literary text types include: stories (e.g., historical fiction, myths, graphic novels), poetry, drama, etc.

Audiences include: Peers (one-to-one), Small group (one-to-group), Whole group (one-to-many)

Emerging

5. *Listening actively* Demonstrate active listening in oral presentation activities by asking and answering basic questions with prompting and substantial support.

6. *Reading/viewing closely*
   a. Explain ideas, phenomena, processes, and text relationships (e.g., compare/contrast, cause/effect, problem/solution) based on close reading of a variety of grade-appropriate texts and viewing of multimedia with substantial support.
   b. Express inferences and conclusions drawn based on close reading of grade-level texts and viewing of multimedia using some frequently used verbs (e.g., *shows that, based on*).
   c. Use knowledge of morphology (e.g., affixes, roots, and base words), context, reference materials, and visual cues to determine the meaning of unknown and multiple-meaning words on familiar topics.

7. *Evaluating language choices* Explain how well writers and speakers use language to support ideas and arguments with detailed evidence (e.g., identifying the precise vocabulary used to present evidence, or the phrasing used to signal a shift in meaning) when provided with substantial support.

Expanding

5. *Listening actively* Demonstrate active listening in oral presentation activities by asking and answering detailed questions with occasional prompting and moderate support.

6. *Reading/viewing closely*
   a. Explain ideas, phenomena, processes, and text relationships (e.g., compare/contrast, cause/effect, problem/solution) based on close reading of a variety of grade-level texts and viewing of multimedia with moderate support.
   b. Express inferences and conclusions drawn based on close reading of grade-appropriate texts and viewing of multimedia using a variety of verbs (e.g., *suggests that, leads to*).
   c. Use knowledge of morphology (e.g., affixes, roots, and base words), context, reference materials, and visual cues to determine the meaning of unknown and multiple-meaning words on familiar and new topics.

7. *Evaluating language choices* Explain how well writers and speakers use specific language to present ideas or support arguments and provide detailed evidence (e.g., showing the clarity of the phrasing used to present an argument) with moderate support.

Bridging

5. *Listening actively* Demonstrate active listening in oral presentation activities by asking and answering detailed questions with minimal prompting and support

6. *Reading/viewing closely*
   a. Explain ideas, phenomena, processes, and text relationships (e.g., compare/contrast, cause/effect, problem/solution) based on close reading of a variety of grade-level texts and viewing of multimedia with light support.
   b. Express inferences and conclusions drawn based on close reading of grade-level texts and viewing of multimedia using a variety of precise academic verbs (e.g., *indicates that, influences*).
   c. Use knowledge of morphology (e.g., affixes, roots, and base words), context, reference materials, and visual cues to determine the meaning, including figurative and connotative meanings, of unknown and multiple-meaning words on a variety of new topics.

7. *Evaluating language choices* Explain how well writers and speakers use specific language resources to present ideas or support arguments and provide detailed evidence (e.g., identifying the specific language used to present ideas and claims that are well supported and distinguishing them from those that are not) when provided with light support.

Texts and Discourse in Context	English Language Development Level Continuum		

B. INTERPRETIVE

	Emerging	Expanding	Bridging
Part I, strands 8–10 Corresponding Common Core State Standards for English Language Arts 8. RL.7.4-5; RI.7.4-5; RH.7.4-5; RST.7.4-5; SL.7.3; L.7.3,5-6 9. W.7.1,8-9; WHST.7.1,8-9; L.7.1-3,6 10.W.7.4-5; WHST.7.4-5; SL.7.4,6; L.7.1,3,5-6 **Purposes for using language** include: describing, entertaining, informing, interpreting, analyzing, recounting, explaining, persuading, negotiating, justifying, evaluating	8. *Analyzing language choices* Explain how phrasing or different common words with similar meaning (e.g., choosing to use the word *polite* versus *good*) produce different effects on the audience.	8. *Analyzing language choices* Explain how phrasing, different words with similar meaning (e.g., describing a character as *diplomatic* versus *respectful*), or figurative language (e.g., *The wind whispered through the night.*) produce shades of meaning and different effects on the audience.	8. *Analyzing language choices* Explain how phrasing, different words with similar meaning (e.g., *refined-respectful-polite-diplomatic*), or figurative language (e.g., *The wind whispered through the night.*) produce shades of meaning, nuances, and different effects on the audience.

C. PRODUCTIVE

	Emerging	Expanding	Bridging
Text types include: **Informational text types include:** descriptions or accounts (e.g., scientific, historical, economic, technical), recounts (e.g., biography, memoir), information reports, explanations (e.g., causal, factorial), expositions (e.g., speeches, opinion pieces, argument, debate), responses (e.g., literary analysis), etc. **Literary text types include:** stories (e.g., historical fiction, myths, graphic novels), poetry, drama, etc. **Audiences include:** Peers (one-to-one), Small group (one-to-group), Whole group (one-to-many)	9. *Presenting* Plan and deliver brief informative oral presentations on familiar topics. 10. *Writing* a. Write short literary and informational texts (e.g., an argument for wearing school uniforms) collaboratively (e.g., with peers) and independently. b. Write brief summaries of texts and experiences using complete sentences and key words (e.g., from notes or graphic organizers).	9. *Presenting* Plan and deliver longer oral presentations on a variety of topics and content areas, using details and evidence to support ideas. 10. *Writing* a. Write longer literary and informational texts (e.g., an argument for wearing school uniforms) collaboratively (e.g., with peers) and independently using appropriate text organization. b. Write increasingly concise summaries of texts and experiences using complete sentences and key words (e.g., from notes or graphic organizers).	9. *Presenting* Plan and deliver longer oral presentations on a variety of topics in a variety of disciplines, using reasoning and evidence to support ideas, as well as growing understanding of register. 10. *Writing* a. Write longer and more detailed literary and informational texts (e.g., an argument for wearing school uniforms) collaboratively (e.g., with peers) and independently using appropriate text organization and growing understanding of register. b. Write clear and coherent summaries of texts and experiences using complete and concise sentences and key words (e.g., from notes or graphic organizers).

Texts and Discourse in Context	English Language Development Level Continuum		
	C. PRODUCTIVE		
	Emerging	**Expanding**	**Bridging**
Part I, strands 11–12 Corresponding Common Core State Standards for English Language Arts 11. W.7.1,8-9; WHST.7.1,8-9; L.7.1-3,6 12. W.7.4-5; WHST.7.4-5; SL.7.4,6; L.7.1,3,5-6 **Purposes for using language include:** describing, entertaining, informing, interpreting, analyzing, recounting, explaining, persuading, negotiating, justifying, evaluating **Text types include:** **Informational text types include:** descriptions or accounts (e.g., scientific, historical, economic, technical), recounts (e.g., biography, memoir), information reports, explanations (e.g., causal, factorial), expositions (e.g., speeches, opinion pieces, argument, debate), responses (e.g., literary analysis), etc. **Literary text types include:** stories (e.g., historical fiction, myths,graphic novels), poetry, drama, etc. **Audiences include:** Peers (one-to-one), Small group (one-to-group), Whole group (one-to-many)	**11.** *Justifying/arguing* **a.** Justify opinions by providing some textual evidence or relevant background knowledge with substantial support. **b.** Express attitude and opinions or temper statements with familiar modal expressions (e.g., *can, may*). **12.** *Selecting language resources* **a.** Use a select number of general academic words (e.g., *cycle, alternative*) and domain-specific words (e.g., *scene, chapter, paragraph, cell*) to create some precision while speaking and writing. **b.** Use knowledge of morphology to appropriately select affixes in basic ways (e.g. *She likes X. He walked to school.*).	**11.** *Justifying/arguing* **a.** Justify opinions or persuade others by providing relevant textual evidence or relevant background knowledge with moderate support. **b.** Express attitude and opinions or temper statements with a variety of familiar modal expressions (e.g., *possibly/likely, could/would/should*). **12.** *Selecting language resources* **a.** Use a growing set of academic words (e.g., *cycle, alternative, indicate, process*), domain-specific words (e.g., *scene, soliloquy, sonnet, friction, monarchy, fraction*), synonyms, and antonyms to create precision and shades of meaning while speaking and writing. **b.** Use knowledge of morphology to appropriately select affixes in a growing number of ways to manipulate language (e.g., *She likes walking to school. That's impossible.*).	**11.** *Justifying/arguing* **a.** Justify opinions or persuade others by providing detailed and relevant textual evidence or relevant background knowledge with light support. **b.** Express attitude and opinions or temper statements with nuanced modal expressions (e.g. *possibly/potentially/absolutely, should/might*). **12.** *Selecting language resources* **a.** Use an expanded set of general academic words (e.g., *cycle, alternative, indicate, process, emphasize, illustrate*), domain-specific words (e.g., *scene, soliloquy, sonnet, friction, monarchy, fraction*), synonyms, antonyms, and figurative language to create precision and shades of meaning while speaking and writing. **b.** Use knowledge of morphology to appropriately select affixes in a variety of ways to manipulate language (e.g., changing *destroy -> destruction, probably -> probability, reluctant -> reluctantly*).

Section 2: Elaboration on Critical Principles for Developing Language & Cognition in Academic Contexts

PART II: Learning About How English Works

Texts and Discourse in Context	English Language Development Level Continuum		
	A. STRUCTURING COHESIVE TEXTS		
	Emerging	**Expanding**	**Bridging**

Part II, strands 1-2 Corresponding Common Core State Standards for English Language Arts

1. RL.7.5; RI.7.5; RH.7.5; RST.7.5; W.7.1-5,10; WHST.7.1-2,4-5,10; SL.7.4
2. RI.7.5; RH.7.5; RST.7.5; W.7.1-5,10; WHST.7.1-2,4-5,10; L.7.1,3-6

Purposes for using language include: describing, entertaining, informing, interpreting, analyzing, recounting, explaining, persuading, negotiating, justifying, evaluating

Text types include:

Informational text types include: descriptions or accounts (e.g., scientific, historical, economic, technical), recounts (e.g., biography, memoir), information reports, explanations (e.g., causal, factorial), expositions (e.g., speeches, opinion pieces, argument, debate), responses (e.g., literary analysis), etc.

Literary text types include: stories (e.g., historical fiction, myths,graphic novels), poetry, drama, etc.

Audiences include: Peers (one-to-one), Small group (one-to-group), Whole group (one-to-many)

Emerging

1. *Understanding text structure* Apply understanding of how different text types are organized to express ideas (e.g., how narratives are organized sequentially) to comprehending texts and to writing brief arguments, informative/ explanatory texts and narratives.

2. *Understanding cohesion*
   a. Apply knowledge of familiar language resources for referring to make texts more cohesive (e.g., how pronouns refer back to nouns in text) to comprehending texts and writing brief texts.
   b. Apply basic understanding of how ideas, events, or reasons are linked throughout a text using everyday connecting words or phrases (e.g., at the end, next) to comprehending texts and writing brief texts.

Expanding

1. *Understanding text structure* Apply understanding of the organizational features of different text types (e.g., how narratives are organized by an event sequence that unfolds naturally versus how arguments are organized around reasons and evidence) to comprehending texts and to writing increasingly clear and coherent arguments, informative/explanatory texts and narratives.

2. *Understanding cohesion*
   a. Apply knowledge of familiar language resources for referring to make texts more cohesive (e.g., how pronouns refer back to nouns in text, how using synonyms helps avoid repetition) to comprehending texts and writing texts with increasing cohesion.
   b. Apply growing understanding of how ideas, events, or reasons are linked throughout a text using a variety of connecting words or phrases (e.g., *for example, as a result, on the other hand*) to comprehending texts and writing texts with increasing cohesion.

Bridging

1. *Understanding text structure* Apply understanding of the organizational structure of different text types (e.g., how narratives are organized by an event sequence that unfolds naturally versus how arguments are organized around reasons and evidence) to comprehending texts and to writing clear and cohesive arguments, informative/explanatory texts and narratives.

2. *Understanding cohesion*
   a. Apply knowledge of familiar language resources for referring to make texts more cohesive (e.g., how pronouns, synonyms, or nominalizations are used to refer backward in a text) to comprehending texts and writing cohesive texts.
   b. Apply increasing understanding of how ideas, events, or reasons are linked throughout a text using an increasing variety of academic connecting and transitional words or phrases (e.g., *for instance, in addition, consequently*) to comprehending texts and writing texts with increasing cohesion.

Texts and Discourse in Context	English Language Development Level Continuum		
	B. EXPANDING & ENRICHING IDEAS		
	Emerging	Expanding	Bridging
Part II, strands 3–5 Corresponding Common Core State Standards for English Language Arts 3. **W.7.5; WHST.7.5; SL.7.6; L.7.1,3-6** 4. **W.7.5; WHST.7.5; SL.7.6; L.7.1,3-6** 5. **W.7.4-5; WHST.7.4-5; SL.7.6; L.7.1,3-6** **Purposes for using language include:** describing, entertaining, informing, interpreting, analyzing, recounting, explaining, persuading, negotiating, justifying, evaluating **Text types include:** **Informational text types include:** descriptions or accounts (e.g., scientific, historical, economic, technical), recounts (e.g. biography, memoir), information reports, explanations (e.g., causal, factorial), expositions (e.g., speeches, opinion pieces, argument, debate), responses (e.g., literary analysis), etc. **Literary text types include:** stories (e.g., historical fiction, myths,graphic novels), poetry, drama, etc. **Audiences include:** Peers (one-to-one), Small group (one-to-group), Whole group (one-to-many)	3. *Using verbs and verb phrases* Use a variety of verbs in different tenses (e.g., present, past, future), and aspects (e.g., simple, progressive) appropriate for the text type and discipline (e.g., simple past and past progressive for recounting an experience) on familiar topics. 4. *Using nouns and noun phrases* Expand noun phrases in basic ways (e.g., adding a sensory adjective to a noun) in order to enrich the meaning of sentences and add details about ideas, people, and things. 5. *Modify to add details* Expand sentences with simple adverbials (e.g., adverbs, adverb phrases, prepositional phrases) to provide details (e.g., time, manner, place, cause) about a familiar activity or process.	3. *Using verbs and verb phrases* Use a variety of verbs in different tenses (e.g., present, past, future), and aspects (e.g., simple, progressive, perfect) appropriate for the task, text type, and discipline (e.g., simple present for literary analysis) on an increasing variety of topics. 4. *Using nouns and noun phrases* Expand noun phrases in a growing number of ways (e.g., adding adjectives to nouns or simple clause embedding) in order to enrich the meaning of sentences and add details about ideas, people, and things. 5. *Modify to add details* Expand sentences with adverbials (e.g., adverbs, adverb phrases, prepositional phrases) to provide details (e.g., time, manner, place, cause) about a familiar or new activity or process.	3. *Using verbs and verb phrases* Use a variety of verbs in different tenses (e.g., present, past, future), and aspects (e.g., simple, progressive, perfect) appropriate for the task, text type, and discipline (e.g., the present perfect to describe previously made claims or conclusions) on a variety of topics. 4. *Using nouns and noun phrases* Expand noun phrases in an increasing variety of ways (e.g., more complex clause embedding) in order to enrich the meaning of sentences and add details about ideas, people, and things. 5. *Modify to add details* Expand sentences with a variety of adverbials (e.g., adverbs, adverb phrases and clauses, prepositional phrases) to provide details (e.g., time, manner, place, cause) about a variety of familiar and new activities and processes.

Texts and Discourse in Context	Emerging	Expanding	Bridging
Part II, strands 6-7 Corresponding Common Core State Standards for English Language Arts 6. W.7.1-5; WHST.7.1-2,4-5; SL.7.4,6; L.7.1,3-6 7. W.7.1-5; WHST.7.1-2,4-5; SL.7.4,6; L.7.1,3-6 **Purposes for using language include:** describing, entertaining, informing, interpreting, analyzing, recounting, explaining, persuading, negotiating, justifying, evaluating **Text types include:** **Informational text types include:** descriptions or accounts (e.g., scientific, historical, economic, technical), recounts (e.g., biography, memoir), information reports, explanations (e.g., causal, factorial), expositions (e.g., speeches, opinion pieces, argument, debate), responses (e.g., literary analysis), etc. **Literary text types include:** stories (e.g., historical fiction, myths, graphic novels), poetry, drama, etc. **Audiences include:** Peers (one-to-one), Small group (one-to-group), Whole group (one-to-many)	**C. CONNECTING & CONDENSING IDEAS** 6. *Connecting ideas* Combine clauses in a few basic ways to make connections between and join ideas (e.g., creating compound sentences using *and, but, so*; creating complex sentences using *because*). 7. *Condense ideas* Condense ideas in simple ways (e.g., by compounding verbs, adding prepositional phrases, or through simple embedded clauses or other ways of condensing as in, This is a story about a girl. The girl changed the world. → This is a story about a girl *who changed the world.*) to create precise and detailed sentences.	6. *Connecting ideas* Combine clauses in an increasing variety of ways (e.g., creating compound and complex sentences) to make connections between and join ideas, for example, to express a reason (e.g., *He stayed at home on Sunday to study for Monday's exam*) or to make a concession (e.g., *She studied all night even though she wasn't feeling well*). 7. *Condense ideas* Condense ideas in an increasing variety of ways (e.g., through various types of embedded clauses and other ways of condensing, as in, Organic vegetables are food. They're made without chemical fertilizers. They're made without chemical insecticides. → *Organic vegetables are foods that are made without chemical fertilizers or insecticides*.) to create precise and detailed sentences.	6. *Connecting ideas* Combine clauses in a wide variety of ways (e.g., creating compound, complex, and compound-complex sentences) to make connections between and join ideas, for example, to show the relationship between multiple events or ideas (e.g., *After eating lunch, the students worked in groups while their teacher walked around the room*.) or to evaluate an argument (e.g., *The author claims X, although there is a lack of evidence to support this claim*. 7. *Condense ideas* Condense ideas in a variety of ways (e.g., through various types of embedded clauses, ways of condensing, and nominalization as in, They destroyed the rainforest. Lots of animals *died*. → The *destruction* of the rainforest led to the *death* of many animals*.) to create precise and detailed sentences.

Section 2: Elaboration on Critical Principles for Developing Language & Cognition in Academic Contexts

PART III: Using Foundational Literacy Skills

Foundational Literacy Skills

See Appendix A for information on teaching reading foundational skills to English learners of various profiles based on age, native language, native language writing system, schooling experience, and literacy experience and proficiency. Some considerations are:

Literacy in an Alphabetic Writing System

- Print concepts
- Phonological awareness
- Phonics & word recognition
- Fluency

- Native language and literacy (e.g., phoneme awareness or print concept skills in native language) should be assessed for potential transference to English language and literacy.
- Similarities between native language and English should be highlighted (e.g., phonemes or letters that are the same in both languages).
- Differences between native language and English should be highlighted (e.g., some phonemes in English may not exist in the student's native language; native language syntax may be different from English syntax).